LONDON STUDIES ON SOUTH ASIA

HINDU AND CHRISTIAN IN SOUTH-EAST INDIA

CENTRE OF SOUTH ASIAN STUDIES
SCHOOL OF ORIENTAL AND AFRICAN STUDIES
UNIVERSITY OF LONDON

LONDON STUDIES ON SOUTH ASIA

5. CRIME, JUSTICE AND SOCIETY IN COLONIAL SRI LANKA
John D. Rogers
6. HINDU AND CHRISTIAN IN SOUTH-EAST INDIA
Geoffrey A. Oddie

LONDON STUDIES ON SOUTH ASIA NO. 6

HINDU AND CHRISTIAN IN SOUTH-EAST INDIA

GEOFFREY A. ODDIE

LONDON AND NEW YORK

First published 1991 by Curzon Press Ltd.

Published 2013 by Routledge
2 Park Square, Milton Park, Abingdon, Oxfordshire OX14 4RN

Simultaneously published in United States of America by Routledge
711 Third Avenue, New York, NY, 10017, USA

First issued in paperback 2016

Routledge is an imprint of the Taylor & Francis Group, an informa business

All rights reserved

© Geoffrey A. Oddie 1991

British Library Cataloguing in Publication Data
Oddie, G. A. (Geoff A) 1932–
Hindu and Christian in South-East India
1. India. Hinduism. Christianity
I. Title II Series
291.0954

ISBN 13: 978-1-138-99221-4 (pbk)
ISBN 13: 978-0-7007-0224-4 (hbk)

CONTENTS

List of figures	vii
Abbreviations	viii
Preface	ix
Introduction	1
1 Legacies and Setting	12
2 Company Policies, Temples and Changing Attitudes, 1800 – 1838	40
3 The Results of the Company's Disconnection with Hinduism	64
4 Sectarian Conflicts within Srivaishavaism: Tengalais and Vadagalais	82
5 The Character, Role and Significance of Non-Braham Saivite *Maths* in Tanjore District	98
6 Aspects of Popular Hinduism	119
7 Brahmans and Christian Conversion	140
8 The Depressed Classes and Christianity	153
9 The Christian Community in a Hindu Setting: Continuities and Change	170
10 Hindu Revivalism and Theosophy	189
Conclusion	217
Appendix 1: Adhinam Temples, Tanjore District, c. 1841 – 1900	232
Appendix 2: Trustees of some Non-Adhinam Temples, Tanjore District	234
Appendix 3: Temple Committees	236
Appendix 4: Temple Lands and Income, Tanjore District	240
Appendix 5: Castes denied Entry into Principal Temples, Tanjore District, c. 1881 – 1901	241
Appendix 6: Peak Attendances at some Religious Festivals: Estimates	242

Appendix 7: Tanjore and Trichinopoly: Religious Communities 244
Appendix 8: Brahman Converts 245
Appendix 9: Religion by Caste 248
Appendix 10: Theosophical Society Members, Trichinopoly and Tanjore Districts, 1883 – 1900 252
Appendix 11: Education by Caste: Hindus, 1888 – 1889 258
Appendix 12: Hindu Tract Society Membership, 1888 – 1889 259
Appendix 13: Enrolments in Government and Missionary Colleges: Tanjore and Trichinopoly Districts, 1881 – 1882 to 1893 – 1894 260
Select Bibliography 261
Glossary 270
Index 273

LIST OF FIGURES

1	Tanjore and Trichinopoly Districts	viii
2	The Kaveri Delta	3
3	North View of Trichinopoly, c. 1785	14
4	Taluks: Tanjore and Trichinopoly Districts	19
5	Raja Serfoji of Tanjore riding in procession	42
6	Temple car being drawn in procession	48
7	Main towns and religious centres: Tanjore and Trichinopoly Districts	121
8	Hook-swinging festival	126
9	Railways completed up to 1894 in Tanjore and Trichiniopoly Districts	132

Note: Figs. 3, 5, 6 and 8 are reproduced with the kind permission of the British Library (India Office Library).

ABBREVIATIONS

A.P.F.	Annals of the Propagation of the Faith
A.R.S.I.	Jesuit Archives, Rome
E.L.M.	Evangelisch Lutherisches Missionblatt
H.F.	Harvest Field
I.A.	Indian Antiquary
I.C.H.R.	Indian Church History Review
I.E.S.H.R.	Indian Economic and Social History Review
I.L.R.	India Law Reports
I.O.R.	India Office Records
J.A.S.	Journal of Asian Studies
J.R.A.S.	Journal of Royal Asiatic Society of Great Britain and Ireland
L.M.S.	London Missionary Society
L.N.	Letters and Notices
M.D.C.R.	Madras Diocesan Committee Report
M.D.Q.R.	Madras Diocesan Quarterly Report
M.F.	Mission Field
M.H.C.	Madras High Court
M.J.P.	Madras Judicial Proceedings
M.M.S.	Methodist Missionary Society
M.P.C.	Madras Public Consultations
M.P.P.	Madras Public Proceedings
M.Q.M.J.	Madras Quarterly Mission Journal
M.R.P.	Madras Revenue Proceedings
O.D.L.	Old Diary Leaves
S.P.G.	Society for the Propagation of the Gospel
S.P.G.Q.R.	Society for the Propagation of the Gospel Quarterly Report
Th	Theosophist
Th Sup.	Theosophist Supplement
T.R.	Tanjore Records
T.R.O.	Tamilnadu Record Office, Madras, Egmore
W.M.M.S.	Wesleyan Methodist Missionary Society
W.M.N.	Wesleyan Missionary Notices
U.S.P.G.	United Society for the Propagation of the Gospel

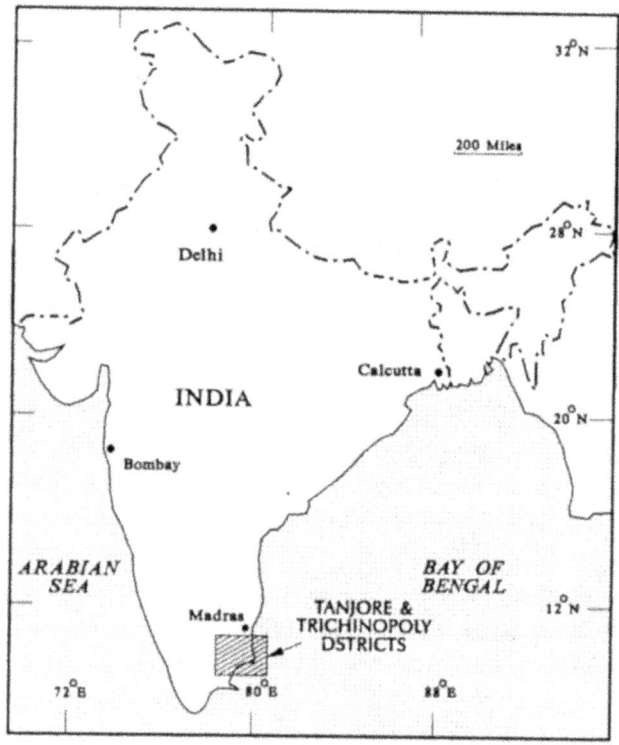

1 Tanjore and Trichinopoly Districts

PREFACE

The section in Chapter 3 dealing with the temple-cart issue appeared in the *Indo-British Review*, Vol. XIII, No. 1, January-June 1987. Chapter 5 on the non-brahman saivite maths in Tanjore district is a slightly modified version of a paper which was published in Kenneth Ballhatchet and David Taylor (eds.) *Changing South Asia: Religion and Society*, Asian Research Service, Hong Kong, 1984. The substance of Chapter 7 on brahmans and Christian conversion was published in Colloques Internationaux du Centre National de la Recherche Scientifique (ed.) *Asie du Sud: Traditions et Changements*, Paris 1979, and Chapter 9 on the Christian community in a Hindu setting is a slightly amended version of an article published in the *Indian Church History Review*, Vol XV, No. 1, June 1981. I wish to thank the editors of these journals and conference papers for their kind permission to reproduce or republish in modified form the material as mentioned above.

I would also like to acknowledge the help and assistance I have received from librarians and archivists in many parts of the world — especially from those in the India Office Library, the School of Oriental and African Studies and the Church Missionary Society, all in London, the Jesuit archives and library in Rome, the Tamilnadu and High Court of Madras archives and the Adyar library in Madras, the United Theological College library and archives in Bangalore, and the Shembaganur archives in the Madurai district, Tamilnadu.

Much of my research necessitated visits to Tanjore and Trichinopoly districts. I was the guest of many pastors and others who gave of their time and effort in helping me locate and make the most effective use of local records. I owe a great deal to my research assistant, Sri Rama Prasad, not only for the work he did on local church records, but also for enlarging my range of contacts and for arranging interviews with the head of the Dharmapuram *math* and a visit to the Tiravavaditurai *math* in January 1980.

Special thanks are due to Faye Sutherland for typing the original manuscript, and to the secretarial staff of the Department of History for their time and assistance. I am also grateful to Virginia Macleod, particularly for the maps and proof reading, and to Greg Baily of La Trobe University for reading the text and for his incisive and helpful comments. I have been greatly helped and encouraged by many others not the least of whom is Professor Ambirajan of the Department of Humanities and Social Sciences in the Indian Institute of Technology, Madras, whose practical help and enthusiasm for Tamil studies has meant a great deal. I also owe much to the patience and understanding of my wife, Nola, who, like the long-suffering companion of many an author, has had to endure the moods and preoccupation which, at least for some, appear to be part of the creative process.

I wish to thank the Australian Research Grants Committee for helping to finance this project over several years and the University of Sydney for further financial support for travel and other expenses. Finally, I would like to express my thanks to the South Asia editorial committee of the School of Oriental and African Studies for their thoughtful comments and practical help.

G.A. Oddie

INTRODUCTION

Recent studies of South India in the nineteenth and twentieth centuries concentrate primarily on political and social issues. Studies of specifically religious developments, of religious encounter, institutions and movements, especially in the nineteenth century, have been few and far between. A small number of publications, mostly chapters in books or articles, have attempted to present a broad Presidency-wide overview of particular types of development relating mostly to Hinduism. These include an analysis of British policies towards religious endowments, a study of the relationship between temples and political developments and a general account of the nature and growth of Hindu revivalism towards the end of the nineteenth century.[1]

In contrast to these general Presidency-wide studies are books and articles much more localized in scope. Conspicious among them are a range of studies of religious conversion movements[2] and a few publications which concentrate primarily on the history of specific institutions.[3]

The purpose of this study is to examine religious institutions, trends and developments in two adjoining districts — thereby adopting a level of focus which falls somewhere between these two extremes of the broadly-based overview and the detailed localized investigation of single religious establishments or movements. This middle level or regional approach has enabled the author to make maximum use of Government and other records organized on a district basis. It has also provided scope for comparison and a limited degree of generalization without ignoring too much of the detail and local variation.

The reason for choosing Tanjore and Trichinopoly districts and focusing on south-eastern India lies primarily in the fact that these districts encompass most of the Kaveri delta — a region which had long been famous as a centre of cultural and religious activity.

The Kaveri river, which has had a profound influence on the history and life of the peoples of south-eastern India, rises in the Coorg mountains and eventually flows in an easterly direction through Trichinopoly district. It bifurcates about nine miles west of Trichinopoly city — the northern branch being known as the Coleroon and the southern continuing as the Kaveri. About seventeen miles below this point the two streams very nearly re-unite. Thereafter the Coleroon turns in a north-easterly direction, forming a natural boundary (in the nineteenth century as well as today) between Tanjore and Trichinopoly districts and Tanjore and South Arcot, before it finally reaches the sea. The Kaveri, turning to the south, splits into numerous branches which spread out over the delta region.

The flat and fertile tracts of the delta, which only begin to widen out in the extreme eastern part of Trichinopoly district, occupy rather more than half the total area of Tanjore district. Hence it was Tanjore rather than Trichinopoly which was the more populous, fertile and intensively cultivated of the two districts in the nineteenth century — its most important product being 'Kaveri' rice which was exported for consumption elsewhere in India and overseas.[4]

The river was and still is regarded as one of the most sacred streams in the whole of India. Like the Ganga, the Kaveri is revered as the embodiment of a deity. According to the *Kaveri Mahatmya Purana*, for example, Kaveri was the faithful daughter of Brahma who, in order to bless her father and the world, resolved to become a river.[5] Bathing in the waters of the Kaveri was therefore considered especially efficacious — the special sanctity of the river being reflected in the fact that, in the 1860s, eight out of the twenty largest festivals in the Presidency took place along its banks.[6] These included the great annual festival held on Srirangam island (which is situated at a point where the river divides) and also popular festivals at Kumbakonam, Mayavaram and Tiruvaiyaru.

The status of the delta as a religious and cultural centre was further enhanced during the medieval period by the Chola rulers who encouraged brahmans to settle in the area. The fertility of the region also ensured the rise of wealthy landed and commercial classes who were able to maintain, if not endow, a large number of temples and *maths* (monasteries) as well as support a large 'unproductive class' of religious functionaries. As a result of these (and possibly other developments) there was a higher percentage of brahmans in Tanjore than in any other Tamil-speaking district in the nineteenth century,[7] as well as a large number of influential non-brahman monks and other religious specialists.

Like other parts of the Presidency in the nineteenth century, the delta was affected by British administration, missionary activity and the rise of a western-educated élite who also became actively involved in religious affairs. Placed by circumstance somewhere between the old and new, between tradition and the new forces and ideas associated with British rule, of all Hindus they appear to have become most fully alive to the need for religious change, or at least adaptation. As we shall see, they became the most ardent and influential advocates of Western

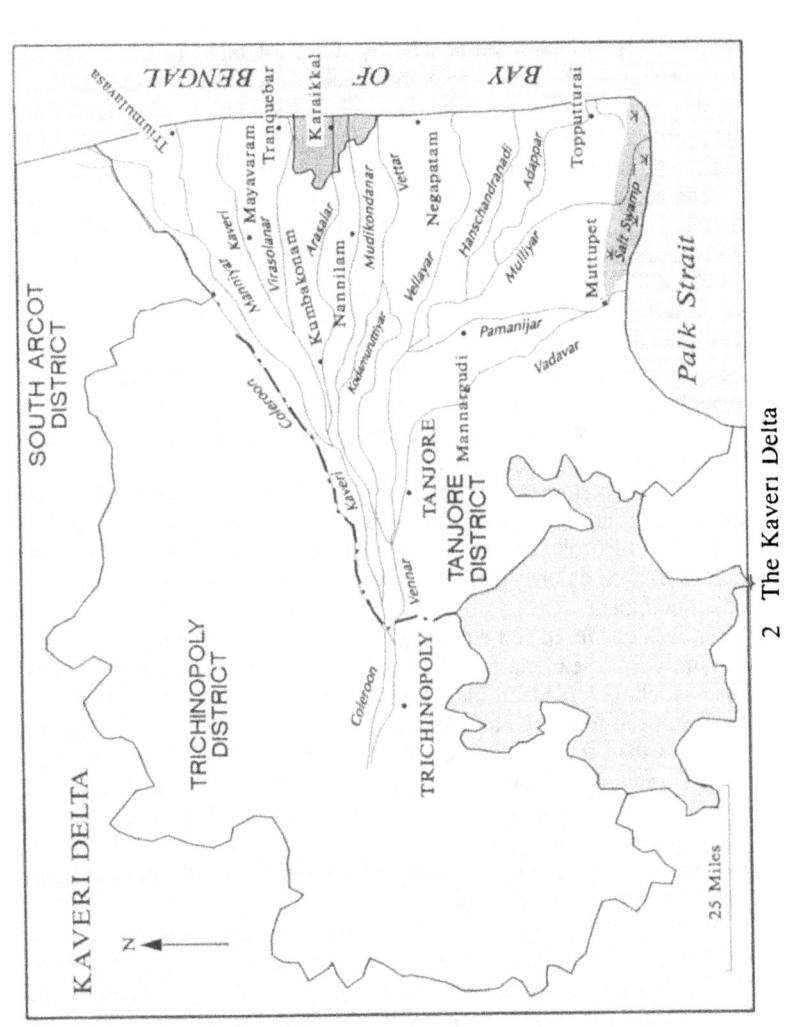

2 The Kaveri Delta

rationalism and of Hindu reform and revival, though not of conversion to Christianity.

As is the case with all historical works the scope and focus of the present study has been influenced by the availability or otherwise of source material. It has also been influenced by a conviction that there is a distinction between the discipline of history on the one hand and studies of contemporary society on the other. Recent anthropological studies and insights, for example, can be extremely helpful in attempts to understand religious developments, customs and institutions in the nineteenth century and extensive use has been made of anthropological and other contemporary studies of Tanjore district and of other parts of Tamilnadu. However, most of the raw material of anthropology, the research data, is drawn from the present and cannot always be used as evidence about what was practised or about attitudes in the nineteenth century. Indeed, the historian has to avoid the temptation of reading the present back into the past — riding roughshod over differences and discontinuities which may well exist between present 'realities' and past developments and practice.

Most earlier studies of religious developments and institutions in South India in the nineteenth century have relied on colonial or missionary records. The present study is based on both these types of sources as well as on additional material including both European and Indian comment.

It is fashionable in some academic circles to play down the value of the purely European material in the study of historical changes such as those which took place in India during the nineteenth century. It is true that European record collections, like other repositories, are limited in scope — that the primary emphasis of record collectors, at least initially, was on the collection of material which had some bearing on European interests and policies rather than on the acquisition of purely exotic sources. But, as we shall see, this does not mean that Indian sources and comment are not included even in, for example, East India Company revenue or judicial records.

Secondly, if it is argued with respect to religion and religious developments in the nineteenth century, that Europeans had their own peculiar nineteenth century view of 'religion' which was different from the view of local people, such as Tamils, then this argument, together with the implication that European comment was somehow inadequate, requires further consideration. While, for example, it may be true that European categories and views of religion were *sometimes* different from those of some Hindus, it is important to recognize that

European views varied and that French Catholics, British or American Evangelicals, Theosophists and other European commentators (such as those referred to in the body of this work) had somewhat different views of what might be described as 'ultimate reality', spiritual progress and ethical behaviour. While, for example, European Theosophists were usually able to incorporate *advaita* Hinduism into their world view, this was not generally true of Christian missionaries who rejected these teachings as false. Furthermore, Catholic and Protestant missionaries were divided among themselves on the merits of caste and on how far Hindu customs could be absorbed into what they liked to think of as 'true religion'. In other words, some Europeans were more in tune with Hindu or Tamil views of the world than others. Moreover, even if one concedes that there was *a* Tamil view of the world, it does not follow that Europeans necessarily misunderstood Tamil ideas or religious practices. Indeed, it could be argued that precisely because of their theistic background, European Christians were well placed in their attempts to understand similar strands, including the importance of temple worship, in Tamil religious practice.

Thirdly, there is the obvious and not unjustified observation that Europeans were outsiders and were therefore unable to discuss Hinduism or, for that matter, Indian Christianity from within. This is, however, a comment which can be made about élite Indian assessments of low-caste movements, about brahman descriptions of untouchability, or about almost any report by one group of people on the attitude or behaviour of almost any other. There is, moreover, a lot to be said for an outsider's comments as he or she can sometimes perceive things the insider takes for granted, or fails to notice. The outsider's view of the world is no less valid than that of the insider and both types of perception can be used to complement each other. Indeed, one of the main difficulties with the material available for this study was not so much lack of Indian or Tamil input, but lack of sources, comprising inside comment, which would balance outside observation.

In one sense the European material was useful as one type of inside comment — in providing the data which is fundamental to an understanding of European attitudes and policies affecting religion and religious developments even at the local level. European officials, Theosophists and missionaries were themselves part of the environment they describe. It was their views and feelings, their policies which, among other factors, began to affect the local religious and social interaction, which constituted part of a dialectic, and which help to explain why Hindus and Indian Christians reacted the way they did.

But this material is also useful as outside comment. In her study of slavery and agricultural bondage in South India in the nineteenth century Benedicte Hjejle has already shown how purely European sources, if used critically and with care and attention, can become valuable and useful tools in reconstructing a great deal of what was happening at the local level.[8] More recently still Ranajit Guha in his book, *Elementary Aspects of Peasant Insurgency in Colonial India*,[9] has shown that there are ways of approaching and using colonial material which can illuminate peasant insurgency movements in India and elsewhere.

As we shall see, Government officials, including collectors and magistrates, were drawn increasingly into the administration and policing of local religious affairs. While many were asked to undertake inquiries and present reports in the normal course of duty, others had, or developed, a very special interest in the local social and religious system. Some, like Charles Lushington, who compiled a detailed report on the internal affairs and functioning of Srirangam temple, were obviously fascinated by what they discovered and some, like H. J. Stokes, who was Sub-Collector of Tanjore in the 1870s and who became something of an expert on local customs, contributed to learned journals.

Perhaps even more than district officers, the missionaries varied considerably in their educational attainments and background. Like Government officers, they were expected to learn the local language, but, unlike the former, spent many more years in the one locality and, generally speaking, had more extensive first-hand knowledge of local conditions. Furthermore, while it is true that most of them lacked a sympathy for Hinduism and were critical of some forms of Indian Christianity, they did little to hide their views and prejudice and thus make it easy for readers to take these biases into account. Their business and special interest was religion and some of them were acute observers who lived and travelled in parts of the country where their compatriots were seldom if ever seen.

In this book, however, the European comment and evidence does not stand alone. European collections contain a considerable amount of indigenous material. Some of the most illuminating petitions relating to sectarian controversies in the great temple at Srirangam, for example, are filed in the Madras Revenue Proceedings in the India Office Records in London. Missionary collections usually include Indian Christian and sometimes Hindu comment, while other records, such as the evidence collected in connection with an inquiry into the management and condition of Hindu *maths* and temples in the 1870s, also includes widespread and diverse Indian (mostly Hindu) commentary and observation. Last, but not least colonial records also incorporate legal material — a valuable respository of indigenous as well as British response and evidence — a source which has been used

INTRODUCTION 7

by Arjun Appadurai and Carol Breckenridge in their studies of Hindu temples in the nineteenth century. It is this material, located in the archives of the High Court in Madras, which provides valuable economic, social and other data on some of the most prestigious religious institutions in the Madras Presidency. These and other European sources, such as periodical literature which contains comments or reports by local Tamils, have, in the present instance, been supplemented by purely indigenous collections or papers. These include the *Hindu* newspaper files, Tamil tracts published by the Hindu Tract Society and autobiographical material such as that contained in Lacombe's biography of Mahadeva Iyer one of the more prominent Christian converts.

One of the main problems with the source material used for this study was not so much lack of indigenous material and comment, but as already indicated, insufficient inside comment. Added to this was the scarcity of sources for what might be described as 'history from below'. There was some useful information in Thurston's volumes on *Castes and Tribes of Southern India*, in Oppert's book *On the Original Inhabitants of Bharatavarsa or India*[10] and in Whitehead's near contemporary study of *The Village Gods of South India*.[11] But apart from information in these sources and scattered references in gazetteers and census reports, there was very little published ethnographic information on popular religion specifically in Tanjore and Trichinopoly districts in the nineteenth century. While, as we have seen, Government officers and missionaries were beginning to develop an interest in the life and customs of particular communities, this had not yet resulted in any marked increase in output of systematic studies of popular or folk religion. Indeed, the lack of ethnographic and other material on popular religion imposed severe restraints on what it was possible to do and made it difficult even to describe the daily rituals of ordinary people during this period without using material that did not clearly relate to the delta region. The evidence available for the study of depressed-class conversion movements during the same period is also fairly limited. In this case, however, sources such as the census and gazetteers and records in different missionary archives have been supplemented by records scattered in various churches throughout the Kaveri delta. These include baptism, admission and marriage registers all of which were useful in reconstructing the character of depressed class movements.

No attempt has been made in this work to present a comprehensive view of religion in Tanjore and Trichinopoly districts in the nineteenth century. It is primarily a study of institutions and movements with a particular focus, not so much on the ideas and teaching of religion, but on the way it operated in practice and functioned within the social system.

Apart from Sastri's work, which deals primarily with religion in premodern South India,[12] there have been few if any attempts to investigate interconnections between different aspects of religion or religious developments in the region. We have therefore been especially conscious of the need for a more holistic approach in our research and study of religion and religious developments in the delta area. We are not only concerned with relationships between Hinduism and Christianity, but also with the interrelatedness of different facets of the Hindu religious system. Even if Hinduism (a word invented by outsiders to describe the religion of the people of India)[13] was never a completely coherent or unified system, this does not mean that there was no link or relationship between different 'Hindu' institutions or movements. One of our tasks was therefore to attempt to understand more about the relationship between aspects of Hinduism which have often been studied separately or in isolation from each other. What, for example, was the relationship between temples and *maths*, or between temples and the different sectarian groupings within the region? Or perhaps, more importantly, what was the relationship between élite institutions on the one hand and popular religion on the other? Should we continue to draw a distinction between the so-called 'great and little traditions'? Can we talk about levels of religion and, if so, what was the relationship between them?

Our major focus has, however, been on the way in which all these various aspects of religious life and development related to the social system. This issue has long been bound up with the debates about levels in Hinduism as mentioned above. While Lawrence Babb is, for example, especially concerned with religious concepts and the idea of a divine hierarchy of gods,[14] Redfield, who first developed the concept of 'great and little traditions', begins with people, 'the reflective few' and 'the unreflective many', and then raises questions about their religious ideas and practice.[15] Implicit, at the very least, in these and other discussions, including the notion of 'Sanscritization',[16] is the central and ongoing problem of the relationship between religious and social levels. To what extent did different groups in the social hierarchy practise different forms of religion and what, if anything, did high and low caste Hindus share in common?

This question, which is dealt with most fully in chapter six, also prompts reflection on the relationship between religion, social status and power. How far were those classes who were dominant economically, socially and politically in local society also dominant in religion? Was it the ritually dominant brahmans who controlled 'the institutions of religion', as Suntharalingam and Visswanathan seem to imply,[17] or were they forced to share leadership and power in religion with high-caste non-brahmans?[18] Was the relationship between power in society and power in religion purely accidental or was religion used by the higher castes and classes as some sort of mechanism for continued control and domination? Furthermore, to what extent was religion utilized by those at the base of the social hierarchy? What was the role of religion in social protest? How far were the depressed classes influenced by ideas of social equality and to what extent were they able to make use of ideas and resources either in Hinduism or Christianity in their struggle for increased power and recognition? These and other questions about the way in which religion was used or functioned within the social system constitute a recurrent theme in the chapters which follow.

Finally, much of what we have to say illustrates the point that the relationship between religion and society, between religious and social developments, was essentially a two-way process — the one affecting the other. If, for example, there is evidence of the way in which the advent of British rule, the rise of the new Western-educated classes and other factors affected religion in the region, there is also evidence of the way in which religion itself continued to affect and change the life of local people. Indeed, religion was important in more than one sense. It not only provided a certain degree of stability and social coherence but was also, in some of its other aspects, a source of disruption and conflict and an agency of social transformation — a very powerful factor in changing identities and social custom and in realigning the balance of forces in local society.

NOTES

1 Chandra Mudaliar, *The State and Religious Endowments in Madras*, Madras 1976; C. J. Baker, 'Temples and Political Development' in C. J. Baker and D. A. Washbrook (eds.) *South India: Political Institutions and Political Change 1880 – 1940*, Delhi 1975 and R. Suntharalingam, *Politics and nationalist Awakening in South India 1852 – 1891*, ch. 7, Arizona 1974.

2 Recent studies of Christian conversion movements in the Madras Presidency during the nineteenth century include a chapter in R. L. Hardgrave, *The Nadars of Tamilnad: The Political Culture of a Community in Change*, Berkeley and Los Angeles 1969; G. A. Oddie, 'Christian Conversion in Telugu Country, 1860 – 1900: a Case Study of One Protestant Movement in the Godavery-Krishna Delta', *I.E.S.H.R.*, Vol. XII, No. 1, January – March 1975; R. E. Frykenberg, 'The Impact of Conversion and Social Reform upon Society in South India during the late

Company Period: Questions concerning Hindu-Christian Encounters with special reference to Tinnevelly', in C. H. Philips (ed.) *Indian Society and the Beginning of Modernization c.1830 – 1850*, London 1976, and S. Manickham. *The Social Setting of Christian Conversion in South India*, Weisbaden 1977.

3 See, for example, A. Appadurai, *Worship and Conflict Under Colonial Rule: a South Indian Case*, Cambridge 1982. See also C. Breckenridge, 'From Protector to Litigant — Changing Relations between Hindu Temples and the Raja of Ramnad' in B. Stein (ed.) *South Indian Temples: An Analytical Reconsideration*, New Delhi 1978.

4 For contemporary or near contemporary material on the physical geography and economic condition and development of Tanjore and Trichinopoly districts in the nineteenth century see especially F. R. Hemingway, *Tanjore*, Madras 1906 and *Trichinopoly*, Madras 1907 as well as S. Srinivasa Raghavaiyangar, *Memorandum on the Progress of the Madras Presidency during the last forty years of British Administration*, Madras 1893, especially Section V. For more recent comment on socio-economic developments in Tanjore district during the same period, see D. A. Washbrook, 'Political Change in a Stable Society: Tanjore District 1880 – 1920' in C. J. Baker and D. A. Washbrook (eds.), *South India: Political Institutions and Political Change*, Delhi 1975, and D. A. Washbrook, *The Emergence of Provincial Politics: The Madras Presidency 1870 – 1920*, Cambridge 1976. For a useful recent analysis of some aspects of economic development, land revenue policies and landed classes in Trichinopoly, see Sara Braunstein, 'British Land Revenue Policy and Social Continuity in a south Indian District: A Study of Trichinopoly District, 1801 – 1824', M.A. Thesis, University of Western Australia, 1976.

5 *Imperial Gazetteer of India*, Vol. XI (new ed.) Oxford 1908, p. 8.

6 D. A. Washbrook, *The Emergence of Provincial Politics*, p. 89.

7 *Census of India*, 1871, Madras, Vol. 2.

8 *The Scandinavian Economic History Review*, Vol. XV, Nos. 1 and 2, 1967.

9 Delhi, 1983.

10 Westminster 1893. Gustav Oppert was Professor of Sanskrit and Comparative Philology in the Presidency College Madras and, amongst other things, Telugu Translator to Government.

11 Although this book was not published until 1921 it included material which had been collected at least fifteen years before. See, for example, H. Whitehead, 'The Village Deities of South India' in *The Nineteenth Century and After*, Vol. LX, 1906, pp. 533 – 46.

12 K. A. N. Sastri, *Development of Religion in South India*, Madras 1963.

13 H. Yule and A. C. Burnell, *Hobson-Jobson*, second edition, Delhi 1965.

14 *The Divine Hierarchy: Popular Hinduism in Central India*, New York and London, 1975.

15 *The Little Community and Peasant Society and Culture*, Chicago and London 1960, p. 41.

16 On the issue of 'sanscritization' see especially M. N. Srinivas, *Religion and Society Among the Coorgs of South India*, Bombay 1952, *Caste in Modern India and Other Essays*, Bombay etc. 1962 and *Social Change in Modern*

India, Berkeley and Los Angeles 1968: J. F. Stall, 'Sanskrit and Sanskritization', *Journal of Asian Studies*, vol. 22, May 1963.
17 See Suntharalingam, op. cit., p. 7 and E. Visswanathan, 'The Emergence of Brahmins in South India with Special Reference to Tamil Nadu', in S. N. Mukherjee (ed.), *Indian History and Thought: Essays in Honour of A. L. Basham*, Calcutta 1982, p. 287.
18 The term 'non-brahman' as used in this book is taken to mean all those Hindu castes between brahmans at the top of the social scale and untouchables at the bottom.

1

LEGACIES AND SETTING

A: TRADITIONAL RULERS, DHARMA AND THE PORTENTS OF CHANGE

Hinduism in the pre-colonial era was clearly interlinked with the political system. Long-established Hindu views of government, in the South as well as in the North, included a belief that it was the duty of the ruler to uphold *dharma* — to foster and protect the existing social and religious system. This tradition of patronage and protection was generally accepted and followed by pre-colonial rulers in both Trichinopoly and Tanjore districts.

It was the Hindu Nayaks of Madura who governed most or all of Trichinopoly district, together with other territory, for more than two centuries until 1736. Judging from the evidence of inscriptions and other sources, they built and repaired temples and often gave land in support of temples and *maths*.[1] They remitted taxes so as to help maintain specific religious ceremonies, bestowed lands and villages on brahmans and even passed orders forbidding the mixing of castes.[2]

Associated with this policy of protection was a comparatively tolerant even-handed approach towards the different religious groups living within their kingdom. They supported both vaishnavite and saivite temples[3] and even bestowed gifts on less exalted deities such as Aiyanar, the god of boundaries and protector of villages.[4] They also granted small amounts of land in support of Muslim religious leaders and mosques[5] and, with one or two exceptions attempted to protect Jesuit missionaries and converts against not infrequent outbreaks of persecution.[6]

The Nawabs of Arcot, who succeeded the Nayaks as overlords of Trichinopoly district in 1736 and who were the immediate predecessors of the British, were distracted by wars and unsettled political conditions and had little opportunity, even if they wished, of developing their own system of administration. They seldom became involved in local religious affairs. When they did, however, they appear to have followed the traditional policies of patronage and toleration. Though they were Muslims, they donated land to Hindu temples[7] and, on at least one occasion, were called upon to help settle Hindu religious disputes at Srirangam.[8]

In Tanjore district the policy of the Maratha rajas was much the same as that pursued by the Nayaks of Madura in the sense that they too were well known as patrons of religious activity and institutions. This included support and encouragement for teachers of *advaita* philosophy as well as for the main theistic forms of Hinduism. The early rajas, however, appear to have been less consistent and at times less tolerant in their attitude towards Christianity — possibly because they recognized that the Jesuit missionaries and converts represented a greater threat to the *status quo* than other communities in the kingdom.[9]

As patrons of literature and learning the rajas presided over the later stages of what has been described as a great 'literary and philosophical revival' which took place in Tanjore during the period from about 1550 to 1750.[10] The early rajas gave much encouragement to the authors of Sanskrit and Telugu religious literature as well as to secular works. These included works on ritual, such as the *Acharanavaneeta* which was a digest of the *Dharmasastra* on the funeral and Shraddha ceremonies, prepared at the request of Raja Shahji (1684 – 1712),[11] a new interpretation of the *Ramayana* by one of the ministers of state under Sarabhoji (1712 – 1718),[12] an exposition of the *Brahmasutras*, a study of *advaita* doctrines, and religious plays and poetry.[13]

Although, in the second half of the eighteenth century, this literary activity was less apparent, the rajas were, nevertheless, still active as patrons of individual scholars, religious leaders and religious institutions. Raja Tuljaji (1763 – 1787), for example, continued to patronize religious writers[14] and set aside revenues in support of *maths* and temples. He and his rani also established a number of *chattrams* for the accommodation of brahmans and other pilgrims *en route* for Rameswaram.[15]

By this time, however, there were growing signs that this policy of patronage and especially of protection was becoming more difficult to sustain as a result of the growing power and increasing activity of the English East India Company. From the Raja's point of view the question was no longer merely one of patronage and of developing existing religious facilities and institutions, but for protecting the very basis of the socio-religious system from the adverse effects of European penetration.

In 1773 Raja Tuljaji was deposed by East Indian Company troops; but then, in 1776, reinstated by order of the Court of Directors. Under the terms of a treaty signed with the English two years later he agreed to accept an English garrison and to cede a part of his territory (the town and seaport of Nagore and 277 towns and villages in Mannargudi district) in payment of the costs involved.[16]

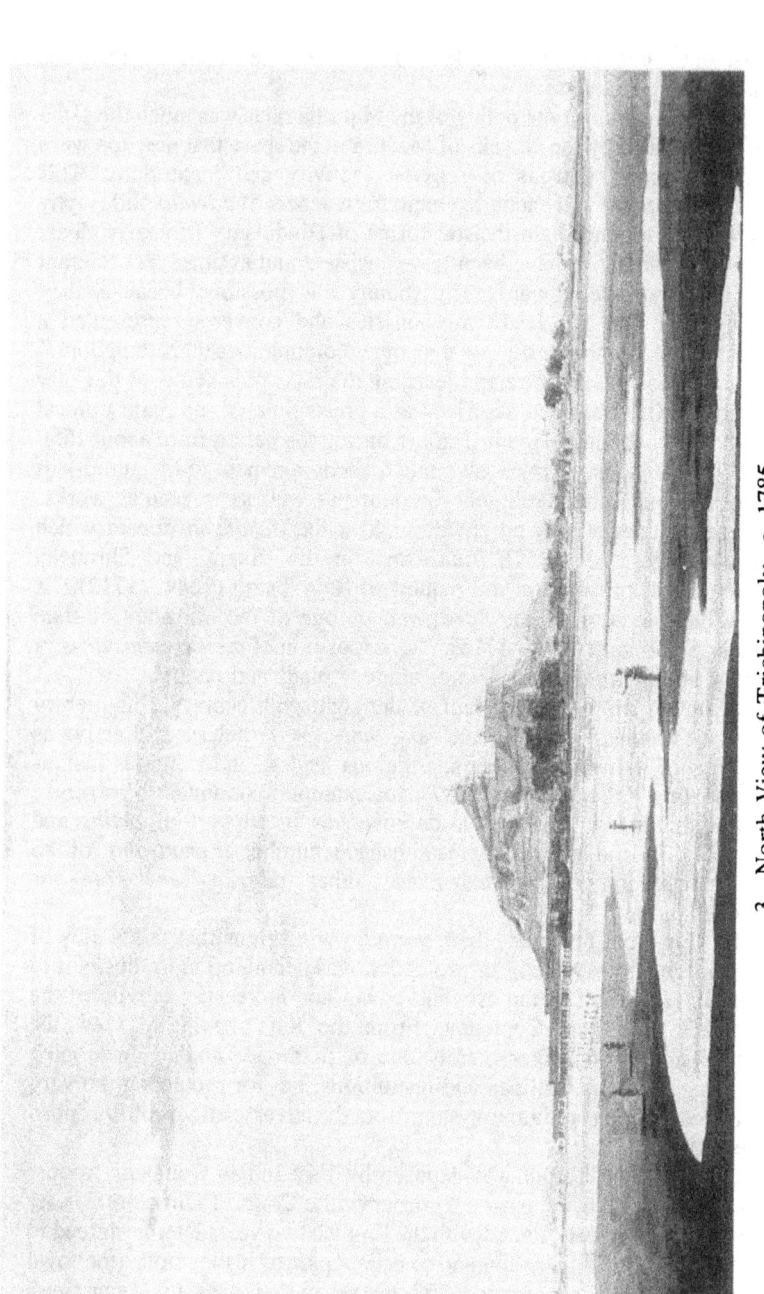

3 North View of Trichinopoly, c. 1785

But in spite of the Raja's obvious subjection and dependence on the Company's support, he insisted on inserting a series of safeguards in the treaty. Three of these conditions which related to the religious and social order may have appeared almost trivial to the English, but were of considerable importance to the Raja as measures in defence of the established religious and social order.[17] One condition was that 'such enams as have been granted for the use of Pagodas [Temples], or charity to Brahmins, of maintaining choultries and water pandalls, shall be continued as formerly. Such spots of land contiguous to Pagodas or Brahmin houses, which are known by the name of Brimh Wast-tow, and which have been rented for money or in kind, or have been let out as choutrums, shall be enjoyed by the present possessors as usual. The charity allowances for the rhut or coach to the Pagoda shall be continued.'

A second condition which reflected the Raja's desire to maintain the coach or car festivals was that 'People shall be sent as usual to draw the rhut or coach of the Pagoda at the times of procession' and a third condition, expressing the Raja's desire to protect both brahmans and sacred places from the effects of pollution by Europeans, was that 'No houses shall be build by the Circar (Company) in villages called Agne where Brahmins reside. No Europeans shall be allowed to dwell near any tanks or ponds belonging to Pagodas or Brahmin villages.'

The threat, however, was not merely from the East India Company but also from the increasing activity of European missionaries who, together with their converts and inspite of periods of persecution, were gradually extending their influence throughout the region.

Among the first Christians to settle in Tanjore and Trichinopoly districts were Portuguese-speaking parava Christians, mostly merchants, who settled in Negapatam and Tranquebar sometime during the second half of the sixteenth century.[18] Branches of the Negapatam settlement were subsequently established at Tirumalavasal in Shiyali taluk and at Karaikkal. There are also reports of Christians in Tanjore city at least as early as 1570, some two decades before the founding of the Madura mission by Jesuit missionaries in 1592.[19] The establishment of this mission, and especially the work of Robert de Nobili, marked a new and important stage in the development and spread of Catholic Christianity in the region — some of de Nobili's converts who were attached to the Nayak's court settling in Trichinopoly when the court was established there in 1626.[20] In subsequent years Jesuit missionaries became increasingly active in both Trichinopoly and Tanjore districts and the number of Christians continued to grow until sometime after the Jesuit Order was suppressed by Papal decree in 1773.

In the meantime, the first Protestant missionaries to arrive in India, Bartholomew Ziegenbalg and Henry Plutschau, German Lutherans, reached the Danish settlement at Tranquebar in July 1706.[21] From Tranquebar the mission spread along the Coromandel coast and into the interior of Tanjore and Trichinipoly districts. In 1721 one of Ziegenbalg's successors, the Rev. Mr Schultze, corresponded with the Raja of Tanjore and was invited to his court.[22] Though this event marked the beginning of what was to become a long and at times intimate association between the Tranquebar missionaries and the Tanjore royal family, this sometimes close and cordial relationship cannot hide the fact that the fundamental purpose of the missionaries was to subvert the religious and to a lesser extent the social order, hoping to replace Hinduism with Protestant Christianity.[23]

However, it was only after the imposition of British rule, the treaty of 1799 annexing most of Tanjore district, and the annexation of the Carnatic, including Trichinopoly district in 1801, that the seriousness of this threat (emanating especially from the Protestant missionaries) became gradually more apparent to the Hindu community.

All the Lutheran mission stations founded by the Tranquebar missionaries in the eighteenth century, with the exception of Tranquebar itself, were (because of the waning of missionary enthusiasm in Europe) transferred to the care of Anglican missionary societies — initially to the Society for the Promotion of Christian Knowledge (S.P.C.K.) and then, in 1826, to the high Anglican Society for the Propagation of the Gospel in Foreign Parts (S.P.G.). Among those who found themselves Anglicans almost by default were former Lutheran congregations at Trichinopoly, Kumbakonam and Poreiar near Tranquebar. In subsequent years the Lutherans themselves, having revived an interest in foreign missions, re-entered the field in the service of the Evangelical Lutheran Mission (E.L.M.) also known as the Leipzig Mission — a name derived from the fact that its headquarters were in Leipzig. The centre at Tranquebar was given a new and important lease of life as the chief seat of Lutheran missionary operations and new stations were opened at a number of places including Poreiar (1842), Mayavaram (1845), Trichinopoly (1850), Tanjore (1851) and Manikramman (1852).[24]

Apart from the S.P.G., several other English Protestant missionary organizations entered the field in the nineteenth century, though only two of these managed to sustain a continued presence. The Anglican Church Missionary Society (C.M.S.) began work at Mayavaram in 1823 but soon withdrew[25] and the London Missionary Society, which opened a centre at Kumbakonam in 1825, transferred its work to the S.P.G. in 1852. It was the English Methodists employed by the Wesleyan Methodist Missionary Society (W.M.M.S.) who, together with the S.P.G. and Lutheran missionaries, became the three most important and active Protestant groups in the delta in the nineteenth century. The Methodists established an influential centre at Negapatam in 1819 and also had mission stations in Trichinopoly, Tanjore and Mannargudi. In the early 1880s these groups were joined by the Salvation Army which also became increasingly active in its own unique way at various centres throughout the delta.

Catholics in the region continued to outnumber Protestants by more than nine to one throughout the nineteenth century.[26] In spite of this, however, it was Protestantism which, at least up until the 1890s, appears to have been perceived as the major threat to Hinduism — especially by the more educated section of the Hindu population.[27] It was the Protestant movement which was comparatively new and which seemed to challenge to a much greater extent the values of established tradition such as caste, forms of worship and even dress.[28] It was more aggressive and more tied up with the power of the State — a force which, far more than Catholicism, threatened to coalesce with the Government in an all out assault on the Hindu religious and social system. Furthermore, the Jesuit missionaries (the most active force for Catholicism in the area) were preoccupied with attempts to reassert control and revive the faith and religious life of existing congregations, and they had very little time and few resources to devote to fresh evangelistic efforts among Hindus. On the other hand the Protestants were able to extend their evangelistic activities throughout the region — especially through the dissemination of Tamil and English language tracts and pamphlets and through forthright preaching in the streets of towns, at Hindu festivals and during journeys through the countryside. They not only adopted a much more abrasive and public profile, but were also able to dominate and very largely control the modern system of higher education in the English language. Indeed it was only when the Catholics, who re-established St Joseph's College in Trichinopoly in 1883, succeeded in attracting more higher-caste Hindus into their programme of education in English and began to win converts from among their pupils, that they too began to provoke an opposition on a scale and intensity which was more comparable with the Hindu reaction to Protestant missionary activity.

B: TEMPLE COMMUNITIES AND TEMPLE SERVICE IN THE EARLY NINETEENTH CENTURY

The two most important Hindu religious institutions in the region were temples and *maths*. Some account of the origin and early history of *maths* is included in Chapter 5 and the purpose of this section is to explore the character of temple communities and the nature of temple service primarily with reference to conditions in the early nineteenth century, before the British intervened to any great extent in temple affairs or introduced major changes in temple administration.

Temples and shrines were and still are the most obvious physical manifestation of religious life in the delta. Studies of temples in South India have included an examination of the part they played in medieval economic systems, the role of temples in the support and extension of royal authority, the way in which their activities related to the social system and the relationship between temples and modern political activity.[29] It is well to remember, however, that temples were primarily religious institutions — the abode of the deity, the focus of ritual activity and the very heart and centre of the worshipping community.

There were thousands of shrines and temples in Tanjore and Trichinopoly districts and it was these institutions which attracted the attention of Company servants anxious to consolidate early British rule. As we shall see, the Company believed its best interests would be served by making as few changes to the existing religious system as possible and by following the traditional Indian practice of protecting existing religious institutions. In practice, this meant that the Company was committed to the idea of ensuring that endowments, including temple endowments, were appropriated for the purposes for which they were established.[30] This entailed considerable work at the local level, collectors frequently being asked to supply detailed information about the number, state and extent of revenues of temples under their jurisdiction.[31]

The most comprehensive early survey of temples in Trichinopoly was made by the Collector, Henry Dickinson, in 1828, and of temples in Tanjore by N. W. Kindersley the Collector there in 1841.[32] Dickinson reported that there were 4,701 'places of Hindu worship' in his district.[33] Three of these, the temples of Srirangam, Jambukeswaram, and the Rock Fort or Tayuman temple,[34] (all located in the upper reaches of the delta and near the district headquarters) were 'far superior in celebrity to all the others'. Their combined annual income of Rs. 62,546 was just over 30 per cent of the aggregate income of all temples in the district. In addition to these were 125 temples of 'note and consequence' which, according to the same report, received 41 per cent of all temple incomes. Lastly, there were 4,576 'petty pagodas' which included temples and shrines dedicated to 'popular' or village deities and whose income was entirely dependent on the contribution of local inhabitants.

Kindersley's report on places of Hindu worship in Tanjore district was less comprehensive as it was restricted to the 2,874 institutions which he stated were 'under the Superintendence of the Government Officers' and did not include 'the almost innumerable village temples' which Dickinson had incorporated into his report on Trichinopoly

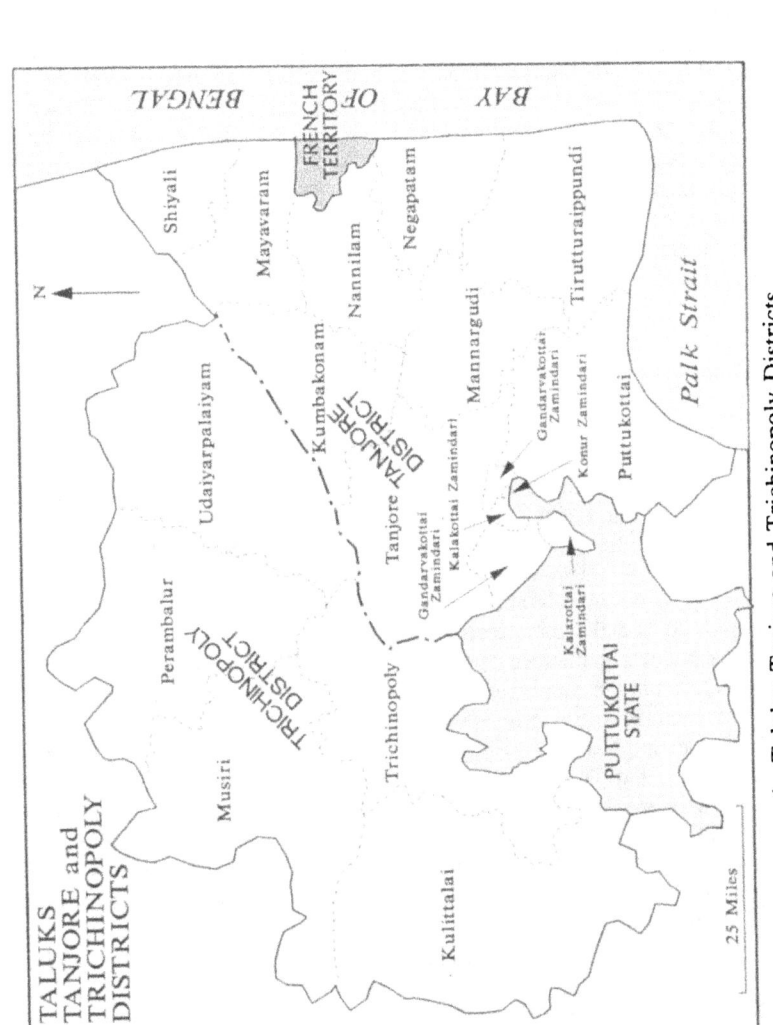

4 Taluks: Tanjore and Trichinopoly Districts

district.[35] It shows that, compared with the latter district, Tanjore had a much greater number of prestigious and wealthy temples. There were 193 temples under the Company's superintendence in Tanjore district whose annual revenue from land and money endowments exceeded 200 chakrams or Rs. 311 – 1 – 9, compared with 63 in Trichinopoly.[36] At least five temples in Tanjore (several of them under the control of non-brahman *maths*) had an annual income greater than that of Jambukeswaram, the second most wealthy temple in Trichinopoly.[37] Furthermore, the Tanjore calculations did not include temples still under the superintendence of the Tanjore Princes — the most famous of which was the great temple at Tanjore itself.[38] Indeed, according to T. V. Row (author of the Tanjore district manual of 1883), the total number of the larger temples in the district was about half the number comprised 'in the whole Presidency'.[39]

Temple Servants and Duties in the Larger Temples

Temple communities comprised at least three different classes of people. Firstly, there were the trustees whose position was usually hereditary and who were sometimes descendants of the original founders of the institution.[40] Secondly, there were the temple staff or employees — those who were, in effect, largely responsible for the upkeep of the temple and the maintenance of the different rituals and ceremony. Lastly, there were the ordinary worshippers, some of whom were major benefactors or their descendants. Though they played no direct part in the running or management of temple affairs they could be very vocal in airing grievances and in pressing for reform.[41]

While these appear to have been the three most distinctive groups within the temple communities in the early nineteenth century, as we shall see, another group of some importance was created by the British in 1863. These were the members of the new temple committees established to supervise the work of the trustees. These officials were also often involved in worship at one of the temples under their supervision.

Early British records relating to the three principal temples in Trichinopoly throw a great deal of light on the duties, social background and remuneration of the temple employees. According to the report submitted to the Board of Revenue in 1818 by the Collector, Charles Lushington,[42] Srirangam, which included a number of sub-shrines or temples within its walls, had by far the largest staff, employing 820 people regularly in the performance of 'ceremonies' within the temple.[43] Jambukeswaram employed 201 people and the

Tayuman temple 146 temple servants making a total of 1,173 people who were listed as performing 'ceremonies' in all three establishments. The specific duties of 225 of this number cannot be ascertained — 107 being listed simply as brahmans 'in attendance' and 148 as having 'general duties'. The remaining 918 temple employees can, however, be divided into six rough categories according to their tasks or occupation.

The first group, (about one per cent), held what might be described as the senior managerial positions. They were the *stullatars* or managers and their assistants in Srirangam and Jambukeswaram who, together with the *tambiran* (non-brahman monk) of the Tayuman temple, supervised the management of their respective establishments.

Secondly, there were 509 people (56 per cent) who were directly involved in rituals and ceremonial. Of these 84 were priests who performed *puja*, or people who either daily or at less frequent intervals made offerings to the deity on behalf of private individuals. There were 84 readers who recited either the Vedas or the *Prabandam* (devotional poetry of the Alvars or poet saints); 48 were described as lamp-lighters; at least 47 were involved in the distribution of betel leaf and nut or sandalwood oil to worshippers. Other employees in this category had the task of carrying, dressing or decorating the deity and of holding ceremonial umbrellas. Last but not least, were 55 musicians or *nattuvans* and 111 dancing girls, nearly three quarters of whom were employed in the temple at Srirangam.

The third category (22 per cent) were temple servants concerned with the supply or preparation of food and drink and other ingredients used in worship. Prominent among them were suppliers of milk, water or rice to the temples, and those who cooked rice or who made cakes in the sacred kitchens. Other duties included the supply of perfumes, the preparation of tumeric and sandalwood oil, and the supply of flowers for garlands and decoration.

A fourth group of temple servants (about one per cent) were *carnums* or accountants and a fifth group (about 10 per cent) were those who were mostly concerned with temple security. Among these were superintendents, guards, watchmen, peons and even, in the case of Srirangam, 'a spy'.

Lastly, there were approximately 94 employees (about 10 per cent) who were craftsmen or who were involved in less skilled occupations. Included among these were potters, iron smiths, carpenters (such as those employed in erecting pandals or sheds), cow keepers, gardeners, monkey and dog drivers, and sweepers.

In spite of the fact that one temple, namely Srirangam, was a vaishnavite institution and the other two were saivite there appears to have been little difference in the type of tasks performed in them. As

Srirangam had by far the largest establishment, employing about 70 per cent of the temple servants listed in Lushington's report, there was probably a greater degree of specialization among employees. It is noteworthy, for example, that some of the sub-categories of servants in Srirangam, such as those who conducted *arccanai* (private worship) or who distributed betel, are not listed in connection with the saivite institutions. This does not mean, however, that these tasks were not performed in saivite temples but rather that they were probably carried out under the heading of more general duties.

The one clear difference in duties which does emerge in the Collector's report, and which reflects sectarian differences, is in the recitation of scripture. In Srirangam, a tengalai vaishnavite institution, 25 individuals were listed as readers of the *Prabandam* poems, which were of special importance in the tengalai tradition,[44] and 20 as readers of the Vedas. In the saivite temples, however, the recitation of the *Prabandam* was much less important. In Jambukeswaram only two individuals, and in the Tayuman temple only one are listed as reading the *Prabandam* compared with 16 persons who recited the Vedas in each of these institutions.

The precise relationship between the caste of employees and the duties they performed in the temples is difficult to ascertain. This is partly because only a minority of those referred to in Lushington's report are mentioned by name and because, when they are, it is not always possible to infer their caste. What evidence there is, however, suggests that, with few exceptions, the most sensitive or important ritual duties in all three temples (those which demanded the highest degree of ritual purity) were performed by brahmans. Judging from the name or names which appear beside each duty it was the brahmans who usually acted as the immediate attendants on the 'swami'. They were the ones who put cloths and jewels on the image, who held his umbrella or who usually acted as his bearers. They were also the ones who brought water required for use in the temple, who boiled the rice and made cakes in the kitchen and who distributed the *prasadam*, including betel and sandalwood, to visitors.

It is important to note, however, that there were still some non-brahman participants in functions which brought them into more or less close contact with the deity. In Srirangam, for example, Custoory Rungumpillay occupied the office which was 'formerly to offer new grain of the Crops grown on Pagoda lands'. As we have seen, some non-brahmans in the saivite temples read the *Prabandam* while, in the Tayuman temple, Appoo Pillay, a non-brahman had the task of tying flowers to the idol.

If non-brahmans were only represented in a very minor degree in the more ritually sensitive areas of temple activity, they were more important or even dominant in some other activities essential to the effective functioning of the institution. Most of the *carnums* in all three temples were non-brahmans as were many of those who supplied the food or who were involved in supervisory activities. The artisan castes, many of those who provided personal service, all the dancing girls and most of the musicians were also drawn from the non-brahman sectors of the population.[45]

Office Holding, Profits and Privilege

Judging from the records relating to Srirangam in particular many of the offices in the principal temples were *mirasi* or hereditary positions. Such positions in Srirangam included the office of *stullatar* or manager, head accountant, cook and cake-maker. Duties such as carrying the idol in procession or guarding the temple jewels were also hereditary.[46] It was also the custom for dancing girls, as well as musicians in the temples everywhere, to train at least some of their children in the tasks they themselves performed.[47]

Office-holding even in the largest and most prestigious temples was not necessarily a lucrative form of employment.[48] Most temple servants appear to have received a fixed salary.[49] At the same time it was also customary in temples such as Srirangam for most employees to pay out a fixed annual rent or *nuzur* for the mere privilege of holding office.[50] Office-holders had to weigh up the cost of rent against their regular salary and any extra income that might come their way.

The situation was made more difficult financially for some time as a result of experiments during the early phases of British rule. Several Collectors attempted to increase the rent from office holders in Srirangam by selling positions annually to the highest bidder.[51] This practice, which was condemned by the *stullatars* as an 'innovation' which drove some office holders into defrauding the temple, led to a situation in which servants were paying more in rent than they received in 'authorized pay and other emoluments'.[52] In 1830, for example, the man who had charge of the *hundi* or sealed pot in which offerings to the deity were placed, had to pay an average annual rent of Rs. 54-2-2, but received only Rs. 18-11-11 ½ as authorized payment and emoluments. Many others, including overseers, those who baked ceremonial cakes, the servants whose duty it was to distribute sandalwood oil and betel leaf and nut to members of the public, and those who sold the surplus cooked rice, all paid rents in excess of their official income.[53]

The imposition of higher rents was, of course, possible only because tenants, in the words of one official, 'plundered'[54] the temple or had other more legitimate sources of income in addition to their authorized pay and emoluments.

N. S. Cameron, Collector of Trichinopoly from January 1829 to February 1831, realizing that the increase in rents had encouraged abuses, attempted to ease the pressure on those in most financial difficulty by making a distinction between office holders who appeared to be largely dependent on their authorized pay etc. and those with access to additional sources of income.[55] The practice of selling some positions annually to the highest bidder, in cases where it was felt that the authorities had little control over the incumbent's income, was continued. In other cases, however, annual sales were abandoned — rents being once again fixed in accordance with customary pre-British practice.[56] In the case of the attendant in charge of the *hundi*, for example, his rent was reduced to a fixed annual charge of Rs. 4 leaving him with an authorized profit of Rs. 14-11-11 ½ — an annual income roughly equivalent to that of an agricultural labourer.[57] The rent to be paid by each of the 40 brahman cooks was also fixed at a reduced rate leaving them with an official annual income of Rs. 16 each.

Not all offices in Srirangam were, however, subject to the payment of an annual rent. It appears from the record of legal proceedings in 1825, for example, that the 34 brahmans in Srirangam who had the right to recite the Vedas behind the *swami* as he was carried in procession, were not required to pay an annual fee.[58] Those joining the group for the first time paid an initial fee of Rs. 12 ½ for the privilege and thereafter received a regular annual payment of Rs. 18. Once again, however, this was a very modest emolument — hardly comparable with the rates of pay which could be obtained by skilled or professional workers in Government employment. In 1859 – 60, for example, twenty-five years later, in spite of the fact that local prices had not even doubled, bricklayers and carpenters employed in the Public Works Department in Trichinopoly district were earning nearly four times as much.[59] In about 1877, when prices were still not double the 1825 rate, most clerks working in the revenue office in the city of Trichinopoly nearby were earning salaries ten times greater than the official payment the brahmans had received for their duties in Srirangam.[60]

While these rates of pay for services in Srirangam can therefore hardly be regarded as excessive, it has to be borne in mind that some tasks or duties were occasional or part-time and that there were also opportunities, at least in some cases, for supplementing 'official' income. Indeed, one cannot be certain that even those servants Cameron classified as being largely dependent on authorized pay were in fact as heavily dependent on that source as he implied. There was no guarantee, for example, that the man in charge of the sealed pot would not solicit donations from the public or that brahman cooks would not sell cooked rice at a profit to themselves.⁶¹ Furthermore, it was recognized by Cameron and others that there was no way of completely controlling the income of many of the other temple employees. These included the general superintendent who conducted notaries to the deity and obtained *prasadam* (sacred remnants of food consumed by the deity) from them 'for which he induces them to give him a fee'; the superintendent of charitable *choultries* established by individuals, those who ground and distributed betel nut, the vendors of boiled rice and others.⁶² Clearly, in these circumstances, the more prestigious, popular and crowded the temple the greater were the opportunities for soliciting money from the public.

There were also special perquisites attached to some positions in the temple. For example, the holder of the offices of astrologer and *tiruppaniseivar* (the pouring of water in the *prakarams* of the temple when the deity was taken around) was entitled to the payment of special dues on the occasion of the marriage of his son. In 1898, in a case contested in the Madras High Court, the incumbent of one such office in Srirangam claimed Rs. 22-2-8 as the amount outstanding after the marriage of his son in 1888.⁶³

Lastly, some temple employees, such as dancing girls, were not wholly dependent on what they earned within the temple precincts. They attended weddings, danced on other public and private occasions and engaged in prostitution outside as well as within the temple precincts.⁶⁴ 'The *devadasis* receive a fixed salary for the religious duties which they perform', wrote Abbé Dubois, 'but as the amount is small they supplement it by selling their favours in as profitable a manner as possible'.⁶⁵ Judging from a petition from one of the *nattuvans* or musicians in the Tyagarajaswami temple, Tiruvalur, it also appears that it was customary for these men (who belonged to the same caste as the dancing girls) to share in the profits of what the girls earned outside the temple.⁶⁶ Moreover, *nattuvans* accompanied *devadasis* at nautch parties and probably also supplemented their income by playing and singing songs in the villages.⁶⁷

Of all the temple servants, dancing girls appear to have been among the most wealthy. What most surprised M. Monier Williams (the well-known Sanskritist and scholar of Hinduism) when he visited temples in southern India in the 1870s was the number and weight of the dancing girls' ornaments. In a subsequent account of his travels he wrote that

> Some wore nose-rings and finger-rings glittering with rubies and pearls. Their ears were pierced all round and filled with costly ear-rings. Their limbs were encumbered with bangles, anklets, armlets, toe-rings, necklaces, chain-ornaments, head-ornaments and the like. One of the Tanjore girls informed me that she had been recently robbed of jewels to the value of Rs. 25,000. No

doubt they drive a profitable trade under the sanction of religion, and some courtesans have been known to amass enormous fourtunes.[68]

It is fairly clear then that while temple employees were paid regular salaries or modest official emoluments depending on their duties within the temple, these payments do not give an adequate or precise indication of their total earnings — dancing girls, for example, accumulating considerable wealth. On the other hand, it is important to note that office-holding, involving the performance of specific duties, was not only linked with emoluments or income but with status, including personal and family reputation. The prestige and standing of individuals and families was sometimes more important than profit and could be greatly enhanced through association with one of the ancient centres of worship. Commenting on a case in which one of the offices in Srirangam (involving participation in ceremonies for one-sixteenth of a day per annum) was purchased for Rs. 200 in 1878 and Rs. 125 in 1888, the district munsiff declared that 'it is evident, that the people of Srirangam, even among the well-to-do classes, sometimes pay a fancy price for the mere dignity of holding some mirassi office in the temple.'[69]

Linked with particular duties and emoluments and implying a certain status within the worshipping community were temple honours. Many of the groups already mentioned, including donors, trustees, temple servants and other worshippers, participated in what Appadurai has described as 'the redistributive process'. This process which was initiated by the donor Appadurai defines as 'the ongoing relationship of exchange, in which goods and services are gifted to the deity, transformed in the process of worship, and reallocated to the worshippers in the form of shares, which are culturally demarcated by publicly received honors.'[70]

The honours which patrons, temple servants and others received as worshippers included sacred ingredients such as *prasadam* given in a specific ritual context, *tirttam* (sacred water left over from the deity's meals or his bath), *alankaram* (decorations such as robes, garlands etc.) and other objects or ingredients such as tumeric paste, sandalwood oil and betel nut. Referring to ceremonies in the Tiruvalur temple near Negapatam in Tanjore district in 1862, for example, the Rev. James Hobday (W.M.M.S.) described the way in which temple servants received honours (*prasadam*) towards the close of the ceremony. He remarked that

An offering of cocoanuts and other things was presented and in the end the servants of the temple came forward, and standing before the idol in the car, and in line received a portion of the sanctified food . . . The food when prepared is first presented to the god, and then divided amongst the temple servants; Panjayats [managers], priests, idol bearers and dancing women.[71]

The right to receive or share in particular honours, as well as the way in which this was done, usually depended upon the individual's generosity as donor or upon his or her ritual function or task within the temple. The receipt of honours therefore symbolized one's precise rank or status within the worshipping community.[72] A generous donor, one who, for example, had endowed the temple with a large portion of land or money, a trustee or a visiting guru or sectarian leader might perhaps receive special honours on a special festival occasion — honours which ordinary temple servants seldom received. Furthermore, some duties within the temple were regarded as more important for the welfare of the deity or of greater ritual significance than others and these differences were also reflected in the receipt of honours such as *tirttam* or *prasadam*. While, especially in the Protestant Christian community, the receipt of the bread and wine, including perhaps the sharing of a common cup, symbolized the spiritual equality of all believers (a point many of the Protestant missionaries in India never tired of making) the distribution of *prasadam* in the Hindu temple symbolized spiritual hierarchy. The order of precedence in which the worshippers received *prasadam* was all important and marked the temple servant's or worshipper's particular status in relation to the deity.

According to the *Koil Olugu* or *Chronicle of Srirangam* the trustees, together with various classes of servants, all received public recognition for their work in the form of honours during the medieval period.[73] Furthermore, the right to honours and precedence in the receipt of honours was one major cause of disputes between vadagalai and tengalai factions within Srirangam temple throughout the nineteenth century. In 1808, for example, tengalais, who regarded vadagalais as usurpers intent on gaining control over the temple, demanded the right to receive *tirttam* first.[74] In 1840 the Collector of Trichinopoly, A. P. Onslow, warned of the likelihood of disturbances over honours and requested the peshkar to enforce adherence to custom and keep the peace after the Jeer of the Ahobilam *Math*, the spiritual leader of the vadagalai sect, had himself performed honours (*satakopan*) in one of the outer shrines of the temple.[75] In 1850 it was complained in another dispute that the sathanies (a non-brahman caste who performed many of the menial services in the temple) had been prevented from exercising not only their *mirasi* privileges and offices but also 'honours' in the temple ceremonies.[76] Furthermore, in 1896, in another dispute involving the dismissal of one of the vadagalai trustees of the temple, the Chief Justice pointed out that the trustee involved had been dismissed the day before the principal day of the festival 'on which special honours would be paid to the plaintiff as trustee'.[77]

Though temples were primarily the abode of the deity, places of ritual and worship and occasionally also, as in the case of Srirangam and the Nachiyarkovil temple, centres of sectarian conflict and rivalry, they were also extremely important social institutions. Association with the more prestigious temples and public recognition in the form of honours were certainly factors in the regulation of local status. For aspiring politicians and for others looking for power, recognition or respect, the position of trustee, or a seat on the temple committee could be one way of gaining wider recognition and public esteem and of improving the individual's or the family's standing in the local community. As we shall see in Chapter 3, membership of a temple committee or appointment as a trustee could also bring with it powers of patronage together with the possibility of dispensing favours and of enlarging one's circle of 'friends' and allies. Amongst other things, temples, especially in the Kaveri delta, were also wealthy institutions. While some temple servants, such as those whose income could not be effectively controlled by temple authorities, were in a position to make moderate or even considerable fortunes, it was, as we shall see, the trustees and members of temple committees in particular who possessed the authority, including access to temple accounts, which could enable them to increase their own wealth at the expense of the institution.

C: RELIGION AND EVERYDAY LIFE

While temple worship and temple festivals were significant aspects of religious life in the region, it is important to note that not all Hindus had access to the major temples such as those described above. Indeed, a listing of castes excluded from the main temples in Tanjore district suggests that, even as late as the second half of the nineteenth century, as much as a third of the population was affected by bans on temple entry. Harijan and fishing castes, valaiyans, whose traditional occupation was hunting, and nadars, the toddy-tapping caste of Tamilnadu, were all excluded from worship at major temples throughout the district.[78]

Effectively excluded from the worship of the greater gods of Hinduism, lower and outcaste communities, in common with most other sections of the Hindu population (not excluding brahmans), were involved in the worship or propitiation of a whole host of less exalted beings. These ranged from deities like the much-loved Ganesh (Vigneswara), the elephant headed son of Siva, who was popular throughout India, through to village, caste and family deities and even demons or malignant spirits.[79]

Almost every village had its own particular *grama devata* (literally village deity) whose protection was seen as especially important for the ongoing life and survival of the village community. While a few of these spirits, including the ancient god Aiyanar, were male, most of them were *shaktis*, female spirits, known as *amma* or mother. They were believed to protect the village from the machinations of evil spirits or from some natural calamity such as drought, famine or disease. Among the more important of the *grama devatas* in Tanjore and Trichinopoly districts were Aiyanar, Madurai Viran, Mariamma, Pidari and numerous other *shaktis*.[80]

The worship of Aiyanar as well as of Madurai Viran (who, as we shall see, was of much more recent origin) was widespread in Tanjore and Trichinopoly districts.[81] Aiyanar, who used his position as chief of ghosts to restrain them from inflicting harm on men, was revered as guardian of boundaries, forests, tanks and rivers. He was reputed to ride out, sword in hand, with his retinue at midnight 'over hills and dales to clear the country of all obnoxious spirits'.[82] While it was believed that anyone who met his hunting party on the road would meet with certain death, he was, according to Oppert, 'much praised for his kindness' by village people who generally requested him 'to grant wealth, to bestow sons, to destroy enemies, to avert drought, to secure the favour of women, to destroy the evil effects of omens caused by lizards, and similar boons'.[83]

Though the *shaktis* had different names they represented much the same principle of power and tended to vary only in the details of the functions they performed. Unlike Aiyanar they were not only protectors, but also spirits which, if sufficiently aroused, could wreak vengeance on the whole community. As a result they were greatly feared and had to be kept happy and under control. Mariamma, who was considered by some of her followers as chief *shakti*, was the goddess of small-pox and disease generally.[84] But as well as being responsible for sickness she was sometimes also blamed for drought. While it was felt that her worship and propitiation, especially through blood sacrifice, was essential for the welfare and prosperity of the village community she, like Aiyanar, was also worshipped by individuals who desired something of her. Another example of a village goddess was Pidari, also worshipped extensively throughout the region.[85] As queen of devils she was considered to have the power to protect the people from devils and, like Mariamma, was also held responsible for drought and other disasters.

Although the *grama devatas* were worshipped regularly on a daily or weekly basis with a variety of offerings, including meat and drink, there were other occasions, during times of crisis, when it was felt especially necessary to placate them with further gifts and attention. Writing in his diary in September 1837, the Rev. J. E. Nimmo, an Anglo-Indian Protestant missionary preaching in the countryside near Kumbakonan, noted, for example that

> Only the other day, I had occasion to go to the village of Korreeyoor, when I happened to find a number of brass vessels, with a bunch of Margosa leaves, saffron, rice etc. set before the pialls of several of the houses, which they call Mahreeyamai, in order to implore her to remove the Cholera, which was then prevailing there . . . There is just now a great bustle in Combaconum about this goddess mareiyamai who they . . . imagine is the author of this fatal disorder.[86]

Aiyanar, Mariamma, Pidari and some of the other village deities were also honoured through the holding of annual festivals. Some of these, like the Mariamma festival at Samayapuram in Trichinopoly district, attracted many thousands of devotees.[87] Goats, swine and cocks were beheaded before their shrines and, in some cases, hookswinging also took place.[88]

Apart from those village deities who, like Mariamma, were worshipped by many different classes in the population, there were also specific caste deities — or patron spirits. For example, the tottiyans, who in Trichinopoly were mostly cultivators, worshipped patron dieties by the name of Bommakka and Mallamma — the spirits of two women who had burnt as satis.[89] The caste goddess of the local reddis was Yellama, whose temple was at Esanai in Perambalur taluk, while the caste deity of the Trichinopoly uppiliyians (whose traditional occupation had been salt manufacture) was Karnvandaraya Boomadeva.[90] According to Hemingway, he had no temple, 'but all Uppiliyans in a village join in offering him an annual sacrifice in Tai (January – February) before the earth is scraped for the first time in the season for making saltpetre'.[91]

In addition to the worship of the greater gods of Hinduism, of village, caste and family deities there was also the worship of the supernatural in living things.[92] The worship of trees such as the fig, the margosa, the banya and the palmyra was not uncommon and was a practice adopted by brahmans as well as by a range of other castes in the local Hindu population. Snakes, especially cobras, were also worshipped by high and low-caste devotees. Cattle were worshipped during Pongal, when the ploughing began and when the treading of the paddy commenced.

Last, but not least, was a widespread belief in the prevalence and power of evil spirits.[93] Indeed, it was believed that one of the principal duties of Aiyanar and other village deities was to prevent devils from harming members of the village community. These spirits, who were feared even by brahmans, were thought to dwell especially in trees, to haunt houses or wander restlessly from place to place preferring to inhabit burial and burning grounds, gibbets and places of execution. Calamities such as fire, flood and drought and all kinds of disease and evil deeds were ascribed to their activity. According to Hemingway, who collected his information on Tanjore district at the end of the nineteenth century, 'all classes' believed that evil spirits could be warded off by talismans, that women were often possessed by devils and that these could be driven out by the charms of a professional sorcerer.

We have already noted that while most of the sensitive and key positions involving the performance of rituals in the major temples were in the hands of brahmans, there is evidence that some non-brahmans played an important part in these temples as religious specialists. The worship, propitiation, or control of village and lesser spirits, including malevolent beings, also required the service of religious specialists. However, many of the priests and functionaries involved in these activities were drawn from lower socio-economic levels of Hindu society. Most of the *pujaris* or officiating priests of village shrines throughout the South appear to have been non-brahmans (including *pandarams*) or untouchables.[94] Untouchables not infrequently carried out the task of beheading animals at village festivals — a task which, though felt to be necessary, was generally abhorrent to brahmans.[95]

There is no reason to believe that the situation in the Kaveri delta was very different from elsewhere in the south, though there is evidence that brahmans acted as *pujaris* in at least two Mariamma temples in Tanjore district.[96] One of these was the Mariamma temple in Negapatam and the other was near the town of Tanjore. There is also evidence which suggests that brahmans took control of a village shrine near Trichinopoly during the latter part of the nineteenth century. Writing in his book published in 1921 Bishop Whitehead stated that 'An old Munsiff of the district told me that he could remember the time when all the pūjārîs were Śūdras. The Brāhmans appear to have secured a footing in the shrine about fifty years ago.'[97] In these instances where the brahmans were priests it is unlikely that animal sacrifices were offered at the central shrine where the brahmans ministered.[98]

Many of the castes other than brahmans were also involved as religious specialists in the propitiation or manipulation of subordinate spirits, though, even in these activities, brahman participation was not entirely absent. For example, some of the Trichinopoly kaniyalar brahmans (a sub-section of the smarthas), usually the women, were noted for their skill in being able to control evil spirits and cause them to possess a man.[99]

The world of spirit was not only felt to be all pervasive, and ever-present reality in daily life, but was also something which, as we have seen, could be used (even manipulated) on behalf of communities and individuals. There were rituals, prayers and formulations which could be used to meet almost everyone's needs — especially the needs of those in trouble or distress. One of the most important of these strategies in the life of the individual was the making of a vow or promise which it was hoped would influence the deity. Referring to this practice in Trichinopoly district Hemingway wrote that

> Throughout the district (as elsewhere) vows are commonly made at the shrines of deities of all classes. They consist of promises (*prartanai*) that the suppliant will do a stated act in honour of the god if his prayers for the grant of a specified boon are answered. Common vows made by those desirous of offspring are that if a child is born to them they will observe the ceremony of the first shaving of his head at the shrine of the deity invoked, or will hang a cradle in the temple. Those whose child is sick vow that if it recovers they will dedicate its jewels, or a sum of money, to the temple or will carry milk and sugar before the god on a *kavadi*. If the suppliant is himself ill, he vows that if he regains his health he will make a stated offering to the deity, or will perform some act of self-mortification such as piercing his tongue with a needle or some part of his body with a spear . . . Other common vows are to roll round and round a temple in the dust, or to give a puppet-show or drama in honour of the god. In the case of the village goddess, the vow is often an undertaking to put up images of heroes, cattle, men, etc. in front of their temples, or to walk through the fire. This latter is especially frequent when Draupadi is the goddess invoked. In the case of Mariyamman, the vow usually includes a promise to carry an earthen pot (*kazagam*) on the head to her temple.[100]

Popular religion was not only vital and relevant to the daily life of individuals and communities, but was also adaptive and far from static. There is evidence, for example, of change in the uses and significance of cultic centres over a very short period and of the appearance of new gods and objects of worship.

On at least two occasions in Tanjore district in the nineteenth century the accidental discovery of images revived an interest in old but long-neglected sacred sites.[101] In 1863, for example, the accidental ploughing up of images of Vishnu and other deities in a field in the Tirutturaippundi subdivision sparked off rumours that these objects were endowed with miraculous powers of healing. Pilgrims flocked to the site, a new temple was erected and numerous people continued to visit the spot thereafter.

It is also clear that some of the deities worshipped in Tanjore and Trichinopoly districts in the nineteenth century were of comparatively recent origin. While, as noted above, some of the caste deities appear to have arisen as a result of the deification of women who were burned as satis, Madurai Viran, one of the most popular village deities in the region, was also comparatively new. According to Hemingway, he was 'the deification of an historical character, a man who was the servant of one of the polygars of Madura and afterwards of Tirumala Nayakkan, king of that town.'[102] Furthermore, many Hindus honoured the new saints or spirits which had arisen as a result of the introduction of Islam and Christianity. Together with pilgrims of other faiths, they adopted the practice of making vows at the *darga* (tomb) of the Muslim saint Miran Sahib at Nagore[103] and also joined with Christians in the annual pilgrimage to the little chapel of Our Lady of Health at Velanganni some six miles from Negapatam.[104]

While, as we intend to suggest, British rule impinged most directly on the institutions and consciousness of higher-caste Hindus, it also had some effects on popular religion — on festivals, including temple-cart processions, and on the practice of hook-swinging. The character of religious festivals, the nature and significance of temple-cart processions, fire-walking and hook-swinging (all matters of some concern to British authorities and therefore better documented than some other aspects of popular religion) will be discussed in subsequent chapters which will also explore the effects of British rule. Our more immediate concern is, however, with the East India Company's initial reaction and perception of its role in religious affairs in the region — a perception which, amongst other things, led to its involvement in the recruitment of labour for temple-cart processions.

NOTES

1 R. S. Aiyar *History of the Nayaks of Madura*, Madras 1924, pp. 53, 255 and Appendix D including inscriptions Nos. 20, 42, 50, 61, 77, 127, 130, 163, 170, 177, 178, 206,215 and 225.
2 Ibid., ins. No. 124−5.
3 Ibid., ins. 50, 73, 130, 170, 177−9, 196.
4 Ibid., ins. 64, 231.
5 Ibid., ins. 198, 232, 237, 241, 261.
6 For an account of the Nayak's attitude towards the Madura Mission see especially R. Sathianathaier, *Tamilaham in the 17th Century*, Madras 1956, Ch. VI.
7 Aiyar, op. cit., ins. 251.

NOTES TO CHAPTER 1

8 See copy of an order issued by Hazarat Nawab Saheb in 1796 in V. N. Hari Rao 'A History of Trichinopoly and Srirangam', Ph.D. Thesis, University of Madras, 1948.
9 Apart from Sathianathaier, op. cit., see especially A. Merrsman. 'The Catholic Church in Tranquebar and Tanjore During the Formative Years of the Lutheran Mission' in *I.C.H.R.*, Vol. 1, No. 1, December 1967, esp. pp. 105–12.
10 K. R. Subramanian, *The Maratha Rajas of Tanjore*, Madras 1928, esp. pp. 33–5.
11 Ibid., p. 33.
12 Ibid., p. 30.
13 Ibid., pp. 33–5.
14 Ibid., p. 58.
15 T. V. Row, *A Manual of the District of Tanjore*, Madras 1883, pp. 235, 237, 239.
16 C. U. Aitchison, *A Collection of Treaties, Engagements and Sanads Relating to India and Neighbouring Countries*, Vol. X, Calcutta 1930, pp. 86–8.
17 Ibid., pp. 87–8.
18 Meersman, op. cit., pp. 94–5 and also his book entitled *The Ancient Franciscan Provinces in India, 1500–1835*, Bangalore 1971, pp. 384–98; F. R. Hemingway, *Tanjore*, p. 161. For an account of the origins and development of the parava community see P. A. Roche, *Fishermen of the Coromandel: A Study of the Paravas of the Coromandel*, Delhi 1984.
19 Meersman. 'The Catholic Church in Tranquebar . . .', p. 103.
20 Sathianathaier, op. cit., pp. 130–1.
21 See especially A. Lehmann, *It Began at Tranquebar: the story of the Tranquebar mission and the beginnings of Protestant Christianity in India*, Madras 1956.
22 Ibid., p. 139.
23 Even though Ziegenbalg, for example, believed that these 'heathens' still possessed some traditions 'out of the Word of God' there can be little doubt that he wanted to destroy and replace much of what he discovered in Hinduism. Writing in the preface to his treatise on the gods of South India and referring to Christ Jesus as the 'Universal Saviour of the World', he prayed that Christ might 'dispel from this pagan country the heathenish darkness, and illuminate it with the light of his saving Gospel. May He destroy and annihilate the false gods, whom they now still worship, and may He alone be adored by them as the King of glory!' (B. Ziegenbalg, *Genealogy of the South Indian Gods* . . . (translated into English by the Rev. G. J. Metzger), Madras 1869, p. XIX.
24 For an account of the revival of Lutheran missionary activity see especially E. R. Baierlein, *The Land of the Tamulians and its Missions*, translated from the German by J. D. B. Gribble, Madras 1875, Chapter III.
25 Ibid., pp. 195–6.

NOTES TO CHAPTER 1   35

26 G. A. Oddie, 'Christians in the Census; Tanjore and Trichinipoly Districts, 1871 – 1901' in N. G. Barrier (ed.), *The Census in British India: New Perspectives*, Delhi 1981.
27 Infra, Ch. 10.
28 Jesuit missionaries like Fr. Walter Clifford were well aware of the need to respect Indian customs where these did not appear to positively contradict the teachings of Christianity. 'Whenever these national prejudices do not hurt in any respect the interests of religion,' he wrote, 'we are obliged to respect them. To try to eradicate them would be useless trouble'(*A.P.F.*, Vol. V, 1844, pp. 188 – 9). Catholicism with its emphasis on the role of priests, devotion to subsidiary spiritual beings, namely the saints and the Virgin Mary, its processions, symbols and elaborate ceremony, pilgrimage and sacred shrines, dovetailed much more easily into the pre-existing patterns of Hindu practice than Protestant forms of religion. This was a point the Protestants themselves were quick to notice with various degrees of disapproval. 'During the past ten days', wrote the Rev. J. M. Thompson, from Negapatam in 1877, 'we have had an exhibition of the kind of work the Church of Rome is doing in the land. They have just celebrated the festival of Corpus Christi; and its accompaniments in the shape of processions, cars containing images, lighted torches, tom-tom beating, and image worship, would certainly have led to the conclusion that the festival was a heathen one, had it not been that the cross was here and there visible.' (*W.M.N.*, 1877, p. 207). See also Infra, Ch. 9.
29 See especially B. Stein, 'The Economic Function of a Medieval South Indian Temple', *J.A.S.*, Vol. XIX, February 1960; R. Nagaswamy, 'The South Indian Temple — As An Employer', *I.E.S.H.R.*, Vol. 2, No. 4, October 1965; G. W. Spencer, 'Religious Networks and Royal Influence in Eleventh Century South India', *Journal of the Economic and Social History of the Orient*, Vol XII, January 1969; Richard Kennedy, 'Status and Control of Temples in Tamil Nadu', *I.E.S.H.R.*, Vol. XI, Nos. 2 – 3, June – September 1974; and C. J. Baker, 'Temples and Political Development', in C. J. Baker and D. A. Washbrook, op. cit.
30 Mudaliar, op. cit., pp. 22 – 3.
31 Ibid., pp. 27 – 30.
32 Dickinson, having had experience as a district officer in Chittor and Nellore was Collector and Magistrate of Trichinopoly, 1826 – 28. (C. C. Prinsep *Record of Services of the Honourable East India Company's Civil Servants in the Madras Presidency from 1741 to 1858*, London 1885). Nathanial W. Kindersley (1794 – 1844) was the fifth child in a family which had a long association with India. His grandfather, Colonel Nathaniel Kindersley (1732 – 1769), joined the army and accompanied Clive to Bengal in 1764. His father, Nathaniel Edward (1763 – 1831), was in banking and business in Madras and later became Collector of North Arcot (1790 – 2). N. W., who entered the Company's service in 1814, hated India at first, but changed his mind while acting as Second Assistant to the Collector and Magistrate of Coimbatore where he was able to indulge his passion for sport and outdoor life. After experience as Head Assistant to the Collector, and Magistrate of Nellore (1822 – 4). Sub-

NOTES TO CHAPTER 1

Collector and Assistant Magistrate of Canara (1824 – 5) and Sub-Collector of Tinnevelly (1825 – 8) he became the longest serving Collector in Tanjore district in the nineteenth century, acting as Collector, with one interval of about 18 months, from 1828 to 1843, when he became Second Member of the Board of Revenue (Prinsep, op. cit., I.O.R. J/1/29; A. F. Kindersley *A History of the Kindersley Family*, printed for private circulation, 1938).

33 Collr. to Sec., 14/2/1828, *M.R.P.*, Ra. 296, Vol. 50, 25/2/1828.
34 The name was apparently derived from a Chola king who first consecrated the *Lingam* on the top of the rock. (Hemingway, *Trichinopoly*, p. 340, n. 2).
35 Collr. to Sec., Board of Revenue, 26/11/1841, *M.R.P.*, Ra. 303. Vol. 32. 16/12/1841.
36 Collr. to Sec., 14/2/1828 including Abstract Statement showing the Receipts and Charges of the Principal Pagodas in the Trichinopoly Division, *M.R.P.*, Ra. 296, Vol. 50, 25/2/1828.
37 These were the Kampharesvaraswami temple, Tirubuyanam and the Mahalingaswami temple, Tiruvidaimarudur, Kumbakonam taluk; the Athmanathaswami temple, Avadayarkoil, Puttukkottai; the Vedaranyesvaraswami temple, Vedaranyam, Tirutturaippundi taluk; and the Vilinathaswami Temple, Tiruvilimalalai, Nannilam taluk.
38 Infra, Ch. 2.
39 T. V. Row, op. cit., p. 226. See also J. Hepburn to Sec., *M.R.P.*, Ra. 292, Vol. 66, 18/5/1818.
40 P. R. Ganapathi Iyer, *The Law Relating re Hindu and Mahomedan Religious Endowments*, Madras 1905, p. CLXVI, Town Munsiff of Trichinopoly to Collector of Trichinopoly, 6/7/1872 and Vakil of the Civil Court of Trichinopoly to Acting Collector of Trichinopoly, 12/8/1872 in *M.R.P.* (henceforth *I.O.R.*, P/383), 18/7/1874.
41 Infra, Ch. 3.
42 Born 5 March 1784, son of the Rev. J. S. Lushington of Newcastle Upon Tyne; joined the Company's service as Writer in 1801; 1803 – 13 had experience mostly of legal work in Rajahmundry; 1813 – 15 Assistant Judge of Kumbakonam; 1815 – 23 Collr. and Magistrate of Trichinopoly (*I.O.R.*, J/1/18 and Prinsep, op. cit.).
43 Lushington to Sec., 19/6/1818. *M.R.P.*, Ra. 291. Vol. 71, 29/6/1818.
44 Infra, Ch. 4.
45 On the status of *devadasis* or dancing girls see especially E. Thurston, *Castes and Tribes of Southern India*, Vol II, Madras 1909.
46 Collr. to Sec., 14/2/1828, *M.R.P.*, Ra. 296, Vol. 50, 25/2/1828; Head Assist. Collr. to Sec., 12/11/1814, *M.R.P.*, Ra. 291, Vol. 23, 17/11/1814; Garrow to Sec., 10/6/1809, *M.R.P.*, Ra. 289, Vol. 32, 15/6/18.
47 G. A. Oddie, *Social Protest in India: British Protestant Missionaries and Social Reforms, 1850 – 1900*, Delhi 1979, pp. 103 – 4.
48 See the Rev. J. Hobday's remarks on temple servants employed in the Tyagaraja temple in Tanjore district (*H.F.*, Vol. 1, September 1862, p. 249).

NOTES TO CHAPTER 1

49 Collr. to Sec., 14/2/1828, *M.R.P.*, Ra. 296, Vol. 50, 25/2/1828; Wallace to Sec., 15/2/1814, *M.R.P.*, Ra. 291, Vol. 1, 24/2/1814; J. A. Dubois, *Hindu Manners Customs and Ceremonies* (Translated ... by H. K. Beauchamp) Third ed., Oxford 1905, p. 587.
50 Garrow to Sec., 10/6/1809, *M.R.P.*, Ra. 289, Vol. 32, 15/6/1809.
51 Dickinson to Sec., 14/2/1828, *M.R.P.*, Ra. 296, Vol. 50, 25/2/1828.
52 N. S. Cameron to Sec., 24/9/1830, *M.R.P.*, Ra. 297, Vol. 60, 7/10/1830.
53 Ibid.
54 Collr. to Sec., 14/2/1828, *M.R.P.*, Ra. 296, Vol. 50, 25/2/1828.
55 Collr. to Sec., 24/9/1830, *M.R.P.*, Ra. 297, Vol. 60, 7/10/1830.
56 Ibid. and Collr. to Sec., 3/7/1837, *M.R.P.*, Ra. 300, Vol. 75, 17/7/1837.
57 Precise data on agricultural wages in Trichinopoly district in the early nineteenth century are difficult to obtain. According to J. A. Dubois, who was familiar with conditions in the Tamil as well as in the Kanada-speaking districts and who finalized the last draft of his manuscript in about 1823, agricultural labourers, when paid in coin, received 'from twelve to twenty rupees a year' according to locality — labourers being paid better along the coast. (Dubois, op. cit., p. 82). Thirty years later J. D. Bourdillion, who had had experience of work in Trichinopoly and was then Collector of Arcot, wrote that 'the earnings of a man employed in agricultural labour [in the fourteen principal ryotwari districts] cannot be quoted at more than 20 rupees a year, including everything' (S. Srinivasa Raghavaiyangar, op. cit. p. xli). Unskilled labour in the process industries apparently earned a little more — a sugar manufacturer reporting in 1848 that he could get as much labour as he wanted at 2 – 3 rupees per month (*Cambridge Economic History of India*, Vol. 2, p. 374, Cambridge 1983).
58 M. S. Thiruvenkata Chari, *A Collection of Papers relating to Sri Runganathasasawmi Temple*, Trichinopoly 1887, p. 13.
59 Srinivasa Raghavaiyangar, op. cit., pp. cxcv – cc. For details of the average price of food grains in Trichinopoly district over five-year periods from 1809 to 1888 see ibid. pp. c – ciii.
60 L. Moore, *A Manual of Trichinopoly District*, Madras 1878, p. 244.
61 Collr. to Sec., 14/2/1828, *M.R.P.*, Ra. 296, Vol. 50, 25/2/1828.
62 Collr. to Sec., 24/9/1830, *M.R.P.*, Ra. 297, Vol. 60, 7/10/1830.
63 *M.H.C.*, Second Appeal, No. 467 of 1898.
64 Oddie, *Social Protest* ..., pp. 103 – 5.
65 Dubois, op. cit., p. 586.
66 Hepburn to President, 6/4/1819, *M.R.P.*, Ra. 293, Vol. 16, 12/4/1819.
67 C. E. Gover, *The Folk-Songs of Southern India*, 2nd ed., Madras 1959, pp. xi – xv; Thurston, op. cit., Vol. V, p. 272.
68 M. Monier Williams, *Brahmanism and Hinduism or Religious Thought and Life in India*, 4th ed. London 1891, p. 451.
69 *M.H.C.*, Second Appeal, No. 1571 of 1891.
70 A. Appadurai, *Worship and Conflict* ..., p. 212.
71 *H.F.*, Vol. 1 September 1862, p. 249.
72 See especially Appadurai, *Worship and Conflict* ..., p. 36.
73 Appadurai, *Worship and Conflict* ..., pp. 76, 85 – 8.

74 Original Suit no. 130 of 1808 in the Zillah Court of Trichinopoly cited in M. S. Thiruvenkata Chari, op. cit., p. 3.
75 Chari, op. cit., pp. 35 – 6.
76 Ibid., p. 45.
77 *M.H.C.*, Appeals Nos. 22 and 23 of 1896.
78 See Appendix 5.
79 For an eighteenth century account of popular religion in South India, much of it based on letters, conferences and interviews with Hindus, see B. Ziegenbalg, *Genealogy of the South-Indian Gods*, (translated into English by G. J. Metzger) Madras 1869. For the most thorough and comprehensive nineteenth century account, especially of village and subordinate deities, see Oppert, op. cit., pp. 450 – 513, 554 – 74, and for slightly more recent discussions of popular religion see H. Whitehead, op. cit., and W. T. Elmore, *Dravidian Gods in Modern HInduism*, Madras 1925.
80 Hemingway, *Tanjore*, p. 68 and *Trichinopoly*, p. 89.
81 A special feature of Aiyanar's shrine, which was usually located in a grove some distance from the village, was a collection of clay horses, elephants, buffaloes and other animals which had been left for him and represented the gifts of devotees, who when they or their families were ill or in distress, vowed to dedicate such offerings to Aiyanar. (Oppert, op. cit., p. 510; Hemingway, *Tanjore*, p. 68).
82 Hemingway, *Tanjore*, p. 68.
83 Oppert, op. cit., p. 506.
84 Ziegenbalg, op. cit., pp. 138 – 40; Oppert, op. cit., pp. 471 – 85; Hemingway, *Tanjore*, p. 69.
85 Ziegenbalg, op. cit., pp. 175 – 6; Oppert, op. cit., pp. 491 – 5.
86 *L.M.S.*, J. E. Nimmo to W. Ellis 20/9/1837, S.I. Tamil, Box 7. The margosa or neem tree is an evergreen bearing white flowers, (*Melia azadirachta*) and was frequently associated with village deities. On some occasions, such as the one referred to above, it was used to symbolize the goddess herself. (Hemingway, *Tanjore*, p. 476; Oppert, op. cit., p. 476; Whitehead, op. cit., p. 37.)
87 Hemingway, *Trichinopoly*, p. 89; Oppert, op. cit., pp. 461, 475 – 6, 498, 512; Zeigenbalg, op. cit., pp. 134, 139.
88 Infra, ch. 6.
89 Thurston, op. cit., Vol. VII, pp. 184, 196.
90 Hemingway, *Trichinopoly*, p. 91.
91 Ibid., p. 117.
92 Hemingway, *Tanjore*, p. 70.
93 Ibid., pp. 66 – 7; Hemingway, *Trichinopoly*, p. 89; Oppert op. cit., pp. 559 – 65. See also Ziegenbelg, pp. 152-5.
94 See especially Ziegenbalg, op. cit., pp. 134, 139, 143; Oppert, op. cit., pp. 460, 469, 503, 510, 512; Whitehead, op. cit., pp. 18 – 20.
95 Writing in his well-known manual in the early eighteenth century Ziegenbalg declared that 'brahmans will have nothing to do with the shedding of blood though they, too, believe the Grama devatas and the chief among devils [Aiyanar] cannot be made propitious except by the shedding of blood'. [op. cit., p. 143].

NOTES TO CHAPTER 1

96 *I.O.R.*, P/3784, *M.J.P.*, 27/81 1890, Hemingway, *Tanjore*, p. 69; Whitehead, op. cit., p. 19.
97 Whitehead, op. cit., p. 105.
98 Ibid., p. 19.
99 Hemingway, *Trichinopoly*, p. 87; Thurston, op. cit., Vol. 1, p. 343.
100 Hemingway, *Trichinopoly*, pp. 91-2.
101 *Madras Times*, 2/6/1863, 24/5/1866; Hemingway, *Tanjore*, p. 283.
102 Hemingway, *Tanjore*, p. 68.
103 Ibid., p. 243.
104 Ibid., p. 250.

2

COMPANY POLICIES, TEMPLES AND
CHANGING ATTITUDES 1800 – 1838

The East India Company's religious policy was much the same in Tanjore and Trichinopoly districts as in other parts of the South.

The Company was primarily concerned with the development of its trade and commerce and hence with the maintenance of a peaceful environment in which these activities would prosper. Once the Company had acquired new territories, officials were anxious to reconcile the people to the new regime and to avoid causing further offence through any unnecessary interference in their customs and way of life.[1] Hence they hastened to inform their new subjects that the Company would protect their religious institutions and respect their religious and social usages.

Fairly typical of these pronouncements was the declaration of 1801 made to the people of the Carnatic, including Trichinopoly district:

Although the Right Honourable the Governor in Council trusts that the experience which the inhabitants of the Carnatic have already had will have rendered it unnecessary for his Lordship to explain the general principles of moderation, justice, protection, and security, which form the characteristic features of the British Government, yet his Lordship in accepting the sacred trust transferred to the Company by the present engagements, invites the people of the Carnatic to a ready and cheerful obedience to the authority of the Company, in a confident assurance of enjoying, under the protection of public and defined laws, every just and ascertained civil right, with a free exercise of the religious institutions and domestic usages of their ancestors.[2]

Well aware of their precarious hold upon the allegiance of the people and of the dangers of innovation, Company officials simply adopted the policy of previous rulers — or, at least, of those rulers who had adhered most strictly to the ideas of protection and toleration.

THE TANJORE RAJAS' RELIGIOUS POLICY AND
ACTIVITY UNDER COMPANY RULE

In Tanjore the implementation of this policy was complicated by the fact that the Tanjore Rajas were permitted to retain their title, together with some of their powers and privileges, even after annexation. The Company took over most of the country's administration, but permitted Raja Serfoji to retain control of the fort at Tanjore and to continue to exercise many of his religious functions.³ He was given a money allowance part of which could be used for the patronage of religion and was also permitted to 'exercise authority and superintendence' over the 59 or so temples in the fort and palace area.⁴ Furthermore, Company officials, anxious to reconcile both Raja and people to the new regime, made some attempt to raise additional revenue so that Serfoji would be able to continue patronizing and celebrating the usual festivals 'so gratifying to the Rajah and his People'.⁵

A part of Tanjore therefore remained, at least for the time being, a type of Hindu enclave — the rajas, within certain given limitations, being able to pursue many of their own traditional religious policies.

Perhaps even more than his predecessors, Raja Serfoji was generous to Christians. He continued to remember with much affection the Rev. C. F. Swartz, the German missionary working with the S.P.C.K., whom the East India Company had appointed as his guardian in 1788, and who died just one year before the annexation.⁶ He gave orders that his Christian servants (civil and military personnel) were not to be prevented from attending church on Sundays or observing their own festivals.⁷ He continued to allow Tamil Christians the right of worshipping in the church within the fort and gave missionaries permission to open a school in the same place.⁸ He also supplied Tanjore Christians with grain during the period of famine and, amongst other measures, established a charitable institution for the education and support of Christian children.⁹

But like Tuljaji and much to the puzzlement of the Rev. H. Pearson, Swartz's biographer, Raja Serfoji does not appear to have contemplated conversion to Christianity¹⁰ and lavished most of his attention on support and promotion of Hindu activities and institutions. During the period of his rule, from 1798 – 1832, he continued with a programme of constructing temples¹¹ and paid particular attention to repairs and improvements in the great Brihadesvara temple a few kilometres from his palace.¹² He repaired all the shrines in the temple, rebuilt the tank at the northern end of the enclosure, constructed new *mandapams* or ceremonial halls, and improved the *prakara* with stone pavements. In 1800 in honour of his favourite concubine the Raja established the largest and most magnificent of the 'Rajah's *Chattrams*' in the district. This institution was intended for the use and accommodation of pilgrims on the road southwards to Rameswaram.¹³ A few years later the Raja erected two sacrificial halls nearby and performed Vedic sacrifices.¹⁴ He was also constant in his efforts to maintain and even increase the scale and splendour of religious festivals. He contributed

5 Raja Serfoji of Tanjore riding in procession

funds towards expenses involved in the celebration of Pongal and the great Mahamagum festival held every twelve years in Kumbakonam.[15] In 1807 he presented the Brihadesvara temple with three new temple carts and, throughout his reign, made special efforts to secure the attendance of an adequate number of labourers to drag these and other coaches at festivals.[16] He also attempted to maintain the usual pomp and display apparent at the annual celebration of the Dasara festival in Tanjore which he expected all senior British officials to attend.[17]

The Raja was not, however, merely patron of existing religious institutions and communities whether Christian or Hindu. He was also known for his increasing personal piety and devotion, principally to saivism. In 1802, he visited and performed devotions in Trichinopoly and on the island of Srirangam in thanksgiving for the Company's confirmation of his title as Raja.[18] In 1813 he followed the example of Amar Singh, his immediate predecessor, in going on pilgrimage to the famous saivite shrine at Rameswaram, where according to the Resident, William Blackburne, he was 'incessantly and zealously occupied in the rites and ceremonies of his religion' and where, in what the Resident regarded as an excess of fervour, the Raja even ordered his Muslim attendants to shave their heads.[19] Like many other Hindus, Raja Serfoji believed that 'the most desirable object to a Hindu is to visit the most Sacred and highly celebrated Kausee [Benares] and to perform ablutions in the Ganges'[20] and, while at Rameswaram, he made a vow to visit Benares. During the journey northwards in 1821 he visited and presented gifts to many well-known temples including Tirupathi and Jaganath and, while in Benares, was able to inspect his own 'charities' — *chattrams* and other facilities established especially for pilgrims from South India.[21]

The Raja's general policies of patronage and support for Hinduism were continued under his son Shivaji (1832 – 1853) though the latter appears to have been much less sympathetic to Christianity.[22] When Shivaji, the last of the line, died without issue in 1853, mourned by the multitudes who lined the streets and by the tens of thousands who accompanied him to his funeral pyre, it was indeed the end of an era and of what many must have come to feel was an ancient and divinely ordained way of life.[23]

THE COMPANY'S INCREASING CONNECTION WITH HINDUISM

In the meantime East India Company officials who had assumed ultimate responsibility for religious affairs in Trichinopoly and for the protection and continued functioning of those temples in Tanjore not under the control of the Raja, discovered that their task was complex and difficult.

Though their predecessors had been active in attempts to finance and support religious establishments in the region, they were seldom involved in the details of temple administration. According to John Wallace, Collector of Tanjore from 1805 to 1813, most of the temple communities in the area had been left largely to their own devices. Writing in 1814 he observed that

> Previously to 1812, the numerous, and in many cases considerable establishments [temples] had, in pursuance of former usage, been left almost exclusively in the Management of the Tumberans [non-brahman monks], Stanikums [superintendents], and other servants belonging to them. In some of the more considerable Churches the Tasildars [chief Government revenue officers] had a general superintendence of their affairs; but . . . were unable to exercise that efficient authority over them, which was necessary . . . The accounts of former years' management, as far as they have been hitherto examined, shew a want of regularity such as might be expected in so extensive and complicated an Establishment, without any efficient Head to superintend the due realization of its Revenues, and to direct the proper application of them to the purposes for which they are intended.[24]

While British officers, like their Indian predecessors, were anxious merely to protect existing religious establishments, they became slowly but surely convinced that this protection was possible only through an increasing interference in the management of religious institutions. The continued and effective functioning of temples and temple ceremony seemed to them to demand increasing intervention until, by the late 1820s, they were involved in the fine details of management, probably to a much greater extent than had occurred before.

One of the problems connected with temples under their direct control or supervision (as distinct from those which were still under the control of the Raja) was the apparent alienation of temple lands. In Tanjore, Wallace found that debts had been incurred by managers of many of the endowed temples by mortgages on land to the value of Rs. 1,99,861 — a considerable sum of money. In 1812 he resumed all these lands on behalf of these institutions.[25] A few years later James Hepburn, Wallace's successor, drew the Board of Revenue's attention to the fact that the Kumbakonam district court had authorized the superintendent of the Paumony temple to sell some of its lands in order to defray the costs involved in temple ceremonies and worship.[26] He expressed the fear that if the lands were sold this would create a precedent leading to the widespread alienation of revenues of different public institutions. The Board in reply directed the Collector to take such measures as he thought necessary 'to prevent the execution of the decree in the first instance and to obtain its reversal in the second instance.'[27] It also sent copies of the correspondence to other Collectors informing them of the Board's opinion 'that a Court of India is not competent to order the sale of alienated lands of this description in satisfaction of private debt.'[28]

Another problem which seemed to require immediate attention was the fact that some of even the most prestigious temples appeared to be in a sad state of disrepair. Collectors or their assistants were soon involved in a wide range of activities connected with repairs and maintenance. These included major projects, such as repairs to the walls of Srirangam, or details such as the replacement of the bamboo poles for carrying the 'swami' in procession and repairs to his pearl umbrellas and robes.[29]

Last, but not least, were a host of problems associated with the internal management and staffing of these institutions. Apart from disturbing rumours which suggested (and which may have been designed to suggest) corruption or maladministration,[30] there was a constant stream of petitions, complaints and requests connected with office holding, including the appointment, salaries, rights and dismissal of temple servants.[31] Temple employees themselves demanded Company involvement in temple affairs. This was partly because of conflict within temple communities, coupled with a belief among temple servants that, if they could persuade the Collector to become involved, they might be able to obtain a decision more favourable to themselves. One example of this was an incident involving a drummer in the temple at Tiruvalur.[32] Having failed to persuade the dancing girls to give him a greater share of the profits derived from their sexual activity outside the temple premises, the drummer asked the Collector to intervene. The latter replied that he could not compel the dancing girls to comply with the drummer's wishes, as it was a private dispute, 'altogether unconnected' with the temple, and that the drummer must therefore, if he was dissatisfied, apply to the Courts for redress. Having tried several times to persuade the Collector to change his mind, the drummer decided to interrupt ceremonies in the temple, 'hoping by this means to compel the Collector to intervene and decide in his favour'. All the musicians were called into the dispute and, not only stopped work until such time as the dancing girls would agree to share more of their earnings, but carried off the great drums so as to be absolutely sure that others would not be employed in their place. The ceremonies were either cancelled or disrupted and the Collector, whose business it was to see that worship was maintained, was forced to intervene.

As well as having to face problems such as these, district officers were frequently asked for information and details about temples and temple accounts by the Board of Revenue. Moreover, in Tanjore, the pressure on Collectors to become further involved in the Hindu religious establishment was greatly increased by the fact that they were expected, whenever necessary, to facilitate the Raja's religious affairs. Raja Serfoji, for example, frequently asked Collectors, through the British Resident, to arrange for the payment of special allowances to temples organizing periodic celebrations.[33] He expected Collectors to secure the ingredients used in worship,[34] to help maintain security in his temples in the town of Tanjore,[35] to organize the recruitment of labour in British territory for drawing temple carts in the palace and fort area, and to make arrangements for his pilgrimage and even for the presentation of gifts to temples in other parts of India.[36]

One of the results of the Company's increased involvement in Hindu religious affairs in the Kaveri delta, as well as in other parts of the Madras Presidency, was that Company officials gained a reputation for managing religious endowments with increased efficiency.[37] Temples were refurbished, ceremonies and festivals conducted with regularity, and revenues gradually increased.

Another result was an increasing tendency to introduce change or innovation, partly because of the emphasis on improving efficiency of existing institutions. Some district officers were not, for example, especially sensitive in their attitude towards hereditary positions. Hereditary trustees were occasionally dismissed; while in the Srirangam temple, some hereditary positions were sold at public auction, a policy which had the effect of bringing outsiders into what had been a traditional and closed preserve.

But even more important for long-term religious developments in the delta, and in the Madras Presidency as a whole, was a growing disquiet in Britain over the company's increasing involvement in Hindu religious affairs. This increasing association with Hinduism coincided with the growth of the Evangelical revival in the United Kingdom and led to increasing public pressure on the Company to withdraw from what many Christians believed was an excessive and inexcusable support and encouragement of 'idolatry'.

THE TEMPLE-CART CONTROVERSY AND GROWTH OF OPPOSITION

One of the most contentious issues (at least in Tanjore district which was famous for the number and splendour of its temple festivals) was the involvement of Company servants in the compulsory recruitment of labour for the drawing of temple-carts during temple celebrations.

Many Christians in Britain and India were already familiar with complaints about the way in which the East India Company appeared to condone the 'horrors' of Jagannath through its regulation of the pilgrim tax and its apparent indifference to the fate of pilgrims who threw themselves to be crushed underneath the pondrous wheels of Jagannath's vehicle.[38] The subject of temple-carts was an emotive issue and, in the Madras Presidency, was also an issue which raised doubts and fuelled the debate about the wisdom of the Company's religious policy. Reports and discussion, centred on the hazards associated with the pulling of temple-carts and on various aspects of the recruitment system, intensified opposition to what was popularly known as the Company's 'connexion with idolatry' and strengthened the movement which eventually forced a change in the Company's religious policy.

Abbé Dubois, the Catholic missionary and author of *Hindu Manners, Customs and Ceremonies*, who spent over thirty years in the Tamil and Kanada speaking districts of South India, describing temple-carts, wrote that

> There is not a single temple of any note which has not one or two processions every year. On such occasions the idols are placed on huge massive cars supported on four large solid wheels, not made, like our wheels, with spokes and felloes. A big beam serves as the axle, and supports the car proper, which is sometimes fifty feet in height. The thick blocks which form the base are carved with images of men and women . . . Several stages of carved planking are raised upon this basement, gradually diminishing in width until the whole fabric has the form of a pyramid. On the days of procession the car is adorned with coloured calicoes, costly cloths, green foliage, garlands of flowers, &c. The idol, clothed in the richest apparel and adorned with its most precious jewels, is placed in the middle of the car, beneath an elegant canopy. Thick cables are attached to the car, and sometimes more than a thousand persons are harnessed to it.[39]

While this description of temple-carts is accurate enough, it gives no indication of how many more than 'a thousand persons' were sometimes required to drag or pull the vehicles. One of the largest cars in Tanjore district was used to carry an image of Siva in the annual procession at Tiruvalur in Negapatam taluk. According to the Rev. A. Bourne, the car, which was drawn by six artificial horses (four of which were three or four times larger than natural horses), required 10 to 12,000 thousand men to move it — the largest of the six ropes used for the purpose being 1,600 feet long.[40] In his analysis of the number of coolies needed for the Mahamagum festival held in Kumbakonam in 1838, the Rev. J. E. Nimmo (L.M.S.) calculated that the number of men employed to move each of the 12 cars ranged from 1,000 *for the*

6 Temple car being drawn in procession

smallest car to 12,000 for the vehicle belonging to the Sarangapani temple.[41] About 5,000 people were required to drag the great car belonging to Rajagopalaswami temple in Mannargudi[42] and 4,000 to draw Sri Ramachandraswami's vehicle from one of Raja Serfoji's temples in the fort.[43] Further evidence and general confirmation of the large numbers involved in dragging individual temple-carts in Tanjore district appears in a statement by the Police Amin of Negapatam who in 1840 remarked that 'no less than 10,000 Men' were required to draw some of the larger cars in the province.[44]

When we translate these figures into more general requirements then the total number of labourers required was very considerable indeed. The Raja of Tanjore, for example, argued that he needed 30,000 men to draw temple-carts during the annual festival in the town of Tanjore and another 20,000 for celebrations in the same centre on other occasions throughout the year.[45] Robert Nelson, Sub-Collector of Tanjore in 1827 – 8, who was especially interested in the issue, stated that 15,000 men were also required for the annual feasts at Kumbakonam, the same number of Madyarjunam (Tiruvadaimarudur) and at Trivalur, and 12,000 at Mannargudi.[46] Taking these and other requirements into account he estimated that as many as 85,000 coolies (eight per cent of the district population) were required on an average of five times a year to perform temple duties.

The recruitment of labour for the dragging of temple-carts in Tanjore was thus a massive operation. It was also one which, over the years, had come to involve Government officers, village officials and *mirasidars* in a great deal of extra work, time and energy.[47] *Mirasidars* were expected to supply a customary number of coolies which was proportional to the amount of land they possessed. Most of the labourers who were gathered together at certain points in the countryside and marched off to temples under the supervision of *tahsildars*, were either the *mirasidar's* own servants (landless labourers) or cultivators who owned cattle and were entitled to a part of the *mirasidar's* crop. During their absence from work in the fields, the latter were entitled to two Madras measures of rice per day, about half the wage normally paid to landless labourers. The *mirasidars'* servants continued to receive their usual pay, the cost of hiring additional labour for work in the fields during their absence being born by the *mirasidars* themselves.

On their arrival at their destination the men were carefully counted and then kept under close supervision to prevent escape until their services were no longer required and they were allowed to return home.

Initially, collectors in Tanjore district do not appear to have raised any objections to the Company's policy of assisting the Raja and temple authorities in the recruitment of labour for temple-cart processions.

John Wallace, who was Collector from 1805 until 1813, appears, for example, to have had no scruples about the way in which the system operated. In 1810, in response to the British Residents' complaints that taluk servants were having considerable difficulty recruiting the necessary labour for the Raja's usual celebrations, he promised to punish 'in an exemplary manner' any *tahsildars* who failed to carry out their duties in obtaining the necessary number of coolies.[48]

However, John Cotton, who had been Wallace's Head Assistant and who became Collector of Tanjore in 1820,[49] was more critical of the way in which the recruitment system operated and was one of the first district officers in the locality to point out the need for reform. Conscious of the way in which some coolies were forced to march long distances for temple service, he ruled, in 1820, that in future they were to be drawn from surrounding taluks only.[50] In the following year, when the Raja asked for additional coolies for processions in connection with his newly-constructed temple at the Muktambapuram *chattram*, Cotton protested in a letter to the Resident that he doubted that he had the authority 'to enforce' the attendance of more coolies than the number normally required for temple service.[51] He explained that if any of the *mirasidars* refused to give assistance, even in the processions which had long been established, then he would have great hesitation in acting under the existing regulations, as he did not believe it was the intention or the desire of Government that the *mirasidars* 'should in any way be *compelled* to support their own Religious Institutions.'

You are no doubt aware [he lectured] that this and most of the other Coach Festivals in this District take place at a most inconvenient season of the year, during the great Harvest, and that the Coolies quitting their Villages from a distance and being absent as many necessarily are for three, four & five days, when the Crops are ready to be cut, must be attended with considerable Inconvenience and loss to the People, and hence it is that the Privilege, which some Villages enjoy by ancient Grants, of being exempt from furnishing Coolies on these occasions, is regarded of such importance, and is held so tenaciously by the Meerasidars, that any infringement of it, attempted, is always immediately complained of or resisted.[52]

In the end Cotton had his way and the Raja had to recruit the extra number of coolies required independently through 'two native officers' and without the Collector's assistance.[53]

In 1828 Robert Nelson, who had served as Sub-Collector for a short period under Cotton before the latter's transfer, wrote to the new Collector Nathaniel Kindersley attacking what he regarded as the 'evils' of the recruitment system and pressing for the Company's total withdrawal from any involvement in recruitment operations.[54] He drew attention to Cotton's views and elaborated on the inconveniences and losses sustained by various classes in the rural population. Underlining the fact that some of the major festivals occurred just when labourers were required for harvest, he pointed out that *mirasidars* were involved in the extra expense of having additional help while the labourers themselves, including cultivators, were faced with losses and inconvenience. 'Whether his field requires watering, his grain gathering in or whatever may be the circumstances of his family', wrote Nelson, 'he must at once depart on this futile errand, and bear the loss and annoyance as well as he may.'

He also highlighted what he felt was the cruelty and unpopularity of the recruitment system. He argued that *mirasidars* not infrequently bribed Government officials so as to escape the burden of having to provide men for temple service and that compulsion was used in the recruitment and subsequent management of labour — a large number of peons always being required 'to prevent the escape of the coolies and to urge them to exertion by threats and even blows'.

Finally, included among other criticisms of the system, was the telling point that the Company itself was adversely affected through its involvement in recruitment operations. Not only was local administration severely disrupted or even halted altogether, for days at a time, while police and revenue officials marshalled as many labourers as possible, but the Government's share of land revenues was reduced because of the crops which were left on the ground and spoiled.

In his reply, Kindersley agreed with his subordinate that the system did entail loss of revenue to the Government and hardship to individuals.[55] But he felt that Nelson's analysis was 'somewhat highly coloured', including his stress on the unpopularity of recruitment; and being a man of some Christian conviction himself, the Collector took up the issue of what position a Christian government should adopt in India. While agreeing, in principle, that 'idolatry' was 'undeniably an evil' and that its support should be 'deprecated', he argued at some length that the Company could not afford to lose the goodwill of the people by withdrawing its support from Hindu religious institutions. He confessed his belief that 'the progress of Christianity in the East' seemed to depend upon 'the permanency of the British Empire in India' and that therefore 'even the most zealous Christians' should be careful not to do anything 'which may tend to weaken the efficacy of this apparently chosen instrument.'

Notwithstanding these differences of opinion with his subordinate, Kindersley agreed to send all the correspondence (including Nelson's letter and his own reply) to the Board of Revenue. The Board, perhaps oversensitive because of growing opposition, especially in England, to the Government's connection with 'idolatry', concurred in substance with the Collector's reply.[56] They recorded their 'decided disapprobation, not only of Mr Nelson's sentiments, but of his conduct also.' They argued that an official in his position had no right to discuss issues such as these and cautioned Nelson 'against a recurrence of such useless and uncalled for discussions'. A few weeks later the Governor-in-Council, having been given copies of the correspondence, strongly endorsed the Board's proceedings.[57]

Nelson may have been silenced, but it is possible his protest had some effect on Kindersley's own attitude towards the temple-cart issue and other aspects of the Company's policy towards Hinduism. After the correspondence with his subordinate Kindersley appears to have become increasingly uneasy about his own official role in relation to Hinduism. In spite of his criticism of Nelson's comments he probably shared the same basic religious and humanitarian outlook[58] and when, in 1833 (five years after the controversy with Nelson), he received a petition from the 'principal inhabitants' (*mirasidars*) of one taluk asking to be relieved of the customary burden of supplying labour for the drawing of temple-carts he willingly acceded to their request.[59]

Nor was Nelson completely alone in his opposition to Company policy. Local Protestant missionaries also opposed the Company's involvement in the recruitment of labour for temple service and almost certainly discussed these 'evils' with friends in the Company's service and supplied them with information. The Rev. A. Bourne, a Methodist missionary stationed at Negapatam in 1830, for example, appears to have lent Nelson a copy of his journal describing the flogging of coolies during temple-cart processions at Tiruvalur (Trivalore).[60] This description was subsequently used as evidence in an appendix to a memorial opposing the Company's involvement in Hindu religious affairs. Moreover, there was a strong feeling against the practice of compelling people to draw temple-carts among some other Company officials in other parts of the Presidency.[61]

The Company's problems in connection with the temple-cart issue continued and, in 1836, a memorial attacking the Government's continued connection with 'idolatry', including its interference in the organization of temple-cart processions, was drawn up and eventually signed by over two hundred Protestant ministers, chaplains, missionaries and military and civil officers, including collectors and magistrates.[62] The authors of the memorial claimed that there was considerable dissatisfaction among 'the great mass of the people' with the compulsory practice of drawing temple carts. They declared that

This onerous task is now only effected throughout this Presidency by the agency of the police; thousands of the poorer class being forced, under the orders of the collector and magistrate, from their homes for the performance of this special duty, without, in the majority of cases, the slightest compensation; and whatever may be the wishes and sentiments of the individuals immediately connected with the pagodas, we are fully assured that this interference is viewed by the great body of the people, both land-owners and their labourers, as a vexatious and oppressive exercise of power, to which they submit only on compulsion. It is, we conceive, therefore, certain that this baneful part of the debasing idolatry of the land is now upheld and carried on in this presidency, solely by the interposition and authority of the British Government.

While this memorial was being circulated for signature, the temple-cart issue was suddenly projected into new prominence by a serious accident which occurred during a festival, not in Tanjore, but in Conjeeveram (Kanchipuram) in Chingleput district. The Assistant Magistrate, R. B. Sewell, who was summoned to the scene, reported that

The manner in which the accident occurred was this: while engaged in drawing the Car and at a moment when (owing to its having received too violent an impetus from the people working the levers behind) it was moving along with great velocity, one of the men at the ropes unfortunately lost his hold, and fell; others fell over him; and before a stop could be put to the ponderous machine, its wheels had passed over the bodies of ten individuals — Of these only two survived.[63]

After the accident almost all the coolies fled and it was only with the greatest difficulty that a few of these, together with people recruited from the streets, could be persuaded to drag the car back to its original point of departure.

In reporting the incident to the Board of Revenue the Magistrate of Chingleput, A. MacLean, remarked that, in his opinion, the most effective method of preventing the recurrence of similar tragedies would be to withdraw the aid and interference of Government in the celebration of these festivals 'more especially as regards pressing individuals contrary to their inclination, into the service of the Car.'[64]

Early in April 1836, a few weeks after the accident, but before the Government issued orders terminating the involvement of Company officials in the recruitment system, the Governor received privately from Daniel Corrie, the Bishop of Madras, a copy of the memorial strongly attacking the Government's connection with 'Idolatry' including the criticism of the recruitment system.[65]

Faced with the evidence of a groundswell against its policy, including considerable discontent among its own employees, coupled with news of the disaster at Conjeeveram, the Government was finally forced to capitulate.

Replying to the Magistrate of Chingleput the Chief Secretary wrote that it was the Board of Revenue's opinion that 'the interference of the Officers of Governmnent in requiring the attendance of the people against their inclination to draw the Cars at the Native festivals' could not but be felt by them 'as a grievous hardship', and that, as 'in the present instance' it has been 'attended with serious loss of life,' the Board requested the Magistrate to discontinue the practice in future and confine his interference on such occasions 'to the preservation of the peace'.[66]

This correspondence was printed and circulated to magistrates throughout the Presidency 'for their information and guidance' and, on 31 May 1836, the Government of Madras, referring to the loss of life at Conjeeveram, passed an order prohibiting Government officers from requiring the attendance of people 'against their inclinations' to draw the cars at 'Native' festivals.[67]

The controversy over temple-carts and the recruitment of labour for temple service highlights some of the principal issues involved in the debate over the East India Company's patronage and support of Hinduism. On the one hand there were many, including Christians, who believed that, in view of the precarious nature of early British rule and the difficulties involved in winning the hearts and minds of the people, there was no alternative but to follow traditional religious policies of upholding and supporting the existing system. This policy was probably reinforced by collectors like John Wallace who felt no special aversion to Hinduism.

At the opposite end of the scale were the growing number of Evangelicals who believed that Hinduism was an evil system which should be totally destroyed.[68] They regarded the Company's 'connexion with idolatry' as virtually a policy of 'supping with the devil', and believed that official measures did a great deal to fortify and enhance Hinduism at the expense of Christianity. This view was put forcefully by the Rev. Edmund Crisp in a letter marked 'private and confidential' to his superior in London in 1831.[69] He declared that, notwithstanding the help he had occasionally been given by Government officers, 'all the means which missionaries employ are most powerfully, though I believe unintentionally counteracted by the course of policy which the Government pursues, in this province especially [Tanjore], in reference to the Heathen Temples.' Referring to the effect of Government patronage of Hinduism on Hindu attitudes at a meeting in Exeter Hall,

London, some years later, Crisp again argued that the Company's policy greatly impeded the spread of Christianity:

> When we point out to them [Hindus], that idolatry is not the worship of God, that it is even contrary to his commandments and his word, they ask, 'How can you say so? Who keeps our pagodas in repair? Who prepared the car, and brings the people to it to draw it? Do you not do it yourselves . . . (identifying us with the British power generally)? If you do these things, where is the reasonableness and the propriety of saying idolatry is sinful? I am not forming an argument, I am merely repeating words which have often been cast in our teeth.[70]

Opponents of the Company's policy were not, however, merely concerned with its effects on the propagation of Christianity. As previously mentioned, Nelson also underlined some of the more serious practical disadvantages of the recruitment system which, in his view, not only left officials with less time for more essential duties, but drew labour away from harvesting and adversely affected the Company's income from land revenue.

But as realistic or as convincing as these latter arguments may have been, they were probably only incidental to the primary thrust of opposition. Apart from concern about the way in which Company policy appeared to favour Hinduism at the expense of Christianity (and therefore put some Christian officers in what they considered was an invidious position) there were important humanitarian considerations involved. These were reflected in the feeling, shared by all the major groups critical of the Company's policy, that the recruitment system was a system of forced labour which entailed a great deal of brutality, hardship and suffering.

Indeed, it is significant that the temple-cart and recruitment controversy coincided, not only with the rise of the Evangelical movement, but also with the humanitarian movement in Britain. In fact, the two movements were often interlinked, Humanitarianism being seen, at least by some, as a necessary corollary of Christian faith. It was this humanitarian aspect of the temple-cart question which was given prominence in Nelson's protest, which was stressed in statements and evidence included in the Madras memorial of 1836 and which forced the Madras Government to act after the tragedy which occurred at Conjeeveram at about the same time.

Finally, what effect did the cessation of official participation in the recruitment of labour have on Hinduism and on temple-cart processions? There is evidence, at least in missionary reports from Tanjore district, that the change in Company policy was still causing disruption to temple-cart processions more than a decade later. This is especially interesting evidence as the missionaries had special reasons for wanting to observe and monitor the effects of the new measures and were unlikely to make claims about the new policy unless they were convinced that it was actually working. Writing in 1859 from Tiruvalur, one of the centres well known for its temple-cart processions, the Rev. W. O. Simpson reported that the temple authorities there had been having difficulty getting the temple-cart moving and that 'for the first time' the god had not been taken out during annual celebrations.[71] Two years later he reported that the trustees were facing similar problems in getting labour to drag the temple-cart at the annual festival at Mannargudi.[72] Writing again from Tiruvalur in 1862, the Rev. J. Hobday commented that

I need not remark that the Government has been most prompt in using measures to put a stop to their native officers forcing the people to help in dragging idol cars. It is sufficient to state that we had no cars moved in March last. The Panjayat [board of trustees] have made attempts for two or three months to drive the cars, but without effect.[73]

While it is clear that the Company's decision to withdraw from all involvement in the recruitment of labour for temple-cart processions was causing some problems, and was also the subject of some Hindu comment and complaint,[74] the long-term and deeper psychological effects on the Government's break with tradition are more problematic. The new Government policy on the temple-cart issue was merely the first in a series of measures to distance the administration from active involvement in Hindu religious affairs and the subsequent dismay felt by some Hindus at the lack of Government support for the recruitment of labour tended to merge with other complaints about the Company's failure to fulfil its traditional religious obligations.

AGITATION AND THE DESPATCH OF 1838

In 1833 the Directors of the Company, under increasing pressure, especially from Evangelicals in England, notified the Governor-General-in-Council of their intention of gradually withdrawing from their association with Hindu ceremonies and institutions.[75] Included in a series of resolutions was a declaration that 'in all matters relating to their temples, their worship, their festivals, their religious practices, their ceremonial observances, our native subjects [shall] be left entirely to themselves.'[76]

The Madras Government appears to have taken very little notice of this despatch. Indeed its failure to sever its direct connection with temple administration, Hindu ceremonies and other non-Christian religious activity, as well as its continued participation in the recruitment of labour for the drawing of temple-carts, was roundly condemned in the memorial of 1836 — a document which, as we have seen, was signed by over two hundred signatories including missionaries and a large number of civil and military officers.

Though, for the reasons already given, the Madras Government was forced to capitulate on the temple-cart issue in May 1836, it still showed no signs of doing anything else about its continued involvement in temple administration and Hindu ceremony and, as a result, some of the Company's own employees began resigning in protest. The most sensational case was that of Sir Peregrine Maitland who resigned as Commander-in-Chief at Madras.[77] A less publicized case was that of Robert Nelson, the former Sub-Collector of Tanjore, whose letter to the Court of Directors resigning his position in the Company's service was published in the London *Times* in May 1838.[78]

In England, feeling, especially among Evangelicals and their supporters, was running high. A Provincial Committee was formed in 1838 for the express purpose of 'diffusing information relative to the connexion [sic] of the East India Company's Government with the superstitious idolatrous systems of the natives, and for promoting the dissolution of that connexion [sic].'[79] Christian ministers and laity in various parts of the country, the missionary societies and individuals (some of them, such as John Poynder, in important positions within the Company's governing structure) all continued to exert increasing pressure on the Court of Proprietors, the Directors, the House of Commons and even the Crown.[80]

In August 1838, Sir John Hobhouse, President of the Board of Control, gave an undertaking in the Commons that the Government would be taking further action. A few days later a despatch was sent to the Governor-General reiterating the Directors' 'anxious desire' that he should

accomplish with as little delay as may be practicable, the arrangements which we believe to be already in progress for abolishing the Pilgrim Tax, and for discontinuing the connexion [sic] of the Government with the management of all funds which may be assigned for the support of religious institutions in India. We more particularly desire that the management of all temples and other places of religious resort, together with the revenues derived therefrom, be resigned into the hands of the natives . . .[81]

The August despatch of 1838, which was a clear indication of the Directors' impatience with the Madras Government's prevarication, finally had its effect in speeding up the latter's withdrawal from its direct connection with Hinduism. As we shall see in the following chapter, this change in policy had important effects on the administration of religious endowments, worship and ceremony, and on other aspects of religious life in Tanjore and Trichinopoly districts.

NOTES

1. Mudaliar, op. cit., esp. pp. 9 – 15.
2. Quoted in J. W. Kaye, *Christianity in India: An Historical Narrative*, London 1859, p. 393.
3. Aitchison, op. cit., Vol. X, pp. 101 – 5.
4. App. No. 234 of 1895, *I.L.R.*, Madras Series Vol. XX, 1897, pp. 421 – 33.
5. *T.R.*, Resident to Collr. Tanjore, 5/2/1801.
6. For a recent assessment of the part played by Swartz in administration and politics in Tanjore and of his role as Serfoji's guardian see Don Wright 'Swartz of Thanjavur: A Missionary in Politics', *South Asia*, Vol. IV, No. 2., December 1981, pp. 94 – 105. The Raja, who had a portrait of Swartz in his palace, erected a marble monument in his memory on which were inscribed the words 'my father, my friend, the protector, and guardian of my youth'. (H. Pearson, op. cit., Vol. II, p. 383)
7. Pearson, op. cit.
8. Ibid., p. 380.
9. Ibid., pp. 380, 388.
10. Ibid., p. 391.
11. *T.R.*, Sirkele to Resident, 11/2/1825, Vol. 4433, p. 44; Resident to Collr., 4/2/1821, Vol. 3429, pp. 58 – 60.
12. *South Indian Epigraphy*, Annual Report, 1923 – 4, p. 120.
13. T. V. Row, op. cit., pp. 232 – 239.
14. *South Indian Epigraphy*, Annual Report, 1923 – 4, p. 121.
15. *T.R.*, Collr. to Sec. Board of Revenue, 11/1/1814, Vol. 3274, pp. 1 – 2.
16. *T.R.*, Resident to Collr. 17/3/1807, Vol. 3491, pp. 133 – 4; Sub-Collr. to Resident 26/3/1807, Vol. 3487, pp. 81 – 3; Resident to Collr., 8/6/1810, Vol. 3431, p. 187; Collr. to Resident 15/6/1810, Vol. 3431, pp. 205 – 6; Resident to Collr., 11/3/1811 and Collr. to Resident, 13/3/1811, Vol. 3431, pp. 501 – 4; Sirkele to Resident 7/6/1816, Vol. 3519, pp. 201 – 2; Collr. to Resident 2/2/1821, Vol. 3429, pp. 26 – 7; Resident to Collr., 4/2/1821; Vol. 3429, pp. 58 – 60; Collr. to Resident, 10/2/1821, Vol. 3429, pp. 56 – 7; Raja to Resident, 15 and 16/2/1821, Vol. 3429, pp. 67 – 8.
17. This was a military and religious festival held in October at the end of the rains and at a time traditionally favoured for the commencement of military operations. It was the most important day of the year among Maratha ruling families. Article 9 of the treaty signed in 1789 stated that, 'the Rajah shall

be treated on all occasions, in his own territories as well as in those of the company, with all the attention, respect, and honour which is due to a friend and ally of the British nation' and, after annexation, Dasara became even more important as the one regular occasion in which the Raja was permitted to hold the centre of the stage and could insist on being treated with 'due respect' as a sovereign prince. He held 'a grand durbar', received the respects of East India Company officials (including the Resident and Collector) and of the principal inhabitants of the district, as well as tribute from the Danish Government in Tranquebar. It was also an occasion in which the Raja participated in *puja* and thus reminded his subjects of his fundamental allegiance to Hindu deities and 'dharma'. (See especially *T.R.*, Garrow (Rev. Dept.) to Collr., 5/4/1802; Resident to Raja 8/9/1817; Vol. 3424, pp. 223 – 5; Resident to Govt., 5/10/1817; Resident to Govt., 16/10/1823, Vol. 4426, p. 282; *W.M.M.S.*, A. Bourne to I. Townley, 26/10/1830, Madras, Box 434.)
18 *T.R.*, Resident to Govt., 18/5/1802, Vol. 3430, pp. 470 – 1.
19 *T.R.*, Resident to Govt., 11/4/1816, Vol. 3434, pp. 292 etc. During the whole of the pilgrimage of about three weeks the Raja, although accustomed to eating meat, adhered 'most rigidly' to a purely vegetarian diet, abstained 'with equal strictness' from bathing and travelled only once in a palanquin (*T.R.*, Resident to Govt., 26/5/1816, Vol. 3434, pp. 338 – 9).
20 *T.R.*, Raja to Governor, Vol. 3438, p. 69.
21 *T.R.*, Vol. 4425, p. 116, Vol. 4429, pp. 203 – 4; Raja to Resident, 6/1/1825, Vol. 4433, pp. 5 – 7.
22 *Athenaeum*, 18/6/1844; T. V. Row, op. cit., p. 238. After a visit to Tanjore in 1845 the Bishop of Madras, Bishop Spencer, complained that, 'Not the slightest encouragement is shown by the Rajah to the Christians; on the contrary, I am persuaded that Christianity is considered in Tanjore as a visitation of the gods.' (C. F. Pascoe, *Classified Digest of the Records of the S.P.G. in Foreign Parts 1701 – 1892*, London 1893, p. 512).
23 W. Hickey, *The Tanjore Mahratta Principality in Southern India*, Madras 1874, pp. 145 – 6.
24 Wallace to Govt., 15/2/1814, *M.R.P.*, Ra. 291, Vol. 1 24/2/1814. See also Nelson's letter enclosed in Kindersley to Board of Revenue, 19/11/1828, *M.R.P.*, Ra. 296, Vol. 73, 11/12/1828.
25 Kindersley to Board of Revenue, 31/8/1833, *M.R.P.*, Ra. 299, Vol. 13, 9/9/1833.
26 Hepburn to Sec., 3/1/1815, *M.R.P.*, Ra. 291, Vol. 31, 12/1/1815.
27 Board to Hepburn, 12/1/1815, *M.R.P.*, Ra. 291, Vol. 31, 12/1/1815.
28 *M.R.P.*, Ra. 291, Vol. 35, 20/3/1815.
29 *M.P.C.*, Ra. 247, Vol. 8, 11/10/1836 (Appendix to Memorial); Lushington to Sec., 24/12/1819, *M.R.P.*, Vol. 44, 3/1/1820; Cameron to Sec., 24/9/1830, *M.R.P.*, Ra. 297, Vol. 60, 7/10/1830.
30 *T.R.*, Collector to Sec., 25/2/1802, Vol. 3206, pp. 292 – 3. See also infra Ch. 3.
31 As examples of *some* of these complaints made by temple servants see G. Garrow to Sec., 10/6/1809, *M.R.P.*, Ra. 289, Vol. 32, 15/6/1809;

NOTES TO CHAPTER 2

Lushington to Sec., 12/1/1819, *M.R.P.*, Ra. 293, Vol. 6, 18/1/1819; G. Saunders to Sec., 4/9/1826, *M.R.P.*, Ra. 295, Vol. 83, 28/9/1826; H. Dickinson to Sec., 24/5/1827, *M.R.P.*, Ra. 296, Vol. 18, 31/5/1827; H. Dickinson to Sec. 16/7/1827, *M.R.P.*, Ra. 296, Vol. 24, 23/7/1827.
32 J. Hepburn to Sec., 6/4/1819, *M.R.P.*, Ra. 293, Vol. 16, 12/4/1819.
33 *T.R.*, Collr. to Board of Revenue, 6/1/1814, Vol. 3274, pp. 1 – 2.
34 *T.R.*, Resident to Collr., 12/3/1824, vol. 4426, p. 425.
35 *T.R.*, Raja to Resident, 14/12/1824, Vol. 4432, pp. 242 – 3.
36 *T.R.*, Raja to Resident, 6/1/1825, Vol. 4433, pp. 5 – 7; Resident to Sirkele, 18/11/1821, Vol. 3429, pp. 240 – 1.
37 Mudaliar, op. cit., p. 31., Rajaram Tawker to Act. Collr. of Trichinopoly, 14/8/1872, *I.O.R.*, P/383, p. 5193; Kumaru V. O. M. Naiynar to Act. Collr. of Trichinopoly, 14/8/1872, *I.O.R.*, P/383, p. 5201; Sami Iyer to Act. Collr. of Trichinopoly, 8/6/1872, *I.O.R.*, P/383, p. 5215.
38 K. Ingham, *Reformers in India, 1793 – 1833*, Cambridge 1956, pp. 33 – 44.
39 J. A. Dubois, op. cit., p. 604. For further information on Abbé Dubois' life and work see P. Hockings 'The Abbé Dubois, an early French ethnographer'. *Contributions to Indian Sociology*, N.S., Vol. 11, No. 2, July – December 1977, pp. 329 – 43.
40 *W.M.M.S.*, Bourne to Morley, 19/4/1830, Madras, Box 434.
41 *L.M.S.*, J. E. Nimmo to W. Ellis, 22/3/1838, S.I. Tamil, Box 8.
42 J. Bush (ed.) *W. O. Simpson: Methodist Minister and Missionary*, London 1886, pp. 257 – 8.
43 *T.R.*, Sirkele to Resident, 7/6/1816, Vol. 3519, pp. 201 – 2.
44 Translated extract of an Arzee from police Amin of Negapatam to Mag. Tanjore 25/5/1840, *M.R.P.*, Ra. 302, Vol. 35, 29/6/1840.
45 *T.R.*, Resident to Collr., 8/6/1810, Vol. 3431, p. 187.
46 Nelson's letter in Kindersley to Board of Revenue, 19/11/1828, *M.R.P.*, Ra. 296, Vol. 73, 11/12/1828.
47 Ibid.
48 *T.R.*, Resident to Collr., 8/6/1810, Vol. 3431, p. 187, Collr. to Resident, 15/6/1810, Vol. 3431, pp. 205 – 6.
49 Cotton, who entered the Company's service in 1801, had already had 11 years experience of work in the district (as well as seven years in Tinnevelly) before becoming Collector and Magistrate of Tanjore — a position he held until 1827. He was elected a Director of the East India Company in 1833 and Chairman of the Court of Directors in 1843 (Prinsep, op. cit.)
50 Nelson's letter in Kindersley to Board of Revenue, *M.R.P.*, Ra. 296, Vol. 73, 11/12/1828.
51 *T.R.*, Collr. to Resident, 2/2/1821, Vol. 3429, pp. 56 – 7; Resident to Collr., 4/2/1821, Vol. 3429, pp. 58 – 60; Collr. to Resident, 10/2/1821, Vol. 3429, pp. 65 – 6.
52 *T.R.*, Collr. to Resident, 10/2/1821, Vol. 3429, pp. 65 – 6.
53 *T.R.*, Raja to Resident, 16/2/1821, Vol. 3429, pp. 67 – 8.
54 Nelson to Kindersley in Kindersley to Board of Revenue, 19/2/1828, *M.R.P.*, Ra. 296, Vol. 73, 11/12/1828. Nelson became a writer in the

NOTES TO CHAPTER 2 61

Company's service in 1816. 1818: Second Assistant to the Collr. and Magistrate of Salem. 1821: Head Assistant to same. Leave to St. Helena and eventually England. 1824: Head Assistant to the Collr. and Magistrate of Madura. 1827: Sub-Collector and Joint Magistrate of Tanjore until 1831 when transferred to Trichinopoly. (Prinsep, op. cit.)

55 Enclosed in Kindersley to Board of Revenue, 19/2/1828, *M.R.P.*, Ra. 296, Vol. 73, 11/12/1828.
56 Sec. to Board of Revenue to Principal Collr., 11/12/1828, *M.R.P.*, Ra. 296, Vol. 73, 11/12/1828.
57 Sec. to Govt. to Board to Revenue, 16/1/1829, *M.R.P.*, Ra. 297, Vol. 1, 19/1/1829.
58 Nathaniel's father, who was looked upon with much affection by his son, is described as having gained 'an early sense of religion' and was much exercised by the same question of Christianity and Hinduism in India. He joined in the public controversy on the admission of Christian missionaries to India suggesting that 'the quiet offer of the Gospel to the Hindoos, through the medium of DISCREET Missionaries and Translations of the Scripture, is not likely to give offence to the Natives'. (N. E. Kindersley *A Letter to the Earl of Buckinghamshire on the Propagation of Christianity in India*, London 1813). N. W. Kindersley himself was described by his son as being 'a religious man'. (A. F. Kindersley, op. cit., p. 132).
59 *M.P.C.*, Ra. 247, Vol. 8, 11/10/1836, Appendix to Memorial. After the episode and debate involving Nelson, Kindersley also began to express dissatisfaction with the part British officials were expected to play in attending Hindu ceremonies. In 1831 he took the unprecedented step of refusing to attend the Raja's annual Dasara celebrations because they took place on a Sunday. This episode highlights not merely the way in which local officials in the Madras Presidency were beginning to resist the Company's official policy of involvement with Hinduism, but also the growing difficulty the Company was experiencing in attempting to reconcile the feelings of Hindus on the one side with the increasingly aggressive demands of the Christian administrators (especially Evangelicals) on the other. In spite of pressure from the Acting Resident, who pointed out how much the Raja's feeling and 'dignity' were concerned in the Collector's attendance, the latter made his stand 'a point of conscience' and refused to budge. The Raja, obviously upset, complained to the Governor of Madras. In his reply, through the Resident, the Governor stated that he saw no reason to impute to the Principal Collector any intentional disrespect to the Raja in not attending a Hindu festival on a Sunday. He reminded the Raja of the attention that was paid to him 'by all public officers' of the Madras and Supreme Governments during his pilgrimage to Benares and on various occasions when his own religious ceremonies and personal considerations were concerned and, finally, he expressed his confidence that the Raja would have a similar regard for 'the Scruples of European gentlemen' who wished to observe 'the ordinances of their religion'. (*T.R.*, Acting Resident to Collr., 1/10/1831, Vol. 4217, pp. 267 – 8; Acting Resident to Raja, 21/11/1831, Vol. 4438, pp. 392 – 3).
60 *M.P.C.*, 11/10/1836, Ra. 247, Vol. 8 (Appendix D to Memorial):

W.M.M.S., Bourne to Morley, 19/4/1830, Madras, Box 434. Writing to the Secretary of his Society in London in 1834 Bourne recommended Nelson as 'a man who fears God' (*W.M.S.*, Bourne to Beecham, 4/3/1834, Madras Box 435).
61 Ingham, op. cit., p. 37.
62 *M.P.C.*, 11/10/1836, Ra. 247, Vol. 8, pp. 2706–99, or *Commons Accounts and Papers*, 1837, Vol. XLIII. Among the signatories who had had some experience of work in Trichinopoly and Tanjore district were H. M. Blair, b. 16/1/1798, Collr. Trichinopoly, 1832–8, host to the Bishop of Madras during his visit to the district in February 1836; J. Bourdillon, b. 6/2/1811, Head Assistant Trichinopoly 1833–5, 1836–7; E. B. Thomas, b. 5/9/1803, Head Assistant to Collr. and Magistrate, Trichinopoly, 1828–30 and, in 1836, Sub-Collr. and Joint Magistrate, South Arcot; C. Whittingham who had been Acting Registrar of the Zillah Court of Kumbakonam and had just been appointed Assist. Collr. South Arcot; E. G. Glass, Acting Judge and Criminal Judge at Kumbakonam 1836, and F. Lascelles, b. 15/7/1795, Acting Judge and Criminal Judge at Kumbakonam 1831–2, and, in 1836, Judge Zillah Court, Chittoor.
63 Sewell to Magistrate of Chingleput, 29/3/1836, F/4/1668 Board's Collection 66793. According to the Tahsildar and other eye witnesses, those killed on the spot had been so completely crushed and flattened by the weight of the broad and heavy wheels, that it was with the greatest difficulty they were recognised by their friends. The legs, arms and other parts of the body of others who died shortly after were 'fearfully torn and mangled'.
64 Magistrate to Chief Sec. Board of Revenue, 7/4/1836, *I.O.R.*, F/4/1668, Board's Collections 66793.
65 *Memoirs of the Right Rev. Daniel Corrie, LL.D. First Bishop of Madras*, compiled . . . by his brothers, London 1847, pp. 606–12.
66 Chief Secretary to MacLean, 21/5/1836, *I.O.R.*, F/4/1668, Board's Collection 66793.
67 *Circular Orders of Government* of 31 May 1836, *I.O.R.*, F/4/1668, Board's Collection 66793.
68 See especially K. A. Ballhatchet 'Some Aspects of Historical Writing on India by Protestant Christian Missionaries during the Nineteenth and Twentieth Centuries', in C. H. Philips (ed.), *Historians of India, Pakistan and Ceylon*, London 1961, and E. J. Sharpe *Not to Destroy but to Fulfil: The Contribution of J. N. M. Farquhar to Protestant Missionary Thought in India Before 1914*, Uppsala 1965, ch. 1.
69 *L.M.S.*, Crisp to Hankey, 6/10/1831, S. I. Tamil, Box 4. See also the memorial signed by other missionaries including the Revs. J. C. Kohlhoff and V. D. Coombes of the S.P.G. mission, Tanjore.
70 *Calcutta Christian Observer*, Vol. VI, November 1837, pp. 595–9.
71 J. Bush, op. cit., pp. 232–3.
72 Ibid., p. 257.
73 *Harvest Field*, Vol. 1, September 1862, p. 248.
74 For references in missionary material to some of the more negative Hindu comments see especially *Madras Quarterly Mission Journal*, Vol. 1, new series, July 1850, Vol 1, pp. 61–2; J. Bush, op. cit., pp. 232–3, 258–9; *Harvest Field*, Vol. 1, November 1861, p. 115 and September 1862, p. 248.

75 A. Mayhew, *Christianity and the Government of India*, London 1929, pp. 150 – 1.
76 J. W. Kaye, op. cit., p. 417.
77 *The Times*, 23/8/1839; J. W. Kaye, op. cit., p. 427.
78 *The Times*, 7/5/1838. After ascertaining from the Court that it really was necessary for him to accept and undertake any office, including those connected with 'the idolatory of the country' he announced he could no longer serve two masters — obeying both the East India Company which required civil servants 'to assist and uphold the idolatrous worship of India' and the Lord Jesus Christ who instructed him to keep himself from idols and 'to flee from idolatry'. Faced with this choice, he declared, he preferred 'to follow the Lord Jesus Christ' and renounce his position in the Company.
79 *The Times*, 23/8/1839.
80 Ibid., 20,22/3. 21/6/1838.
81 See copy of despatch dated 8/8/1838, *Commons, Accounts and Papers*, Vol. XXXIX, 1839.

3

THE RESULTS OF THE COMPANY'S DISCONNECTION WITH HINDUISM

THE 'NO LAW PERIOD' AND THE ESTABLISHMENT OF TEMPLE COMMITTEES

In 1841, in a directive to the Government of Fort St. George, the Government of India conveyed the Directors' opinion that the measures which had been fully carried into execution in every other part of British India for withdrawing from interference with 'native' religious establishments should 'now without further delay' be completed under the Madras Government, and it asked that 'immediate consideration' be given to 'the best mode of fulfilling the instruction of the Hon'ble Court of Directors'.[1]

According to principles determined by the Governor-General-in-Council the management of religious institutions was to be left to those best qualified and belonging to the same faith for which the institution was established; these officials, together with their subordinates, were to be held responsible to the Court of Justice for any breach of duty or trust and, lastly, lands belonging to these institutions were to continue to be managed by the Company's revenue officers, but the proceeds given to the 'native' administrators. The implementation of these directives in the Kaveri delta, as in other parts of the Madras Presidency, involved a series of carefully planned measures. They included the handing over of responsibility for the management of temples, either to individuals or committees; the commutation of money allowances into grants of land, and the disposal of surplus funds which had been acquired during the period in which temples were under the supervision of Company officials.[2]

Collectors were asked to nominate trustees and, in making arrangements for the transfer of responsibility for these institutions, they generally took into account the relative wealth or prestige of the temples concerned.

In Tanjore the Collector made over the smaller Hindu temples under his supervision, those with an income which did not exceed 30 *chakrams* (Rs. 46-10-8) per annum, 2,247 in number, 'to the *entire management* of their respective Stanicks' [hereditary trustees].[3] Those with an annual income of between 30 and 200 *chakrams* (Rs. 311-19), 434 in number, were placed in charge of *panchayats*, or committees 'of the most respectable individuals of the Villages in which they are respectively situated.' Lastly, their remained 193 temples in the Collector's wealthiest category — those with an annual income which exceeded 200 *chakrams*. Control of 17 of these temples was left in the hands of non-brahman *maths* while the management of the remaining 176 other temples in the same class were, in each case, placed in the hands of a *panchayat* comprised of 'the most respectable inhabitants of the sect, or sects connected with it' from the village or town in which it was situated.

In Trichinopoly, where there were fewer temples and far fewer wealthy institutions, the transfer of power was not such a massive operation. There were 113 smaller temples under Government supervision. A few of these appear to have been handed over to the *zamindar* of Toriore or to other individuals, but in most cases the Collector, A. P. Onslow, transferred supervision to small *panchayats* or committees.[4] He commented that

> The individuals selected as dhurmakurtahs are for the most part inhabitants of the villages in which the pagodas are situated, or of the villages in their vicinity. They are principally the head men of the village; in some instances they are merchants, and in all, the most respectable who could be found willing to engage in the undertaking. The number of dhurmakurtahs proposed to be appointed is seldom less than three for each institution; but in a few cases it is proposed that the administration should be entrusted to a single individual, as being the heir of the founder of the institution.

Apart from these proceedings special detailed arrangements were made for the management of the three principal temples in the district (Srirangam, Jambukeswaram and the Rock Fort temple) — measures which will be discussed in some detail later.[5]

During the period from their official installation up until 1862 the trustees of these and other temples in the Presidency were left alone without any check on their use of power except the restraint which could very occasionally be brought to bear through individual or corporate action in the courts. Rumours of mismanagement and embezzlement of temple funds became widespread and increasing dissatisfaction with the experiment of leaving trustees very largely without supervision or control led to the passing of the Religious Endowment Act XX of 1863.[6] This Act, as we shall see, marked a further stage in the process of opening up temples to the management and control of a wider section of the population.

Act XX of 1863 established specially constituted temple committees to supervise the work of trustees.[7] These committees were composed of three or more persons and usually had jurisdiction over a number of temples or a 'circle'. Thus in 1864 the Collector of Trichinopoly established separate temple committees for each of the five taluks of Trichonopoly, Musiri, Perambulur, Udaiyarpalayiam and Kulittalai.[8] In Tanjore district three larger committees were established each with responsibility for temples in several taluks. The Kumbakonam temple committee was responsible for temples in Kumbakonam, Mayavaram, and Shiyali taluks, the Negapatam committee for temples in Negapatam, Nannilam and Tirutturaippundi sub-divisions, and the Tanjore committee for the taluks of Tanjore, Mannargudi and Pattukkottai in the west and south-western part of the district.[9] No member of a temple committee could at the same time hold office as a trustee or manager of an institution under the committee's jurisdiction. Members of the committee were to hold office for life unless removed for misconduct or unfitness by an order of Court. Vacancies were supposed to be filled by election[10] though this regulation was often ignored in practice.

The primary task of the committee was to call for and supervise the trustees' annual accounts. The committee's powers, including its right to appoint, suspend or dismiss trustees, were left somewhat vague — a vagueness which, as shall become apparent, was the source of bitter contests and litigation.

SOCIAL GROUPINGS AND THE ISSUE OF TEMPLE CONTROL

The Collector's selection and appointment of individuals as trustees in the early 1840s and the subsequent establishment and staffing of temple committees in the early 1860s, raises the question as to whether these measures enabled new groups or classes in the population to exercise an increased influence over temple affairs. What evidence is there, for example, that people in the Kaveri delta belonging to hitherto unrepresented or poorly represented occupational groupings, sects, or castes, took advantage of these new opportunities to gain increased power and representation on the new committees? And how far, if at all, are there signs of what Richard Kennedy has alleged was a successful brahman attempt to establish themselves 'firmer than ever' as 'the secular leaders', especially of the wealthy institutions?[11]

While nominating trustees, Collectors in Tanjore and Trichinopoly districts paid some attention to hereditary positions, usually leaving hereditary trustees in their place. However, many new and additional positions were created.

The new *panchayats*, which were established as boards of trustees to supervise the larger temples may have included hereditary trustees, but they also required the recruitment of extra personnel.[12] In both districts the *panchayats* usually included village headmen[13] who were probably influential landed proprietors,[14] and the principal officers or priests of the institution — some of whom had never acted as trustees before. Referring to new groups who gained control over some temples in Trichinopoly in the 1840s Rangasami Aiyengar (*mirasadar* and manager of Srirangam temple) explained that

> Many . . . temples in these localities, being those built by Carnatic kings in ancient days and endowed with inams, were taken care of by the Government but were, however, handed over in 1842 to trustees who were either privileged men entitled Theer thakorars, or Servants, or Pundarams, or Othewans. These men were all, in fact, pagoda servants whose forefathers had never, for a moment, entertained an idea towards the improvement of the pagodas and had simply lived upon the charity of the institution.[15]

The changes introduced in the 1840s and 1860s not only enabled some groups in the community, who hitherto had little or no say in the running of temples, to exert an influence or even control temple affairs, but also intensified competition and conflict among rival sectarian groups seeking positions and increased power through these new committees. The establishment of the boards and committees opened the way for vadagalais to exercise greater power and control especially over Srirangam temple where the tengalais were forced on the defensive.[17]

Finally, what effect did the new arrangements have on brahman/non-brahman control of temples in the region? How far, if at all, does Kennedy's argument that the brahmans were involved in a successful bid to extend their control (especially over the larger institutions) apply to developments in the Kaveri delta?

The first point to note is that, irrespective of what actually happened, Collectors in Tanjore and Trichinopoly districts do not appear to have had a policy of deliberately favouring brahmans in appointments either as trustees or as members of temple committees. All the evidence suggests that they were not especially interested in whether appointees were brahmans or non-brahmans. Nor, as we have seen, were they totally oblivious to the need to respect the hereditary character of the office where this was clearly established. From their point of view what usually seems to have mattered more than caste was class — wealth, probity and respectability — qualifications which they believed would carry weight and meet the wishes of the most important and influential groups in the local community. When selecting trustees in 1841 Onslow, the Collector of Trichinopoly, explained that he had attempted to transfer the management of temples 'to the most respectable individuals' he could find, men who, while professing the Hindu faith, seemed 'best qualified to conduct the administration of them with fidelity and regularity' or were parties 'of good reputation, and acceptable to their countrymen'.[18] N. W. Kindersley, Collector of Tanjore, was also determined to select the most 'respectable' individuals as trustees,[19] while his successor, G. L. Morris, writing in January 1863, stressed that the chief difficulty he had encountered in establishing temple committees was in finding persons of 'character and respectability' who were willing to act on these committees.[20]

But perhaps more relevant than British policy is what actually happened. Is there evidence that, notwithstanding the attitude of district officers, brahmans were able to exercise increasing control over temples in the region?

Unfortunately, comprehensive lists of trustees of temples in the Kaveri delta before and after what Kennedy regards as the key period, 1841 – 1863, are unavailable. It is possible, however, to obtain information on the caste background of the trustees of the three most celebrated and wealthy temples in Trichinopoly district (Srirangam, Jambukeswaram and the Rock Fort temple)[21] for the periods under consideration.

In the early nineteenth century the control of Srirangam temple affairs was largely in the hands of two well-established Brahman families — the Bhattas and the Uttamanambis.[22] In 1818, the number of *stulattars* (managers) listed in the Collector's report was six and in 1828 seven — all of them brahmans with the exception of one who was 'not a Brahman but a Satany'.[23] The latter's position, which was also described as hereditary, was of special significance as satanis were tengalai non-brahmans who, according to M. Monier Williams, were 'opposed to Brahmanical usages.'[24]

Brahmans remained dominant in the administration of Srirangam affairs throughout the nineteenth century though, contrary to what might be expected from Kennedy's argument, the non-brahman representation appears also to have persisted. In 1891 and 1898, for example, two trustees were brahmans and one a mudaliar or vellala.[25] Clearly there was no particular trend either way in the caste of trustees — the balance between the two communities, brahman and non-brahman, in Srirangam remaining largely unchanged.

During the early part of the nineteenth century the conduct of affairs at Jambukeswaram was in the hands of a single brahman trustee.[26] The

Collector replaced him with a non-brahman (Chundrashaikarum Pillay) in 1842[27] and there is evidence that a non-brahman was also trustee during the period from 1889 to 1894.[28] However, towards the end of the century, when the temple was under the management of two trustees, at least one of these was a brahman.[29]

If there was no consistent pattern in the caste of trustees at Jambukeswaram the picture is clearer with respect to the trustees of the Rock Fort temple. All the evidence suggests that the temple remained in non-Brahman hands throughout the century even though the *tambiran*, an appointee of the Dharmapuram *math*, was not always the effective manager.[30] Once again, in the case of this temple too, there was little, if any, change and certainly no indication of brahmans taking control from non-brahman trustees.

The story seems to have been much the same in Tanjore district where the data available also suggests little change in the caste of trustees. Here non-brahmans were more dominant and securely in control of the principal institutions than they were in Trichinopoly district.

In Tanjore, temples could be divided into two basic categories: *adhinam* and non-*adhinam*. *Adhinam* temples were those under the management of the non-brahman saivite *maths*. The heads of these *maths*, such as those of Dharmapuram and Thiruvavaduturai, enjoyed hereditary right to appoint their own disciples (*tambirans*) as trustees. Although in 1841 these temples were only 17 out of a total of 2,874 places of Hindu worship listed in the Collector's report, they controlled nearly half of all temple lands and received an income which amounted to 36 per cent of all temple revenues in the district.[31] The right of heads of non-brahman *maths* to continue to appoint managers to these 17 temples was respected in 1841 and again in 1863 when many other temples passed under the supervision of temple committees.[32] By the end of the century the heads of Dharmapuram and Thiruvavaduturai between them appointed managers to 42 temples in Tanjore and elsewhere.[33] In Tanjore their control over temples was probably greater than it had been in 1841. Their rights were not only firmly recognized in practice, but they appear to have extended control over the management of a number of additional temples including the Sri Mayuranathaswami temple in Mayavaram.[34]

According to the Collector's report of 1841 non-*adhinam* temples (those which were not under the control of *tambirans*) received 15 per cent of the money allowances and 57 per cent of the temple revenues derived from land. These temples could be subdivided into two categories: firstly, those under the control of the Tanjore royal family who like the *tambirans* were non-brahmans and secondly, the remaining temples which were under the management of neither the royal family nor the non-brahman saivite *maths*.

The rajas (and after 1863 the ranis) were the hereditary trustees of about sixty temples most of which were located in or around Tanjore town.[35] Among them was the famous Brihadesvara (or Rajarajesvara) temple which, in 1905, had an endowment of Rs. 8,000 from the palace estate and an income of some Rs. 1,500 from other sources.[36]

The second category of non-*adhinam* temples included most of the important vaishnavite shrines in the district. Evidence is available on the caste background of some of the trustees connected with 14 of these non-*adhinam* temples — including the caste of trustees of the Chakrapani, Sarangapani, Ramaswami temples in Kumbakonam, the Rajagopalaswami temple in Mannargudi, the Nachiyarkovil temple in Kumbakonam taluk, and Kayarohanaswami temple in Negapatam — all of them among the most prestigious and wealthy institutions in the district. Though in most cases the names of trustees appeared in documents only at a particular time, the trustee's term of office could extend over many years. According to these data (see Appendix 2) in three temples the trustees were brahmans; in three, both communities were represented, and in the remaining seven the trustees were non-brahmans. While the information is certainly limited and incomplete, what there is again points to the dominance of non-brahmans (at least in the second half of the nineteenth century) and suggests that if there had been any significant change in the caste of trustees controlling temples, it is more likely to have been from brahman to non-brahman control rather than towards increasing brahman dominance as suggested by Kennedy's article.[37]

But what of the caste of members of the new temple committees? Does evidence on this point suggest increasing brahman domination?

The caste of those appointed to temple committees in Tanjore and Trichinopoly districts in 1864 is set out in Appendix 3. The caste of one of the 19 members of temple committees in Tanjore district is unclear. Of the remaining 18 members, 12 were non-brahmans and 6 were brahmans, while in Trichinopoly brahmans outnumbered non-brahmans by 12 to 11. The higher representation of non-brahmans compared with brahmans on temple committees in Tanjore reinforced what appears to have been the non-brahman numerical superiority and predominance among trustees. Even in Trichinopoly, where brahmans had the edge, non-brahmans were still playing a significant part in the management and supervision of temples.

Only half of the committees appear to have survived into the 1890s — a trend which suggests that in some taluks there was a lack of interest in them, including an absence of social groups (brahmans or non-brahmans) anxious to use the system as a method of increasing control over temples. Where committees did survive, as in the case of the

Kumbakonam, Negapatam, Musiri and Trichinopoly temple committees, the caste of new members appointed or elected to fill vacancies after 1864 has also been included (whenever the information was available) in Appendix 3. Quite clearly the balance between the two communities on temple committees tended to fluctuate from time to time as a brahman replaced a non-brahman or *vice versa*. However, there is no obvious trend in any particular direction — certainly not towards a general and increasing brahman domination of the committees as the nineteenth century progressed.

Finally, what of the argument, implicit in the Kennedy thesis, that irrespective of the actual outcome brahmans as brahmans consciously competed with non-brahmans for greater control of temples? If there was competition for the position of trustee or for membership of temple committees, how far was this due to brahman/non-brahman rivalry including brahman attempts to achieve power or consolidate their position?

When, in the Kaveri delta, members of the public did have an opportunity to seek appointments, to stand as candidates or vote in *devastanam* elections, brahman/non-brahman rivalry was seldom apparent. As we have seen, in some taluks there was little or no desire to serve on committees. In Trichinopoly and Kumbakonam taluks, however, there was bitter rivalry and intense campaigning for positions on the temple committees. For the most part these conflicts had little to do with brahman/non-brahman competition. In Trichinopoly, the struggle was over which sect, tengalais or vadagalais, would control Srirangam,[38] while in Kumbakonam competition for places on the temple committee was prompted very largely by factional rivalry which cut across caste lines.

A factional dispute seriously disrupted the *devastanam* elections in Kumbakonam several times in the 1880s. The local political arena became increasingly divided between S. A. Saminatha Iyer, a leading lawyer, *mirasidar* and property owner, and his followers on the one hand, and Veerayyah Vandayar, an extremely wealthy landholder, and his followers on the other.[39] Both leaders, with considerable resources and influence at their disposal, fought 'desperately' to obtain a majority on the temple committee which in 1888 and 1889 was equally divided with three members, a brahman and two non-brahmans, on each side.[40] The filling of a vacancy for the seventh place was crucial for the balance of power; and when Punnusami Nadar, a well-known toddy contractor, supported by Vandayar and his party, polled the largest number of votes in August 1888 and again in April 1889, the election was declared invalid by the opposing groups of the temple committee.[41] In May 1889, after a second impasse, the District Judge was finally forced to intervene appointing the nadar to the vacancy.

While factional rivalry dominated the Kumbakonam *devastanam* elections at least until Saminatha Iyer's death in 1899, new elections which were held in November 1899 did begin to take on the appearance of inter-caste rivalry.[42] On that occasion, Sundralinga Tambiran of the Tiruppanandal *math* defeated V. Krishna Iyer in a contest which according to the *Hindu* became increasingly 'a mere caste question'. This type of conflict was, however, unusual and the weight of evidence suggests that, even if brahmans and non-brahmans were sometimes conscious of a rivalry between the two communities, they were, nevertheless, generally content to share power and co-operate in temple management.

MALADMINISTRATION AND PUBLIC CONCERN

One of the more obvious results of the British withdrawal from all connection with Hindu establishments was the mismanagement of temples and temple estates and evidence that temples were no longer conducting ceremonies and worship as efficiently, or in the same grand manner, as they had been during the earlier decades of the nineteenth century. Linked with these changes was public anxiety and speculation about the extent of corruption and misappropriation of temple funds and gloom and frustration at what some Hindus perceived as the decline of Hinduism.

It was widely acknowledged throughout the Presidency that the Act of 1863 failed to protect religious endowments. Between 1874 and 1900 six attempts were made in the Madras Legislative Council to introduce bills which would remedy defects in existing legislation.[43] The first bill, submitted by V. Ramiengar in 1871, was rejected by the Government of Madras on the grounds that it was 'radically incomplete and would certainly fail to attain its object'[44] and successive bills were blocked for various reasons, including a feeling that the time was not ripe, that the intended bill was not in sufficient harmony with the Act of 1863, or that it was too wide in scope. The net result of the Madras Government's continued inability to secure the passage of legislation was that nothing effective was done to improve the administration of temples and temple estates, the condition of which continued to deteriorate throughout the nineteenth century.

One of the defects in the act of 1863 was that it exempted from any form of supervision a whole class of temples defined as 'hereditary' institutions. These included the temples under the control of monastic institutions — many of the most prestigious temples in Tanjore district.

But the act was also defective in that it failed to provide temple committees with sufficient clearly defined powers and authority over trustees.[45] The nature and limit of powers vested in committees were not clearly specified — a condition which was bound to lead to conflict between temple committees and the trustees who, not surprisingly, accused the committees of undue interference in temple affairs.

Replying to inquiries from the Collector of Tanjore in 1872, K. Regunatha Row, a member of the temple committee for the Kumbakonam circle, complained that

> The Committees have to struggle with great difficulties in procuring accounts periodically from the Trustees, and much more in making inquiries concerning doubtful items of receipts and expenditure. The only power the Committees have over the Trustees, though not expressly stated in the enactment, but inferred from the decisions of the High Court, is to suspend or dismiss the latter as the case may be. But though the Committees exercise this, their only power, in many instances it has had very little effect upon the Trustees who, having possession of the pagodas and its properties in their hands, treat the orders of the Committees with the greatest contempt, and would hold the office in spite of all that might be done by the Committees. Such resistance on the part of the Trustees is not considered by the local Magistrates as criminal trespasses, and the Committees are obliged to sue the dismissed Trustees in Civil Courts for ousting them from the possession of the pagodas and their property. But the Committees having no public funds at hand, such as a course is never followed.[46]

It should not be assumed however that temple committees always acted in the public interest or were models of probity solely concerned with the efficient and effective management of the temples under their jurisdiction. In Trichinopoly district, for example, the Trichinopoly Taluk Committee was the only one which met together to do any work. Members of the Committee spent much of their time in appointing, dismissing or reappointing trustees at least partly with the object of trying to secure advantages for trustees with whom they had a particular relationship. Some trustees were friends, creditors or potential creditors of members of the committee or were in a position to recommend special favours such as temple honours. And while trustees could be of value to members of the temple committee the reverse was also true. For their part the temple committee had no direct control over temple funds but did have the authority to recommend which particular trustee in each of the temples under their supervision would have the right and privilege of administering the temple funds.

One of the results of this system was that factional relationships tended to develop — temple committees splitting up as members formed or consolidated alliances with different trustees. Competition for appointments either as trustees or for membership on temple committees (a competition which was especially keen in the Trichinopoly and Kumbakonam taluks) meant that it was in the interests of rival groups or factions to spread rumours and accusations about each other.[47] This makes is extremely difficult to gauge the real as opposed to the rumoured extent of misappropriation, fraud and embezzlement. Rumours of widespread corruption circulated throughout the delta creating a climate of opinion in which the very worst excesses were easily imagined. Some claims and counter-claims could be checked but there were other stories the truth of which could never be ascertained. Commenting on the difficulties involved in auditing temple accounts H. J. Stokes, Sub-Collector of Tanjore in 1872, remarked, for example, that it was easy enough for auditors to ascertain if any of the valuable jewels or cloths in the temple were missing, to discover indirect alienations of landed property, to form a 'general opinion' as to whether ceremonies were conducted on a regular basis, or to see if repairs entered into the accounts had been done.[48] But, he continued, there were other ways in which the temple could be 'plundered' and which were more difficult to discover. For example, no accounts could be checked for receipts from charitable donors 'on account of vows etc.', and who was to prove that omissions had been made from the accounts? Then again there was no foolproof method of checking how much food was distributed to people on festival occasions or how much oil etc. was consumed in the temple. If an entry of Rs. 5,000 occurred in an account for the distribution of food, how could it be proved that only some of the food to this value had in fact been distributed?

While it is important to recognize that some individuals involved in temple management were already wealthy men and that some managers contributed to temple revenues out of their own pockets[49] and were apparently honest and anxious 'to do good to the institution', the fact remains that prominent district officers (who did not necessarily believe in unsubstantiated rumour) were convinced that there was widespread misappropriation of temple funds in the delta during the second half of the nineteenth century.

Stokes who, as we saw, was well aware of the need to examine critically the factors involved, declared his opinion that 'at present where there is misappropriation, it is wholesale and unchecked. No money is spent on repairs, and very little on ceremonies; the money is simply taken by the trustees for their private purposes.'[50] Though A. S. Rau, Deputy Collector during the same period, was inclined to defend trustees as a group, he did not deny instances of 'fraud' as well as mismanagement.[51] The Tahsildar of Negapatam who undertook an extensive investigation of the situation in the area under his jurisdiction, declared his belief that 'many of the trustees are only intent upon embezzling religious and charitable funds, and not in devoting their time for the improvement of those funds.'[52] Referring to cases of

'Malversation, Mismanagement and Alienation of Endowments etc.' which had come before courts in the Tanjore district between 1863 and 1876, A. C. Burnell, the District Judge, drew attention to the fact that temples possessed many valuable jewels and stated that even where receipts had been given 'jewels answering the descriptions in the receipts, but of less value, are often substituted.'[53] Even though lack of incentive, including legal costs and the difficulty of obtaining accounts, discouraged worshippers from taking action against trustees in the courts there were three convictions against trustees for the misappropriation of funds in north Tanjore from 1873 – 5.[54] In another case it was found that the temple committee itself had 'illegally and dishonestly made away with, and converted to their own use, the sum of Rupees 2,950, being part of the funds of the Sikkal Pagoda.'[55]

The problem was not confined to the substitution and theft of jewels, the theft of money and manipulation of temple accounts, but also appears to have involved elaborate schemes for acquiring income more directly through the control and alienation of the revenues from temple estates. K. Regunatha Row, of the Kambakonam Temple Committee, argued that

> There is little doubt that in most cases the present Trustees have been guilty of flagrant misappropriations of the funds in their hands. The landed estates under their trust are generally leased out for nominal rents, and the amounts collected from the tenants, etc., are concealed, being seldom entered in the accounts. In most cases the Trustees themselves are the virtual lessees of the estates. They often get the lease executed in the name of some relative or friend of their own. Thus the operation of selfish influences has deprived the pagodas of the benefits of their landed estates, which the Trustees enjoy under the terms of a permanent lease for a nominal rent.[56]

Sethu Row, Tahsildar of Musiri, together with several other Government officers, believed that members of some temple committees were also engaged in the business of appropriating revenues from temple estates. He remarked that, in some cases, members of the committee

> removed the trustees who would not agree with them and kept the office open for a long time, getting the duties of the trustees performed by their own men. In renting out inam villages of the pagodas they have underhand dealings with the renters, converting to their own use the profits secured by the fraud. They appoint as Amins their own men, and, by their [sic.] means, fill their pockets, allowing them, at the same time a large margin for misappropriation . . . The trustees of the Vishnu temple at Therunarayanapuram and that of the Siva

temple at Iyalore have long been removed and their places are still kept open. There are entire inam villages attached to the devastanams, and they are managed by the Committee members' own men.[57]

Referring specifically to temple lands under the management of non-brahman monks Stokes commented that

The fields of Pandarams more often than others are the subject of remission inquiries. Many of these Pandarams live in a style altogether inconsistent with their position, and some have contracted heavy debts. In some cases the temple lands have been sold for arrears; and there is reason to suspect that what the temple has lost, the trustees or their relations have purchased.[58]

It is impossible to say how far the smooth functioning of temples and the conduct of festivals was undermined by the inexperience and incompetence of boards and committees and how far by the calculated misappropriation of temple revenues.[59] But in the Kaveri delta at least, the effects of incompetence, greed and embezzlement all added up to much the same thing. The amount of money which had been spent on the restoration and upkeep of buildings, on the payment of temple staff and on the performance of rituals and ceremony was no longer available for the same purpose.

There was indeed abundant evidence of the visible and physical effects of mismanagement and neglect.[60] In the 1890s it was reported that important festivals in some of the more celebrated temples in Trichinopoly had stopped,[61] while worshippers in the Tiruvarur temple Tanjore district were reduced to keeping up services 'by raising loans and by begging'.[62] Complaints about the disruption and cessation of worship continued[63] and in an address presented to the Governor in 1898, drawing attention to the need to protect temple funds, Tanjore *mirasidars* complained that in their district the closing of 'the most important temples' had become 'an ordinary occurrence'.[64]

Temple servants were also in a difficult position. Complaints in the 1860s and 1870s that pay was in arrear[65] were echoed later in the century. Commenting on proposals for new legislation aimed at improving the management of temples one correspondent from Trichinopoly writing in the *Hindu* in 1887 remarked that:

At present the servants of many temples have their pay in arrears for months and months. In many cases they even resort to Courts of law to recover the wages due to them for the service rendered.[66]

But perhaps an even more obvious sign of mismanagement and neglect was the deteriorating fabric and disrepair apparent in temples which had once been more carefully maintained. 'Of the 2,874 temples in this district', wrote the Tahsildar of Negapatam in 1872, 'some are in ruins, some in good condition, and many requiring thorough repair. Of these about 3 per cent I suppose are properly managed.'[67] At the same time officials and others in Trichinopoly district reported that many temples there had 'gone to ruin' or were 'out of repair'.[68] A few years later, after a visit to the Jambukeswaram temple in the same district, Monier Williams, who described it as 'one of the most important and interesting shrines in India', remarked that it was 'in a somewhat decaying condition'.[69] Neglect and mismanagement also continued to affect the state of temples in Tanjore district where, according to T. V. Row writing in 1883, 'the general neglect of the buildings' as well as the usual service in the temples was the 'universal complaint in Tanjore district as elsewhere'.[70]

The withdrawal of the East India Company's supervision of and involvement in Hindu affairs not only led ultimately to the neglect and mismanagement of Hindu temples in the region, but also appears to have had deeply felt repercussions — a loss of morale (certainly among some middle-class Hindus) together with an expectation that Christianity would ultimately become the dominant religion.

These views and reactions are reflected in the reports of Hindu conversations with Christian missionaries. In 1850, for example, an S.P.G. Missionary reporting a conversation that took place between himself and a young mudaliar who lived not far from Negapatam, quoted him as saying that

ever since the Company's Government had discontinued their connection with idolatry, by prohibiting their officers from being present at the celebration of heathen festivals, and especially from attending the drawing of cars, it has not only lost much of its importance, but what was worse, that the offerings presented on such occasions had become considerably diminished.[71]

The following year the Rev. J. Little, a Methodist missionary stationed at Mannargudi, remarked that he and his colleagues had been 'surprised' to note the opinion which prevailed in Hindu society 'that their religion will be overthrown and demolished, and Christianity will be universally established'.[72]

While it might be suspected that some of these remarks (particularly the comment about the growing importance of Christianity) may have been made by Hindus who were anxious to please the missionaries by telling them what they wanted to hear, there is also independent evidence that by about 1880 other Hindus feared the worst. Referring to prevailing misgivings about the future of Hinduism, one Hindu correspondent to the *Theosophist* writing from Tiruvadi (Trivadi) in Tanjore taluk in April 1882 declared that converts to Western science and religion had been 'so sapping the foundations of Hinduism' that 'it was feared that, before hardly half a century should have run its course, the beautiful edifice of Indian society, reared by the wisdom and sagacity of generations of sages, would tumble into ruin.'

One of the first and most obvious signs of the time, referred to in the young mudaliar's comments, had been the Government's refusal to assist in recruiting labour for temple-cart processions — a change in policy which affected the scale and magnificence of processions at a number of centres in Tanjore district.[74] Then again there were the rumours and reports — the very widespread conviction — that since the Government's withdrawal, heads of monasteries, as well as managers of temples, were involved in plundering and undermining the effectiveness of Hindu institutions. Fears and anxiety were spread, not merely by allegations of corruption in high places, but by the evidence there for everyone to see of temples falling into disrepair and of rituals and ceremonies no longer being conducted in the same efficient manner. Furthermore, Christian missionaries were increasingly active and, though they had not as yet made converts from among the higher castes, there was always the possibility that this might happen, especially in view of the fact that they were extending the mission school system which continued to attract brahmans and other high-caste Hindus.

These were the changes, fears and misgivings which appear to have affected at least some of the middling and high-caste Hindus prior to the Hindu 'revival' and which created a sense of forboding and unease — a climate of opinion which, as shall be suggested in a subsequent chapter, helps to explain why Olcott, Blavatsky and other Theosophists were welcomed with such enthusiasm as saviours of Hinduism and as very effective allies in the struggle against the disruptive forces of Rationalism and especially Christianity.

NOTES

1 Chandra Mudaliar, op. cit., p. 36.
2 Ibid., pp. 36–40.
3 Kindersley to Sec., 26/11/1841, *M.R.P.*, Ra. 303, Vol. 32, 16/12/1841.
4 Onslow to Sec., 4/9/1841, and Sec. to Onslow, 23/5/1842. *I.O.R.*, L/Parl/Coll.No. 418A.

5 Infra, pp. 68-9.
6 Mudaliar, op. cit., pp. 40-4.
7 For details of the Act and discussion of its defects see Mudaliar, op. cit., pp. 44-51.
8 *Fort St George Gazette*, 23/2/1864.
9 Ibid., 5/4/1864.
10 For the rules framed by the Madras Government for the election of temple committee members see P. R. Ganapathi Iyer, op. cit., Appendix VIII.
11 Kennedy, op. cit.
12 Hurry Row to Acting Collr. Trichinopoly, 16/8/1872, *I.O.R.*, P/383, p. 5212.
13 R. Ramanatha Iyer, *The Madras Hindu Religious Endowments Act (Act II of 1927)*, Madras 1931, p. 410; Onslow, to Sec. 4/9/1841, and Sec. to Onslow, 23/5/1842, *I.O.R.*, L/Parl./Coll. No. 418A.
14 A. Strinivasa Rau, Deputy Collr. to Officiating Collr. of Tanjore, 23/12/1872, *I.O.R.*, P/383, p. 5162.
15 Rangasami Aiyengar to Acting Collr. of Trichinopoly, 12/8/1872, *I.O.R.*, P/383, p. 5217.
16 Ibid.
17 Infra, Ch. 4.
18 Onslow to Sec., 4/9/1841, *I.O.R.*, L/Parl./Coll. No. 418A.
19 Collector to Sec., 26/11/1841, *M.R.P.*, Ra. 303, Vol. 32, 16/12/1841.
20 Collector to Sec., 30/1/1863, *M.R.P.*, Ra. 315, Vol. 5, 17/2/1864.
21 Supra, Ch. 1.
22 The Uttamanambi family appears to have risen into prominence in the fourteenth century. They maintained close connections with the Vijayanagar court and not only gave land grants and other gifts to the temple but encouraged chieftains and others to follow suit. Associated with the rise of this family was the establishment of a *math* at Srirangam. Its head, who was known as the Sriranganarayana Jiyar, was an Uttamanambi. He and his successors were given several duties and privileges in the temple and came to occupy a prominent position in the temple's administration (V. N. Hari Rao, op. cit., pp. 334-5; A. Appadurai, *Worship and Conflict*, pp. 86-9).
23 Lushington to Sec., 17/6/1818, *M.R.P.*, Ra. 291, Vol. 71, 29/6/1818; H. Dickinson to Sec., 14/2/1828, *M.R.P.*, Ra. 296, Vol. 50, 25/2/1828.
24 M. Monier Williams, op. cit., p. 125. See also infra, Ch. 4, n. 17.
25 *M.H.C.*, Second Appeal No. 1571 of 1891; Second Appeal No. 467 of 1898.
26 Dickinson to Sec., 14/2/1828, *M.R.P.*, Ra. 296, Vol. 50, 25/2/1828; Lushington to Sec., 17/7/1818, *M.R.P.*, Ra. 291, Vol. 71, 29/7/1818.
27 Onslow to Sec., 29/7/1842, *M.R.P.*, *I.O.R.*, L/Parl./Coll. No. 418A; *M.R.P.*, 6/10/1842, *I.O.R.*, L./Parl./Coll. No. 418A.
28 *Hindu*, 30/1/1895, 14/3/1899.
29 Ibid., 14/3/1899.
30 Lushington to Sec., 17/6/1818, *M.R.P.*, Ra. 291, Vol. 71, 29/6/1818; Dickinson to Sec., 14/2/1828, *M.R.P.*, Ra. 296, Vol. 50, 25/2/1828; Onslow to Sec., 14/2/1840, *M.R.P.*, Ra. 302, Vol. 37, 27/7/1840, Onslow

to Sec., 31/7/1840, *M.R.P.*, Ra. 302, Vol. 39, 20/8/1840; Onslow to Sec., 29/7/1842 and 6/10/1842, *I.O.R.*, L/Parl./Coll. No. 418A; *I.L.R.*, 10 Mad. 464; *Hindu*, 13/12/1889, 26/11/1890.
31. Kindersley to Sec., 26/11/1841, *M.R.P.*, Ra. 303, Vol. 32, 16/12/1841.
32. Ibid., and Mudaliar, op. cit., pp. 37, 45.
33. *Hindu*, 16/7/1900; Hemingway, *Tanjore*, p. 232.
34. See Appendix I.
35. Appeal No. 234 of 1895, *I.L.R.*, Madras Series, Vol. XX 1897, p. 426.
36. Hemingway, *Tanjore*, p. 271; *Hindu*, 16/8/1898.
37. Another way of assessing the overall situation in Tanjore district with regard to the brahman or non-brahman caste of trustees of major temples towards the end of the nineteenth century is to take T. V. Row's list of 1884 of the 23 'most celebrated of the principal temples in the district'. (T. V. Row, op. cit., pp. 228 – 9). Some evidence relating to the caste of trustees was available in connection with just over half of these institutions. During the period for which there was evidence one of them was managed by the Tanjore royal family, 11 by non-brahman monks and, of the remaining three, two were under non-brahman management and *one* had both brahman and non-brahman trustees.
38. Infra, Ch. 4.
39. D. A. Washbrook, *The Emergence of Provincial Politics*, p. 111; *Hindu*, 22/8/1888, 20/4/1889, 26/4/1889, 17/5/1889, 1/6/1889.
40. *Hindu*, 24/8/1888.
41. Ibid., 23/7/1888, 6, 12, 22, 24/8/1888, 20, 23, 24, 26, 27, 29/4/1889, 13/5/1889.
42. Ibid., 26, 28/10/1899, 4, 8, 10, 11/11/1889.
43. R. Ramanatha Iyer, op. cit., pp. 13 – 31; Mudaliar, op. cit., pp. 53 – 8.
44. Mudaliar, op. cit., p. 53.
45. Ibid., pp. 48 – 9.
46. K. Regunatha Row to Collr. of Tanjore, 19/8/1872, *I.O.R.*, P/383, p. 176. See also Pattabhiram Pillai, Huzur Sheristadar to Act. Collr. of Trichinopoly, 6/1/1873, *I.O.R.*, P/383, p. 5191.
47. According to A. Strinivasa Rau, Deputy Collector of Tanjore, this tendency to take every opportunity of condemning the system of management by trustees or non-official committees, and of accusing them of fraud and mismanagement was also encouraged by 'natives of rank and influence' when they visited temples and felt they were no longer treated with consideration by the managers of the temples. (Deputy Collr. to Collr of Tanjore, 23/12/1872, *I.O.R.*, P/383, p. 5161).
48. Sub-Collr. to Collr. of Tanjore, 14/6/1872, *I.O.R.*, P/383, p. 5181.
49. Deputy Collr. to Collr. of Tanjore, 23/12/1872 and Vakil of Civil Court of Trichinopoly to Act. Collr. of Trichinopoly, 12/6/1872, *I.O.R.*, P/383, pp. 5163, 5210.
50. Stokes to Collr. of Tanjore 14/6/1872, *I.O.R.*, P/383, p. 5181.
51. A. S. Rau to Collr. of Tanjore, 23/12/1872, I.O.R., P/383 p. 5161.
52. Tahsildar of Negapatam to Collr. of Tanjore, 16/5/1872, *I.O.R.*, P/383 p. 5168.

53 Burnell to President of the Hindu Religious Endowment Law Committee, 9/11/1876, *I.O.R.*, P/1426, *M.J.P.*, 10/1/1879.
54 *I.O.R.*, P/1426, *M.J.P.*, 10/1/1879.
55 See statement showing cases of malversation, mismanagement and alienation etc. *I.O.R.*, P/1426, *M.J.P.*, 10/1/1879.
56 K. Regunatha Row to Collr. of Tanjore, 19/8/1872, *I.O.R.*, P/383, pp. 5177–8.
57 Tahsildar of Musiri to act. Collr. of Tanjore, 19/8/1872, *I.O.R.*, P/383, p. 5225. See also Deputy Collr. of Tanjore to Collr. of Tanjore, 23/12/1872, *I.O.R.*, P/383, p. 5162.
58 Stokes to Collr. of Tanjore 14/6/1872, *I.O.R.*, P/383 p. 5181.
59 For an account of the way in which a dispute between trustees and tenants, as well as deliberate misappropriation, drastically reduced the income of the celebrated Thayagarajeswami temple at Trivalore in Tanjore district see R. Vengatrayaloo, Tahsildar of Negapatam to Collr. of Tanjore 16/5/1872.
60 *Hindu*, 6/4/1887, 25/5/87, T. R. Row, op. cit., p. 228.
61 Tahsildar of Musiri to Act. Collr. Trichinopoly, 17/8/1872, *I.O.R.*, P/383, p. 5225.
62 Tahsildar of Negapatam to Collr. Tanjore, 16/5/1872, *I.O.R.*, P/383, p. 5169.
63 *Hindu*, 15/8/1885, 6/4/1887; T. V. Row, op. cit., p. 228.
64 Ibid., 12/4/1898.
65 Tahsildar of Negapatam to Collr. Tanjore, 16/5/1872, *I.O.R.*, P/383, p. 5169. *I.O.R.*, P/1426, *M.J.P.*, 10/1/1879.
66 *Hindu*, 25/5/1887.
67 Tahsildar of Negapatam to Collr. Tanjore 16/5/1872, I.O.R., P/383, p. 5170. See also the findings of the District Court of North Tanjore, *I.O.R.*, P/1426. Tahsildar of Kulittalai to Act. Collr. Trichinopoly 9N.D.O. *I.O.R.*, P/383, p. 5169; Zamindar of Arealur to Act. Collr. of Trichinopoly 14/8/1872, *I.O.R.*, P/383, p. 5201; Srinivasa Thathachariar Rau to Act. Collr. of Trichinopoly 18/8/1872, *I.O.R.*, P/383, p. 5206 and T. Appaji Rau to Act. Collr. of Trichinopoly, 30/5/1872, *I.O.R.* P/383, p. 5223.
68 Tahsildar of Kulittalai to Act. Collr. Trichinopoly (N.D.) *I.O.R.*, P/383, p. 5169; Zamindar of Arealur to Act. Collr. of Trichinopoly 14/8/1872, *I.O.R.*, P/383, p. 5201; Srinivasa Thathachariar Rau to Act. Collr. of Trichinopoly 18/8/1872, *I.O.R.*, P/383, p. 5206 and T. Appaji Rau to Act. Collr. of Trichinopoly, 30/5/1872, *I.O.R.*, P/383, p. 5223.
69 M. Monier Williams, *Brahmanism*, pp. 445–6.
70 T. V. Row, op. cit., p. 228.
71 *M.Q.M.J.*, No. 1, New Series, July 1850, Vol. 1, pp. 61–2.
72 *W.M.N.*, 1852, p. 5. See also *L.M.S.*, J. E. Nimmo, Annual Report, 31/12/1840, S. I. Tamil, Box 8.
73 *Th.*, Vol. III, June 1882, p. 235.
74 *H.F.*, Vol. 1, November 1861, pp. 14–15 and September 1862, p. 248; J. Bush (ed.), op. cit., pp. 232–3, 257–8.

4

SECTARIAN CONFLICTS WITHIN SRIVAISHNAVISM: TENGALAIS AND VADAGALAIS

I

So far we have been considering some of the ways in which the imposition of British rule and other changes, including the rise of the evangelical movement in Britain, began to affect the traditional relationship between the ruler on the one hand and Hinduism on the other. We have discussed the effect of these changes on temple administration and on the ongoing life and activity associated with temple communities. The purpose of the next few chapters is to explore other continuities and changes in Hinduism including developments which were also, to a greater or lesser degree, affected by the new influences and forces at work in local society. The subject of the present chapter is sectarian conflict and some of the ways in which traditional sectarian rivalry was affected if not intensified in the region in the nineteenth century.

Many of the traditional differences between vaishnavites and saivites, including differences in theology, ritual and worship, were preserved and maintained, especially among the higher castes, in South India during this period.[1]

The census reports for the Madras Presidency from 1871 to 1891 classified most Hindus as belonging to one or other of these sectarian[2] categories. These reports, which suggest that vaishnavism was predominant in the Telugu country and saivism in Tamilnadu, give the percentages of saivites and vaishnavites in Trichinopoly and Tanjore district as shown in Table 1.[3]

As the nineteenth century progressed, however, the census commissioners became increasingly dissatisfied with the accuracy and usefulness of this type of classification — a category which they finally decided to abandon after 1891. While, in their view, the distinction between vaishnavites and saivites was an important division among high-caste Hindus, it had little relevance or meaning further down the social scale.[4] Not only were lower-caste Hindus often ignorant of the

Table 1. Percentages of Saivites and Vaisnavites.

Year	Trinchinopoly		Tanjore	
	Saivites	Vaishnavites	Saivites	Vaishnavites
1871	75.5	24.3	86.5	13.5
1881	73.7	26.3	86.0	14.0
1891	74.1	25.9	85.6	14.2

more fundamental differences between the sects but, even among the higher castes, the division no longer appeared to be as socially significant as it had been earlier. According to the census report for 1901, for example, no 'active proselytism' was maintained by either group, while the 'antagonism' between the two no longer awakened the enthusiasm it once did.[5]

In fact, the most intensely bitter and socially disruptive sectarian feuds among Hindus in nineteenth century Tamil society were not between vaishnavites and saivites, but were within the vaishnava (or srivaishnava)[6] movement itself — between the vadagalais, (or 'northerners') and tengalais (or 'southerners').[7] According to M. Monier Williams, who visited South India in 1883, these two sects within the srivaishnava movement were 'far more opposed to each other than both parties are to Saivas,'[8] and the same observation was made by others.[9]

The origin of these disputes between tengalais and vadagalais dated back to preferences for different texts, theological and other disparities which began to emerge among the followers of Ramanuja some time after his death in 1173. Ramanuja himself appears to have drawn no distinction between Sanskrit and Tamil works and treated them both as equally useful in religious worship. Some of his followers, however, known subsequently as tengalais, came to prefer Tamil literature including the *Prabandam* (or hymns of the *alvars* or saints). Others (the vadagalais), without denying the significance of the Tamil hymns, made greater use of Sanskrit texts.[10] Disputes between these two groups tended to arise especially over the question of the priority to be given to the recitation of the *Prabandam* of the Vedas in temples.[11]

Linked with the linguistic and textual division were doctrinal differences including conflicting views as to the means and availability of salvation — views which, as Stein has pointed out,[12] have very different social implications. According to Ramanuja, the *bhakta*, or devotee, was saved through *prapatti* (resignation or self-surrender). However, differences arose over how far, if at all, *prapatti* involved preparation or effort on the part of the individual.[13] Tengalais taught that *prapatti* was the means of 'unreservedly placing oneself in his [God's] hands, and ridding oneself of all notions of securing salvation by self-effort'.[14] In their view, the devotee was in a position analogous to that of a kitten which, without any effort on its part, is picked up and carried to safety in its mother's mouth. On the other hand, vadagalais held that some kind of effort was required as a preliminary to *prapatti* in just the same way as a young monkey has to cling to his mother's back as she hops from place to place. They not only had a more limited view of the efficacy and extent of God's saving grace, but believed that knowledge about how to achieve salvation was confined very largely to specialists. They insisted that brahmans alone were qualified to instruct devotees in all spiritual knowledge and denounced the tengalai view that this knowledge could be obtained even from low-caste teachers.[15] Furthermore, unlike tengalai brahmans, vadagalai brahmans refused to teach non-brahmans the *astaksari-mantra* or eight-syllabled holy prayer[16] (a prayer to Vishnu supposed to be recited thrice daily), displaying what was perhaps an attitude of greater indifference to the spiritual condition of the lower castes.

The tengalai school with its use of Tamil, special veneration of the *alvars* (who included low-caste Hindus) and stress on the availability of spiritual knowledge and salvation irrespective of 'caste, colour or creed' had a greater appeal than the more Sanskritic and socially conservative vadagalai movement. The former appears to have spread more rapidly and widely among low and outcaste groups and continued as the more socially radical and popular division among srivaisnavites in the nineteenth century.

Nineteenth century census reports do not give figures on the number and caste of non-brahman adherents of either sect, but there is no reason to doubt Bhattacharya's claim that the tengalai division continued to include a larger proportion of 'sudra' adherents.[17] Furthermore, tengalai brahmans continued to practise what were essentially non-brahman rituals and customs to a greater degree than their more 'orthodox'[18] counterparts. According to the census, there was little difference between tengalai and vadagalai brahman communities in the age at which girls were married or in the proportion of widows among them;[19] but tengalai brahmans, unlike vadagalais, did not shave their widows' heads and quoted several texts in support of the practice.[20] Nor did they observe the daily ritual of *homa*,[21] a practice among vadagalai and other brahmans dating back to Vedic times whereby offerings of clarified butter, rice, etc., were made to fire. Furthermore, the marriage ceremony among tengalai brahmans, especially in Chingleput and north Arcot districts, was simpler and had more affinity with low-caste customs and ritual than marriage ceremonies in the vadagalai brahman community.[22] Not only did tengalai brahmans share more in common with non-brahmans but, compared with vadagalai brahmans, they expressed more tolerant and accommodating social attitudes. According to A. Govindacarya, the tengalai author of an article published in the *Journal of the Royal Asiatic Society* in 1910,[23] vadagalais still taught that 'a *Prapanna* [one who practises resignation] but who is an inferior caste is deserving of only so much respect as may be displayed by the tongue' whereas tengalais taught that 'no such limitations can be tolerated. A *prapanna* must be regarded completely as a *prapanna* irrespective of caste, creed, or colour. No inequality begat by caste or other such formalities and conventions ought to separate the godly from the godly.'

It appears then that, by the nineteenth century, doctrinal and other tensions between tengalais and vadagalais had not only hardened into social divisions among the brahmans (intermarriage between them being extremely uncommon)[24] but had also developed into two somewhat conflicting social movements. The desire on the part of vadagalais to preserve brahman dominance (including doctrines and rituals based on a knowledge of Sanskrit texts) was opposed by leaders of the tengalai movement who espoused a more conciliatory and popular system — one which accommodated, to a much greater extent, the religious and social needs and aspirations of lower-caste Hindus.

II

Given the more rapid spread and successful establishment of tengalai vaishnavism in most parts of Tamilnadu it is hardly surprising that eventually vadagalais attempted to check their opponents and, as Appadurai has pointed out, 'looked for new areas in which to promulgate and institutionalize their beliefs'.[25] In the nineteenth century, in the Kaveri delta as elsewhere, they appear to have been on the counter-offensive — in most cases taking the initiative in attempting to penetrate temples under tengalai control.

The most intensive and protracted struggle in the delta took place over vadagalai attempts to penetrate the Sriranganatha temple — the chief shrine on the island of Srirangam and one which had long been recognized as a tengalai institution. The conflict, which continued intermittently throughout the nineteenth century and which occasionally flared into violence, was all the more desperately and keenly fought because of the important place Srirangam (the common name for the temple itself) occupied in Hindu sentiment; indeed, whichever sect managed to dominate and control the temple, dominated and controlled one of the wealthiest and most famous religious centres in the whole of India.

The temple, regarded by many Hindus as inferior only to Benares,[26] was by far the largest in Southern India — its massive walls which formed a series of quadrangular enclosures, with its shrines and other buildings occupying 165 acres. It was in the words of M. Monier Williams, one of several notable European visitors to the island in the second half of the nineteenth century, 'rather a sacred city than a temple'.[27] Its chief shrine dated back to at least as early as the eighth century A.D. and is mentioned in the works of all the *alvars* but one.[28] It became the headquarters of the vaishnava movement during the medieval period — Ramanuja spending many years there as chief *acharya* and devotee of Sriranganatha. The sanctity of the place was also enhanced by its location, not only at the confluence of two rivers (a site generally revered by Hindus) but also by the fact that one of these rivers was the Kaveri whose waters, according to the *puranas*,[29] wash away all sin.

During the nineteenth century Srirangam continued to attract pilgrims from all over India. Official estimates of the numbers attending the temple's main festival in December were as high as 90,000 in 1874 and 1879 — though the figure was much lower in some other years owing to the outbreak of cholera or for other reasons.[30] The temple also continued to attract endowments and remained an extremely wealthy institution, making control over its resources an even more desirable objective. In 1841, according to the Collector's report, its annual income (mostly from private donations and government grants, rather than from land) was four times greater than that of any other temple in Trichinopoly district and accounted for nearly one-third of the total revenue of the 113 larger temples listed in the district returns.[31] Furthermore, Srirangam was famed for its jewels, gold vessels and other precious ornaments.[32]

Even after the growth of divisions within the srivaishnava movement vadagalais and tengalais continued to visit each other's shrines[33] and, in Srirangam, several hundred vadagalai families were permitted to continue residing within the precincts of the temple, provided they adhered to custom and accepted tengalai dominance.[34] In 1803, however, only two years after the British assumed responsibility for the administration of the Carnatic, including oversight of Srirangam, disputes broke out between the two parties over the customary right of tengalai brahmans to perform funeral rites in vadagalai houses.[35]

In attempting to settle this and other issues, including vadagalai claims to the Vedantacarya shrine within the temple precincts, John Wallace the Collector, in 1803 laid the basis of an official policy which lasted for the next 30 years. He ruled firmly in favour of tengalais and a continuance of the *status quo*. He declared that, as the entire temple was manned by tengalais (brahmans and non-brahmans alike), vadagalais could not claim any connection with it: that the various ceremonies were to be conducted according to custom as they had been before British rule, and that anyone who went against custom was to be punished in the chief court and exiled from the shrine.[36]

Wallace's ruling, however, appears to have had little effect in curbing disputes. The vadagalais were well aware of the fact that positions held by local British officials were temporary, that there were frequent changes in civil service personnel and that, with the appointment of each new collector, judge or magistrate, they could try again, testing for cracks in official policy.[37] In 1808, after the vadagalais had taken the issue of their alleged rights in Srirangam to court, R. H. Latham, the District Judge, confirmed tengalai 'superiority' over the temple, including their right 'to direct the ceremonies with all the privileges appertaining thereto'.[38] In 1818 C. M. Lushington, who was then Collector, rejected a petition from vadagalais, declaring that they 'had no title to any privileges as of their own right, but that they must act in subserviency to the Tengallayars, and only perform such ceremonies as were prescribed by them'.[39] These decisions in favour of tengalai predominance and rights within Srirangam were again confirmed by G. W. Saunders, the Collector, in 1824 by a decision in the District Court of Kumbakonam in 1825 and by H. Dickinson, the Collector, in 1827.[40]

But then vadagalai persistence was suddenly rewarded, for in 1832 occurred the first in a series of developments which gradually began to weaken tengalai control and authority within the temple.

In 1829, when it came to the knowledge of N. S. Cameron, the new Collector, that vadagalais were once again reciting Vedas in the temple contrary to regulations, he issued a proclamation requiring all parties to conform to the decision contained in Judge Latham's decree of 1808. Though he warned that anyone disobeying his orders, and hence Latham's decree, would be 'liable to a heavy fine' vadagalai brahmans ignored his warning and were subsequently fined.[41]

Initially, the vadagalais appeared to accept this punishment, but then in 1832, three years later, they discovered in George Garrow, Acting First Judge, someone who they believed would act on their behalf. They appealed against Cameron's proclamation and the fines that had been imposed. Garrow thereupon issued a precept recalling the proclamation and returning the fines,[42] an unprecedented action which had the effect of removing the legal restraints against vadagalais reciting the Vedas within the temple.

In defending this sudden reversal of a long-standing policy, Garrow argued that his decision had nothing to do with the merits of the case as between the contending parties, but that Cameron's proclamation had been 'illegal'.[43] But, while it is debatable as to whether Garrow was technically correct, tengalais believed the real reason for his decision had nothing to do with the niceties of legal argument. In their view, Garrow was prejudiced in their opponents' favour — having 'in his Court and household' a number of individuals 'that is to say Public and Menial Servants all of Vadagala Schism'.[44]

The immediate effect of Garrow's precept was to encourage violence. According to the Collector, 'the very night' after its publication about two hundred vadagalais

rushed tumultuously into the Pagoda, and read Vehdaparayenum setting at defiance the authority of the Devastanum Peshcar [chief assistant] and knocking down the Peons who attempted to prevent their entrance, saying that the order against their performing ceremonies there had been recalled. This outrage was repeated on the following day . . .[45]

Although order was eventually restored and 25 of the ringleaders punished with a fine, and a higher court eventually declared Latham's decree final — confirming tengalais in their rights and restoring what was regarded as the *status quo*,[46] Garrow's intervention had long-term effects. For the first time since the introduction of British rule an official decision had been made which failed to protect established custom and which questioned tengalai rights in Srirangam. It not only enhanced the status of vadagalai claims to a greater control of temple affairs but, in the words of the Collector in 1832, was 'most mischievous' in 'reviving the pretensions of the Vadagalais which had been proved to be totally unfounded'.[47]

A second development which affected tengalai control of Srirangam in the nineteenth century was the Company's decision to reorganize the temple's management so as to facilitate the Company's general policy of withdrawal from all connection with Hindu religious establishments.[48] The Collector, A. P. Onslow, suggested that the management of Srirangam should be left in the hands of 'the hereditary officers of the institution, headed by a *jeer* (religious devotee)'.[49] By 'hereditary officers' he meant the hereditary *stulattars* or trustees, who were four in number, the hereditary principal *archikar* or *pujari* (priest) of the temple and, lastly, the *jeer* or *sannyasi* who was to have 'the immediate adjustment of all disputes; the disputants being at liberty to apply to the usual courts of justice for the final settlement'. In the Collector's view one of the main advantages of this proposal was that the management of the institution would be 'in exact accordance with Hindoo usage' and acceptable to the Hindu community. The hereditary officers were tengalai and, if Onslow had had his way, the management of the temple would have remained just as securely in tengalai hands as hitherto.

The Board of Revenue in Madras, however, was not only less wedded to tradition but was also sceptical about the practicality of these suggestions.[50] They argued that the conduct of affairs under the guidance of a *jeer* 'who by his vows as a sunniyasee, is bound to renounce all wordly cares and occupations', did not seem to them 'to hold out a fair expectation of ensuring the efficient control of the large expenditure, or of preserving inviolate the accumulated wealth of that institution'. They feared that there would be 'discord' between the hereditary trustees and the *archikars* and, apparently dismissing as unimportant traditional methods of selecting trustees, suggested the possibility that outsiders (such as the Tondamon family) might well become associated with the temple's management.

In view of these objections, the Collector was forced to abandon his essentially conservative policy and opted for experiment and innovation. The idea of appointing the *jeer* and head priest to the committee was abandoned[51] and instead two non-hereditary 'independent and respectable persons', Chundrashaikarum Pillay, a large *mirasidar* in Tanjore and Trichinopoly districts, and Krishna Rao, formerly a legal officer in Trichinopoly, were appointed as the new trustees 'in conjunction with two of the pagoda stullaters [sic] all the four officers of that description officiating on the committee in alternative years'.[52] Krishna Rao and possibly also Pillay were tengalais and according to the tengalais themselves, all went well for the first three years — the committee continuing to conduct the affairs of the temple according to custom and without challenging tengalai predominance.[53]

However, Krishna Rao died in 1845 and, for reasons which are unclear, Onslow set the *stulattars* aside and appointed two non-vaishnavite public servants as sole trustees — notwithstanding a general government directive that the management of religious institutions was to be handed over to those belonging to the same faith for which the institution was established.[54] One of the appointees was Veerasawmien of the madiva sect, Head Writer of the Commissariat Office Southern Division, and the other, Conjamala Moothely, was a saivite and Cash Keeper at the Collector's Cutchery.[55]

Thus for the first time the hereditary trustees of the temple appear to have had no voice in its management. Not only was tengalai control of the temple at stake but tengalais feared, not without some justification, that this control would pass into the hands of their traditional opponents. In a memorial to the Court of Directors in 1848 they complained that already vadagalais were permitted to introduce their distinctive practices such as 'reciting the Vedas during processions of the Swamy and at marriage ceremonies'.[56] They asserted that vadagalais were also performing rituals in vadagalai houses within the temple complex — a privilege tengalais had long claimed as their own

— and also that affrays in the temple were becoming even more common. That these protests to London had no effect is suggested by subsequent events when, apparently for the first time, a vadagalai was appointed as one of the trustees[57] — a measure which was not only contrary to centuries of practice but which could hardly have been better calculated to inflame sectarian feeling. Temple affairs were plunged into disarray and violent riots broke out as tengalais protested against the appointment.

A third development which affected the position of tengalais at Srirangam, which increased the uncertainty of their being able to control the composition of the board of trustees and which broadened the arena of sectarian conflict, was the government's establishment of temple committees in 1863.[58] In Trichinopoly that section of the act which provided that temple committees were to be appointed from persons professing 'the same religion' as the one the institution belonged to, was deliberately set aside. The Acting Collector, M. J. Walhouse, argued that nothing was to be gained by appointing separate committees for saivite and vaishnavite temples, or by taking differences between tengalais and vadagalais into account.[59] Referring to Srirangam, he declared that he could not see how the dispute could be 'mended' by appointing a separate committee for each party. Srirangam was therefore placed under the jurisdiction of a temple committee which was composed of Hindus of different sectarian affiliations, viz., two saivites and three vaishnavites — the latter including two tengalais and one vadagalai.[60]

In the previous 'no law period' the trustees had come to include non-tengalai or even vadagalai members. Now, under these new arrangements, a mixture of sectarian interests was even more carefully preserved on the temple committee — the members of which, as we have seen, were appointed for life. The stage was set for alliances between members of the same sect on the temple committee and board of trustees — for vadagalais on the temple committee, for example, to work through trustees already sympathetic to their cause or to appoint their own men as trustees and, through these means, introduce more of their own ceremonies and gain greater control of the temple. Indeed, as legal records for the period 1883 to 1893 suggest,[61] whichever party was able to dominate the temple committee was also able to influence the composition or membership of the board of trustees — with, amongst other things, serious consequences for the good order and effective management of the temple itself.

During the period 1888 to 1893 Srirangam was under the management of three trustees two of whom (V. A. Bhuttar and T. R. Mudaliar) occupied positions which were not in dispute.[62] The real contest between the two sects was to see which of their men would occupy the third place on the board of trustees, and this depended on the balance of power on the temple committee.

In February 1888 there was a saivite, a vadagalai and three tengalais on the temple committee. In November 1890 the three tengalais were dismissed 'for some negligence' by order of the Court. The disappearance of the three tengalais from the committee was soon followed by the resignation of the tengalai trustees 'under pressure from the committee'. The tables were soon turned, however, as in January 1892 the High Court reinstated the three tengalai members of the temple committee and the tengalai trustee was then reappointed.

A little later, however, the temple committee lost two of its three tengalai members. One resigned in February 1892 and the other died about a fortnight later. Of the three remaining members of the committee one was a saivite, one was a vadagalai and the third (T. V. Chetti) the only remaining tengalai representative. According to the District Judge who presided over the case, Chetti was a weak character 'vascillating and easily impressed'. He was persuaded to join with his two colleagues in dismissing once again the tengalai trustee — appointing K. S. Aiyengar, a vadagalai, in his place. The new appointee was a cousin of the vadagalai member of the temple committee and was also Chetti's creditor.

But K. S. Aiyengar, like the others, was not to remain a trustee for long. T. V. Chetti died in June 1892, reducing the numbers on the temple committee to two. Two months later there was a riot in Srirangam apparently in reaction to vadagalai attempts to introduce vadagalai rituals, and in October 1892 the District Judge finally decided to fill up all three vacancies on the temple committee[63] bringing it up to its full complement of five. All three new incumbents were tengalais. In December the Committee, now with a tengalai majority, suspended K. S. Aiyengar as a trustee on the grounds that 'he had caused loss of property and money to the temple . . . and had conducted things in the temple contrary to custom so as to cause a disturbance of the peace'. He was dismissed in February 1893.

It is fairly clear from these events that the district judges were not insensitive to the need to keep at least some tengalai representatives on the taluk temple committee.[64] But the fact is that this committee usually included at least one vadagalai representative as well, and the very existence of the committee provided vadagalais with a new weapon and new machinery through which they could appoint their own people as trustees and exercise greater control over what had previously been a tengalai stronghold.

III

The issues dividing tengalais and vadagalais in the nineteenth century were not very different from what they had been in the pre-modern period. What was new was the way in which the parties attempted to achieve their aims through the new political structure and new legal system. The struggle was conducted not merely in the temple itself but outside through the new temple committees and in the law courts; and appeals were made not only to local officials but to authorities in Madras and even overseas.

In Tanjore district in 1864 an unwarranted attempt led by vadagalai members of the newly-appointed Kumbakonam temple committee to dismiss trustees of the Nachiyarkovil temple (who belonged to neither party) and a move to appoint vadagalais in their place were frustrated by the decisions of British legal authorities who argued that there were no 'good and sufficient grounds' for the dismissals.'[65] But if, in this case, the British effectively maintained the *status quo*, the effect of their activities with respect to Srirangam was very different. Garrow's ruling, which appeared to overthrow previous decisions in favour of the temple being under tengalai management and to remove legal impediments to vadagalais reciting the Vedas within the temple, increased apprehension among tengalais and encouraged vadagalais to press their claims. The action by collectors in replacing hereditary trustees by outsiders (non-tengalais and, in at least one case, a vadagalai) and the establishment of a supervisory temple committee in 1864 representing different sects including vadagalais, opened the way for greater vadagalai influence and more effective control over rituals and ceremony.

These disputes undoubtedly played a part in undermining the effectiveness and efficiency of the temple's administration. The dissension among trustees[66] and on the temple committee, the uncertainty that existed in some cases with regard to tenure on the board of trustees and frequent changes in its membership, according to whether tengalais or vadagalais obtained the upper hand, were factors which not only distracted attention from the main task of management, but which must also have made it extremely difficult for even conscientious trustees to function effectively. Indeed, there were frequent complaints in the press during the last quarter of the century of mismanagement[67] — of the temple servants not being paid regularly, of buildings falling into disrepair, of festivals not being conducted properly and of what were simply called 'irregularities'.

While the party leadership in these disputes was predominantly if not exclusively brahman the warring factions also included non-brahman adherents. Some of these were, for example, members of the Trichinopoly temple committee[68] and some were possibly active in the demonstrations and more violent affrays which erupted from time to time. Disturbances in the temple led to the destruction of property, interrupted ceremonies and, on at least one occasion, forced the temple's closure.[69] The litigation which resulted from these feuds helped line the pockets of the legal profession and plunged several rich Trichinopoly families into poverty.[70] Nor were the effects of these disputes confined to one locality. Disputes in Srirangam and in connection with the Nachiyarkovil and Rajagopalaswami temples in Tanjore district were, as mentioned above, part of an even wider sectarian conflict — a struggle which was taking place concurrently in many other srivaishnava centres — in the Sri Partasarati Swami temple in Triplicane, at Srivilliputtur in Tinnevelly, at Conjeeveram in Chingleput and in other parts of Tamilnadu.[71] The infighting, litigation and violence was given wider publicity through the press so that what happened at one centre was likely to inflame feelings elsewhere — each party being extremely sensitive to news of encroachments or supposed 'injustices' committed by the other.

Last, but not least, sectarian bitterness and rivalry increasingly scandalized some of the Western-educated Hindus — especially those conscious of the need to unify Hinduism in the face of Christian missionary aggression.[72] It is hardly surprising then that several if not most of those Hindu reform and revival organizations established in South India in the 1880s had as one of their objectives the aim of promoting harmony and goodwill among the sects as well as castes of India.[73] Nor according to the editor of the *Hindu* were these divisions acceptable among people struggling to achieve some measure of national unity. Writing in an editorial published in January 1899, he declared that

The dreadful outbursts of religious fanaticism, marked by fearful breaches of public tranquility, between Sivaites on the one hand and Vaishnavites on the other, have now become harmless memories of the past . . . The more unnatural feud, however, is that between the Tengalais and the Vadagalais; and it has from the time of its commencement continued to rage with unabated, nay, with steadily increasing fury . . . Is it not desirable then, before trying or even planning to fuse the heterogenous peoples of India into one homogenous nation, with one political aspiration and one national church so to speak, to attempt the less ambitious task of closing the ever-widening gulf between two sects professing the same faith and approaching the same deity, the same in name and form, through very slightly different modes of worship?[74]

NOTES

1 For a discussion of these differences see especially J. Gonda, *Visnuism and Sivaism: A Comparison*. London, 1970.
2 Though the terms 'sect' and 'sectarian', with their Western and Christian connotations, may not be entirely satisfactory as concepts which can be applied to Hinduism, they are arguably just as suitable as any other alternative. 'Sect' has generally been used to describe Christian groups which were, in a sense, splinter groups, which defined themselves over and against 'church' and which, as Brian Wilson has pointed out, were 'movements of religious protest' rejecting the authority of 'orthodox' religious leaders. While Hindu groupings, such as saivites and vaishnavites or tengalais and vadagalais, can hardly be described as sects in this sense they were, nevertheless, divisions within a larger religious tradition and, in that very general sense, shared something in common with Christian sects. The term 'sect' was used by Hindus when writing in English to describe these divisions among themselves (see for example the *Hindu*, 9/9/1898 and 21/1/1899) and it is still used by scholars, such as Renou and Appadurai, when discussing the same phenomenon. (L Renou (ed.) *Hinduism*, New York, 1962, pp. 45-51; A. Appadurai, *'Worship and Conflict . . .'* Ch. 2). Furthermore, unlike possible alternative terms, such as the Sanskrit 'sampradaya' or 'tradition', 'sect' gives us 'sectarian' and 'sectarianism', words which serve to underline the fact that these groups were, or had been, involved in intensive and bitter religious conflict and rivalry.

For further discussion of this problem see especially B. Wilson *Religious Sects: A Sociological Study*, London 1970, and Anncharlott Eschmann, 'Religion, Reaction and Change: the Role of Sects in Hinduism' in *Religion and Development in Asian Societies, Proceedings of the International Workshop*, Colombo 1975.
3 *Census of India*, 1881, Madras, Vol. 1, p. 36; Vol. XIII, 1891, p. 71.
4 Ibid., 1891, Madras, Vol. XIII, p. 70.
5 Ibid., 1891, Madras, Vol. XIII, p. 70.
6 The srivaisnavas, who were followers of Ramanuja's teaching, added the prefix 'sri' to their name, indicating that they were the worshippers of Vishnu united with or accompanied by His Divine Consort the Goddess Sri also called Lakshmi (J. B. Carman, *The Theology of Ramanuja*, New Haven and London, 1974, p. 158).
7 In this context 'north' means the northern part of the Tamil country with its capital at Kanchipuram (the seat of Sanskrit learning) and 'south' meant the Kaveri delta with its capital at Srirangam — one of the centres of Tamil culture. (N. Jagadeesan, *History of Sri Vaishnavism in the Tamil Country (Post Ramanuja)* Madurai 1977, p. 183; A. Govindacharya, 'Tengalai and Vadagalai', *J.R.A.S.*, 1912, p. 714.
8 M. Monier Williams, 'Brahminism . . .', p. 125.
9 *I.O.R.*, P/383 Kristnyer (Town Munsif of Trichinopoly) to Collector 6/7/1872; *Hindu*, 21/1/1899.

NOTES TO CHAPTER 4

10 Jagadeesan, op. cit., p. 178; T. V. Mahalingam, *Administration and Social Life Under Vijayanagar*, Part II, *Social Life*, Madras 1975, pp. 195 – 6.
11 Jagadeesan, op. cit., p. 190; S. M. Sastri, 'The Origin of the Srivaishnavas of Southern India', *I.A.*, September 1884, p. 255.
12 B. Stein, 'Social Mobility and Medieval South Indian Sects' in J. Silverberg (ed), *Social Mobility in the Caste System: An interdisciplinary symposium*, The Hague, Paris, 1968 pp. 82 – 6.
13 A. Govindacarya, 'The Astadasa-Bhedas, or the eighteen points of doctrinal differences between the Tengalais (Southerners) and the Vadagalais (Northerners) of the Visistadvaita Vaishna School, South India', *J.R.A.S.*, 1912, pp. 1105 – 10.
14 'The Artha-Pancaka of Pillair Lokacarya', (translated by A. Govindacarya) *J.R.A.S.*, 1910, p. 584.
15 Jagadeensan, op. cit., pp. 184, 192 – 3.
16 A. Govindacarya *J.R.A.S.*, 1910, p. 1112.
17 J. N. Bhattacharya, *Hindu Castes and Sects*, Calcutta 1896, p. 346. The report for 1871 does, however, enumerate the numbers of satanis, a mixed group of tengalai non-brahmans whose 'principal occupation' appears to have been some kind of service in the temple. Among other things, they made garlands, carried the torches during the god's procession and swept the temple floor. They also made umbrellas, flower baskets and boxes of palmyra leaves, and prepared the sacred balls of white clay and saffron powder. According to the same source they made up over 10 per cent of the Hindu population in Trichinopoly and 2.7 per cent in Tanjore district. (*Census of India*, 1871, Madras, Vol. II, pp. 307 – 317; *Census of India*, 1891, Madras, Vol. XIV, pp. 270 – 1; E. Thurston, op. cit., Vol. VI, pp. 297 – 304).
18 *Census of India*, 1891, Madras, Vol. XV, pp. 116 – 17.
19 Orthodox in the sense that vadagalai brahmans tended to reflect the ethos and way of life of the majority of vaishnavite brahmans including those in the north.
20 V. N. Narasimmiyengar, 'Tonsure of Hindu Widows', *I.A.*, Vol. III, 1874, pp. 135 – 7; S. M. N. Sastri, op. cit., pp. 254 – 5.
21 S. M. N. Sastri, op. cit., p. 255.
22 Ibid.
23 Govindacarya, 'The Astadasa-Bhedas . . .,' p. 1110.
24 *Census of India, 1881*, Madras, Vol. 1, pp. 107 – 8; *H.F.*, Vol. IV, April 1884, p. 320.
25 A. Appadurai, 'Kings, Sects and Temples . . .', p. 69.
26 C. M. Lushington to Sec., 17/6/1818, *M.R.P.*, Ra. 291, Vol. 71, 29/6/1818.
27 Monier Williams, 'Brahminism . . .', p. 448. For other descriptions and comment see *A.P.F.* (a Jesuit's impression) Vol. XV, 1854, pp. 161 – 2 and Hemingway, *Trichinopoly*, pp. 319 – 22.
28 For details of the temple's early history see V. N. Hari Rao, op. cit., which includes a translation of the *Koil-Olugu*, a Tamil chronicle of the temple.
29 Hari Rao, op. cit., p. 26. See also supra, Introduction.
30 Infra, Ch. 6.

NOTES TO CHAPTER 4

31 A. P. Onslow, to Sec., Board of Revenue, 4/9/1841 in *I.O.R.*, L/Parl./Coll. No. 418A *Papers on the Connexion of the Government of India with Idolatory, or with Mahometanism*, pp. 44–52.
32 *I.A.*, Vol. I, 5 April 1872, p. 131.
33 *Madras Times*, 8/1/1864.
34 Memorial, 21/2/1848, *M.R.P.*, Ra. 307, Vol. 61, 8/5/1848.
35 Ibid., Hari Rao, op. cit, Appendix, pp. 172–6.
36 Hari Rao, op. cit., Appendix, pp. 172–6; *M.R.P.*, Ra. 307, Vol. 61, 8/5/1848.
37 Collr. to Sec. 11/7/1832, *M.R.P.*, Ra. 298, Vol. 146, 23/7/1832.
38 R. A. Bannerman to Govt., 30/7/1830, *M.R.P.*, Ra. 298, Vol. 48, 30/7/1832; Memorial (Supplementary Documents nos. 2 and 3), *M.R.P.*, Ra. 307, Vol. 61, 8/5/1848.
39 H. Dickinson to Sec., 29/11/1827, *M.R.P.*, Ra. 296, Vol. 41, 6/12/1827.
40 Ibid., and Memorial (Supplementary Documents nos. 9 and 10) *M.R.P.*, Ra. 307, Vol. 61, 8/5/1848.
41 H. M. Blair to Sec., 11/7/1832, *M.R.P.*, Ra. 298, Vol. 46, 23/7/1832; Bannerman to Govt., 30/7/1832, *M.R.P.*, Ra. 298, Vol. 48, 30/7/1832.
42 Ibid.
43 Blair to Sec., 11/7/1832, *M.R.P.*, Ra. 298, Vol. 46, 23/7/1832.
44 Memorial, *M.R.P.*, Ra. 307, Vol. 61, 8/5/1848.
45 Blair to Sec., 11/7/1832, *M.R.P.*, Ra. 298, Vol. 46, 23/7/1832.
46 Govt. to Board of Revenue, 7/8/1832, *M.R.P.*, Ra. 298, Vol. 49, 16/8/1832.
47 Blair to Sec., 11/7/1832, *M.R.P.*, Ra. 298, Vol. 46, 23/7/1832.
48 Supra, Ch. 3.
49 Onslow to Board of Revenue, 22/2/1842 *I.O.R.* L/Parl./Coll. No. 418A. For an account of the way in which certain families came to be associated with the management of Srirangam during the medieval period see V. N. Hari Rao, op. cit.
50 Board of Revenue to Onslow, 23/5/1842. *I.O.R.*, L/Parl./Coll. No. 418A.
51 *I.O.R.* L/Parl./Coll. No. 418A, Onslow to Board of Revenue, 27/7/1842 and extract from *M.R.P.* 6/10/1842.
52 Onslow to Board of Revenue 29/7/1842 and extract from *M.R.P.*, 6/10/1842, *I.O.R.* L./Parl./Coll. No. 418A.
53 Memorial *M.R.P.*, Ra. 307, Vol. 61, 8/5/1848.
54 Mudaliar, op. cit., p. 36.
55 Memorial, *M.R.P.*, Ra. 307, Vol. 61, 8/5/1848.
56 Ibid.
57 *M.H.C.*, Appeal No. 22 of 1896 (R. D. Broadford's Judgment).
58 Supra, Ch. 3.
59 Walhouse to Sec., 5/12/1863, *M.R.P.*, Ra. 315, Vol. 5, 20/1/1864.
60 *M.R.P.*, Ra. 315, Vol. 5, 20/1/1864 and 25/2/1864; *Fort St George Gazette*, 23/4/1864.
61 *M.H.C.*, Appeal No. 22 of 1896.
62 Ibid.
63 *Hindu*, 17/10/1892.

64 All three appointed by the Judge in 1892, for example, were tengalais (*M.H.C.* Appeal No. 22 of 1896; *Hindu*, 17/10/1892.)
65 *M.H.C.*, Regular Appeal, No. 16 of 1867.
66 *Hindu*, 25/5/1899.
67 Ibid., 23/1/1888, 20/6/1888, 31/3/1889, 29/6/1889, 25/5/1899, 5/9/1900.
68 *M.H.C.*, Appeal No. 22 of 1896.
69 *Hindu*, 17/1/1890, 10/2/1894.
70 *I.O.R.*, P/383, 18/7/1874, p. 5184; *Hindu* 21/1/1899.
71 See for example *I.L.R.*, Madras Series, Vol. XII, 1889, pp. 580 – 586, Vol. XXVI, 1903, pp. 376 – 384; *I.A.*, Vol. III, May 1874, p. 126, *Hindu*, 21/1, 15/7, 6/12, 1889, 2/12/1892, 13/1, 26/3/1894; Appadurai, op. cit., Hemingway, *Tanjore*, p. 226.
72 For attacks on sectarianism see especially *Hindu*, 3/2/1891, and 21/1/1899.
73 *Th.* Sup. October 1881, p. 3; July 1882, p. 4. See also R. Suntharalingam op. cit., pp. 290 – 311 and G. A. Oddie 'Anti-Missionary Feeling and Hindu Revivalism in Madras: the Hindu Preaching and Tract Societies, c. 1886 – 1891' in F. W. Clothey (ed.) *Images of Man: Religion and Historical Process in South Asia*, Madras 1982, pp. 217 – 34.
74 *Hindu*, 21/1/1899.

5

THE CHARACTER, ROLE AND SIGNIFICANCE OF NON-BRAHMAN SAIVITE *MATHS* IN TANJORE DISTRICT

I

The importance of asceticism in ancient Indian society was reflected in the teachings of the Upanishads and also in the ideal of the four stages (*ashramas*) of life. According to this ideal, set out in detail in the *Laws of Manu*,[1] one who belonged to the 'twice-born' class, having studied the Vedas and fulfilled his role as a householder and family man, was expected gradually to turn his mind from earthly cares to concentrate increasingly on his quest for *moksha* or liberation. In the third stage of his life he was to leave his home and live as a hermit, or with his wife, practising austerities and meditation. In the last stage, as a very old man, he would become a homeless wandering *sannyasi* with all worldly ties broken.

While this was probably more of an idealized model than a generally accepted and practised way of life, it nevertheless reflects the high regard which 'twice-born' castes had for the life of renunciation and for a life-style which was, at least initially, associated with Hindu *maths* or monastic institutions.

In its original and narrow sense the term *math* (or mutt) meant the residence of an ascetic.[2] However, in the nineteenth century the term was also used to describe the residence of a number of ascetics or monks who together (and sometimes with monks in other monasteries) constituted a particular community or monastic order. The order, according to a recent study of Hindu monastic life in Orissa, was 'organized around the concept of a teaching tradition (*sampradaya*) related to a famous teacher (*acharya*) who first enunciated the philosophical-religious system of the order'.[3] The residence of an ascetic or *math* was naturally a place which attracted the attention of those seeking spiritual guidance and the lone hermit or *sannyasin*, if willing to teach, became a special type of *guru*. In this way some *maths* became centres of learning, places where disciples desirous of learning spiritual truths could congregate and meet their *guru* for instruction.[4] Some *maths* were richly endowed by Hindu rulers, landowners and others[5] and, by the nineteenth century, had become wealthy, highly-organized complex institutions providing for a range of religious, educational and other services in Hindu society. The more important monastic centres were usually *adhinams*, viz. central *maths* exercising control and supervision over subordinate *maths* and other institutions such as temples.[6]

The development of these more complex organizations was, initially, overshadowed in importance by the rise and growth of Buddhist and Jain monastic centres. It was not until the time of Shankara (?A.D. 788 – 820) that there is much evidence of an influential and well-organized Hindu monastic system. Shankara, who is well-known as the founder of his own school of *Advaita Vedanta* and is credited with giving the final blow to Buddhism in India, was not slow to perceive the advantages of monastic organisation.[7] He selected four places each in a different quarter of the subcontinent for the establishment of monastic centres. They were at Badri in the north, Dwarka in the west, Puri in the east and Sringeri in Karnataka in the south. The Sringeri *math* was the chief monastery headed by Shankara himself. Its rulers styled Jaget-Guru (or *guru* of the world)[8] claimed ultimate authority over all *advaita sannyasis*. Shankara also created ten suborders (*dasanamis*) of ascetics. Three of these, known as the *dandi* (staff-holding) subsects, initiated brahmans only while the others also accepted other members of the 'twice-born' *varnas*.

II

In South India in the nineteenth century different *maths* or groups of *maths* not only tended to represent different traditions or sects within Hinduism, but were also separated into brahman and non-brahman organizations. Most brahmans in the Tamil country could be divided into smarthas, or followers of Shankara, and srivaishnavites, or the followers of Ramanuja. According to census returns in 1871, about 75 per cent of brahmans in Tanjore district were *smarthas* — who worshipped both Vishnu and Siva, though principally the latter.[9] Many if not most of these looked to Jaget Guru of Sringeri or the head of the brahman *math* at Kumbakonam (who claimed some independence from Sringeri) as their spiritual head.[10] Most of the remaining brahmans in the district were srivaishnavites and, as was the case in other parts of Tamilnadu, they could be divided into vadagalais and tengalais. Differences between them included some divergence in social attitude and practice as well as differences in theology and ritual.[11] Throughout the nineteenth century most of the Tanjore vadagalai brahmans (who were nearly three times as numerous as the tengalai brahmans in the district),[12] appear to have acknowledged the *Jeer* or head of the Ahobilam *math* in Kurnool district as their spiritual head. At the end of the century, the headquarters of the *math* which had branches all over South India, was in fact relocated near Kumbakonam.[13] The tengalai brahmans had their own *maths* perhaps the most important of which was Vanamamalai in Tinnevelly district which had considerable revenues and two hundred subordinate *maths* scattered over different parts of India.[14]

While generalizations about the nature of these brahman *maths* are dangerous in view of the absence of detailed research, it is perhaps possible to identify some of their more common characteristics. The heads were *sannyasis* in a recognized line of succession going back to the founder of a particular tradition. Like most other *gurus* they appear to have initiated their own disciples and appointed their own successors.[15] Their *maths* became, as already suggested, a type of seminary where they received visiting lay disciples, *sannyasis* and brahman pundits, and where they organized discussions and perhaps also taught brahman boys the Vedas and other sacred literature.[16]

The effectiveness of the *mathapadi* (or head of the *math*) in helping to preserve and propagate particular sectarian traditions, whether this was *Advaita Vedanta* or varieties of srivaishnavite teaching, was strengthened by the fact that they exercised some control over temple priests and ritual. The head of the Kumbakonam *math*, for example, appointed managers of three temples, one of which was at Conjeeveram in Chingleput district, while the *Jeer* of Ahobilam *math* was *dharmakarta* or trustee of the Viraraghava temple at Tiruvalur and other temples whose income amounted to more than Rs. 25,000 p.a.[17]

Among a number of other activities carried out by the heads of brahman *maths*, such as the performance of *puja* and arbitration in disputes, were those that were not necessarily confined to the *math* itself. During the nineteenth century *mathapadis* not infrequently went on tour accompanied by disciples and servants and with a great deal of pomp and ceremony.[18] The purpose of these expeditions varied and, among the factors which appear to have prompted them, there was the desire to undertake pilgrimages to shrines such as Tirupathi or Rameswaram, the need to visit sub-*maths* and inspect temples, the desire to meet with disciples in more distant parts of the country, to hold audiences and perform *puja* and perhaps even the need to collect funds for the *math* itself. Whatever the motive, however, these journeys served to affirm and enhance the *mathapadi's* status and spread his renown in the Hindu community. In spite of criticism by Western-educated critics who believed that *maths* had outlived their usefulness to become centres of corruption, intrigue and easy living, they still retained (at least according to the *Hindu*) 'all their old influence' over the mind of the masses. Referring to the installation of a new head of the Sankaracharya *math* at Kumbakonam, the paper explained that

> The procession the other day, at Kumbakonam, which took the new guru round the chief streets of the city, was thronged by thousands of pious disciples and believers who would willingly make large sacrifices on account of the ancient seat (of Vedantic learning) as they call it and resent any attempt against its power, dignity or wealth.[19]

While the non-brahman saivite *maths* in Tanjore district were largely modelled on these brahman institutions there were important differences between them. They not only catered for different castes (brahmans in the one instance and high-caste non-brahmans in the other) but were somewhat different in their cultural and linguistic interests and approach. In the brahman institutions, such as the Kumbakonam Shankacharya *maths*, the accent was on the study of the Vedas and other Sanskrit literature whereas, in the non-brahman *maths*, study was much more commonly, though not exclusively, in the vernacular and included a heavy emphasis on Tamil texts.[20] Through their knowledge of Sanskrit and Sanskrit texts *sannyasis* (the brahman ascetics) such as those connected with the four main Sankaracharya *maths*, though living in different regions and language areas of India, could communicate with each other through Sanskrit[21] and shared the same corpus of Sanskrit literature. On the other hand, the non-brahman *saivite maths* were essentially regional, not only because teaching and study was mainly, if not entirely, through Tamil, but because *Saiva Siddhanta* (the particular philosophical-religious teachings these *maths* espoused) was primarily, if not exclusively, a regional interpretation.

III

The chief non-brahman saivite *maths* in Tanjore were the Tiruppagalur *math* in Nannilam taluk, the *math* at Tiruppanandal in Kumbakonam taluk and the Thiruvavaduthurai and Dharmapuram establishments both of which were located in the Mayavaram subdivision.[22] All except the *math* at Tiruppanandal, which was staffed by disciples from Dharmapuram,[23] were strictly speaking *adhinams*. Of the three *adhinams*, Tiruppagalur was clearly the least important. It was different from the other non-brahman saivite *maths* in that it contained no monks (*tambirans*) except for the head ascetic.[24] Furthermore, it was unable to exercise as much influence as the others, controlled fewer temples and possessed much less wealth and landed property than either Dharmapuram or Thiruvavaduturai.

Both Dharmapuram and Thiruvavaduturai were founded as a result of the growth of Saivism in South India. They trace their origins back to the first line of disciples of Meykandar the thirteenth century 'saint' and author of *Siva Jananabodam*, a work in Tamil regarded as the basic text of *Saiva Siddhanta*.[25] *Saiva Siddhanta* was an essentially theistic form of religion — the emphasis which Meykandar and other non-brahman leaders placed on the centrality of loving devotion to Siva contrasting with the brahman advocacy of Shankara's *Advaita Vedanta*. In thirteenth century inscriptions, which confirm the existence of Dharmapuram, Tiruvavaduturai and other non-brahman *saivite maths* at this time, there is in fact some evidence that their teaching and activity was opposed by brahmans.[26] In one instance, for example, the non-brahman *math* at Tiruvanaikkaval in Trichinopoly district appears to have been taken over by brahmans and, in another, disturbances resulted in the appointment of a brahman teacher.

The origin of *maths* at Dharmapuram and Tiruvavaduturai, like the origin of similar establishments elsewhere, was however not only linked with a desire to perpetuate and propagate a particular tradition but also with ideas of renunciation and individual salvation. The *math* existed perhaps as much for the *guru* and his disciples as for propaganda and organizational purposes. According to the judge in the Madras High Court summing up evidence in an important case involving Dharmapuram and Tiruppanandal *maths*, the parties to the appeal were ascetics or hermits who professed not only to have renounced all family ties and all desire for wealth and women, but who devoted themselves to religious study, contemplation and service 'in view to secure immunity from future births (to which according to their faith, they believe they are liable), and spiritual happiness.'[27]

The *guru*, who as head of the non-brahman *adhinam* was called the *Pandara Sannadhi*, was seeking salvation both for himself and also for his disciples whom he was expected to guide and teach.[28] But while he was the focal point and source of authority in the *math* (something of this authority being reflected in the fact that he alone, like heads of brahman *maths*, chose his successor) the precise nature of his spiritual power and authority could vary depending on the particular order or *adhinam* concerned. While, for example, accounts of *Pandara Sannadhis* performing miracles occur in official 'histories' of Dharmapuram and Tiruvavaduturai and imply a belief that both these men had extraordinary spiritual powers,[29] differences in the *datum* or gift ceremonies conducted in connection with the disciples' initiation clearly suggests that the head of Tiruvavaduturai was held to be less god-like than his counterpart at Dharmapuram. In a ceremony in the latter *math* the *tambiran* or disciple solemnly made a gift of his body, soul and wealth to the *Pandara Sannadhi*, while in Thiruvavaduturai, in what was otherwise a similar ceremony, this gift was made not to the *Pandara Sannadhi* but to God.[30]

Apart from having celibate disciples or *tambirans* in his *adhinam* and in subordinate *maths* and temples under his control, the head of Thiruvavaduturai (and probably also of Dharmapuram) had lay followers as well. According to Hemingway he was *guru* to a number of 'private persons' who visited him and gave him presents on the anniversary day of the founder of the *math*.[31] Like the head of the Shankaracharya brahman *math* at Kumbakonam, he, together with some of his immediate disciples, was accustomed to going on tour of other districts including, in this case, Trichinopoly, Tondamandalam, Tinnevelly, Ramnad and even Malabar.[32] This was not only for purposes of inspection or for his own private religious reasons but also to enable him to receive the respect of *mirasidars*, temple servants and others and to hold audiences with lay disciples amongst whom were included low as well as higher caste devotees. He had, for example, a number of lay followers or disciples in Madras city some of whom were *nattuvans* (a general term for dancing instructors and musicians) and who were therefore, as we shall see, lower in status than the *Pandara Sannadhi* and *tambirans* resident at Tiruvavaduturai.[33]

In 1869 there were 30 disciples, as well as secular servants, living at Dharmapuram and in 1900 about 20 disciples there, and about 50 at Thiruvavaduturai.[34] Some Brahman *maths* appear to have occasionally admitted women into their order[35] and there is clear evidence that women could be ordained or initiated into the order of Dharmapuram.[36] However, in the only case in which the name of a Dharmapuram nun appeared in the records which have been examined so far, it is clear that she was living at Chidambaram and there is nothing which would suggest that any of those who took vows and were living in the chief non-brahman saivite *maths* in Tanjore district were females.

Individuals who became *tambirans* or monks attached to the Dharmapuram or Thiruvavaduturai *adhinams* appear to have been mostly vellalas[37] though they had not always belonged to the same subsection or *jati* group within the vellala community. Meykandar, the common preceptor of both *adhinams*, and Guru Jnana Sambandha, who is said to have been the founder of Dharmapuram, were both, for example, karkatha vellalas,[38] those who were supposed to have originated in the Pandyan country. On the other hand, many of the *tambirans* attached to Dharmapuram and Thiruvavadaturai during the nineteenth century were *pandarams*.[39] The traditional occupation of this caste or subgroup was to serve as priests of the vellala community.[40] They were staunch saivites and strict vegetarians who in actual practice had adopted a variety of occupations. According to Thurston some were 'respectable people' who had settled down as land-holders. Others continued to act as priests, while others, taking a vow of celibacy, became *tambirans* in *maths* such as those at Dharmapuram and Thiruvavaduturai. It was these *pandaram tambirans* who rose into prominence as *Pandara Sannadhis* or heads of these institutions and it was they who superintended most of the important Siva temples in Tanjore district.[41]

While little is known about why certain individuals decided to become *tambirans* at Dharmapuram and Thiruvavaduturai, it is clearly apparent that most of them were recruited from one fairly specific social group — a group that already possessed a tradition that some of its members entered monastic institutions. Furthermore, there is some evidence that this trend was, if anything, reinforced by customary practice within certain families — in one case, a nephew or possibly two nephews (brothers) adopting their uncle's profession in becoming monks.[42] Added to the influence of custom was the expectation of gaining religious merit and, possibly also, more worldly considerations — such as the increased status in becoming a monk — especially one associated with a well-known and prestigious institution.

The probationary training and ordination of monks in the two *adhinams* was much the same.[43] If a layman wished to become an ascetic he donned a red cloth, began his religious studies and was taught different forms of prayer. The duration of probation depended on the *Pandara Sannadhi* and, so long as it continued, the novice or probationer was free to change his mind and return to his family.

When the *Pandara* was satisified with the probationer's progress he summoned him to a room in the *math* set apart for worship of the titular deity. There in the presence of the image the disciple took his vows. He was formally asked if he would give up his family and his desire for women and land; and if he answered in the affirmative, 'the answer was accepted as a solemn renunciation of the world'.[44]

After taking vows consistent with the ideas of celibacy and renunciation, he was then initiated into the order. The *Pandara* taught him the *mula mantra* or distinct doctrine or text of his order and invested him with a consecrated red cloth (*mantra kashayam*) as a visible symbol of initiation and gave him, for his personal worship, an idol (probably a *lingam*)[45] made of special sandalwood. Then followed the ceremony, already mentioned, where the disciple made a gift of his body, soul and wealth either to his *guru* or to God.

After his initiation or ordination, the *tambiran* remained at the *adhinam* and continued his religious study until he became 'a learned ascetic'. He was expected to study the history of the *adhinam*, to visit subordinate *maths*, to undertake pilgrimages and to advance the cause of religion and 'charity' generally. Judging from a petition to the Collector in 1815, the monks at Thiruvavaduturai also spent much time in prayer and contemplation. Explaining that they were indeed 'the Monks of Seva Religion' living in the monastery of Thiruvavaduturai and observing celibacy, they added that 'Our daily Duty is to study our Religious Doctrines of Theology, rehearsing the Holy names of God,[46] contemplating in his Glory and praying for the welfare of the Public, as well as of those under whose Government we do reside.'[47]

One of the results of the establishment of *maths* such as those at Dharmapuram and Thiruvavaduturai was that rajas, wealthy *zamindars* and others endowed these institutions with landed properties for their upkeep and also induced the monks to undertake the management of temples, *katlais* (specific endowments within temples) and other 'charities' — with what the *Hindu* newspaper described as 'the mistaken impression that these devotees to asceticism would make the most disinterested managers of places of sanctity.'[48]

By late nineteenth century Thiruvavaduturai was endowed with 25,000 acres of land in the Tinnevelly district, 1,000 acres in Madura and 3,000 acres in Tanjore.[49] In addition, *tambirans* from these two *adhinams* (including those at Tiruppanandal) were responsible for the management of thousands of acres of temple land and other endowments in the Madras Presidency and elsewhere.[50] They were, in fact, placed in the difficult and seemingly ironic position, on the one hand, of having taken a vow renouncing their desire for lands and wealth while, on the other, they were heavily involved (with public approval) in the management of extensive properties and in financial affairs.

The difference between ideal and reality and the tension between vows on the one hand and practice on the other is apparent not only in occasional reports of the monks' sexual misconduct,[51] but more especially in legal records relating to wealth and landed property,

Certainly there are difficulties in knowing precisely what the vow of poverty was intended to mean in practice. If, as the judges of the Madras High Court argued, the vow was supposed to prevent *tambirans* 'from owning or managing property for personal enjoyment',[52] it is not clear whether this means that the monks, such as those at Tiruppanandal, were ignoring their vow by sharing in the joint ownership of property in order to pay for their own living expenses within the *math*, or were breaking the rules by using income from this property to buy presents for relatives and for secular employees.[53]

There is, however, less doubt in some other cases that *tambirans* were not as indifferent to the attractions of property and wealth as their vows intended. For example, it appears from a will dated November 1874[54] that the *Panadara Sannadhi* of Dharmapuram had been busy acquiring private property even after he was appointed head. In his will he stated that

> After I was initiated in the ascetic life in the said Dharmapuram Mutt and after I was made its head, I have made some self acquisitions. They are in my possession; and they are moveable and immoveable properties noted hereunder . . . After I was made the Head of the Mutt . . . I purchased landed properties with my own earnings . . . they belong to me and the potta thereof stands in my name. They consist of nanja [wet land], punja [dry land] etc. properties and go for kaunis 20 and odd [26.44 acres].

Revenue records show that the *tambiran* appointed by the head of Dharmapuram as manager of the Rock Fort temple in Trichinopoly was also living in a manner which hardly fitted the traditional image of an ascetic or one who had renounced all desires for lands and wealth. In a report to the Board of Revenue in 1828 the Collector of Trichinopoly explained that

> The Office of Tumbooran is a very rich one, for in this District he holds fifteen entire villages, and lands in ten other villages, which produce him a revenue of Rupees 9,427-8-4 a year, while in the Provinces of Tanjore and Madura and in Tondiman's Country, he also has extensive possessions which produce him a very considerable Revenue. In consideration of these emoluments he performs ceremonies in the Pagoda which are computed to cost him about 4,500 Rupees a year, the remaining balance being spent as he pleases.[55]

It was the sole right of *Pandara Sannadhis* to nominate and appoint their disciples as managers of what came to be known as *adhinam* temples in Tanjore and other districts.

Some idea of the character and economic importance of these temples can be gained from Kindersley's report on religious establishments in Tanjore district submitted in November 1841.[56] This shows that, while *adhinam* temples numbered only 17 in a total of 2,874 places of worship, they received one-quarter of all money allowances and 43 per cent of all temple revenues derived from land. Their lands extended over 42,409 acres which amounted to 46 per cent of all temple lands in Tanjore district.

Ten out of these seventeen *adhinam* temples were under the management of Dharmapuram, one was under the control of Thiruvavaduturai and the remaining six were managed by other *maths* at least two of which were located outside the district. The temples connected with Dharmapuram received 17 per cent of all the revenues paid in support of temples in the district and part of this income was derived from the produce of 18,824 acres or 21 per cent of all temple land in Tanjore. Furthermore, Dharmapuram, like its counterpart at Thiruvavaduturai, had control of saivite temples outside the district. One of the best known of these was the Rock Fort temple in Trichinopoly[57] which was also an extremely wealthy establishment.

There is some evidence that after 1841 additional *adhinam* temples were constructed or consecrated.[58] Some temples or important endowments within them appear to have changed hands — the heads of rival *maths* being anxious to extend their control and influence as far as possible. By about 1900 the Dharmapuram *Pandara Sannadhi* supervised the management of 27 temples in Tanjore and other districts while the head of Thiruvavaduturai, according to Hemingway, appointed 'managers and priests' to some 15 temples in Tanjore and elsewhere.[59]

Asked by the Board of Revenue to explain the function and powers of *tambirans* in temples in Tanjore in 1835 the Collector, obviously referring to temples where *tambirans* were general managers, remarked that

The Tumberans have general control and management of the Established periodical feasts and ceremonies and attest all accounts of receipts and disbursements. They are not authorized to appoint or dismiss or otherwise punish Pagoda Servants — but their representations on these points are alluded to.[60]

In some of these temples the *tambiran*'s duty as custodian of temple property not only included tasks such as supervising the activity of secular servants in the collection of revenue from temple lands, the keeping of accounts and the maintenance of repairs in the building,[61] but also the management of *katlais* — special endowments established for specific services, such as midday worship, or for the conduct of 'religious charities' such as the feeding of pilgrims.[62]

However, it should be stressed that the authority of *tambirans* appointed as managers did not necessarily or always extend to all endowments in the temple — especially if it was one of the bigger institutions. The Collector's reports and evidence in Hemingway, for example, suggest that, during the period from 1841 until the end of the century, the head of Dharmapuram *math* appointed *tambirans* as managers of the Sri Amritakadesvaraswami Temple in the Mayavaram taluk.[63] The temple had seven *katlais* and yet at no time during this period did the *Pandara Sannadhi* ever control or claim to control all seven endowments.[64] The Dharmapuram *math* which owned and managed four of them in the early 1860s acquired a fifth through purchase in 1868 – 69. The other two *katlais* connected with the temple remained 'distinct institutions' — one, the second richest of all seven with nearly 1,000 acres, continuing under the management of a vellala family and the other (of less importance) under the management of a chetti.

On the other hand, the influence of *tambirans*, and through them the head of their *adhinam*, was not restricted to temples where *tambirans* acted as general managers. Some *tambirans* had minor roles in ordinary non-*adhinam* temples supervising *katlais* and occasional ceremonies or acting as trustees of temples. The heads of both the Dharmapuram and Tiruppagalur *maths*, together with other parties, were, for example, trustees of the Sri Tyagarajaswami temple at Tiruvalur in Negapatam Taluk.[65] The temple consisted of eight *katlais* or separate establishments — the money for general repairs etc. being deducted from these endowments.[66] The Dharmapuram *Pandara Sannadhi* and his representative Palaniappa Tambiran were responsible for what was known as the rajan (Raja's) *katlai* which was the third richest with lands worth Rs. 5,024 p.a. The Vithilinga *Pandata Sannadhi*, the head of the Tiruppagular *math*, was trustee of the *abishekatlai* (institution for bathing or anointing the god) valued at Rs. 7,613-9-8 and of the *annathan* (institution for the distribution of boiled rice) valued at Rs. 4,829-3-1. As the combined income of these two institutions amounted to 47 per cent of the total income of all endowments in the temple, this made the *Pandara Sannadhi* of Tiuppagalur the wealthiest trustee. Other trustees included two brahmans, one Armuga Pandaram, and a fourth trustee who was apparently a *sannyasin*. In this case, then, *tambirans* from different *maths* were employed in the same temple together with agents of other trustees — each responsible for his own *katlai* or *katlais*.

The complexity of the relationship between *maths* and temples and the different powers and responsibilities of *tambirans* employed in temples can be further illustrated by reference to the records of the Tiruppanandal *math* which was placed in the hands of a receiver in 1887. In his inventory of property in 1890 the receiver mentions the names of 16 temples.[67] All activities in at least four of them (including temples at Benares and Tiruppanandal) appear to have been managed by the *math*. In seven other temples the *tambirans* were responsible for the maintenance of one or more *katlais* in addition to activities such as daily *puja* (public worship) and *arccanai* (private worship).[68] In four temples, one in Trichinopoly and three in Tanjore district, the *math* was responsible for *mandapappatis* (the feeding and entertainment of the deity during halts in his or her procession within the precincts of the *mandapam* or terraced hall). In two other temples the *tambiran's* only responsibility was the feeding of brahmans.

Apart from the management of temples and *katlais*, including the performance of saivite ceremony and ritual, these *maths* especially Thiruvavaduturai played an important part in promotion of Tamil studies including the patronage of Tamil scholars.[69] Amongst the most famous names associated with Thiruvavaduturai during the nineteenth century were Sabapathi Navalar and Mahavidan Meenakshi Sundaram Pillai (1815 – 1876), both of them scholar-poets, the latter attracting many followers including musicians to the *math*.

The *maths* also contributed to the maintenance and development of the pilgrimage system maintaining rest houses and providing facilities for saivite pilgrims (brahmans and non-brahmans alike) at different centres in different parts of the subcontinent. In a petition to the Collector in 1815 asking for financial support, the *tambirans* of Thiruvavaduturai, for example, pointed out that former rajas had granted them allowances out of the Government's share of local produce, not only for the maintenance of the monks residing in the monasteries but also for the maintenance of 'Religious Travellers passing and repassing by the way'.[70]

While both Dharmapuram and Thiruvavaduturai catered at least to some extent for the needs of pilgrims,[71] it was Tiruppanandal which had been established primarily for their benefit and with the idea of raising funds in South India for the support of a saivite establishment at Benares. *Tambirans* from Tiruppanandal also maintained subordinate *maths* at Morangi in Nepal, and at Chitambaran and Rameswaram in the Madras Presidency.[72] They appear to have had special duties and responsibilities at Benares (the most sacred of these centres) such as the task of receiving and arranging for the disposal of the bones of the dead;[73] but apart from that they carried out many similar duties at the different centres. They managed a temple at Benares and apparently were expected to participate in *puja* wherever they went.[74] They also spent time in the maintenance of properties, the supervision and keeping of accounts and, in some cases, providing food and accommodation for pilgrims.[75] In 1890 the *math* was, in fact, maintaining a total of 19 *choultries*,[76] simple buildings used by travellers as a temporary resting place where they could sometimes also obtain food and water. Nine of these were in Benares, nine in Rameswaram and one in Chitambaram. In addition to this Tiruppanandal maintained three *chattrams*, superior rest houses for high-caste pilgrims. It also organized the feeding of pilgrims in three temples, including the famous vaishnavite temples of Srirangam and Triplicane, and maintained places where travellers could obtain water.

A further aspect of the *math*'s role in providing facilities for pilgrims, especially for those who wished to visit Benares, was the use of *hundies* or bills of exchange. The operation of this system was explained in a legal document signed by the head *tambiran* and a revenue officer in July 1853:

> Persons going on pilgrimage to Benares from this province [South India], usually pay us according to their means the amounts required for their expenditure there, and take from us hundi addressed to the said Chitambaranatha Kumarasami Tambiran avergal [the *tambiran* at Benares], with directions to pay over the said accounts at Benares to the said respective persons.[77]

Through this system, which was apparently still in operation in 1888 or thereabout, the *tambirans* at Benares also issued *hundies* which could be cashed in the south.[78]

The effectiveness of *maths* as organizations for carrying out certain specific roles within Hindu society depended to a large extent on the competence and probity of the monks themselves. If they were inept as managers or simply exploited the situation for their own ends the smooth functioning of important temples, the regular and proper performance of religious ceremonies and other activities were bound to suffer.

There had probably always been some abuses within the monastic system, but in the latter decades of the nineteenth century concern with these abuses, including corruption and mismanagement, appears to have reached new heights of intensity. This was partly because of an increased emphasis on litigation as a method of solving disputes involving monasteries[79] and also because of the growth of the modern press and a Western-educated class better informed and critical of traditional institutions.

The origin of at least part of the problem lay in the attitude of laity who, out of the misguided notion that holy men were necessarily holy, entrusted *maths* with a considerable degree of independence. British administrators, anxious not to offend Hindu religious susceptibilities, were also reluctant to interfere unless it could be proved that misappropriation of the state's resources was involved. Furthermore, unlike most monasteries of Western Europe, these *maths* were not under inspection or supervision of religious leaders (bishops or others) outside the system. Not only was the *Pandara Sannadhi* revered as a great *guru* and allowed to go his own way, but he himself was often unable to enforce discipline over his own disciples.[80] If they disliked his attempts at control they could easily leave his *math* and join another.

Some *tambirans* appear to have acted with great skill in protecting the funds of their institution even if this meant denying the Board of Revenue income which it considered its own. In 1825, for example, the Sub-Collector of Tanjore received complaints 'that great frauds had been practised' with regard to the income of seventeen villages belonging to the Tiruppanandal *math*.[81] On investigation it appeared that revenue officials including the *Tahsildar* had been bribed to make out and return false estimates of crops for the following year, that the *math* had evaded payment of 'a considerable increase of revenue' and that the *tambirans* 'must have connived at the whole proceedings'. When, therefore, the British officials accused the *tambirans* of being involved in scandal and 'misappropriation' what they really meant was that the *tambirans* had avoided paying the Government some of its revenue. Far from being disadvantaged by these proceedings the *math* itself may have been better off, there being no evidence that, in this case, the monks were using the revenues withheld from the Government for their own private purposes.

There were other instances, however, where the evidence of misappropriation is more compelling and where it is quite clear that *tambirans* knowingly misused *math* funds.

During the nineteenth century a number of more ambitious men in charge of sub-*maths* attempted to break away from the control of the parent institution and establish their own autonomous *maths*. For example, the *tambiran* at Auchiram in Travancore,[82] the *tambiran* at the Rock Fort Temple[83] and *tambirans* successively in charge of the *math* at Tiruppanandal all attempted to assert their independence from Dharmapuram. There is no reason to believe that ambition and rivalry among *tambirans* was a new phenomenon in the nineteenth century; but what appears to have been new was the way in which *tambirans* attempted to solve disputes such as these by resorting to litigation. The implication of this was serious as *tambirans* were then under constant pressure to use funds available in the *math's* treasury to meet the increasing costs of these proceedings. Indeed, it can be argued that one of the reasons for the prosperity of the new Western-type legal profession in the Madras Presidency in the nineteenth century was precisely because members of the profession acquired so much wealth from these traditional monastic institutions.

The tussle between Triuppanandal and Dharmapuram (the focus of public attention for at least twenty years) was especially significant in undermining the financial viability of both institutions and in lowering *maths* in general in the public's estimation. Differences of opinion between the heads of these two *maths*, which began over questions of property and appointments at the sub-*math* at Benares, eventually came to a head in 1880 when Ramalingam was in charge at Tiruppanandal.[84] He was especially angered by his failure to gain control of a temple under the management of Dharmapuram[85] and in his will in 1880 broke completely with tradition by appointing as his successor one Kumarasami Tambiran, a disciple not of Dharmapuram but from the rival establishment of Thurivavaduturai. Ramalingam died a few months later and the *Pandara Sannadhi* of Dharmapuram contested Kumarasami's appointment first in the subordinate court in Kumbakonam and then, when this failed, on appeal to the High Court of Madras in 1885. In his decision, the judge declared that Tiruppanandal was virtually an independent establishment. Kumarasami's appointment was, however, disallowed on the ground that the heads of Tiruppanandal had always been selected from among the disciples of Dharmapuram.

This decision led to further litigation over questions of property and over who, among Dharmapuram disciples, should be appointed to the vacancy at Tiruppanandal.[86] Nor could *tambirans* at Dharmapuram easily forget the role the *Pandara Sannadhi* of Thiruvavaduturai had apparently been playing in encouraging Tiruppanandal's 'pretensions'. Relations between the two *adhinams* in the 1890s could hardly have been worse. Charges and counter charges[87] appear to have led to yet another sensational case — one in 1900 — in which the *Pandara Sannadhi* of Dharmapuram was accused of 'criminal breach of trust, criminal misappropriation and fabrication of false evidence' in relation to properties in the Vydeeswaram temple.[88] He was convicted by the Joint Magistrate of Kumbakonam and sentenced to two months' imprisonment and a fine of Rs. 1,000. This sentence was however reversed by the District and Sessions Judge and the *Pandara Sannadhi* was eventually acquitted.[89]

One effect of these disputes and litigation was to impair the effectiveness of administration in at least some of the temples under the control of the *maths* involved. A correspondent in the *Hindu* in January 1890,[90] for example, described conditions in the Tiruvarur temple (one of those under the partial control of Dharmapuram) as 'chaotic'. Lamenting the fact that this famous temple had been drawn into 'the vortex of Dharmapuram litigation' he explained that

> The servants of the temple have to serve two masters, one the Thambiran the duly appointed agent of one party, the other, his lay deputy, now his rival, being the protege of the opposition party. Each disposes of the temple property according to his own sweet will, and gives directions probably the exact reverse of those of his rival. We are not quite sure that the sacred ceremonies of the temple are performed regularly or are performed at all. One thing everyone is able to observe, that there are not now so many lights as there should be, and that the processions do not take place as regularly and punctually as they ought.[91]

Secondly, costs of litigation (including bribery) weakened the financial viability of all three *maths*. When a receiver was appointed in charge of the *math* at Tiruppanandal in 1887 he discovered that for some months or years past a 'major portion' of the sums which ought to have been spent on charities outside the *math* were applied 'towards the expenses of litigation'.[92] Not only was the cash chest empty, but some of the *math*'s most valuable jewels, gold and silver vessels were missing. The head of the *math*, Kumarasami Tambiran, had pledged jewels and valuable articles with a *chetti* from whom he had borrowed Rupees 12,250 on two occasions. He had also 'given away' a diamond ring to his Vakil in the High Court, four ornaments to the *Pandara Sannadhi* of Thiruvavaduturai and one ornament to his junior in the same *math*. The *tambirans* at Tiruppanandal were not, however, the only ones dissipating endowment and other funds in expensive litigation. Commenting on the effect of litigation on all three *maths* the Hindu remarked in 1900 that it was 'an open secret' that every one of these *maths* was 'in a chronic condition of poverty'.[93]

Lastly, there was the effect of misappropriation and scandal on the attitude of families or the descendants of families who had made endowments, and on the attitude of the Hindu laity in general. As a result of mismanagement at Tiruppanandal the Raja of Puttukkottai who had conducted certain 'charities' through the *math* resumed the lands and, like the Raja of Travancore, also discontinued money payments.[94] In 1888 the receiver appointed to look after the *math's* affairs reported that, because the charities were not being conducted properly, some important villages granted for the support of the work at Benares, Rameswaram and elsewhere had been 'attached or wrongly interfered with' by the donors' descendants.[95] In 1889 he also reported that one of the *zamindars* of North Arcot had also been attempting to resume *math* lands 'alleging that the non-performance of charities by the Tambiran gave him the right to resume the villages.'[96]

Reports of corruption and mismanagement of *maths* not only in Tanjore but in other parts of India.[97] and rumours that all was not well in the brahman *math* in Kumbakonam[98] merely served to reinforce a strong feeling, especially among many Western-educated Hindus, that institutions like Dharmapuram were 'perfectly effete for any good, and only alive for mischief'.[99] On the other hand, there were others who were especially appreciative of some aspects of work *maths* were continuing to perform (e.g. their role in the promotion of Tamil studies)[100] and who cared enough about these institutions to want reform.

It remained to be seen, however, not only whether reform was possible so that the saivite *maths* could play their traditional and useful roles more effectively, but whether they could also adapt to the needs and challenges of the twentieth century. Certainly the outlook in this latter respect did not look promising, as almost the only area in which the *maths* were showing signs of being able to adapt to change was in their involvement in the new Western-style committees and associations. The head of the Tiruppanandal *math*, for example, quickly took advantage of the new legislation of 1863 creating temple committees by making sure he was a member of the Kumbakonam committee.[101] Nor was the Dharmapuram *Pandara Sannadhi* slow to perceive the importance of the new nationalist movement. Both he and the head of the brahman *math* at Kumbakonam sent delegates to represent their establishments at the meeting of the Indian National Congress held in Madras in 1887.[102] But these changes perhaps did little more than illustrate the point that *tambirans* were still very much concerned with questions of power and politics. More cynical observers could continue to argue that all that was really happening was that these monks were still trying to protect their own interests only, this time, more effectively through their adoption of new methods more appropriate to the changed political circumstances of the nineteenth century.

Last, but not least, what role, if any, did these *maths* play in preparing the ground for the rise of the non-brahman movement in the early twentieth century?

Even if the *maths* were founded in the midst of the brahman/non-brahman conflicts in the medieval period there is little evidence of continued conflict between the *tambirans* and brahmans throughout most of the nineteenth century. On the contrary, these non-brahman *maths* employed a large number of saivite brahmans as secular servants, in the management of *math* lands, as accountants, cooks and in other capacities.[103] They administered *chattrams* used by brahmans and special endowments for the feeding of brahmans. They supported the work of brahman scholars such as Peria Vaidyanatha Iyer and Maha Vaidyanatha Iyer.[104] Furthermore, as we have seen, the head of Dharmapuram *math* willingly associated himself with the India-wide Congress movement which some critics claimed could lead to a brahman raj.

But in spite of all this evidence of the *tambirans'* goodwill and desire to co-operate with and assist brahmans in the nineteenth century, there is also some evidence of the beginning of conflict with brahmans over representation on at least one temple committee in Tanjore towards the end of the period. After a vacancy occurred on the Kumbakonam Temple Committee in August 1899 the head of the Tiruppanandal *math* decided to contest the seat against V. Krishna Iyer, also a saivite but a brahman.[105] In this contest, which according to the local correspondent of the *Hindu* became increasingly 'day by day a mere caste question', the *tambiran* was elected by 1,655 votes to 457. Moreover, even though conflicts such as these between *tambirans* and brahmans for public office (and indirectly for control over religious institutions) appear to have been rare indeed, the non-brahman *maths* were, nevertheless, helping to develop what came to be regarded as a distinctive non-brahman culture. The emphasis on Tamil rather than on Sanskrit and the study and propagation of *Saiva Siddhanta* (which, subsequently, was often accepted as the original Tamil religion)[106] contributed towards the growth of a sense of Tamil identity — a regional consciousness and ideology which during the early decades of the twentieth century were utilized by leaders of the non-brahman movement in their struggle against brahman dominance.

NOTES

1. *The Laws of Manu*, trans. Georg Buhler, New York, 1969, esp. VI: G. S. Ghurye, *Indian Sadhus*, 2nd ed., Bombay 1964, Chs. II and III.
2. *I.L.R.* Vol. 10, Madras, section 386: T. V. Row, op. cit. (Index).
3. D. M. Miller and D. C. Wertz, *Hindu Monastic Life and the Monks and Monasteries of Bhubaneswar*, Montreal and London, 1976, p. 4.
4. *Hindu*, 27/1/1900.
5. For reference to Hindu texts extolling the virtues of giving to Hindu temples and other religious institutions see especially J. C. Oman, *The Mystics, Ascetics and Saints of India*. London 1905, pp. 249 – 50.
6. H. R. Pate, *Tinnevelly*, Vol. 1, Madras 1917; N. Desikacharya, *The Origin and Growth of Sri Brahmatantra Prakala Mutt*, Bangalore 1949, pp. 13, LXVII – LXVIII; H. V. Nanjundayya and L. K. Anantha Krishna Iyer, *The Mysore Tribes and Castes*, Vol. II, Mysore 1928, p. 457; *Hindu*, 20/1/1900.
7. See Ghurye, op. cit., ch. V for a detailed account of Shankara's monastic system.
8. C. H. Rao (ed.), *Mysore Gazetteer*, Vol. 5, Bangalore 1930, p. 1178.
9. *Census of India*, 1871 Madras, Vol. I, p. 293.
10. *Hindu*, 22/5/1889, 5, 13/6/1889, 4/6/1890, 28/6/1898.
11. Supra, Ch. 4.
12. *Census of India, 1891* Madras, Vol. XIV, p. 373.
13. *Hindu* 19/1/1900; E. Thurston, *Castes and Tribes*, Vol. I, p. 349.
14. Pate, op. cit., pp. 400 – 401.
15. C. H. Rao, op. cit., p. 1178; Hemingway, *Tanjore*, p. 218; *Hindu*, 19/1/1900; Pate, op. cit., p. 400; Desikacharya, op. cit., p. 40.
16. *Hindu*, 20/8/1888, 19/1/1900.
17. Hemingway, *Tanjore*, p. 218; *Hindu*, 6/8/1888, 19/1/1900. See also Pate, op. cit., p. 314.
18. *Hindu*, 2/6/1890, 20/12/1890, 28/6/1898, 9/6/1899, 19/1/1900; C. H. Rao, op. cit., p. 1178; Desikacharya, op. cit., pp. LXIX – LXXIII, CLVII – CLXIII.
19. *Hindu*, 4/6/1890.
20. T. V. Mahalingam, op. cit., p. 230.
21. For an example of heads of brahman *maths* conversing with each other in Sanskrit see Desikacharya, op. cit., p. XCV.
22. Hemingway, *Tanjore*, pp. 72, 222, 229 – 30, 232, 239 – 40.

NOTES TO CHAPTER 5

23 Ibid., p. 222.
24 Hemingway, *Tanjore*, pp. 239 – 40.
25 M. Rajamanikkam, 'The Tamil Saiva Mathas Under the Cholas (A.D. 900 – 1300)', in C. T. K. Chari (ed.), *Essays in Philosophy presented to Dr. T. M. P. Mahadeven on His Fiftieth Birthday*, Madras 1962, pp. 221 – 2; V. A. Devasenapathi, *Saiva Siddhanta*, Madras 1974, pp. 1 – 2.
26 *Madras Epigraphy. Annual Reports*, 1909, para. 53, pp. 103 – 5; B. Stein, *Peasant State and Society in Medieval South India*, Delhi 1980, pp. 235 – 7.
27 *I.L.R.*, 10 Mad. 385; M. Arunachalam, *Guru Jnana Sambandha of Dharmapuram*, Dharmapuram 1972, p. 21.
28 M. Arunachalam, op. cit., p. 55.
29 Ibid., p. 40; *A Short History of the Thiruvavaduthurai Adheenam*, 1973, p. 15.
30 *I.L.R.*, 10 Mad. 338 – 9.
31 Hemingway, *Tanjore*, p. 232.
32 See especially 'Memorial of the Nattavars and other Principal Inhabitants of Madras', 29 May 1826 (*T.R.* Vol. 4196).
33 Ibid., and Thurston *Castes and Tribes*, Vol. V.
34 *M.H.C.*, Regular Appeals, No. 59 of 1869; Hemingway, *Tanjore*, pp. 230, 232.
35 Ghurye, op. cit., 92 – 3.
36 *M.H.C.*, App. No. 13 of 1885, Exhibit 1338. Will dated 19 November 1874.
37 For Dharmapuram see especially Hemingway, *Tanjore*, p. 230 and *M.H.C.*, App. No. 13 of 1885, Exhibit 1338.
38 K. K. Pillay, *The Caste System in Tamil Nadu*, Madras 1977, p. 24; Arunachalam, op. cit., pp. 8 – 9; *A Short History of the Thiruvaduturai Adheenam*, p. 9.
39 Hemingway, *Tanjore*, p. 82; T. V. Row, op. cit., p. 182.
40 T. V. Row, op. cit.; E. Thurston, *Castes and Tribes*, Vol. VI, pp. 45 – 50.
41 T. V. Row, op. cit., p. 182; Hemingway, *Tanjore*, 1906, p. 82.
42 *I.L.R.*, 10 Mad. 450, 452, 458.
43 Ibid., 389.
44 Ibid., 388.
45 Thurston, *Castes and Tribes*, Vol. VI, p. 45.
46 It might be mentioned in this connection that while searching the library at Thiruvavaduturai in January 1980 the author discovered a large-sized volume which contained nothing more than the word *Siva* printed tens of thousands of times.
47 *T. R.*, Vol. 3192, pp. 437 – 9, 22/11/1815.
48 *Hindu*, 1/6/1888.
49 Hemingway, *Tanjore*, pp. 230, 232. In 1900 the *Hindu* reported that the annual income of lands and properties possessed by Dharmapuram was 'about a lac of rupees' (*Hindu*, 19/10/1900).
50 See Appendix 4.
51 *Hindu*, 10, 12/4/1900; *I.L.R.*, 10 Mad. 470.

52 *I.L.R.*, 10 Mad. 387.
53 *M.H.C.*, App. No. 13 of 1885. See evidence and Lower Court's findings in connection with Tiruppanandal, 1887.
54 *M.H.C.*, App. No. 13 of 1885. Exhibit 1338. Copy of Doc. No. 5 of 1874.
55 H. Dickinson to Sec., 14/2/1828, M.R.P., Ra. 296, Vol. 50, 25/2/1828.
56 Supra, Ch. 1, Ch. 3, and Appendix 4.
57 Dickinson to Sec., 14/2/1828, *M.R.P.*, Ra. 296, Vol. 50, 25/2/1828.
58 *M.H.C.*, App. No. 13 of 1885. exhibit No. 1456; *I.L.R.*, 10 Mad. 430.
59 Hemingway, *Tanjore*, pp. 229, 232; *Hindu*, 16/7/1900, 19/10/1900.
60 *T.R.*, Vol. 4224, pp. 185-6 (25 May 1835), Vol. 4240, p. 35 (2 July 1835).
61 A. P. Onslow to Sec., 14/2/1848, *M.R.P.*, Ra. 302, Vol. 37, 27/7/1848. See especially the Moochalika or agreement signed 25/1/1838.
62 *I.L.R.*, Vol. XVII, Madras series, p. 200.
63 Hemingway, *Tanjore*, p. 232; *M.R.P.*, Ra. 303, Vol. 32, 16 December 1841.
64 *M.H.C.*, Appeals Nos. 115 and 120 of 1894.
65 *M.H.C.*, Regular Appeal, No. 85 of 1868.
66 *I.L.R.*, Vol. XVII, Madras Series, esp. p. 201.
67 *M.H.C.*, App. No. 13 of 1885. Report of Receiver appointed for Tiruppanandal Mutt . . . 15 December 1890.
68 For discussion of ceremony and rituals in South Indian temples see especially A. Appadurai and C. A. Breckenridge. 'The South Indian temple: authority, honour and redistribution', *Contributions to Indian Sociology* (N.S.) Vol. 10, No. 2, 1976, pp. 187–211.
69 See especially *A Short History of the Thiruvavaduturai Adheenam*, p. 16; *Hindu*, 5/8/1898; K. V. Zvelebil, *Tamil Literature*, Wiesbaden 1974, p. 8.
70 *T.R.*, Vol. 3192, pp. 437–9, Petition dated 22 November 1815.
71 *I.L.R.*, 10 Mad. 484.
72 Ibid., 432, 484, 404.
73 *M.H.C.*, App. No. 13 of 1885, Exhibit No. 988 (1848).
74 Ibid., Exhibit No. 1478 (1 Feb. 1872).
75 Ibid., Exhibit No. 642 (3 March 1848).
76 Ibid., Report of the Receiver appointed for Tiruppanandal Mutt, 15 December 1890.
77 *M.H.C.*, App. No. 13 of 1885. Exhibit No. 611.
78 Ibid., Report of the Receiver appointed for Tiruppanandal, 18 June 1888; *I.L.R.*, 10 Mad., 392.
79 Mudaliar, op. cit., p. 45.
80 According to the *Hindu* newspaper 'the orders and bulls of excommunication' passed by the head of one *math* were not binding on others; hence the moment one priest excommunicated one of his fold, another priest offered to take him as his disciple defying the excommunicating priests. 'About 5 years ago', continued the editor, 'a Swamy of Uttaradi Mutt excommunicated a few of his disciples, who ran up to the Swamy of another Mutt for admission into it. Such things are of every day occurrence'. (*Hindu*, 5/6/1899).

81 Sub-Collr. to Principal Collr., Tanjore 25/2/1825, *M.R.P.*, Ra. 295, Vol. 27, 18/4/1825; Cotton to Sec. 26/4/1825; *M.R.P.*, Ra. 295, Vol. 29, 2/5/1825; *T.R.*, Vol. 4194, pp. 165–9, 185–8, 247–57, 283–97, 339–46.
82 *M.H.C.*, App. No. 13 of 1885, Report of Receiver Appointed for Tiruppanandal Mutt, 17 December 1889.
83 *I.L.R.*, 10 Mad. 464.
84 For an account of this dispute see *I.L.R.*, 10 Mad. esp. 450–73.
85 *I.L.R.*, 10 Mad, 471; *M.H.C.*, App. No. 13 of 1885, Original Suit No. 38 of 1881 in the Subordinate Court at Kumbakonam.
86 *I.L.R*, 13 Mad. 339–343; *M.H.C.*, App. No. 108 of 1891; *Hindu*, 20/4/1889, 8/10/1890.
87 *Hindu*, 13/7/1888, 18/4/1900, 19/10/1900.
88 *Hindu*, 18/4/1900.
89 Ibid., 27/12/1900.
90 Ibid., 11/1/1890.
91 See also *Hindu*, 6/10/1899.
92 *M.H.C.*, App. No. 13 of 1885. Report of the Receiver appointed for Tiruppanandal Mutt, 18 June 1888.
93 *Hindu*, 19/10/1900. See also *Hindu*, 1/6/1888 (editorial).
94 *M.H.C.* App. No. 13 of 1885 Lower Court Findings 1887 (10th Witness).
95 *M.H.C.*, App. No. 13 of 1885. Report of Receiver appointed for Tiruppanandal Mutt 17 December 1888.
96 Ibid., 17 December 1889.
97 *Hindu*, 19/10/1900.
98 Ibid., 20/8/1888, 31/10/1888, 4/6/1890.
99 Ibid., 4/6/1890. See also 22/10/1885, 1/6/1888, 7/6/1889, 28/10/1898.
100 Ibid., 5/8/1898.
101 *Fort St. George Gazette*, 5/4/1864; *Hindu*, 24/8/1888, 20/4/1889, 10,11/11/1899.
102 *Report of the Indian National Congress*, 1887, pp. 177–8.
103 *M.H.C.*, App. No. 13 of 1885 including Report of Receiver for Tiruppanandal Mutt, 18 June 1888.
104 *A Short History of the Thiruvavaduturai Adheenam*, p. 16.
105 *Hindu*, 26, 28/10/1899, 8,10,11/11/1899.
106 E. F. Irschick, *Politics and Social Conflict in South India: The Non-Brahman Movement and Tamil Separatism, 1916–1929*, California 1969, pp. 292–4. It is still a matter of dispute among scholars as to how far *Saiva Siddhanta* can be regarded as a purely Tamil system. See Devasenapathi, op. cit., pp. 1–2.

6

ASPECTS OF POPULAR HINDUISM

In the last few chapters discussion has focused primarily on aspects of élite religion, including the part the higher castes played in the functioning and development of temples and *maths* and on high-caste leadership and activities in sectarian disputes. But what of those who appear to have had little voice in these affairs? What of the religion of ordinary people and those at the bottom of the social scale? Is their religion (referred to briefly in chapter 1) best described as popular religion? What was popular Hinduism and how far can it be identified or separated from the religious views and practices of the dominant classes?

The term popular Hinduism as used in this book is taken to mean those aspects of Hinduism which usually attracted widespread popular support and which were largely, *though not exclusively*, associated with the subordinate classes, with ordinary people, including those at the bottom of the social scale.

This definition avoids the pitfalls inherent in L. S. S. O'Malley's use of the term popular Hinduism in his book on the subject published in 1935.[1] He not only equates popular Hinduism with 'the religion of the masses', but draws a clear unbroken line between popular religion on the one hand and 'the belief and practices of the cultured classes' on the other. This is very close to Robert Redfield's subsequent distinction between great and little traditions, between the great tradition of 'the reflective few' and the little tradition of 'the largely unreflective many'.[2] Both authors in fact make the same mistake of exaggerating the differences and of drawing too much of a hard-and-fast distinction between the religion of the élites and the religion of subordinate classes or common people.

What we have already shown in chapter 1[3] is that some high-caste Hindus held beliefs in common with many other more ordinary people and that, like other members of their village community, they participated in the worship of village deities and in attempts to control malignant spirits. In other words, the so-called 'cultured classes' not infrequently indulged in what O'Malley characterizes as 'the religion of the masses' and any definition of popular religion has to take account of this élite participation.

It is certainly not our intention to minimize the overall differences between the religious attitudes, ethos and life of the dominant classes (who were primarily brahmans and other high-caste Hindus) compared with the religion of the masses of the population. Though high-caste Hindus, including brahmans, were involved in popular Hinduism much of their interest and energy in religious matters was directed elsewhere. They were not only more educated and more influenced by Vedic or classical culture, but can also be differentiated from the subordinate classes by virtue of their power and position as trustees and priests of the major temples, as gurus and disciples in *maths* and as the organizers of Western-style religious associations. Furthermore, their participation in popular religion was not without qualification — fear of pollution and caste taboos, especially among brahmans, apparently preventing them from performing a number of village rituals. These included hook-swinging at village festivals and the spilling of blood of animals at village shrines.[4]

Nevertheless, as already mentioned, higher-caste Hindus inherited within their own particular traditions and ways of life aspects of popular religion. It was their involvement in popular religion rather than low-caste participation in what might be termed classical Hinduism which proved most effective in producing a common religious culture — a common stream of values, ideas, faith and action which cut across all the main divisions in the social hierarchy flowing and merging into the main stream of popular religion.[5]

As explained in the introduction, our discussion of particular aspects of popular religion in what follows has been restricted by the availability of source materials. Our primary focus is on aspects of popular Hinduism which involved, at least in some way, most if not all the main classes in the Hindu population. The discussion includes, amongst other things, reference to some of the more important regional festivals, to fire-walking and hook-swinging — all aspects of popular practice which attracted the attention of British authorities in the nineteenth century.

Writing to his superior from Negapatam in Tanjore district in 1864 Brother Bradey, a Jesuit missionary, expressed something of his astonishment at the people's enthusiasm for travelling for religious purposes. He declared that

When it is a question of making a pilgrimage, or visiting some place of devotion, nothing is capable of stopping them. And here we may put both Christians and Pagans in the same class. The Pagans, however, are much more given to this rambling life than the Christians. They will undertake journeys of some hundreds of miles, in order to be present at some great festival, or to fulfil

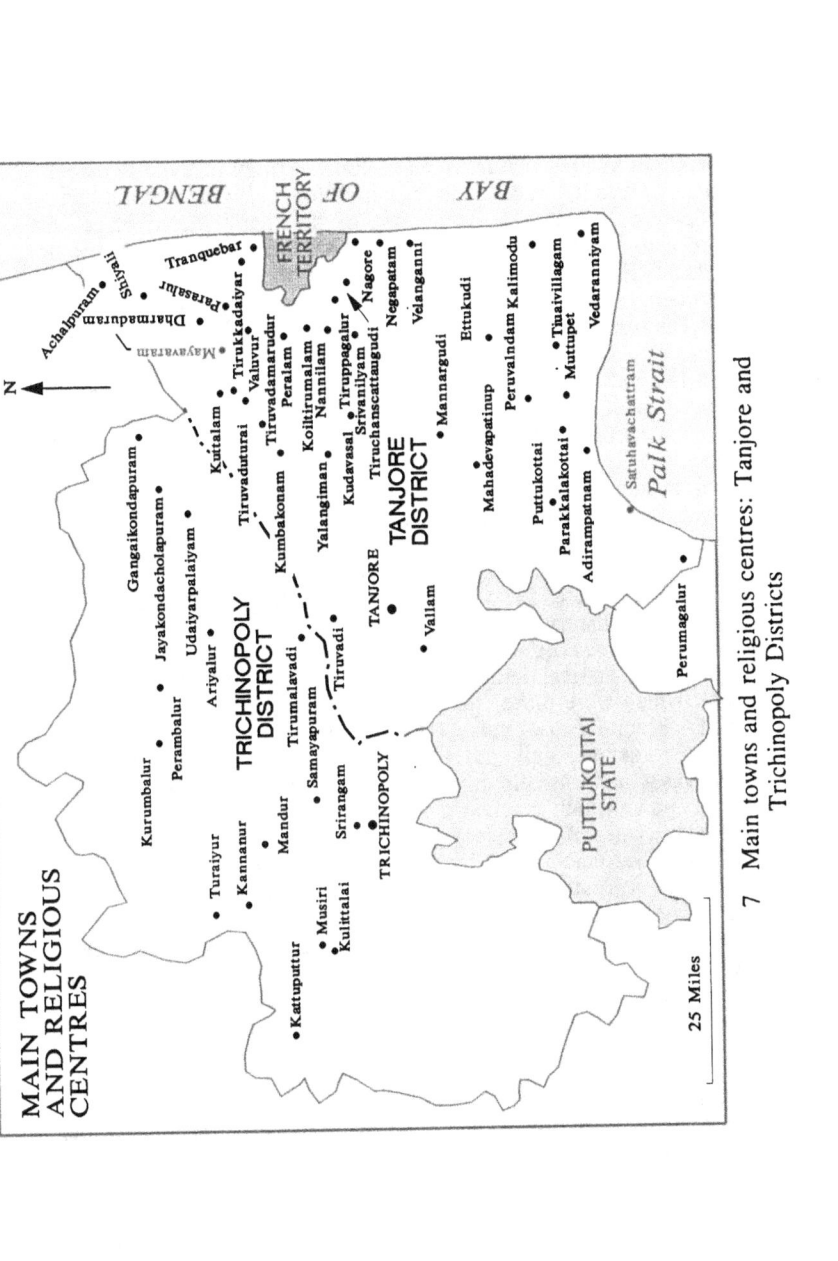

7 Main towns and religious centres: Tanjore and Trichinopoly Districts

a vow made to some of their favourite idols, or to visit spots considered among them as sacred for some particular events that may have taken place there.[6]

Apart from visiting local shrines and holy places some pilgrims went further afield visiting centres such as Rameswaram or even Benares.[7] While they travelled outside the region, others came in — joining with local devotees intent on visiting one of the many sacred places in Tanjore and Trichinopoly districts. Some idea of the importance of these local places is suggested by the fact that in 1868 an official Government publication listed four annual festivals in Trichinopoly and nine in Tanjore district which attracted an average of 10,000 visitors or more.[8]

Each temple of the least importance, and even some of the shrines associated with village deities, had their own particular festivals, annually or recurring at intervals throughout the year. In many villages the people were, for example, accustomed to celebrating Aiyanar — Tirunal an annual festival in honour of Aiyanar.[9] As we have noted, there was also an annual festival in honour of Mariamma and in some places, such as at Samayapuram in Trichinopoly district, this was a major event attracting thousands of devotees.[10]

Apart from these local celebrations relating to the deity and mythology or history of particular places there were India-wide or regional festivals. These included celebrations such as Shivaratri, in honour of the classical deities of Hinduism, and other festivals, such as Pongal, which were more closely related to the changing seasons.

In Trichinopoly the most famous festival relating to classical Hinduism was the Vaikunth Ekadashi — a special festival of the vaishnavas which was held during the Tamil month of *Magali* (January/February) and which reached a climax on Ekadashi day when it was believed the gates of paradise would be open to all pious persons. While this festival was celebrated all over India it was believed to have special significance at Srirangam.[11] The festival there lasted for a period of twenty days attracting, according to the estimates of 1868, an annual average of 50,000 pilgrims from many parts of the subcontinent. Ekadashi day occurred on the tenth day of the festival when, in true symbolic fashion, 'heaven's gate', on the northern entrance of the second innermost enclosure, was opened to the multitudes of pilgrims who, according to Hemingway, believed that if they saw the swami as they passed through the entrance on that occasion they would surely attain *moksha*.[12]

M. Monier Williams who joined the crowds on that special day during one of his visits to South India, wrote that

a vast throng — probably fifty thousand persons — crowded for hours through the contracted passage, amid deafening shouts and vociferations, beating of drums, and discordant sounds of all kinds of music . . . Not a single human being passed through that strait and narrow portal without presenting offerings to the idol, and gifts to the priests.

Speculating on the motives of the pilgrims, he declared his belief that the majority was actuated by a firm conviction 'that the passage of the earthly heaven's gate, kept by the priests, and unlocked at their bidding, would be a sure passport to Vishnu's heaven after death.'[13]

Another annual festival which drew even larger crowds (some estimates being as high as 80,000)[14] was the Tula festival in Mayavaram, Tanjore district, at a point where the river Ganges was supposed to come and mingle her waters with the Kaveri.[15] According to the *Agni-Purana*, bathing in the sacred waters of the Kaveri 'not only expiates all sins but also confers on the bather every sacrificial bliss, every desire and *moksha* in the end.'[16] A bath in the river Kaveri at Mayavaram during the month of *Tula* (October/November) was held to be especially efficacious.

In addition to these larger and more celebrated annual festivals was one other event of special importance in the religious life of the region. This was the Mahamagum festival which occurred at Kumbakonam once every twelve years. It took place in the month of *Magum* (February/March) and continued over a twelve-day period. It was not only the biggest, but perhaps also the best known festival in the Kaveri delta — a celebration which attracted enormous numbers during the second half of the nineteenth century — the largest crowd being estimated at half a million in 1897.[17] Pilgrims came from as far away as the Punjab and the United Provinces, as well as from Cuddapah, Bellary, Mysore and other parts of the South, with the special intention of bathing in the sacred tank on the south side of the great temple of Sarangapani. In his description of the festival in 1838 the Rev. J. E. Nimmo wrote that

Here the brahmans, soodras and pariahs seemed to have forgotten all distinctions of caste, and to mingle themselves together in bathing in the sacred Tank, so renowned for the removing of all bodily and spiritual pollution.

Among those who bathed in the tank was the Raja of Tanjore and, in 1885, heads of brahman and non-brahman *maths*, *zamindars* and the Raja's relatives.[18]

The tank, known as the Mahamagum tank, was believed to possess miraculous virtues at that particular season when, according to the legend, the Goddess Ganga revisited the tank to cleanse herself from the pollution contracted by her 'in consequence of so many thousands of human beings bathing in her waters and leaving their sins behind'.[19]

The purifier came to be purified and would, at the same time, purify from sin and heal from disease the multitudes who bathed in her waters.

A succinct account of the main events connected with the festival was given by the *Madras Times* in February 1873:

> During this festival the pilgrims to Kumbhakonam bathe first in the waters of the *Mahâ Mâgam*, then in the tank of the Golden Lotus (*Pon thamarei thadagam*) and, lastly, in the river Kâveri. There are twelve temples at Kumbhakonam, each having its presiding deity, the chief of the twelve being *Kumbhaśwaram*. These twelve deities are placed in their respective cars and dragged each round his own temple. They are all then carried on the shoulders of men in grand procession, with banners, incense, and fireworks, to the great tank, on the banks of which are erected twelve shrines, one for the reception of each idol. In the shrine which is built in the centre of the tank certain ceremonies are then performed, the trident being planted within it and besprinkled with holy water and incensed by the officiating *guru*. After the completion of these ceremonies, the people, who stand around the tank in anxious expectation, make a sudden plunge into it, as if the healing virtue would affect only the first who entered.[20]

The reason why people visited sacred places in the delta on these occasions probably varied considerably. Some appear to have visited shrines and holy places primarily in order to purify themselves from sin or to attain salvation. Bathing in the waters of the Kaveri at Tiruvadaimarudur (Madhyarjunam), or a dip in the sea at Vedaranniyam on auspicious occasions, as well as bathing at the appropriate time in some of the places already mentioned (such as the Mahamagum tank) could, it was believed, confer lasting benefits on the individual — such as expiation of sins or even *moksha*.[21] But multitudes also flocked to holy places to be cured of bodily ailments or disease. It was held, for example, that the water at Tiruvadi, rendered ten times more sacred during the annual festival known as the Saptasthalam, possessed 'all healing qualities'.[22] Hindus of all classes also flocked to the Christian shrine at Velanganni in the Negapatam taluk where the Virgin Mary known as 'Our Lady of Health' was believed to heal the afflicted. The annual festival, which according to an estimate in 1868 attracted an average of 20,000 pilgrims, brought visitors from many parts of the Presidency 'in the hope of obtaining relief from sickness.'[23]

Hindus also visited sacred sites on auspicious occasions to pray for other types of temporal benefit — perhaps for the blessing of children, in order to drive out devils or even for success in litigation.[24] These prayers, and those for the recovery of health, were sometimes accompanied by a vow. Vows were made at the *darga* (tomb) of the Muslim saint, Miran Sahib, at Nagore,[25] as well as at Hindu shrines and holy places, to give something of value or to undergo some type of self-discipline or suffering in the event of the prayers being answered. The fulfilment of vows was in fact a special feature of the festival in honour of Mariamma at Samayapuram in Trichinopoly district which attracted up to 30 or 40,000 pilgrims during a ten-day period in *Panguini* (March/April). Salt, jaggery, cotton seeds, grain, fowls, sheep and goats were all offered up while, according to Hemingway, many vows of 'self-torture or degradation' were also performed.[26]

But many thousands also appear to have joined in festivals with no specific religious or spiritual purpose in mind. As we have noted, thousands of those who took part in processions drawing the temple-carts were either conscripted or hired especially for the occasion. Beggars and thieves naturally mingled with the crowds,[27] while the concentration of so many people in the same place also attracted entertainers, small traders, cattle dealers and others interested in business.

The Rev. P. Percival, in his description of festivals in India, explained that 'at Shreringam, near Trichinopoly, in the month of December, the annual festival is a vast fair for the transaction of business. Cattle are brought from the adjacent provinces for sale, and wares of every description are sold or exchanged.'[28] The Rev. W. O. Simpson, who attended an annual festival in honour of Raja Gopalaswami in Mannargudi in Tanjore district in 1861, was also struck by the commercial character of the occasion and remarked that

> These feasts resemble our fairs, travelling merchants come in with their stores, confectioners adorn their stalls with Oriental substitutes for gingerbread and brandy snaps; and amongst the sports, the whirligig stands conspicuous. There is little religion in the whole matter.[29]

Another aspect of popular religion which involved high as well as low-caste Hindus was the practice of hook-swinging. This custom was followed in 125 towns and villages in Tanjore district and in at least 10 villages in Trichinopoly during the earlier decades of the nineteenth century.[30] It was described in some detail by J. A. Dubois in his well-known account of Hindu manners and customs in South India:

> At many of the temples consecrated to this cruel goddess [Mariamma] there is a sort of gibbet erected opposite the door. At the extremity of the crosspiece, or arm, a pulley is suspended, through which a cord passes with a hook at the end. The man who had made a vow to undergo this cruel penance places himself under the gibbet, and a priest then beats the fleshy part of the back until it is

8 Hook-swinging festival

quite benumbed. After that the hook is fixed into the flesh thus prepared, and in this way the unhappy wretch is raised in the air. While suspended he is careful not to show any sign of pain; indeed he continues to laugh, jest, and gesticulate like a buffoon in order to amuse the spectators, who applaud and shout with laughter. After swinging in the air for the prescribed time the victim is let down again, and as soon as his wounds are dressed, he returns home in triumph.[31]

The swinging usually took place at periodic festivals in connection with female deities and especially in honour of Mariamma the mother of smallpox. In many parts of South India it was combined with acts of self-inflicted pain and suffering and with the slaughter of animals — one of the main objectives apparently being to placate the deity and thereby ensure an abundance of rain or a period free from smallpox or some other disease.[32]

While hook-swinging was one among a number of rituals which it was believed would help to ensure the well-being and prosperity of the community as a whole, it was also undertaken for personal or family reasons. Individuals who swung (like many of those who practised some other austerity or who made offerings to Mariamma at Samayapuram) often did so in order to fulfil vows made in times of illness or distress.

In Trichinopoly and Tanjore districts, as in other parts of the presidency, those who agreed to swing appear to have been low-caste or outcaste Hindus. According to the Magistrate of Trichinopoly who made inquiries into the practice in 1853, hook-swinging there was undertaken 'chiefly by the lower castes of Hindus, such as the Pullars, Pullies and Pariahs, though many of the Soodrahs of all denominations will attend to witness the performance.'[33] Kaikolans, members of a weaver's caste, also participated in swinging in Trichinopoly district in the nineteenth century.[34] In Tanjore those who swung appear to have had much the same social background as their counterparts in Trichinopoly. In his report on a swinging ceremony which occurred in Valambagudi village in 1890, the Superintendent of Police stated that only pariahs from Palyaputty (a neighbouring village) were permitted 'to perform the vow'.[35] There is also evidence that a man who swung at a subsequent festival in Elanthurai village, Kumbakonam taluk, in 1893 was a kurava — one of a 'gipsy tribe' who lived by basket-making and fortune-telling.[36]

High-caste Hindus were sometimes mentioned as being among the spectators at swinging ceremonies while, in some parts of the Presidency, they swung 'by proxy'.[37] Indeed, it was these castes, together with the landed classes, who were at least partially responsible for keeping the custom alive. Some harijans, for example, agreed to swing, not so much in order to influence the deity, but because they were paid to swing by wealthier or higher-caste Hindus, anxious to perpetuate the system. As a result of an inquiry into the death of a pariah after a hook-swinging festival which took place at Bheemanaikenpoliem near Trichinopoly in 1893, it was revealed that the well-to-do ambalagars (cultivators and village watchmen) derived considerable profits for their temple from the swinging ceremony and that they had encouraged the men to swing with what were alleged to be 'false' promises of lands and money.[38] Further evidence of landlord or high-caste involvement in hook-swinging is contained in the report on the swinging festival which took place after the Mariamma car festival at Valambagudi village, Tanjore taluk, in 1890, which shows that the priest and trustee of the Mariamma temple was a brahman named Swamy Iyer and that he, as well as the pariahs, profited 'to a certain extent' from the alms given by the people who witnessed the ceremony.[39] So influential were managers of temples in keeping the custom going that Henry Forbes, Magistrate of Tanjore in the 1850s, believed that his best chance of stopping the practice was not to approach directly the men who swung, but to put pressure on the managers of temples to give a written undertaking to discontinue the observance.[40]

A third aspect of popular religion in the Kaveri delta was fire-walking.

In a reference to this practice, which he claimed was still followed in 415 places in Tanjore district in 1854, the local magistrate explained that

A space of about five feet diameter is covered with small sticks of the tamarind tree which are lighted, and when the flame is exhausted and the smouldering charcoal alone remains, those who desire to perform the ceremony run hastily over the fire, and stand in a trench of water previously prepared opposite the idol which is to be worshipped.[41]

Fire-walking was sometimes conducted in honour of local deities, but in the Kaveri delta, as in other parts of Tamilnadu, it was often linked with the worship of Draupadi the legendary heroine of the *Mahabharata*.[42] According to the Sanskrit version of the epic she was born of fire and became the voluptuous and attractive wife of all five Pandava brothers, living with each one in turn. In an expanded version of the account which was prevalent in Tanjore, apart from being born of fire, she was supposed to have had to enter fire 'on account of the impurity she underwent from the touch of Kichaka's body'. According to H. J. Stokes, Collector of Tanjore, who wrote an account of fire-walking in

1873, there was probably 'some confusion in the popular mind between Draupadī and Sītā, who had to prove her purity by fire'.[43]

The worship of Draupadi was especially popular among the vanniyars or pallis, an agricultural community who had seen military service under the Nayaks and who were especially active in claiming *kshatriya* status throughout most of the nineteenth century.[44] The name vanniyar appears to have been derived from the Sanskrit *vahni* meaning fire and the vanniyars, who claimed that, like Draupadi and the Pandavas, they too were born of fire, were the mainstay and leading proponents of the fire-walking cult. They not only acted as priests in Draupadi temples but were especially prominent in the recitation and re-enactment of passages from the *Mahabharata* (which many of them knew 'uncommonly well') which preceded the annual fire-walking ceremonies.[45]

In India as elsewhere fire has often been regarded as a purifying agent. The walking over fire may therefore have symbolized the destruction of one's impurity or sins, whether this was already accomplished through fasting or other rituals, or by the fire itself which cleansed in a magical way. But there were also overtones of sacrifice which had come to be attached to the Draupadi cult, at least in Tamilnadu. Animals were sometimes slaughtered near Draupadi shrines and, in some parts of the country, the fire-walking ceremony was believed to secure for the villagers 'their cattle and crops, and protection from dangers of all kinds'.[46] In some cases devotees practised varied forms of self-suffering of self-mortification such as occurred at Turaiyur in Trichinopoly where, throughout the performance, participants struck the backs of their necks with swords.[47]

But whatever communal purpose fire-walking may have had and whatever meaning is implied by the rituals and symbolism used, most participants (like many of those who underwent hook-swinging) took part in the practice primarily or wholly because they wanted to fulfil a vow. This point is reiterated in reports on fire-walking in the different districts in 1853 and is clearly reflected in the records of an inquest into the death of a young man named Pakkiri who died while walking through fire in Tanjore district in 1873. Referring to the dead man, his elder brother stated that Pakkiri had had an attack of jaundice and 'we made a vow to Dropati, saying "Mother, if he recovers we shall tread on your fire"'.[48] Another one of the fire-walkers who was present stated that

I live in the next street to the temple of Draupati. When I was away in Mauritius I was for eight years ill with dyspepsia, and made a vow to the goddess of this temple to walk through fire if I got well. Four years ago I recovered, and last April I returned to my village from Mauritius.[49]

Though the Draupadi cult was dominated by vanniyars, the practice of fire-walking was being introduced into Mariamma worship[50] and there can be little doubt that, like other forms of popular Hinduism, the practice was open and available to the lowest as well as highest segments in the population. Brahmans and high-caste Hindus participated in fire-walking in Nellore district[51] and there is no reason to think they were not involved, at least to some degree, in ceremonies elsewhere including Tanjore and Trichinopoly districts. A major difference between fire-walking and hook-swinging was, however, the prominence of low-caste non-brahmans in fire-walking compared with the much greater preponderance of harijans in the swinging ceremonies. In other words, fire-walking was generally practised by those who had a higher social status and who were certainly making claims for greater social recognition. Furthermore, fire-walking, as already suggested, was clearly linked with India-wide mainly Sanskritic literature and, in that sense, was much more a part of what Srinivas, Singer and others have described as the great tradition than hook-swinging which was apparently unrelated to any significant religious literature.

While lack of source materials, including contemporary comment, precludes a comprehensive analysis of movements and trends within popular Hinduism in Tanjore and Trichinopoly districts in the nineteenth century, there is some evidence of changes in popular practice which were taking place either directly or indirectly as a result of British policies and administration.

One important development affecting popular religion, especially pilgrimage, was the introduction and extension of railways linking Tanjore and Trichinopoly districts with other parts of the Presidency and facilitating the transport of pilgrims within the region.[52] A line running from Trichinopoly in an easterly direction through Tanjore and Trivalur to Negapatam on the coast was completed in 1861. Seven years later a line from Trichinopoly to Erode in Coimbatore district was opened. This linked Trichinopoly and parts of Tanjore with the south-western railway running from Madras, via Erode, through to the Malabar coast. Links with other parts of the Presidency were further extended in 1870 when the metre gauge line from Madras, which passed along the Coromandel coast and inland through south-eastern India to Tuticorin, was completed. This line passed through Shiyali, Mayavaram, Kumbakonam, Tanjore and the junction at Trichinopoly (all of them important stops for pilgrims) before passing through Madura and Tinnevelly districts. In 1894 the two main lines within the region (the one running from west to east and terminating at Negapatam and the other branching off at Tanjore towards the north-east) were linked by a third line completing a triangle and running in a southerly direction along the Tanjore coast. This linked Mayavaram with what then became a junction at Tiruvalur and terminated at Mutupet in Tirutturaippundi taluk.

All these developments, including the construction of several smaller branch lines such as the line from Negapatam to Nagore, greatly facilitated the flow of pilgrims through the region. More people were encouraged to travel, not only because travelling was easier and more comfortable than by road, but also because the service was frequent (for example, to Kumbakonam during the Mahamagum festival)[53] and because cheap return tickets were available, such as those which could be purchased by pilgrims attending the annual festival at Tiruvadi near Tanjore in 1872.[54]

The importance of railways as a factor in increasing the number of pilgrims visiting centres such as Srirangam, Tiruvadi, Kumbakonam and Tiruvalur is apparent in figures relating to the Mahagum festival held every twelve years. In 1873, after the opening of railways and provision for a stop at Kumbakonam, estimates of the numbers attending the festival were very much higher than they had been on the previous occasion — pilgrims coming from as far away as the Punjab, Benares, Cuddpah, Bellary and Mysore.[53] In 1885, when estimates were higher still, it was reported that 87,553 passengers arrived at Kumbakonam by train between the 15th and 28th of February and that, of these, 23,794 came from the north and 63,759 from the south.[56]

While the development of railways was conducive to greater attendance at festivals, especially in the last quarter of the nineteenth century, other factors imposed considerable restraints on attendance and help to explain fluctuations in the size of crowds, for example, at Srirangam. Records relating to the Ekadashi festival are fairly detailed[57] and suggest that, when attendances fell, this was largely due to one or a combination of two or three factors.

In the first place, the timing of the festival was extremely important. If it coincided with the Christmas holiday (when public offices were closed and public servants and other employees and their families could attend) this had the effect of increasing numbers. If, on the other hand, it coincided with Pongal ('which should be kept by Hindus in their own houses')[58] this tended to reduce attendance. On a number of occasions in the 1870s and 1880s attendance appears to have been adversely affected because of the clash with Pongal or because the festival was held either before or after the Christmas holidays.[59] In 1879, however, it was held at the optimum time. The crowds were apparently larger than in any of the three previous years. According to the official report, this was partly due to the fact that the festival commenced almost

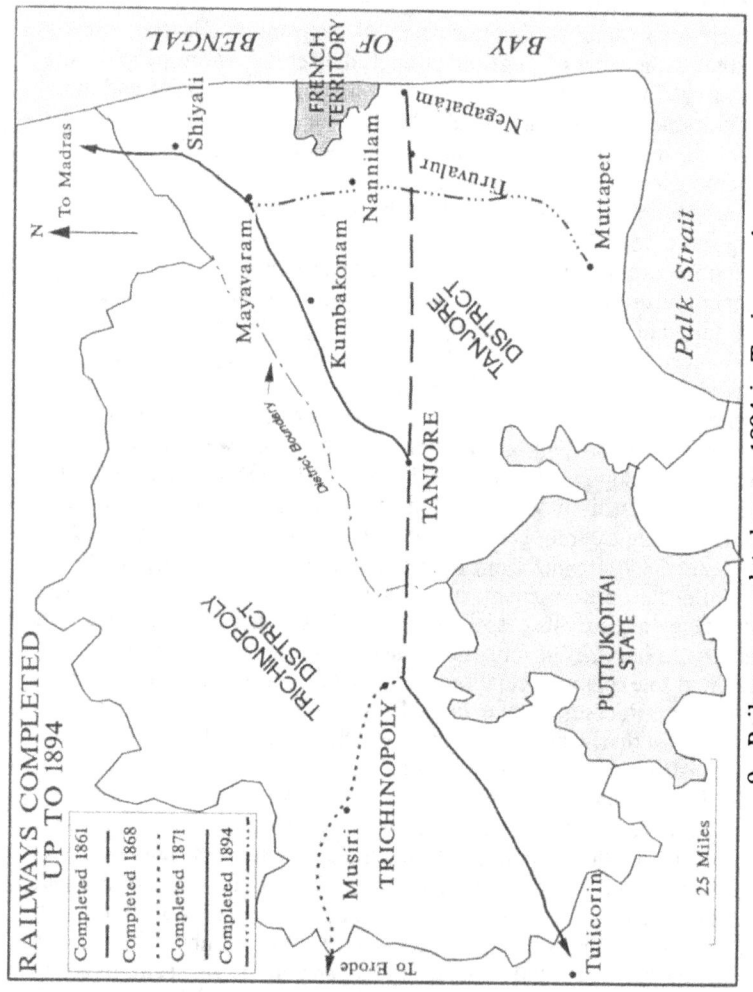

9 Railways completed up to 1894 in Tanjore and Trichiniopoly Districts

simultaneously with the Christmas holidays and because the big day occurred nearly one week before Pongal.[60]

A second and very important factor was the incidence of epidemic diseases. Thus attendances at Srirangam were largely affected by outbreaks of cholera and by widespread publicity of this in Government notices in 1870 – 1, 1876 – 7, 1882 – 4 and in 1888.[61] Referring to Government measures to prevent the spread of cholera in Srirangam during the festival which began 16 December 1887 one Government official reported, for example, that

> Because of prevalence of cholera efforts were made to dissuade those travelling a distance from attending and notices were posted in railway stations warning of risks. Measures reduced numbers from other districts from an average of 15,000 to about 5,000 and also curtailed their stay greatly. Epidemic was at its worst when they began to arrive.[62]

Another factor which also affected attendance (though one which was not often mentioned as a serious deterrent) was the inclemency of the weather. The most striking incidence of this was the cyclone of 21 November 1880[63] which brought with it heavy and continuous rain and which breached several roads and cut the railway line into Srirangam in several places just before the celebrations were due to begin. The estimate on that occasion was that numbers attending the festival were down by two-thirds on the previous year.

Apart from the changes in connection with attendance at festivals there was a marked decline in hook-swinging during the nineteenth century. The practice appears to have been already declining in Tanjore and Trichinopoly, as well as in other parts of the Presidency, before the Government decided actively to discourage the custom in 1854. After detailed inquiries (prompted by a despatch from the Court of Directors reporting on measures adopted in British Guiana for the suppression of hook-swinging among Indian immigrants in the colony) the Government of Madras left it to district officers to use what influence they had to discourage the practice. Forbes, the Magistrate of Tanjore, needed little encouragement to try to suppress what he regarded as a 'cruel and revolting' custom[64] and within a few weeks of receiving instructions he was writing back to the chief secretary of the Public Department to explain that the managers of 78 temples had been prevailed upon to sign written engagements renouncing the custom and that hook-swinging had been 'entirely abandoned throughout Tanjore'.[65] In the following month the Magistrate of Trichinopoly stated that the custom had similarly been abandoned in the district, the managers of the 18 temples where it had prevailed having also given a written undertaking to entirely discontinue the practice.[66]

While these measures appear to have had an important effect in eliminating hook-swinging at festivals in many parts of the region, they were not (in spite of Forbes' confident prediction) entirely successful. There is evidence, for example, that in spite of official discouragement the swinging at Valambagudi village in Tanjore taluk, Tanjore district continued uninterruptedly throughout the period from about 1860 to 1890 while, in another instance, the practice was revived at Bheemanaikenpoliem near Trichinopoly in 1893.[67]

The custom was also 'revived' from time to time in other parts of the Presidency[68] and the Madras Government came under increasing pressure from western-educated Hindus (notably those associated with the *Hindu* newspaper), missionaries and others, not just to discourage the practice, but to forbid it altogether. W. S. Caine M.P., a well-known crusader on behalf of reform in India, raised the issue in the House of Commons in February 1893. In the following year, after it was discovered that a man had died from the effects of the swinging at Bheemanaikenpoliem in Trichinopoly district, the Government of Madras announced that the ceremony would in future be prohibited by orders under section 144 of the Criminal Procedure Code which gave magistrates increased power to prevent a recurrence of the practice.

In 1854, after inquiries into fire-walking (conducted along similar lines to those into hook-swinging), the Government of Madras decided to clamp down on that practice as well — the best methods of discouraging the observance again being left 'to the discretion of the different Magistrates.'[69] But while in the case of hook-swinging most local authorities were determined to eradicate the practice they seem to have been less enthusiastic in attempts to suppress fire-walking. This was partly because hook-swinging was regarded by many district officers not only as dangerous, but 'barbarous' and 'disgusting' while fire-walking came to be seen increasingly as a comparatively harmless, though perhaps 'idle and foolish' custom.[70] The missionaries and their supporters, together with the English-language press in Madras, were more concerned with bringing about the complete suppression of hook-swinging than with getting further Government action on the fire-walking issue and, as already mentioned, when an especially unpleasant accident in connection with hook-swinging occurred in the 1890s, the Government of Madras was again forced to intervene. In the meantime, fire-walking ceremonies were allowed to continue — often noted in Government gazetteers as something of a picturesque or even quaint curiosity.[71]

It cannot be assumed, however, that because fire-walking was still quite common at the end of the century the original order discouraging the practice had no effect. One reaction against the banning of hook-swinging in the Madras Presidency had been the substitution of sheep for people in the swinging ceremony[72] and it appears that the attempted suppression of fire-walking also encouraged an emphasis on alternative forms of ritual. Commenting on Government policy in an article on firewalking published in 1873 H. J. Stokes, Collector of Tanjore, remarked that

> I have heard of a case in the district where, since Government set its face against the ancient practice, the people use flowers instead of fire, and tread on them devoutly in honour of the goddess. Could any reform have a happier ending?[73]

It has already been noted that while Hindu élites were able to participate in popular religion (unless restrained through fears of pollution etc.) the lower orders not only had more difficulty in gaining access to the classical Sanskritic texts but were also excluded from many of the major Hindu institutions. It should not be imagined, however, that this was a situation lower castes always readily accepted, and another of the important changes taking place during the nineteenth century was the attempt by lower-caste groups (e.g. the nadars) to gain rights to temple entry or positions on temple committees and to emulate higher-caste religious and social customs.

An attempt at self-improvement and upward social mobility usually went hand in hand with implicit claims to participate in the religious rites and activity of higher-caste Hindus. In Tanjore and Trichinopoly districts this desire for change was reflected in the attitude of a variety of different castes. These included valaiyans, a hunting caste, who in Tanjore district in 1901 accounted for nearly seven per cent of the Hindu population; the shanars, who preferred to be called nadars; the pallis or vanniyans (who in 1901 represented more than 11 per cent of the population in both districts); the kallans, especially those in the western taluks of Tanjore; udaiyans (cultivators); karaiyans (sea fishermen); vaniyans (oil pressers), and others who were all reported to be claiming a higher status and were imitating brahman customs.[74]

If, in some cases, these changes were limited to alterations in outward observance (such as burning the dead and banning the remarriage of widows) in other cases caste communities went further in attempting to secure for themselves greater access to the religious ideas and rituals associated with the great tradition. Valaiyans, vaniyans and kallans were beginning to employ brahman priests (thus opening the way for further changes in ritual and religious ideas) while the karaiyans were not slow in asserting their claims to an association with Vedic gods.

Another type of reaction to the higher-caste monopoly over certain aspects of Hinduism was not to challenge or attempt to acquire higher-caste religion from within, but to opt out altogether. This type of reaction was reflected in the conversion of low and outcaste Hindus to Christianity — movements which involved changes in communal affiliation and which are discussed in Chapter 8. Alongside these Christian movements was a somewhat weaker trend towards Islam (presumably from among low and outcaste Hindus) which, like conversion to Christianity, is reflected in census figures of the latter half of the nineteenth century.[75] During the period from 1871 to 1901, when figures were more reliable than estimates made in the 1850s and 1860s, the growth rate of the Muslim population was 55 per cent higher than the Hindu population in Tanjore district and 89 per cent higher in Trichinopoly. During the same period the growth rate of the Christian population was conspicuously higher than the growth rate for Muslims and well over double the growth rate for Hindus in both districts.

NOTES

1 *Popular Hinduism: The Religion of the Masses*, Cambridge 1935.
2 *The Little Community and Peasant Society and Culture*, p. 41.
3 Supra, Ch. 2.
4 *Census of India*, 1891, Madras, Vol. xiii, p. 59, T. V. Row, op. cit., p. 169; Ziegenbalg, op. cit., p. 143; Whitehead, *The Village Gods of South India*, pp. 18 – 20.
5 Specific religious disabilities preventing lower-caste Hindus from becoming more familiar with classical religious teachings and even temple culture were considerable. As we have seen, a third of the population in Tanjore district was affected by bans on temple entry while, in addition to this, there was still a great deal of prejudice against lower-caste Hindus studying Sanskrit literature. See, for example, correspondence in the *Hindu*, 18/3/1889.
6 *Letters and Notices*, Vol. III, pp. 1 – 2.
7 See especially, supra, Ch. 5.
8 *Lists of Festivals, Fairs, etc., occurring within the limits of the Madras Presidency*, Madras 1868.
9 Ziegenbalg, op. cit., p. 134.
10 Hemingway, *Trichinopoly*.
11 P. V. J. Ayyar, *South Indian Festivities*, New Delhi, 1892, pp. 171 – 78.
12 Ibid., p. 169, Hemingway, *Trichinopoly*, p. 322.
13 *Brahmanism*, p. 450.
14 *Lists of Festivals, Fairs etc.*
15 Hemingway, *Tanjore*, p. 231.
16 P. V. J. Ayyar, *South Indian Shrines*, New Delhi, 1882, pp. 271 – 2.
17 *M.P.P.*, Vols. 275, 1873; 2594 – 2595, 1855; J. A. Dubois, op. cit., (1897 ed.,) p. 196.

18 *L.M.S.*, Nimmo to Ellis, 22/3/1838, S. I. Tamil, Box 8; *M.P.P.*, Vols. 2594 – 5, 1855.
19 Ayyar, *Shrines*, p. 323.
20 *Madras Times*, 12/2/1873 quoted in *I.A.*, Vol. 2, May 1873, p.152. See also *L.M.S.*, Nimmo to Ellis, 22/3/1838, S. I. Tamil, Box. 8.
21 Ayyar, *Festivities*, pp. 31 – 4; Hemingway, *Tanjore*, 1906, p. 284.
22 *I.A.*, Vol. 1., 5 July 1872, p. 226.
23 Hemingway, *Tanjore*, p. 250, also pp. 249, 260.
24 Hemingway, Ibid., pp. 227, 260.
25 Ibid., p. 243.
26 Hemingway, *Trichinopoly*, p. 318.
27 *L.M.S.*, Nimmo to Ellis, 22/3/1838, S. I. Tamil, Box 8. *Hindu*, 4/6/1888.
28 P. Percival, *The Land of the Veda: India Briefly Described*, London 1854, p. 230; See also *I.O.R.*, *M.P.P.*, Vol. 3511 (1889).
29 J. Bush (ed.) op. cit., p. 257.
30 *I.O.R.*, V/23/139 Sel. Mad., No. 7. *Reports on the swinging Festivals and the Ceremony of Walking through Fire*, Madras 1854 (henceforth Sel. Mad.) pp. 2, 8.
31 J. A. Dubios, op. cit., p. 598.
32 G. A. Oddie, 'Hook-Swinging and the Popular Religion in South India during the Nineteenth Century', *I.E.S.H.R.*, Vol. XXIII, No. 1, January – March 1986.
33 Sel. Mad., p. 2.
34 Thurston, op. cit.
35 *I.O.R.*, P/3784, M.J.R., 7/8/1890, P 145.
36 *Hindu*, 19/5/1893, C. G. Todhunter, the Sub-divisional Magistrate of Negapatam, witnessed a hook-swinging exhibition at Patnacheri in Karaikkal (a small French enclave situated on the coast between Tranquebar and Negapatam) in 1893. In his report to the Tanjore District Magistrate he wrote that 'the ceremony is always practised here in honour of the goddess Mariamman, in most instances by the caste of fishermen but sometimes also by the shepherds. It has no religious sanction or obligation but is regarded as a general penance on behalf of the community, having at the same time a particular efficacy as a vow on the part of individuals . . . The temple at which it [hook-swinging] is performed belongs to a small fishing community, who regard the hook-swinging festival, so far as I could ascertain, as a yearly penance for the offence given to the goddess by the killing of fish. It is carried out in a most regular and orderly way and with no design of filling the coffers of the temple, the people appearing to sincerely believe that a cessation of it would bring ruin on the village. At the same time it is regarded as of great efficacy in vows, two of the men attributing their recovery from cholera to the fact that they had vowed to the goddess to be swung up if they lived, while a third who was childless believed that it would procure him a son'. (I.O.R., P/4409, M.J.P. 21/12/1893).
37 Oddie, 'Hook-swinging . . .'
38 *I.O.R.*, P/4621, M.J.P. 24/9/1894.
39 *I.O.R.*, P/3784, M.J.P. 27/8/1890.

40 Sel. Mad., pp. 8, 18A. When the practice was revived in Negapatam in 1892 the trustee of the temple admitted that as far as the temple authorities were concerned 'the performance was encouraged solely in order to increase the temple's popularity and with no religious object whatever.' (Sub-divisional Magistrate of Negapatam to District Magistrate, Tanjore, 7/9/1893, I.O.R. P/4409, M.J.P. 21/12/1893.)
41 Sel. Mad., pp. 26–27.
42 See especially Alf Hiltebeitel, 'Sexuality and Sacrifice: Convergent Subcurrents in the Firewalking Cult of Draupadi' in F. W. Clothey (ed.) *Images of Man: Religion and Historical Process in South Asia*, Madras 1982; Sel. Mad. p. 20, 23, 24, 32; W. Francis, *South Arcot*, Madras 1906, Vol. I, p. 99; F. J. Richards, *Salem*, Madras 1918, Vol. I, pp. 107, 115–16; Hemingway, *Trichinopoly*, p. 294; E. Thurston, *Ethnographic Notes in Southern India*, Madras 1906, pp. 471–4; G. Oppert, op. cit., pp. 94–99, 477.
43 H. J. Stokes, 'Walking Through Fire', *I.A.*, Vol. 2, July 1873, p. 191.
44 See Hiltebeitel, Oppert and Francis, op. cit.
45 Francis, op. cit., p. 99.
46 Thurston, *Ethnographic Notes*, p. 471.
47 Hemingway, *Trichinopoly*, p. 294.
48 Stokes, '*Walking Through Fire*', p. 191.
49 Ibid., p. 190.
50 Oppert, op. cit., p. 477. In such cases the fire-pit had to be lit with a brand brought from a Draupadi temple (Francis, op. cit., p. 99).
51 Sel. Mad., pp. 31–2.
52 See especially *History of Indian Railways Constructed and in Progress Corrected up to 31 March 1955*. Government of India, Ministry of Railways (Railway Board) publication.
53 *I.A.*, Vol. 2, May 1873, p. 152.
54 Ibid., Vol. 1, July 1872, p. 226.
55 *M.P.P.*, Vol. 274, 1873 (Magistrate's report 28/2/1873).
56 *M.P.P.*, Vol. 2595, 1885; *Hindu*, 12/12/1885.
57 See Appendix 6.
58 *M.P.P.*, Vol. 1038, 1876.
59 Ibid., Vol. 1038, 1876; Vol. 1746, 1881; Vol. 2348, 1884; Vol. 3043, 1887.
60 Ibid., Vol. 1393, 1879.
61 Vol. 272, 1871; Vol. 1038, 1876; Vol. 1039, 1877; Vol. 1925, 1882; Vol. 2118, 1883; Vol. 2348, 1884; Vol. 2284, 1888.
62 Ibid., Vol. 3284, 1888.
63 Ibid., Vol. 1746, 1881.
64 Sel. Mad. p. 18A.
65 Ibid., p. 18A.
66 I.O.R., P/3784, *M.J.P.*, 27/8/1890. Precis of Orders on the Swinging Festival, including extracts from Minutes of Consultation 24/2/1854 and 8/5/1855.
67 *I.O.R.*, P/3784, *M.J.P.*, 27/8/1890, Acting Inspector-General of Police to the Chief Sec. to Govt., 12/8/1890; *I.O.R.*, P/4621, M.J.P., 26/9/1894, Inspector-General of Police to Chief Sec. to Govt. 8/9/1894.

68 Oddie, 'Hook-Swinging . . .'
69 Sel. Mad., p. 19.
70 Ibid., pp. 5, 15, 18, 18A, 20, 23.
71 Writing in 1893 the Sub-divisional Magistrate of Negapatam reported that firewalking was still practised 'more or less' all over Tanjore district. (C. G. Todhunter to District Magistrate, Tanjore, 7/9/1893, *I.O.R.*, P/4409, *M.J.P.*, 21/12/1893).
72 Oppert, op. cit., p. 477; Whitehead, op. cit., p. 59.
73 *I.A.*, Vol. 2, July 1873, p. 191.
74 *Census of India*, 1891, Madras, Vol. XV, pp. 130, 158, 171, 178, 182-3; Hemingway, *Tanjore*, pp. 82 – 3, 84, 87, and *Trichinopoly*, pp. 106 – 110; T. V. Row, op. cit., p. 190.
75 See Appendix 7.

7

BRAHMANS AND CHRISTIAN CONVERSION

One of the most striking aspects of Christian missionary activity in India throughout most of the nineteenth century was the continued failure of missionaries to convert significant numbers of the brahman class. This was in spite of the fact that missionaries sometimes placed considerable emphasis on the need to win over brahmans (whom they regarded as the religious élite) so that other castes would follow.[1] While harijans and other castes at the base of the Hindu hierarchy begged and clamoured more and more loudly for admission into Christian churches the brahmans in general remained aloof.

It is true that census returns for the Madras Presidency show that there were 3,697 Christian brahmans in 1871.[2] However, 3,604 or 97.5 per cent of these were Konkani-speaking Catholics in South Kanara — the descendants of migrants who were said to have been 'forcibly converted to Christianity by the Portuguese'.[3] Of the remaining 93 converts, 54 were Catholics scattered in five other districts and 39 were Protestants scattered in seven districts — 14 of the latter in South Kanara and 9 in Madras.

Even if the census-takers overlooked or failed to record a few other brahman converts, these figures still convey some idea of how difficult and unusual it was for missionaries to baptize even a single brahman. Indeed some missionaries had given up hope and regarded further efforts directed towards conversion of brahmans as a waste of time.[4]

The situation in Tanjore and Trichinopoly districts was not very different from what it was in most other parts of the Presidency. Very few brahman converts were baptized (perhaps less than ten in all the missions) during the first three-quarters of the nineteenth century, while none of them were shown as residing in the region in the census of 1871.

Of the Protestant missionaries the Methodists had the most success, but even they succeeded in baptizing no more than four additional brahman converts in the last quarter of the nineteenth century.[5] In the meantime, however, quite extraordinary developments were taking place in the Catholic mission. In the 1890s the Jesuits, who like the Protestants had been greatly disappointed by the lack of response among brahmans, gradually became aware of new feelings in favour of Christianity among some of the students at St. Joseph's College, Trichinopoly. This resulted in the growth of a brahman conversion movement which appears to have been unprecedented elsewhere in the Madras Presidency in the nineteenth century.

During the period from 1894 to 1900 21 brahmans (most of them students from St. Joseph's College) were baptized into the Catholic Church. The movement continued to develop in the early decades of the twentieth century until the small colony of brahman converts which had been established at St. Mary's Tope Trichinopoly contained about fifty families[6] — some other brahman converts living separately elsewhere in the region.

The Methodist and Jesuit missionaries not only appear to have been the most active and successful in converting brahmans in the region but have also left some of the most detailed and best-documented accounts. The purpose of this chapter is to utilize this material in attempting to understand both the missionaries' failure and their comparative success. What factors help to account for the baptism of brahmans into Methodism and Catholicism during the period 1850 – 1900? Why was the number of those converted and baptized brahmans so few especially during the period 1850 – 1894? How does one account for the increase in the number of brahmans baptized in the Jesuit mission after 1893?

Before discussing these issues and providing some social and biographical information about the converts involved, it is important to clarify the meaning of the term 'conversion'. In this context, as well as in other parts of the book, it is taken to mean the process whereby individuals or groups opted out of one religious community and joined another. But while in some cases (perhaps in most) conversion meant little more than change of community, in other cases it was accompanied by significant changes in conduct or inner life, or marked the beginning of a slow process of change and reorientation in the life of the group or individual.[7]

At least 34 brahmans were baptized in connection with the Methodist and Jesuit missions in Tanjore and Trichinopoly districts during the period 1850 – 1900. Of these 25 were males, mostly students from mission schools and colleges, and 9 were females, either wives or widows.[8] Of the 34 converts, 8 of them (all males) became Methodists and 26, including the nine females, became Roman Catholics.

The great majority of these 34 converts appear to have come from Tanjore district. Information on caste is available in the case of 23. Of these 19 were Tamil brahmans, 17 of them Iyers or smartas, and 2 Iyengars or srivaisnavites. Three of the four remaining brahmans were Marathas and one was simply described as a 'vaisnavite'. Thus 17 out of a total 23, or approximately three out of every four, were smartas or followers of Shankara's teachings. This represented very roughly the proportion of smartas in Tanjore's brahman population.[9]

Many, though not all, of the brahman converts came from a fairly well-to-do background. Information on the parents' occupation was available in the case of 14. Five were sons of domestic priests, (two of these being sons of the pensioned *sastri* of the Raja of Cochin). One convert was the son of a chief priest in a temple. The eight remaining converts were all children of fathers who were, or had been, in Government service — either in education or in the legal profession. There was therefore nothing especially unusual in the fathers' occupations — unless perhaps it was in a high proportion of fathers who were priests.

Where information is available it appears that the ages of converts at the time of baptism (omitting the one infant baptism) ranged from about 15 to 30 years — the average age in the case of 15 converts being 21. This reflects the fact that a majority of converts were students. Lastly, the responsibilities and position of converts within the family varied. At least four were eldest sons (and hence would be expected, in Hindu tradition, to perform their father's last rites, but as converts would be unable to do so), one was the youngest in a family of fourteen and many were middle children.

Evidence, not only in missionary reports but also in the converts' own accounts and even in legal proceedings, suggests that while the character and rate of conversion began to change in 1894, *some* of the reasons for the converts' initial interest in Christianity and for the final decision to seek baptism remained much the same throughout the entire period 1850–1900.

Somewhere in almost every case of conversion is reference to the influence, impact or example of some other person or persons. These people included priests and missionaries, other inquirers and even converts in other missions.[10] The role and influence of European and other 'recognized' Christian leaders was much greater in the case of these brahmans (at least up until 1894) than it was among the lower-caste mass movement converts who were more influenced by friends and relatives and had less contact with missionaries. But that is not to say that the influence of class mates and other inquirers on brahmans was of no significance at all. Small groups of brahmans in the Methodist mission for example appear to have prayed, read the Bible and discussed Christianity together. The apparently lone individual, prepared to stand out and persevere, was often the end product of some kind of general ferment or movement towards Christianity in which others had been involved.[11] The example of brahmans from the same school or even from other missions who had been converted and baptized on some previous occasion could also be infectious and encouraged others to follow suit.[12]

A second important and not unrelated influence on the Catholic side was the example of the priests' corporate life at St. Joseph's. Appusamy Iyer, referring to the circumstances which led to his accepting the Catholic faith in 1891, noted especially 'the spectacle of the life of the Fathers so industrious and so innocent' which made an impression upon him.[13] P. J. Doraisamy Iyer made similar comments. Referring to the reasons for his conversion and baptism in 1894 he wrote that

> I used to see the young Fathers of the College piously reciting their rosary in the college grounds towards nightfall. This made a very great impression on me. Their peaceful demeanour and happy lives, their concord and charity in spite of their being different nationalities, was in great contrast with the lives of Hindu *sanniasis*, two of whom cannot live in peace together in a *mutt*. It was this that prompted me to enquire into the tenets of the Catholic Religion.[14]

Another more general factor in the conversion and baptism of brahmans appears to have been their exposure to more critical attitudes and, linked with this, increasing dissatisfaction with Hinduism. During this period both Methodist and Jesuit missionaries were strongly critical of Hinduism. While he was careful not to antagonize students by denouncing Hinduism, Fr. Billard, for example, went out of his way to stress the fundamental differences between the Catholic faith on the one hand and Hinduism on the other. He was especially critical of what he described as 'le principe de l'indifferentisme',[15] the idea that all religions are equally good and true. The encouragement of a more critical approach, including a comparison of Hinduism with Christianity, began to affect a number of students, including not a few sons of *sastris* and others who had previously been regarded as champions of their own tradition.[16] According to P. J. Ramaswamy Iyer, who was baptized in 1899 and whose brother was already a Christian, one of the chief instruments in the conversion of brahmans was 'earnest and sincere comparative study of religions by the seekers of truth'.[17]

There may be nothing especially significant in the fact that three-quarters of the brahman converts were smartas since this, roughly speaking, represented the proportion of smartas in the brahman population. But, as previously mentioned, smartas were traditionally the followers of the teachings of Shankara (one of the greatest exponents of *Advaita* or Monism) and at least some smartas found, or were beginning to find, these views unsatisfactory. Appusamy Iyer, for example, claimed that when he was still a Hindu he was unable to accept what he described as 'the fundamental dogma of brahmanism which identified God with this material universe, and obliges me to see in my miserable person a portion of the divine.'[18]

Lastly, a very powerful incentive affecting the attitude of many converts and reinforcing their determination to receive baptism was an almost desperate desire to save their souls and 'flee from the wrath to come'. Generally speaking both Methodist and Catholic missionaries continued to preach during that period the 'awful' fate that awaited those outside the Christian Church.[19] This obviously struck sensitive chords of fear in the minds of not a few brahmans who, like other high-caste Hindus, were especially concerned with issues such as the nature and fate of the soul after death. When asked in court why he wished to become a Christian, one young Methodist convert replied that it was because he wanted to save his soul.[20] This sentiment or something similar was echoed by others.[21] Describing the agony preceding his baptism into the Catholic Church, P. J. Ramaswamy Iyer explained that he was torn between 'the pain of deserting my parents in their lonely condition on the one hand, and fear of damnation of my soul for eternity, on the other.'[22]

These then were some of the general factors encouraging the conversion and baptism of brahmans during the period 1850–1900. But why were baptisms not more common and how do we explain the sudden increase in the number of baptized Catholic converts after 1893?

Some of the obstacles which made it extremely difficult for brahmans to join the Christian churches become more clearly apparent when we focus on what happened in the Methodist mission every time a single brahman was baptized.

In the first place, Methodist missionaries, like most of their Protestant colleagues, had long held the view that the retention of caste was incompatible with the profession of Christianity.[23] Hence they expected their converts to renounce caste before being admitted to the Christian Church.[24] In actual practice this usually meant that converts were expected to discard their sacred thread or *poonul* and to eat with Europeans,[25] or with low-caste or pariah Christians, as a sign and symbol that all were one in the fellowship of the Christian Church.

From the point of view of the brahman community itself this step was tantamount to social suicide or death[26] and was regarded with no less abhorrence. To become a Christian was the same thing as losing one's caste, cutting one's *poonul* or becoming a pariah.[27] 'The pariah's religion' was the brahman's usual name for Christianity and consistent with this idea was the belief that conversion to Christianity was 'identical with a dissolute life'.[28] No matter how much affection the parents and relatives still felt for the individual convert, his approach and proximity was dangerous and likely to affect the purity and spiritual welfare of the rest of the household. Conversion to Christianity therefore meant enforced physical and social separation unless, as happened on a few occasions, converts could be persuaded to undergo expensive expiatory rites.

Added to the family's sense of personal loss and grief at inevitable separation was the scandal, the disgrace and possible loss of status involved. Kalyana Raman's mother summed up the feeling of many parents when she pleaded with her son 'not to bring a disgrace upon the caste and family'.[29] Presumably because of the extent of the contamination involved, a conversion in a family could even affect the validity of domestic rites. Explaining why he wished for a delay in his baptism, John Narainswami pointed out that two of his sisters were to be married and that 'if he were baptized during the marriage festivities, all the ceremonies would be rendered invalid, and his two sisters would be condemned to a lifelong widowhood.'[30]

In view of all this it is scarcely surprising that friends and families tried their utmost to dissuade young men from accepting baptism.[31] Brahmans interested in Christianity were not infrequently abused in the streets, confined to the home, beaten and even tortured in attempts to deflect them from their purpose. If these methods failed, and the convert took refuge with the missionaries, then the parents usually instituted legal proceedings charging the missionaries with kidnapping or some other offence. Promising inquirers suddenly disappeared, converts were abducted both before and after baptism and, in at least two cases, young men were forced to go on pilgrimage and undergo ceremonies readmitting them back into Hinduism.

If the combined effect of parental, wider family and caste reactions was not enough to deter the individual, knowledge of what could happen to the individual convert *after* his baptism was sufficient to dampen the ardour of many a young inquirer. Once baptized, the convert was placed in an extremely difficult position. Added to the shock of confrontation with parents, relatives and even friends, and to various trials and persecution, was the impact of finding himself in a completely alien social and cultural environment. Once within the Christian community he was, as we have seen, expected to mix and eat with pariahs and low-caste people. There were usually no other brahman converts with whom he could share his feelings. Furthermore, because of the opposition of the Hindu brahman community, converts such as these usually found it difficult to obtain employment outside the mission.[32] The breach with parents was usually irreconcilable, and judging from what happened to Subrahmanyam Iyer (baptized in 1892) any attempt to revisit the home village was deeply resented.[33]

The trials and difficulties experienced by brahman converts to Catholicism were not very different from those experienced by Methodists — at least up until the mid 1890s. In spite of the Jesuit policy of allowing converts to retain and practice their own caste customs[34] they were still rejected and despised by the Hindu community as if they had actually broken caste and sunk to the level of 'pariahs'.[35] No matter how hard the convert tried to keep himself pure and unsullied and clung to his brahman customs, such was the image of Christianity that Hindu brahmans could not believe that he remained as untainted as themselves. This point emerges clearly in the story of Appusamy Iyer.[36] He and his wife were baptized together in about 1891. The couple, who had suffered much and been forced to fend for themselves, continued to follow brahman customs. When Appusamy's parents came to see him in an attempt to persuade him to return to Hinduism, the young man showed them into his kitchen, explained that he was still a brahman, and stated that in becoming a Christian he had no intention of giving up the privileges of his caste. Though his parents appear to have been impressed with his efforts to maintain his 'purity', he was apparently still regarded as an outcaste by other members of the brahman community. When he and his wife did want to return to Hinduism a few years later they were forced to undergo expensive purification ceremonies in order to gain readmission.

This then was the situation and these were some of the main difficulties involved when, on New Year's day 1889, the Rector of St. Joseph's College, Trichinopoly (Fr. Faseuille) stressed the need for the Fathers to make a more determined effort to convert higher-caste Hindus.[37] In a letter to his Superior in Rome later that same year, he explained that there were already a few brahmans in the College asking for baptism.[38] But, he said, the best policy was one of delay. Instead of baptizing one or two converts as soon as possible, it would be better to wait patiently for the development of a group or corporate movement so that when the time for the baptism of a young brahman did arrive, the others would follow suit. In this way the converts would be able to help and look after each other when rejected by their families. Without this, added the Rector, one needed a miracle to persevere.

It is not clear how far the Rector's views were endorsed by his colleagues. But if any doubts remained as to the dangers involved in the isolation of brahman converts and of their need for the companionship of their own people, these doubts were dispelled a few years later by the defection of Appusamy Iyer. The loneliness, the temptations and problems he and his wife had tried to face had been too much to endure and, as we have seen, he was readmitted into Hindu society. Fr. Lacombe, one of those on the staff, wrote

La leçon fut très pénible pour nous tous ici au collège. Nous nous intéressions tant à ce couple de convertis! Nous en tirâmes une conclusion bien pratique, à savoir: *It est inutile d'essayer de convertir les Brahmes et les autres Hindous de haute caste, si on ne leur fournit pas les moyens de vivre séparés des paiens et suivant les exigences de leur état social.* Ce fut alors que nous vint la première idée de fonder une colonie de convertis de haute caste où les néophytes pourraient se trouver avec gens de leur rang et être protégés contres les tentations du paganisme.[39]

The idea of founding a colony of high-caste converts which emerged as a result of these events coincided with the views and plans of one of the leading converts who was as yet unbaptised. In a letter to Fr. Billard in October 1892 Mahadeva Iyer argued that if he was baptized by himself this would create the usual problems and fail to impress the public. If, on the other hand, four or five other brahmans could be induced to do the same the advantages could hardly be overrated:

In the first place, it will give greater strength to everyone and to the whole body, and will enable anyone to resist ridicule and censure. And since you are for preserving caste (God forbid that you should think otherwise!) it will give greater scope for mutual sympathy. In the second place, the conversion of, say, five Brahmins together will, in my opinion, be an epoch in the annals of India, and the public instead of ridiculing and censuring us, will begin to consider our conversion as an accomplished fact and begin to wonder. We shall become objects of enquiry and serious talk, rather than objects of hatred. Whilst at the same time there is little fear of the converted Brahmins turning apostates.[40]

Mahadeva Iyer, who succeeded in winning his wife's support, waited and was eventually joined by two other converts. The Jesuits were already convinced that the converts needed their own separate colony where they could live together after baptism. But the question was where? The converts themselves had firm ideas which eventually prevailed. In a petition to the Rector of the College[41] they opposed the idea that they should live anywhere near other Catholic converts whom they said were 'supposed by Hindus to be of dirty habits'. The converts wanted a site further away from these associations where they could retain their status and identity as brahmans, where they would be in a better position to attract brahman visitors and help change brahman attitudes towards Christianity. In their statement they declared that

We wish to show by the practice of Christian vitues . . . side by side with an outward conformity to Brahman habits and customs, that Christianity does not mean drinking, wearing hats, boots and trousers, or surrender of caste dignity, but a vivifying influence which raises man to the highest perfection of his moral nature.[42]

Immediately before and after the baptism of these three converts (together with Mahadeva's wife and child) in September 1894 there were the usual signs of outrage, fear of pollution and rejection by the Hindu brahman community. Before their baptism the converts were implored to give up their new doctrines, since by becoming Christians they would dishonour the whole caste.[43] When, after his baptism, Mahadeva went to his father-in-law's house to seek out his wife, he was told 'your presence here is a disgrace to us . . . you pollute us'.[44] And when his wife's people, who were holding her prisoner, realized that they could no longer keep the fact of her baptism secret, they contemplated making her undergo purificatory ceremonies that would enable them 'to keep her in the family without pollution'.[45]

In spite of these initial reactions and persecution, the Christian brahman colony which was established and named St. Mary's Tope, not only survived but began to grow. For the first time in recent history — at least in that part of South India — newly-won brahman converts were able to live in a viable brahman Christian community. The very existence of the colony attracted others. The sense of solidarity and fellowship, strengthened in adversity, was further encouraged by the fact that many of these converts were related to each other.[46] Moreover, as the colony expanded, the shortage of women and inbreeding which may have become a problem, was at least partially overcome by alliances with Catholic brahman women from Pondicherry and elsewhere.

The high degree of publicity which was focused on the converts in 1894 and thereafter was a decided advantage. Initially, when Mahadeva's wife was still being kept prisoner, the young converts (at considerable cost to Fr. Billard) were forced to employ a Hindu brahman cook.[47] When the Hindus tried to persuade the cook to leave, the latter, wishing to keep his position, defended the converts. 'Come', he is reported to have said to anyone who would listen, 'come and see if these young men are not quite as good Brahmins as you are. Do they eat meat? Haven't they the cord just like you?' Some of the curious did arrive and could find nothing to criticize. They could detect no change in customs or in the general appearance of the converts.[48] Apparently the days were gone when Christians, such as these, felt compelled to imitate the style of Europeans or, even worse, fraternize with pariahs! P. J. Ramaswamy Iyer, who was contemplating baptism and whose brother was already a Christian, was able to make the most of this new situation. Anxious to win his wife to the Catholic faith, he was able to take her to his brother's house and show her that there was nothing strange in the customs and manners of brahman Christians.⁴⁹

Slowly Hindu brahman attitudes towards these converts began to change. There could no longer be any doubt that the converts were extremely strict, even fastidious, in adhering to the rules of their caste and that they were less 'contaminated' than other Catholic Christians living in a different part of the town. Their relationship with parents, relatives and former friends very gradually improved. Some of the parents began to pay friendly visits to St. Mary's Tope and even went so far as to accept cooked food from their children — a sure sign of reconciliation.⁵⁰ Other Hindu brahmans also began to fraternize with the converts. Some of them used the public library of Catholic books established in the grounds of St. Mary's Tope.⁵¹ Employees, students and others came to walk in the cool of the evening or to play tennis with Christian friends — accepting water when offered.⁵²

Commenting on the increasing number of brahmans converted to Christianity in Trichinopoly the *Hindu* newspaper declared in February 1898 that

Up until now, the greatest obstacle to conversions was the social ostracism which condemned anyone wishing to convert to Catholicism. Now that these converts have multiplied to the point of forming a colony sufficiently numerous, and have nothing to lose in social status, it is believed that there will be a greater number of conversions in Trichinopoly.⁵³

These predictions proved correct — the number of brahman converts rising to about 150 in 30 years.⁵⁴

As we saw, this increase in numbers was brought about very largely through changes in Catholic missionary policy. Missionary policy has not always been effective or even relevant in some other instances involving the spread of Christianity in India, but in this case it proved to be of the utmost importance. As a result of many trials and disappointments the Jesuit fathers and the converts themselves realized, in the words of Mahadeva Iyer, that 'it is much more difficult to persevere to the end as a Christian than to become a convert'.⁵⁵ This led to greater attention being paid to the needs of converts after baptism. 'After care' was the primary issue and, as Fr. Billard, Mahadeva and others pointed out, this meant that brahman converts would have to live in a brahman colony or community of their own. Here, without being subject to continual persecution and without exposing their faith, they were able to support and care for each other. Moreover, living quite separately from the older Christians who were all 'of an inferior caste'⁵⁶ they were in a better position to preserve and practise their own customs, demonstrating once for all that in becoming Christians it was not necessary to sink to the level of 'pariahs'.

Some of the reasons for continued brahman conversion during this period remained much the same as before, but added to these attractions were other very powerful considerations. In becoming a Christian, one did not necessarily have to forfeit the love and affection of parents and friends or lose one's status and identity as a brahman.

Methodist policy in relation to brahmans remained basically unchanged and, as a result, Methodist missionaries failed to attract many more brahman converts in the last part of the nineteenth century than they had in previous decades. The trend of events in the Jesuit mission, however, not only demonstrated how important a change in policy could be, but also showed that the old pattern of brahman conversion or baptism, which involved the expulsion of individuals from the Hindu community, discontinuity and isolation, was not the only type of brahman conversion which could occur. It was possible for brahmans to change their religion with a minimum of social disruption and in a way which was roughly parallel with what was happening among depressed-class converts who preserved existing social relationships and retained many of their distinctive cultural traditions.

The change in Hindu attitudes was also significant. As we have argued, brahman hostility and opposition to the conversion of members of their own community began to subside when they became convinced that these converts were retaining their 'purity' and social and cultural customs. This suggests that brahman objections to conversion had been based more on social and cultural rather than on theological or abstract considerations. Indeed, from the Hindu point of view it appears to have mattered very little what the individual thought or believed provided he continued to adhere to the rules and customs inherent in the social system and, mainly for this reason, the new Trichinopoly brahman converts were more acceptable in Hindu society.

NOTES

1 See, for example, accounts of Roberto de Nobili in A. J. Cronin, *A Pearl to India: The Life of Roberto de Nobili*, London 1959; and S. Rajamanickam, *The First Oriental Scholar*, Tirunelveli, 1972 and of Protestant educational policy in M. A. Laird, *Missionaries and Education in Bengal, 1793 – 1837*, Oxford 1972.
2 *Census of India*, 1871, Madras, Vol. II, p. 100.
3 Ibid., Vol. 1, p. 133. In his report the Census Commissioner also noted that 'they still retain some caste customs, such as refraining from eating the flesh of the cow, etc., but are said to be extremely observant of the rites and ceremonies of the Romish Church.'

4 L. Lacombe, *L'Oeuvre de la Conversion des hautes castes au College St. Joseph, Trichinopoly*, Rome (N.D.), p. 28.
5 See Appendix 8.
6 See especially N. Mooney and G. V. I. Sama (eds.) *The History of St. Mary's Tope; The Origin, Development and Spread of St. Mary's Tope, the Catholic Brahmin Colony, Tiruchi*, Palayamkottai, 1977.
7 For further discussion of the concept of conversion see G. A. Oddie (ed.) *Religion in South Asia: Religious Conversion and Revival Movements in South Asia in Medieval and Modern Times*, Delhi 1977, pp. 4-5.
8 For these and other details see Appendix 8.
9 *Census of India*, 1871, Madras, Vol. 1, pp. 291-6; T. V. Row, op. cit., p. 168.
10 Among the most influential missionaries on the Methodist side were the Revs. Hobday and Evers (both Anglo-Indians with a thorough knowledge of Tamil) and the Rev. W. O. Simpson. Outstanding among Catholics was the Italian Jesuit Fr. Francis Billard (Professor in English and Mathematics at St. Joseph's College) — a man of extraordinary patience whose name recurs frequently in accounts of brahman conversions.
11 *W.M.M.S.*, J. N. Thompson to E. E. Jenkins, 19/10/1885, Negapatam and Trichinopoly, Box 436. *W.M.N.*, 1856, p. 194; 1877, p. 206; *H.F.*, Vol. 1, May 1863, p. 165; C. H. Monohan, *Theophilus Subrahmanyam, The Story of a Pilgrimage*, London, 1922, p. 27.
12 *H.F.*, Vol 1, June 1862, p. 191; Vol. 2, April 1863, p. 134.
13 R. P. Auguste Jean, *Le Maduré, L'ancienne et la Nouvelle Mission*, Tome II (N.P.,) 1894, p. 223.
14 L. Lacombe, *A Great Indian Convert: Rao Sahib V Mahadeva Aiyer*, Trichinopoly, 1923, p. 21.
15 Lacombe, *L'Oeuvre de la Conversion*, pp. 10-11.
16 *W.M.M.S.*, P. J. Evers to E. Hoole 23/6/1857; Lacombe, *A Great Indian Convert*, 1923, pp. 3-4, 7, 23-24.
17 See his article on 'Brahman Conversion', together with other articles by converts, in N. Money and G. V. I. Sama (eds.), op. cit.
18 Auguste Jean, op. cit., pp. 222-3; Lacombe, *A Great Indian Convert*, 1923, p. 25.
19 For Protestant views see G. A. Oddie, 'India and Missionary Motives, c. 1850-1800', *Journal of Ecclesiastical History*, Vol XXV, No. 1, January 1974, pp. 67-70.
20 *H.F.*, Vol. 1, May 1862, p. 165.
21 *W.M.M.S.*, A. Burgess to E. Hoole, 11/6/1857 and P. J. Evers to E. Hoole, 23/6/1857, Madras, Box 438; *H.F.*, Vol. 2, April 1863, p. 134; *W.M.N.*, 1877, p. 206; Lacombe, *A Great Indian Convert*, pp. 7, 11, 26.
22 *Ways of Grace in India*, Vol. XXI, p. 35.
23 G. G. Findlay and W. W. Holdworth, *The History of the Wesleyan Methodist Missionary Society*, London, 1925, Vol. V, pp. 138-9; *W.M.N.*, 1852, pp. 139-40; 1854, p. 182.
24 Findlay, op. cit., p. 139.

25 *W.M.M.S.*, P. J. Evers to E. Hoole, 23/5/1857; Madras, Box 438; J. N. Thompson to E. E. Jenkins, 20/5/1887, Negapatam and Trichinopoly, Box 426; *H.F.*, Vol. 1, May 1862, p. 164.
26 J. Bush (ed.), op. cit., p. 273; C. H. Monohan, op. cit., p. 77.
27 *W.M.M.S.*, P. J. Evers to E. Hoole, 23/6/1857, Madras, Box 438; *H.F.*, Vol. 1, May 1862, p. 164; Vol. 2, April 1863, p. 138; J. Bush, op. cit., p. 274.
28 *L.N*, Letter from Fr. Billard, November 1894, Vol. XXIII, No. CXX, July 1895, p. 162; Lacombe, *A Great Indian Convert*, p. 31.
29 *H.F.*, Vol. 1, June 1862, p. 191.
30 *W.M.N.*, Vol. VIII, 1885, p. 254.
31 For some of the more detailed accounts of the methods used see *W.M.M.S.*, A. Burgess to E. Hoole, 11/6/1857 and P. J. Evers to E. Hoole, 23/6/1857, Madras, Box 438; J. N. Thompson to E. E. Jenkins, 20/5/1887, Negapatam and Trichinopoly, Box 426; *H.F.*, Vol. 1, May 1862, pp. 163–6; Vol. 2, April 1863, pp. 134–139; C. H. Monohan, op. cit., pp. 60–63; J. Bush, op. cit., pp. 145–150, 265–275.
32 See Appendix 8.
33 Monohan, op. cit., pp. 85–6.
34 On Jesuit attitudes towards caste Infra, Ch. 9.
35 Lacombe, *L'Oeuvre de la Conversion*, pp. 27, 29–30; P. Suau, *L'Inde Tamoule*, Paris, 1901, p. 119; Auguste Jean, op. cit., pp. 223–8.
36 Suau, op. cit., p. 119; Auguste Jean, op. cit., pp. 223–8.
37 *Father Louis Lacombe S. J.*, Trichinopoly 1930, p. 29.
38 *A.R.S.I.*, Maduré 1005–VI, 2, Faseuille to Fr. General, 4/2/1889. See also Maduré 1005–VII, 3, Faseuille to Fr. General, 3/2/1890.
39 Lacombe, *L'Oeuvre de la Conversion*, p. 30.
40 Lacombe, *A Great Indian Convert*, p. 12.
41 Ibid., pp. 30–32.
42 Ibid., p. 31.
43 Ibid., pp. 36–7.
44 Ibid., p. 39.
45 Ibid., p. 53.
46 See Appendix 8.
47 Lacombe, *A Great Indian Convert*, p. 46.
48 *L.N.*, Vol. XXIII, No. CXX, July 1895, pp. 162–3.
49 *Ways of Grace in India*, Vol. XXI, p. 36.
50 Suau, op. cit., p. 131.
51 *A.R.S.I.*, Maduré 1006–11, 19, Lacombe to Fr. General, 31/1/1899.
52 Saua, op. cit., p. 131.
53 Quoted in Suau, op. cit., p. 131.
54 Lacombe, *L'Oeuvre de la Conversion*, p. 34.
55 From his speech in April 1915 to former students of St. Joseph's College (Lacombe, *A Great Indian Convert*, p. 66).
56 *A.R.S.I.*, Maduré 1006–11, 19 Lacombe to Fr. General, 31/1/1899.

8

THE DEPRESSED CLASSES AND CHRISTIANITY

During the 30-year period from 1871 to 1901 the growth rate of the Christian population in the Madras Presidency was just over four times greater than that of the population as a whole. The total population increased by 22.2 per cent while the number of Christians rose by 90.6 per cent.

There was, however, less difference between Christian and population growth rates in Tanjore and Trichinopoly districts — although the difference was still substantial. In Tanjore the population increased by 13.8 per cent and the number of Christians by 31 per cent. In Trichinopoly the population increased by 20.4 per cent while the number of Christians increased by 46.8 per cent. These statistics are presented in Table 2.

The increase in the proportion of Christians in the population was largely due to conversion — the process whereby individuals and groups deliberately chose to join the Christian community.[3]

Table 2. Growth rate of the Christian population.

Year	Total population	Percentage increase	Christian population	Percentage increase
	Madras Presidency[1]			
1871	31,597,872		545,120	
1901	38,623,066	22.2	1,038,854	90.6
		Tanjore[2]		
1871	1,973,731		66,409	
1901	2,245,029	13.8	86,979	31.0
		Trichinopoly		
1871	1,200,408		52,222	
1901	1,444,770	20.4	76,660	46.8

More detailed information on population and Christian growth rates can be obtained through an analysis of census figures on religion by taluk.[4] These figures highlight variations in the extent to which growth in the number of Christians was (except in one subdivision) outstripping growth rates in the population. In the Negapatam taluk, for example, the Christian population increased at nearly four times the rate of the population as a whole, in the Mayavaram taluk at more than twice the rate, while in Perambalur, in Trichinopoly district, the proportion of Christians in the population remained almost stationary during the thirty-year period. Judging from these figures it also appears that the proportion of Christians in the population of Tanjore district was increasing most rapidly in the eastern and central taluks, including Negapatam, Mayavaram, and Nannilam, and in Trichinopoly district, in Udaiyarpaliyam in the north-east and in Kulittalai in the west.

As we intend to show, the people involved in these movements were mainly drawn from the depressed classes. This term refers to those groups who were normally classified as being outside the Hindu *varna* system. Other terms, such as untouchables, panchamas (fifth class) harijans and adi-dravidas etc. refer to the same class of peoples.[5] In Tanjore and Trichinopoly they could be divided into three main communities — the pariahs and pallars, who were mainly agricultural labourers, and the chakliers (leather workers) who represented only a small proportion of the total. Taken together these different communities constituted 15.5% of the population in Tanjore district in 1871 and 13.1 per cent of the population in Trichinopoly.[6]

There had been depressed-class converts among the earliest Christians in the region. The first Christians to settle at Negapatam included parava Christians from the Malabar coast,[7] while converts from among the pariah community were baptized by de Nobili at Trichinopoly early in the seventeenth century.[8] The Census of 1871 (which used the term 'pariah' in a generic sense to include pariahs proper as well as pallans and other untouchables) shows that there was, even then, a very much higher proportion of depressed-class people in the Christian community than in the Hindu population. Forty-nine per cent of Christians in Tanjore and 38.3 per cent in Trichinopoly were from the depressed classes — even though Tanjore district in particular had a higher proportion of high-caste converts, including vellalas, than many other districts in the Presidency.[9] (See Table 3.)

Although a movement of depressed-class peoples into both the Catholic and Protestant churches had been taking place over previous generations, the movement appears to have accelerated in various parts of the South (especially in the Telugu country) round about the time of the great famine of 1876–8.

Table 3. *Percentage of Pariahs in the Hindu and Christian Population, 1871*

	Hindu population	Hindu Pariahs	%	Christian population	Christian Pariahs	%
Tanjore	1,803,787	274,558	15.22	65,262	32,011	49.1
Trichinopoly	1,115,776	137,606	12.33	50,822	19,453	38.3

The situation in Tanjore and Trichinopoly districts after 1871 is reflected in detail in baptismal and other registers scattered in churches throughout the region. These suggest that the increase during the period from 1871 to 1901 was largely due to the influx of people from the depressed classes into the Christian churches. During the late 1880s and the 1890s the movement of pariahs in particular gained considerable momentum, especially in Tanjore district.[10] What had been a multi-caste Christian community at the beginning of the century became increasingly a pariah-dominated community by the 1890s. Although pallars were still being converted in some parts of the delta, by far the most conspicuous movement was among pariahs.

One of the best ways of illustrating what was happening is to compare some of the baptismal registers, which reflect the traditional pattern of slow growth still evident in some urban areas in the 1890s, with registers which indicate the rapidly changing situation in rural areas — especially in East Tanjore. Lutheran registers, such as those in Zion Church, Trichinopoly (1892 – 1900) and in the Holy Comforter Church, Tanjore, (1898 – 1900), continue to mirror the dominant pattern of church growth apparent in many churches in previous decades.[11] The baptism of adult converts was noted only occasionally; converts were usually drawn from a wide variety of different castes; the baptism of single individuals without relatives present was not uncommon and, lastly, some of these converts came from other regions or far away and in that sense were marginal or not fully integrated in local society.[12]

The picture revealed through the study of baptismal registers in East Tanjore in the 1880s and 1890s is, however, rather different. Converts were being baptized at centres such as Tranquebar, Karikal, Manikramman, Mayavaram and Nangur in much larger batches in single ceremonies. The great majority of these converts, who in Mayavaram numbered nearly two thousand people, were of the one caste (pariahs). Again, they almost all lived in villages near where they were baptized and, unlike many of the earlier converts, especially in the towns, had strong roots in local society.

The spread of the movement, which appears to have been almost entirely a rural phenomenon, was facilitated by both social and economic factors. As in other parts of India where comparable 'mass' movements were taking place, individual initiative and leadership was important. In some cases children who were being educated in Christian schools were the first to accept baptism and this event was followed sometime later by the baptism of their parents.[13] In some instances it was the woman, perhaps with her children, who was the first to seek baptism — the husband holding back;[14] while, in other cases, it was the man who was baptized first, his baptism being followed sometime later by that of his wife.[15]

Most converts, however, waited until they could move with the rest of the nuclear family and perhaps also with other relatives as well.[16] The close relationship between many of the depressed-class converts is, for example, clearly apparent in the Manikrammam baptismal register of 9 February 1896. Entries refer to two instances where three brothers with their wives and families were baptized together[17] and one case where two brothers and their wives and families were also baptized at the same time.[18] Many other instances of the interrelatedness of converts is also apparent in other registers in East Tanjore.[19]

These family connections not only acted as some kind of cushion, protecting converts against isolation and some of the worst effects of harassment or persecution, but also greatly facilitated communication. Relatives and families already converted were scattered in different villages and the distribution of these family linkages and networks helps to explain why Christianity developed in some parts of the locality and not in others.

Economic relationships were also important. Different caste groups (such as pallars and pariahs) mixed together in agricultural operations. In many parts of the region landlords strongly opposed the Christian movement. However, there is some evidence that near Tanjore township the attitude of some landlords was rather different. Anglican records usually give the occupation of converts and it appears from the register in St. Peter's Anglican Church, Tanjore, that during the period 1876 – 7 some landlords as well as tenant cultivators and landless labourers were converting to Christianity.[20] Hence, instead of reflecting elements of class conflict, the movement in that part of Tanjore district appears to have been facilitated by traditional patron/client relationships — tenants and landless labourers following landlords into the Christian church.

While the pattern of economic and social relationships helps to explain how and why the movement spread in the way it did these same factors do not really explain why the depressed classes became interested in Christianity in the first place.

Unfortunately pariahs, like so many other illiterate and oppressed peoples in history, have left few records of their own. Hence, in attempting to explain their increasing interest in Christianity in the 1880s and 1890s, we are forced to rely to a considerable extent on missionary sources and on circumstantial evidence which also helps to explain the increasing attractiveness of the new religion.

In the first place, it is fairly clear the movement was not the result of dramatic social disruption during the last half of the nineteenth century. As Washbrook has pointed out, Tanjore district was a remarkably stable society.[21] While famines, for example, increased the level of starvation and suffering among the depressed classes, especially in East Tanjore during the last quarter of the century,[22] there was no obvious breakdown in the economic and social system such as occurred in some of the worst hit famine areas of the South where, in Forrester's view, 'the general loosening of social links within the community set the depressed caste groups free to fend for themselves, to look for new patrons, perhaps, or to change their life-style and religious commitments without the old pressure to conform to norms of the village community being enforced by the higher castes.'[23] The economic and social system in Tanjore district remained very largely intact with landlords still clearly dominant and in control of their tenants and landless labourers. Nor does it appear that there were other dramatic or sudden changes likely radically to upset existing world views — changes which Horton and others have argued prompted the search for new explanations and meaning, and further encouraged the spread of Christianity in some other societies.[24]

Nor is it likely that the movement into Christianity was the result of a growing desire for upward social mobility. The pariahs' acceptance of Christianity on previous occasions and as far back as the eighteenth century had led to little, if any, changes in their status within Tanjore society — a fact that must have been patently obvious to non-Christian pariahs who were thinking of joining the Christian community. A few individual pariahs, such as catechists or teachers, were treated by higher-caste Christians with a greater degree of respect than ordinary pariah Christians; but, generally speaking, pariahs were shunned by the rest of the Christian community. Writing after some years of experience as a pastor in villages near Kumbakonam, the Rev. I. Ignatius wrote that

> The Pariah Christians in villages, like the heathen Pariars, [sic] have their houses generally built as huts; and keep always their compounds unclean, filled with dust, and heaped with bones of dead animals which they eat. They still serve in common for their food the heathen miràsdàrs, and Christians too if any, as landlords, for the cultivation of their paddy fields, etc; bear funeral

notices to different villages for high caste men; beat ton-tom (drum) for their funerals and marriages; and perform their duty as Vettians (menial officers in a village) by burning the dead bodies of the heathen in the village they live in; and differ from high caste men also in the mode of eating and drinking.

Under these circumstances, high caste Christians dislike to have any social intercourse with common Pariah Christians, from a fear of forfeiting all their wordly pride and gain in the sight of their heathen neighbours . . . Animated by the selfish motives of honor and respect among their heathen neighbours, they never freely put their feet in a low caste street, nor touch any Pariah Christian if there be any there . . .

To whatever denominations of Mission Churches they may belong, these abuses are equally the same in all Mission Churches, and form every day's experience among native converts.[25]

As this statement makes clear, high-caste Christians who shunned Christian pariahs were merely reflecting Hindu attitudes which remained unchanged in spite of the pariahs conversion to Christianity.

If then the basic economic and social structure in Tanjore remained largely unchanged and if converts to Christianity could not expect a higher social status as a result of their joining the Christian churches, what factors explain the rapidly increasing momentum of the Christian movement?

One possible explanation was suggested by the Rev. J. Kabis, a Lutheran missionary, in a paper read before the Madras Missionary Conference in August 1897.[26] Kabis, who when stationed at Mayavaram, had baptized more than 1,000 pariahs declared that

every missionary who had even a little experience of work among Pariahs with all his enthusiasm knows very well that it would be quite wrong to overestimate in the present movement of Pariahs towards Christianity, the spiritual influence at work amongst them. There can be no doubt that, very often, one of the chief reasons which leads them to move towards Christianity is their need of a protector, who shall help them to claim and gain the rights which they are beginning to understand are theirs, and that they hope by becoming Christians to better their miserable condition and to find in the missionary a friend in need and a champion in their oppressed situation. Such and other mercenary motives have no doubt generally something to do with the conversion of people of the depressed classes . . .

If any one thinks that he can do mission work among Pariahs by purely spiritual methods, only by preaching and teaching, he has only to try it, and he will soon find out his mistake. Any missionary who wants to work successfully among these people must be prepared to become to them not only a teacher, but also a pleader and almoner. Let us not forget that the movement of them towards Christianity is in the first instance not a spiritual one. One who thinks so would be under a delusion. It is their distress in various ways which leads them chiefly to us.

An increasing awareness among pariahs of their own personal worth and civil rights (a highly significant development referred to in Kabis' comment) was probably the result of gradual changes over a long period of time. One of these changes was the experience some of them had had of travel and temporary migration overseas to countries such as Malaya, Mauritius and Ceylon.[27] Another factor in raising their consciousness was the gradual infiltration of British notions of equality before the law; while a third, no less important development, was long-term contact and increasing acquaintance with Christian missionaries including, in some cases, opportunity to study in elementary mission schools. In 1881, for example, there were well over three thousand pupils in Protestant elementary schools in Tanjore district alone, some of them belonging to the depressed classes.[28]

Linked with a slowly dawning recognition of rights and legal status among the depressed classes was a rejection of the idea that they were always bound to accept their lot in life, and a growing desire for improvement. The search for a way out, for relief from burdens (which perhaps seemed heavier than ever) was not easy. Most caste Hindus were unsympathetic and there was no political organization during this period seriously interested in helping pariahs. Furthermore, migration, which may have appeared attractive, was in reality only possible for a minority within the community.[29] On the other hand, Christian missionaries and especially Protestants were, as we have seen, becoming increasingly active among pariahs in areas such as East Tanjore and, for many pariahs, the missionary and the Christian movement must have appeared as the only alternative, the only hope in a world which (because of their increasing consciousness) was less bearable than before. 'Between the Hindu community proper and the Pariahs there is little love lost,' wrote the editor of the *Hindu* newspaper in 1891.[30] 'Apart from the help of the missionaries', stated the paper on another occasion, 'the Pariahs have no chance of rising above their present condition of extreme poverty and degradation'.

A high proportion of depressed-class families were almost totally dependent on landlords for economic survival. It was in this context that the new religion appeared to offer a better future — at the very least a shift in dependence on landlords alone to dependence on both landlords and mission with the possibility of curbing something of the landlord's power.

Whatever the missionaries might have preached there can be little doubt that it was the material advantages and welfare aspects of Christianity which were among the most tangible and easily understood aspects of the new religion.[31] Furthermore, men like Kabis stressed that they were 'not only messengers of faith but also of love' and that they were bound to meet bodily as well as spiritual needs.[32] In fact, all the missionaries were concerned especially with the care and protection of converts — a service which some of them considered doubly necessary in view of the way in which some landlords and high-caste Hindus treated the new Christians.

Writing in 1851 one of the Jesuit fathers reported that

> In this district [Tanjore] the Christians are almost all lower caste cultivators in the service of pagans upon whom they are dependent . . . In order to withdraw little by little these Christians from this damnable servitude, the missionaries have been searching to procure uncultivated land at a low price to give them at the same time a refuge and an occupation.[33]

Most if not all the missions established schools and orphanages and provided some form of medical assistance.[34] Catholics maintained refuges for catechumens (converts under instruction) while the Lutherans established printing presses and industrial schools for their adherents. Catholics and Lutherans also established special refuges for widows, while Anglican missionaries conducted a 'Tanjore Widows' and Pension Fund'.[35] Missionaries were also prepared to intervene actively in cases involving individuals or groups who appeared to be unable to help themselves. In some cases the missionaries went to special lengths to uphold civil rights and, in one instance, pariahs were brought out of prison with the missionaries' assistance.[36] Missionaries also attempted to redeem Hindus or Christians from slavery or agricultural bondage and were also prepared to institute legal proceedings in cases of severe oppression.[37]

Drawing attention to the distress among members of his poor congregation in 1893, the Rev. George Lazarus (S. P. G. Nangur) wrote that

> Most of them look to me for help in the form of clothes and cash, and I am obliged to help them whenever they are in extreme need and poverty. I am also obliged to help the funeral expenses whenever poor and helpless people die. On my visit to the poor villages, I sometimes help the poor Christians when I see their utter misery and needy circumstances.[38]

In these circumstances, it seems reasonable to assume that missions were perceived, at least in part, as a source of help and protection — as something which pariahs and others could utilize, not only in times of conflict with landlords, but on other occasions of difficulty and distress. The Rev. Mr. Winkel, who took over from Kabis at Mayavaram, declared that Christians baptized during the famine years had turned out to be 'seed sown among thorns' and quoted a lapsed Christian as saying 'we came because of hunger, now we are no longer hungry, so we needn't come any more.'[39] In 1892 two Indian pastors speaking at the Lutheran synod in Tranquebar contended that many had come for bread and left when they no longer needed it,[40] while, five years later, the Rev. Mr Zehme expressed his conviction that lapses were due to those Christians who did not get what they expected from the mission.[41]

But while it is likely that material advantages, including aid and protection, weighed fairly heavily in the minds of many of the depressed classes who converted to Christianity, it would be unwise to dismiss the entire movement as if the theological content of missionary preaching, religious ideas, feelings and convictions played no part in the process. Because of the lack of source materials there is, for example, no way of knowing what precise effect the missionaries' constant stress on the need for repentance, on heaven and hell and on Christ, as the only way of salvation, had on the inner life and thought of the people.[42] Nor is it possible to measure precisely the impact and appeal of teachings which stressed the essential equality and brotherhood of man and which provided the depressed classes with an ideology they could utilize in their opposition to higher-caste Hindus. Furthermore, if the desire for material advantage and protection was the only consideration, how does one explain the tenacity and perseverance of some converts who, in spite of material losses and persecution, still adhered to the mission?

High-caste converts were not the only ones who suffered harassment and persecution. Some depressed-class Christians were rejected by relatives or had to face hostility from other people within their own community.[43] The main opposition, however, came from landlords and was based very largely on fear and self-interest. The *mirasidars* feared that if their labourers became Christian they would no longer be under their complete control and would refuse to perform their usual agricultural and religious services. What, for example, would happen if Christians refused to work on Sundays or wasted time attending a Christian service?[44] Who would beat the drums, or draw temple-carts, or perform other religious duties if these people accepted the new religion? How could the landlord control his labour if workers could complain to the missionary? And what would happen if depressed-class children were educated? Perhaps they too would refuse to submit to their landlords' control or even demand higher wages?[45]

While a few landlords themselves accepted Christianity or were simply indifferent to evangelism among their workers, others were openly hostile and took measures to arrest the movement. In some cases *mirasidars* informed their workers that, as they were now Christians, they could no longer expect the usual perquisites on the occasion of births, deaths and marriages in their family, but that they should turn to their padre for assistance.[46] Some converts were denied the use of ponds and wells, were deprived, at least temporarily, of work (especially if they absented themselves from the fields on Sunday) or were faced with even more severe penalties, such as expulsion from home, for becoming Christian.[47]

Faced with these difficulties some converts returned to Hinduism. Others, however, remained within the Christian community presenting missionaries and pastors with the difficult problem of what to do with members of their congregation who had lost so much.[48]

Inspite of the steadfastness and endurance of some converts however,[49] it has to be recognized that the depressed-class movement into Christianity was something like an open system. While there was a flow of converts into the churches there was also a leakage back into Hinduism. Furthermore, even if converts remained within the confines of the Christian church they were not always adverse to changing denomination.

Among the more interesting records in Lutheran churches in the region are admission registers (as distinct from baptismal registers) which provide information on individuals seeking to join the Lutherans from some other denomination or who, having lapsed into Hinduism, were seeking readmission. The registers are in fact the record of people who had changed their religion or denominational affiliation *at least twice* after baptism — once when they apostasized (or joined another mission) and twice when they rejoined the Lutheran church. In one instance a little more information is provided which shows that one woman in Mayavaram changed her allegiance not twice but thrice. After her baptism into the Lutheran church she relapsed into Hinduism. She then joined the Roman Catholics and was finally readmitted into the Lutheran church in September 1888.[50]

While it is impossible to know how many or what proportion of depressed-class converts changed their denominational allegiance, these admission registers do give some information on the denominational background of converts (most of them belonging to the depressed classes) who changed their affiliation by joining or rejoining the mission. Information was available on nearly 600 people in six centres (five of them in Tanjore district) at different stages during the period 1870 to 1900.

Sixty-three per cent (334) of these converts admitted to the Lutheran church came from Roman Catholic churches, 18 per cent (96) came from Protestant denominations, chiefly the Anglican and Methodist mission, and 19 per cent (104) were lapsed Lutheran converts seeking readmission.

As will later become apparent, many higher-caste or 'sudra' converts changed their affiliation over questions of caste practice and privilege.[51]

Table 4. Lutheran Church — Admissions

	Trichinopoly			
	1870-74	1887-91	1892-1900	Percentage of total excluding 'not given'
Catholics	54	60	26	70.4
Other Protestants	37	2	11	25.1
Lapsed Lutherans	4	2	3	4.5
Not Given	2	35	–	
Total	97	99	40	

	Tanjore					
	Tanjore 1898-1900	Mayavaram 1883-1900	Tranquebar 1888-1900	Karaikkal 1898-1900	Manikrammam 1892-1900	Percentage of total excluding 'not given'
Catholics	24	103	42	7	18	56.2
Other Protestants	5	18	13	8	2	13.3
Lapsed Lutherans		89	6	4	6	30.4
Not Given		14			3	
Total	29	224	61	19	29	

Depressed-class converts were, however, less affected by caste considerations and sometimes changed their denominational affiliation because of marrying someone in a different mission[52] or because another mission appeared to offer benefits greater than did their own. The Anglican pastor in change of the Nangur-Tranquebar mission complained, for example that

> The greatest of all our discouragements is the abolition of the Tanjore Widows' and Pension Fund. This has been the backbone as it were of the mission and a great hold upon our agents from going away with their congregations to the

Lutherans who are very strong in the district with a permanent Pension Fund and other encouragements to their agents.[53]

Perhaps, however, an even clearer indicator of the peculiar instability, even fragility, of the Christian movement is evidence relating to apostasy. Figures on the overall incidence of lapses in Tanjore and Trichinopoly districts were again unavailable, but something of the nature of the problem is reflected in Lutheran church records in the Holy Emmanuel Church, Mayavaram.

Table 5. *Apostates from the Lutheran Mission, Mayavaram 1883 – 1900.*

Year	Converts baptized whose history is known	Minimum no. of those who had apostasized by 1907	% of Apostates to converts
1883	68	9	13.0
1884	81	5	6.0
1885	375	11	3.0
1886	220	85	39.0
1887	80	6	7.5
1888	29	2	7.0
1889	20	4	20.0
1890	18	4	22.0
1891	–	–	
1892	21	2	
1893	12	–	
1894	28	–	
1895	14	11	78.0
1896	107	19	18.0
1897	89	16	18.0
1898	124	48	39.0
1899	139	12	9.0
1900	543	85	
Totals	1,968	319	Average 16.2

In 1907 one of the missionaries, or his assistant, went through the baptismal register with a blue pencil marking the adult converts whom he knew had returned to Hinduism since 1883. There is no indication as to what happened to about one-third of the 2,894 adult (mainly depressed-class) converts baptized during that period. Of the remaining 1,968 converts a few had died, some had moved elsewhere, some remained faithful members of the congregation, and some had become apostates. Information on the percentage of apostates among those whose post-baptismal history was indicated is set out in Table 5.

Three hundred and nineteen or 16 per cent of those whose future after baptism was known had lapsed by 1907 — the proportion of those returning to Hinduism varying considerably from year to year. Thus 3 per cent of those adult converts baptized in 1885 (whose future was known) had lapsed by 1907, while 39 per cent of those baptized in 1886 and 18 per cent of those baptized in 1896 had returned to Hinduism by 1907. While, on the other hand, there is always the possibility that an even greater number of adherents, for example, more of those baptized in the 1890s lapsed *after* 1907, it is equally possible that some of those recorded as lapsed in 1907 rejoined the mission at a later date.

If on reflection the reason for conversion to Christianity, or for converts remaining Christian, appear to be more varied and complex than they may at first appear, the same complexity is also true of apostasy where a variety of factors appear to have been in operation. As we have already noted, some converts who decided to return to Hinduism had discovered, especially under persecution, that Christianity did not fulfil their early expectations but, on the contrary, involved them in considerable troubles and deprivation.[54] Some converts returned to Hinduism in order to marry a suitable partner[55] and some of them lapsed because of lack of pastoral care. While this deficiency in care and guidance was especially apparent in Catholic missions which had too few priests and too many congregations from the very beginning of the nineteenth century,[56] there is also evidence of neglect in Protestant missions — coolies, for example, sometimes lapsing into Hinduism apparently through neglect and lack of encouragement while in temporary employment overseas.[57]

Added to neglect, disappointment, the desire to marry Hindus, and other factors, was the growing pressure on Christians from neighbours and relatives to return to Hinduism. These social factors, including family and village ties, which facilitated conversion could also facilitate apostasy. In some cases, all the members of a joint or nuclear family appear to have lapsed together[58] while, in other cases of apostasy, families were again divided.[59]

Finally, what of those converts who remained more or less permanently in the Christian fold? What were some of the more obvious and general effects of the depressed-class movements on the Christian community, or on the way it was perceived?

In the first place, the churches in Tanjore and Trichinopoly districts became even more closely identified with the pariah community. The movement reinforced the feeling among both brahmans and high-caste non-brahmans that to become a Christian was to become polluted and to associate with those at the bottom of the social scale.[60] Secondly, because of the sudden increase in the number of converts and the solidarity of the groups involved, it became increasingly difficult for missionaries and pastors to eliminate pre-Christian customs and practices carried over into the churches. The Christian community as a whole became more rural and more strongly influenced by depressed-class culture than in previous generations. Lastly, the missionaries were faced with a higher proportion of psychologically and economically dependent people. Because of their poverty and position at the bottom of the social ladder most depressed-class peoples could only ever hope for a better landlord or patron and, in becoming Christian, transferred part of their dependence on landlords to some degree of dependence on the mission.[61] The influx of large numbers of these people, therefore, made it even less likely that the churches would be able to develop into self-sufficient and independent-minded communities either willing or able to challenge western missionary domination. The mission was, among other things, a means of survival and, so long as much the same economic and social conditions prevailed, depressed-class converts were not only likely to remain dependent but were also likely to continue to regard Christianity as the source of material as well as spiritual benefits.

NOTES

1 *Census of India*, 1871, Madras, Vol. II, pp. 31 – 5; *Census of India*, 1901, Vol. XV, Madras, Part I, p. 46.
2 See Appendix 7.
3 For some discussion of this concept see supra Ch. 7.
4 See *Census of India*, 1871, Madras, Vol. II, pp. 292, 297 and *Census of India*, 1901, Vol. XVB, Madras, Part III, p. 31.
5 M.S.A., Rao, *Social Movements and Social Transformation*, Madras 1979, p. 20.
6 *Census of India*, 1871, Madras, Vol. II. pp. 90 – 91.
7 Hemingway, *Tanjore*, p. 161.
8 Hemingway, *Trichinopoly*, pp. 73 – 4. For a more recent account of the early Madura mission, including Christianity in Tanjore and Trichinopoly districts, see R. Sathianathaier, op. cit.
9 *Census of India*, 1871, Madras, Vol. II, pp. 87 – 94. See also Appendix 9.
10 See especially baptismal registers: Anglican, St Peters, Tanjore, 1875 – 1898, Kartiruppu (Nangur) 1865 – 1900; Lutheran, Tranquebar, 1878 –

1900, and Karaikkal, 1896 – 1900 (located at Tranquebar), Manikrammam, 1888 – 1900, Holy Comforter Church, Tanjore, 1863 – 1868, 1898 – 1900, Holy Emmanuel Church Mayavaram.

11 Holy Comforter Church, Tanjore, 1863 – 1882; Zion Church, Trichinopoly 1892 – 1900. See also Christ Church Fort, Trichinopoly (Anglican) baptismal register (adults) 1855 – 1897, and Catholic registers such as those at St Mary's Trichinopoly, 1841 – 1859, and in the Sacred Heart Cathedral archives, congregation under Rome, 1850 – 1893 and congregation under Goa 1874 – 1893.

12 Typical of the tendency, especially common among converts attempting to escape the unpleasant consequences of baptism at home by having the ceremony performed in some other more distant locality, was the baptism, in Zion Church Trichinopoly, of a single male naidu from Arkonam, North Arcot district, and members of a patnulkaran (silk weaving) family from Salem (Zion Church baptismal register, no. 167, 1/1/1898 and nos. 188-192, 20/11/1898).

13 Baptismal register, Holy Emmanuel Church, Mayavaram, nos. 4781 – 3, 27/6/1883; 4856, 11/5/1884 and 5376 – 7.

14 Ibid., 4861, 11/6/1884, 5102, 11/5/1885; baptismal register, Karaikkal no. 49, 1899.

15 Baptismal register, Mayavaram, Nos. 4866, 11/6/1884 and 4892, 20/7/1884.

16 For a discussion of present-day internal structure and family among pariahs in a village in Tamilnadu see M. Moffatt, *The Untouchable Community in South India: Structure and Consensus*, New Jersey, 1979, ch. V.

17 Manikramman baptismal register, Nos. 1097 – 1100, 1121 – 2, 1134 – 7; 1117 – 1120, 1123 – 5, 1131 – 2.

18 Ibid., Nos. 1087 – 90, 1111 – 1116.

19 See, for example, baptismal register, Karaikkal, 1892 – 1900.

20 See nos. 548 – 604.

21 Baker and Washbrook, op. cit., pp. 20 – 65.

22 Hemingway, *Tanjore*, pp. 147 – 149; *E.L.M.*, A.R. 1885, p. 324, 1893, p. 386; *A.P.F.*, Vol. XXXVIII, pp. 318 – 9; *M.D.Q.R.*, No. LXVIII, January 1902; *W.M.N.*, 1878.

23 D. Forrester, 'The Depressed Classes and Conversion to Christianity, 1860 – 1960' in G. A. Oddie (ed.), *Religion in South Asia*, pp. 41 – 2.

24 See especially R. Horton, 'African Conversion', *Africa*, Vol. 41, no. 2 1971, and R. M. Eaton, 'Conversion to Christianity among the Nagas, 1876 – 1971,' *I.E.S.H.R.*, Vol. XXI, No. 1, January to March 1984.

25 *Inquiries made by the Bishop of Madras, regarding the removal of caste prejudices and practices, in the Native Church of South India together with the Replies of the missionaries and native clergy sent thereto*, Madras, 1868, pp. 36 – 8.

26 *H.F.*, third series, Vol. VIII, January – December 1897, pp. 360 – 73, 415 – 22.

27 *M.D.Q.R.*, No. 13, October – December 1886, p. 41; *H.F.*, third series, Vol. VIII, October 1897, p. 420.

28 *Statistical Tables of Protestant Missions in India, Burma and Ceylon*, 1881; *H.F.*, January 1864, p. 57. In 1888 – 1889, in addition to Christians and Muslims of harijan origin, there appear to have been nearly 687 'Hindu' pariahs in Tanjore district and 352 in Trichinopoly enrolled in Government primary schools. *(Report on Public Instruction in the Madras Presidency, 1888 – 1889*, Appendix B, pp. XXXVI – XXXVII).
29 *H.F.*, third series, Vol. VIII, October 1897, p. 420.
30 *Hindu*, 7/8/1891.
31 There was often a difference between what missionaries thought they were saying and the impression (or unspoken message) they actually conveyed. See especially M. Hollis, *Paternalism and the Church, The Study of South Indian Church History*, London, 1962.
32 *H.F.*, third series, Vol. III, October 1897, pp. 368 – 70.
33 Memoir sur la Mission du Maduré, Maduré, 1001 – XVI, 10. See also *E.L.M.*, 1887, p. 22.
34 *A.P.F.*, Vol. XXV, 1864, pp. 296, 307; Vol. XXI, 1870, pp. 65, 70; *M.D.Q.R.*, No. XXXII, July – September 1892, p. 27; No. XXXVII, October – December 1893, p. 167.
35 *M.D.Q.R.*, No. LXVIII, January 1902, p. 84. In 1897 out of 1,475 Lutherans in the Mayavaram mission more than ten per cent were widows. (*E.L.M.*. 1897, p. 423).
36 *E.L.M.*, 1891, p. 89.
37 *H.F.*, third series, Vol. VIII, November, 1897, pp. 416 – 7; *A.P.F.*, Vol. XXVII, 1866, p. 91; *M.D.Q.R.*. No. XXIV, April – June 1890, pp. 181 – 2; No. XXXVII, October – December 1893, p. 165
38 *M.D.Q.R.*, No. XXXVII, October – December 1893, p. 164. See also *E.L.M.*, 1893, p. 386.
39 *E.L.M.*, 1891, p. 87.
40 Ibid., 1892, p. 151.
41 Ibid., 1897, p. 424. See also *E.L.M.*, 1860, p. 281.
42 For an example of the way in which one Lutheran missionary attempted to bring pressure to bear by painting heaven and hell in the most vivid colours see *E.L.M.*, 1888, pp. 228 – 229.
43 *E.L.M.* 1865, p. 23; *M.D.Q.R.*, No. XXXVII, October – December, 1893, p. 167.
44 *E.L.M.*, 1886, pp. 23 – 4; *H.F.*, third series, Vol. VIII, Jan. – Dec. 1897, pp. 364 – 5; *M.D.Q.R.*, No. XII, July – September, 1886, pp. 58 – 59.
45 *H.F.*, third series, Vol. VIII, October 1897, pp. 364 – 365, November 1897, p. 419; *E.L.M.*, 1888, p. 233; *M.D.Q.R.*, No. XII, July – September 1886, pp. 57 – 58; No. XXXVII, October – December 1893, p. 165, No. LV, October – December 1898, p. 158.
46 *E.L.M.*, 1873, p. 358.
47 *H.F.*, third series, Vol. VIII, October 1897, pp. 364 – 366; *E.L.M.*, 1888, p. 229 – 232, 321 – 322; *M.D.Q.R.*, No. XII, July – Sept 1886, pp. 57 – 59, No. XXIV, April – June 1890, p. 182, No. XXXVII, October – December 1893, pp. 165, 167, No. LV, October – December 1898, p. 158.
48 *H.F.*, third series, Vol. VIII, November 1897, p. 419.

THE DEPRESSED CLASSES AND CHRISTIANITY 169

49 For an account of the hardships endured by one of these converts, a middle-aged man at Nangur, who suffered considerable persecution from his Hindu neighbours and was ultimately responsible for the accession of a large number of his fellow villagers to Christianity, see *S.P.G. Annual Report*, 1865, p. 130. See also *E.L.M.*, 1888, pp. 229 – 232, 321 – 322; *M.D.C.R.*, 1868, p. 68.
50 Admission register, Holy Emmanuel Church, Mayavaram, 1883 – 1900, no. 14, 21/9/1888.
51 Infra, Ch. 9.
52 *M.F.*, September 1885, pp. 261 – 264; See also comments in the admission registers referred to above.
53 *M.D.Q.R.*, No. LXVIII, January 1902, p. 34. See also No. XIII, October – December 1886, p. 37.
54 *E.L.M.*, 1860, p. 281; 1891, p. 87; 1892, p. 151; 1897, p. 424.
55 *M.F.*, 1 September 1885, pp. 363 – 364. Tranquebar admissions register no. 16, 1/5/1885, and no. 54, 1/7/1900; Manikrammam admissions register no. 16, 25/12/1894.
56 Even as late as 35 years after the Jesuits resumed work in the Madurai mission Fr. Barbier, who was stationed at Trichinopoly, complained that some Catholic villages remained three, five or even ten years without seeing a priest (J.Ar., Maduré, 1004 – II 33). See also P. J. Bertrand (ed.) *Lettres Edifiantes et Curieuses de la Nouvelle Mission de Madura*, Vol. II, p. 114 and *H.F.*, Vol. 1, November 1861, p. 21.
57 *S.P.G. Annual Report*, 1858, (Nangoor).
58 See especially baptismal register, Holy Emmanuel church, Mayavaram, nos. 5614 – 5681 from the village of Voorkudi.
59 Ibid., nos. 5459, 5528, 6866 and 7475.
60 *M.D.Q.R.*, No. LXVIII, January 1902, p. 31; L. Lacombe, *A Great Indian Convert*, p. 21.
61 See especially *E.L.M.*, 1892, pp. 152 – 153.

9

THE CHRISTIAN COMMUNITY IN A HINDU SETTING: CONTINUITIES AND CHANGE

In the two previous chapters brahman and depressed-class conversion to Christianity were explored. The purpose of this chapter is to examine more closely the results of these and other conversion movements into Christianity — to see how far during the period 1850 – 1900 Christians (some of whose forebears were converted in the sixteenth century) continued to follow Hindu tradition and social customs, or were developing a social system and style of life recognizably different from Hindus. Had the acceptance of Christianity and Christian teaching produced by this time something distinctive and new, or had Christianity itself become 'Hinduized' to the extent that there appeared to be little difference between its adherents and Hindus?

Before we can attempt to answer these and other questions it is necessary to say something more about the number, distribution, denominational affiliation and caste of Christians in Tanjore and Trichinopoly districts during this period.

According to the earliest official estimates of the population of Tanjore and Trichinopoly districts, in 1856 – 7 there were 85,581 Christians, 3.5 per cent of a total population of 2,466,865. Subsequent quinquennial estimates and the census reports for 1871 to 1901 suggest a very definite though somewhat unsteady rise in their number and proportion in the population.[1] In 1901 the combined number of Christians in both districts was 163,639, about 4.5 per cent of the total population.

Their distribution in the population was, however, uneven. Though their numbers were smaller, they were better represented in Trichinopoly than in Tanjore district. They were also better represented in the population of some taluks than in others.[2] And finally, there was a higher proportion of Christians in the urban than in the rural population — this reflecting partly the effect of a heavier concentration of missionary resources and institutions in towns such as Trichinopoly, Tanjore, Kumbakonam and Negapatam.

Outside the towns the number and proportion of Christians scattered in hundreds of different village communities also varied — some Christian families living in greater isolation and probably being put

Table 6. *Religious Communities: Percentages in the Total Population*[3]

		Trichinopoly			Tanjore		
Year	Area	Hindus	Muslims	Christians	Hindus	Muslims	Christians
1881	Rural	93.50	1.96	4.57	91.73	4.80	3.46
	Urban	80.25	10.30	9.36	86.86	8.70	5.25
1901	Rural	92.95	2.26	4.80	91.87	4.50	3.62
	Urban	81.30	9.15	9.53	83.90	10.72	5.23

under greater Hindu pressure to conform than others. In the 1880s, for example, one report shows that there were about 4,000 Catholics in an area around Vallum in Tanjore district living in 56 villages (the average number in each settlement being 71) while the average number in villages in the area around Pattukkottai was well under half that figure.[4]

According to the census of 1871 Catholics outnumbered Protestants by 18 to 1 in Trichinopoly and by 6 to 1 in Tanjore — the proportion of Catholics in the Christian population in the former district (94 per cent) being higher than in any other district of the Madras Presidency.[5] As we have seen, the Protestants included Lutherans (the earliest Protestants in the South), Anglicans affiliated with the S.P.G., and Methodists. If these latter groups were divided among themselves so too were the Catholics who were sharply divided into two rival factions — the 'Goanese' priests and congregations who supported the Padroado (the right of the Archbishop of Goa and, through him, of the Crown of Portugal to make ecclesiastical appointments); and their opponents, the Jesuits and their congregations who recognized the authority of the Vicar Apostolic appointed by Rome and who regarded 'Goanese' priests as 'schismatics'. Although, after their return to the region in 1837, the Jesuits succeeded in winning over most of the Catholic congregations[6] the schism remained — impeding what one Jesuit priest described as 'almost all our projects of amelioration' and arresting 'even the good and regular administration of a large number of important villages'.[7]

Information on the caste of Christians, including Catholics and Protestants, obtained from baptismal and marriage registers, as well as from the census of 1871, is set out in Appendix 9.

As the conversion of brahmans to Christianity was extremely rare, it was the vellalas who, in most places, constituted the highest and most respected caste among Christians and it was these people who sometimes dominated church affairs. According to the census report for

1871, which used this term fairly loosely (to include agamudaiyans, kavores, kammas, reddies and other landed groups), vellalas were well represented in the Christian community, although in a slightly lower proportion than among Hindus. In Tanjore 19 per cent of Hindus and 11 per cent of Christians and in Trichinopoly 17.5 per cent of Hindus and 11.6 per cent of Christians were classified as vellalas. The kammalas (including blacksmiths, carpenters and other artisan groups), were also well represented among Christians; but apart from these two castes (the vellalas and kammalas) there were few other high-caste groups conspicuous among Christians. Not only were brahmans generally missing, but the proportion of high status, or even middle status, non-brahmans in the Christian community throughout this period was far lower than among Hindus. The lower castes and especially the untouchables were much more numerically dominant. Pariahs, pallans, chakkiliyans, valluvans and others described in the 1871 census as 'outcaste tribes' taken together constituted 49 per cent of the Christian population in Tanjore and 38 per cent in Trichinopoly — just over three times their percentage among Hindus in both districts.

Caste also varied to some extent according to denominational background.[8] The report of 1871 shows that while the higher castes were slightly more predominant among Protestants than among Catholics in Tanjore, the superior status of Protestants was even more apparent in Trichinopoly. There 31 per cent of Protestants were returned as vellalas as against 11 per cent of the Catholic community, while the latter also included twice the proportion of pariahs compared with the Protestant group.

How far then did these Christians continue to follow Hindu tradition and social customs? What was their attitude to caste and how far did they continue to observe caste taboos and regulations?

The first point of note is that Catholic and Lutheran missionaries and pastors, who between them exercised control over about 95 per cent of Christians in the area, did very little to try to suppress caste practices in their respective communities.

The Jesuits, who re-entered the mission field in 1837, were inclined to accept and even uphold caste custom provided it did not contradict 'the ordinances of the Church'. At least some of them regarded caste among Christians as a purely civil distinction much the same as class differences in Britain or Europe.[9] Furthermore, as the successors of Robert de Nobili and others in the Madura Mission, they inherited a well-established policy of toleration of caste and other customs. Although some were not uncritical of the 'ridiculous and often unreasonable extreme' to which caste practices were carried, it was also felt that to challenge openly the system would invite disaster. It would not only prove ineffective, but might even 'excite revolution' and damage the long-term interests of the Catholic religion. Caste distinctions therefore were not only condoned in most instances but continued to flourish in the Catholic church.

Writing to his brother in the 1840s, Fr. Gury explained something of the way in which caste feeling continued to operate among Christians affecting even the way in which he himself was obliged to work.[10] As he was pastor of a caste village, the caste people attempted to prevent him from visiting sick pariahs in a nearby hamlet for fear that he too would become polluted. Eventually a compromise was reached 'that I might go into the church, but that no pariah should put his foot in while I was there; and that I should not stop, either to eat or drink in that place.' The next day Fr. Gury was permitted to administer the sacraments, including baptism and mass, in the same pariah hamlet, but at the door of the church, 'the Christians being outside, while I remained within.'

It was, no doubt, complications such as these which led to the appointment in Kumbakonam and elsewhere of catechists called *pandarams* who were set aside especially for work among pariahs.[11] In Tanjore different castes worshipped or held their feast days in the same church but at different times[12] and, in a number of villages throughout the region, high and low-caste groups had their own special chapels.[13] In at least some villages, pallars and pariahs (bitter rivals for generations) refused to worship together[14] and at Negapatam caste and outcaste Catholics were buried in separate plots.[15]

Perhaps the most fundamental of all caste restrictions was the prohibition on intercaste marriages, and here it is clear that the vast majority of Catholics, like Hindus, continued to marry within their own caste group.

An analysis of nearly seven thousand Catholic marriages in the Tanjore and Trichinopoly districts during the period 1853 – 1900 produced the results shown in Table 7.

As will be seen from the table the proportion of intercaste marriages varied somewhat throughout the region being highest in this survey in Trichinopoly where there were Catholic orphanges as well as a cantonment area including many Eurasian troops. Those intercaste marriages which did take place were frequently between people belonging to castes very similar or almost identical in status to their own — a type of intercaste marriage which was certainly not unknown among Hindus during the same period.[16] According to the registers there were at least 27 vellalas (mostly men) who took partners from another caste. Of these partners 13 were mudaliars (a title sometimes adopted by the vellalas themselves), 5 were kallas, 2 were naidus, 2 were chetties and 1 was agamudaiyan.

Table 7. Catholics: Intercaste Marriages

Place	Dates	No. of Entries	Intercaste Marriages	Percentage
Trinchinopoly (St. Mary's)	1853 – 1900	3,332	104	3.12
Tanjore (a)B.V. de Dores (Padroado)	1877 – 1888	1,635	9	0.55
(b)Tanjore District (Jesuit)	1863 – 1893	1,245	6	0.48
Kumbakonam	1882 – 1900	595	13	2.18
Total		6,807	132	1.94

An even higher proportion of intercaste marriages took place lower down the social scale. In fact, half the total number of intercaste marriages involved untouchable castes (53 pariahs and 13 valangais) and of these at least 30 married East Indians (Eurasians). The other untouchables married a wide variety of partners belonging mostly to the lower castes. Where a marked difference in status occurred in these or in other cases the individuals concerned often came from situations in which the pressure to conform to Hindu practice was minimal. Such persons included orphans (from the Catholic orphanage in Trichinopoly) and individuals or couples who came from distant places such as Ceylon, Madras city or Bangalore.

The Lutheran missionaries claimed (not without some justification) that they were as strongly opposed to caste within the Christian church as were other Protestant missionaries. However, in actual practice they adopted much the same conciliatory approach as Catholics. Like Catholics they preferred to avoid forcing the issue and, instead, supported the idea of gradually weakening caste feeling through education and by raising the level of the lower castes.[17]

It was therefore primarily the Anglicans and Methodists who confronted their congregations with the issue and tried to eradicate the practice by more uncompromising methods.[18] The fact that they were very largely unsuccessful is a clear indication of the strength and importance of caste practice even in congregations where there was considerable stress on the equality of all believers.

As a result of complaints from several of his clergy in 1824, Bishop Heber instituted inquiries into the effects of caste on Anglican congregations throughout the Madras Presidency. In their reply to the

Bishop's letter,[19] the Tanjore missionaries made it quite clear that their congregations (inherited indirectly from the Lutherans)[20] continued to keep their caste customs. It was revealed that high-caste Christians sat on the right and low-caste on the left of the churches, that no separate chalice was used during holy communion but that high and low castes went up to the altar at separate times. It was also stated that high and low-caste Christians mixed and sat together in schools, but that the high castes 'do not intermarry nor eat with those of the low caste'.

Following the premature death of Bishop Heber, it was left to Bishop Wilson and others to deal with the problem as best they could. In 1833 Wilson, influenced especially by a conviction that the retention of caste encouraged apostacy, issued his famous circular letter to Anglican missionaries throughout his diocese in which he declared that 'the distinction of castes . . . must be abandoned decidedly, immediately, finally.'[21] Although his letter, which was read in all the churches, did not insist on the renunciation of caste among adult Christians already admitted to Holy Communion, it did stipulate that 'all overt acts which spring from Caste', including separate seating for high and low castes and the custom of different castes approaching the altar at different times, were to cease. The letter also stated that all those preparing for baptism should be advised that they 'must' renounce caste and that children of native Christians would not be admitted to Holy Communion without first renouncing caste.

These measures not only led to the temporary or permanent secession of sudras (mostly vellalas) from Anglican congregations in Tanjore and Trichinopoly districts, but also appear to have had the immediate effect of intensifying caste feeling. Describing the situation in 1834 the Rev. E. Crisp (L.M.S. Kumbakonam) declared that the Bishop's efforts had been 'violently' withstood by the sudra Christians who 'both at Tanjore and Vepery . . . [Madras city] . . . have withdrawn in a body from the usual place of worship, & formed themselves into a distinct congregation'. Not only had 'Native Ministers', catechists and schoolmasters resigned but the people had become 'more tenacious of their observances, and more strong in their aversions, than ever.'[22]

In 1834, 1,500 Christians, chiefly sudras, left Anglican congregations in the Tanjore circle.[23] Although about 785 rejoined two years later, it is by no means clear that the rest followed suit.[24] Defections over the caste issue continued to occur either to the Lutherans or Catholics or both in 1850 and 1851[25] and, in a report in 1860, it was frankly acknowledged that 'all the missions of the Tanjore circle' were suffering 'more or less diminution' in consequence of the measures taken to suppress caste practices.[26] The effect of these measures is also reflected in Protestant statistical tables[27] which not only show a decrease in the number of Anglicans in Tanjore district, but a sharp rise in the number and proportion of Lutherans — phenomena which may be explained in part as the result of the more conciliatory Lutheran attitude towards the caste issue (see Table 8).

Table 8. Protestant Christians: Tanjore District

Year	Lutherans	Anglicans	Methodists	L.M.S.	Total
1851	2,459 (33%)	4,740 (64%)	67	207	7,471
1881	6,590 (30%)	2,883 (30%)	317	–	9,790

Many if not all of those high-caste Anglicans who eventually returned to the fold were won back through compromise, the pastor of the church in Tanjore, for example, promising that the missionaries 'would not officially interfere with their domestic habits and customs, but only for the present insist upon their coming and receiving the Lord's Supper promiscuously, without distinction of caste.'[28]

Replies to inquiries 'regarding the repression of caste in the Diocese of Madras' received in 1867 are further evidence that, despite all their efforts, the Anglican attempt to suppress the practice in Tanjore and Trichinopoly districts had little effect in modifying the more fundamental caste observances.[29] Reports from a number of centres in the Tanjore district (viz. Tanjore, Negapatam, Canandagudy, Vediarpuram, Kumbakonam and Nangur) indicate that the former practice whereby high and low castes approached the altar and took communion separately had been abandoned and that, in some cases, catechists of pariah origin were permitted to enter the homes of caste people and even read the funeral service over the remains of a caste man.[30]

But beyond these few concessions Anglican Christians for all intents and purposes still appear to have adhered to the caste system in much the same way as Hindus. The statement by the Rev. J. Guest of Tanjore that he had never adopted 'any measure to further the abandonment of caste distinctions in eating and drinking, and in general social intercourse amongst any *communicants*' was echoed in replies from Tranquebar, Kumbakonam and Vediapuram in Tanjore District and from Erungalore in Trichinopoly.[31]

Referring to social interaction between ordinary Christians in and around Kumbakonam, the Rev. I. Ignatius remarked that all the usual taboos regarding commensality still applied — Christian pariahs, pallars and shoemakers, as well as high and low castes, refraining from eating together and refusing to accept food from a caste lower than their own. And this, according to the same informant, was a custom 'still in force with Christians of our own day in every hut and palace.'[32] Furthermore, like Hindus, caste Christians continued to live in villages separately from those of untouchable origin while Christian pariahs and pallars themselves continued to live in hamlets or streets separate from each other.[33]

But while reports such as these suggest that most Protestant Christians, when not actually attending Church, continued to *practise* caste customs there can be little doubt that some obvious and some more subtle changes in regard to caste were in fact taking place.

As we saw, some high-caste individuals, including Protestants of brahman origin, renounced caste completely, ate with low-caste Christians and even married women of a different caste. The number of Christians who took this step during this period was never great; but their break with custom was complete enough to provoke the hostility of friends and family alike and to lead to their expulsion from Hindu society.[34]

Secondly, some Protestant Christians (and possibly Catholics as well) gave up intermarrying with Hindus of a similar caste and began to form their own distinctive caste group. Referring to Anglicans and writing from Trichinopoly in 1891 the Rev. J. L. Wyatt complained that

Our great obstacle in the way of conversions from the heathen lies in the fact that our Christians are isolated from the heathen members of their caste. Most of our Christians belong to the second or third generation of Christians; they claim no relationship with other members of their caste, they seek no connection with them . . . They form a caste of their own; and very frequently they intermarry with members of the Roman Church or the Lutheran.[35]

Thirdly, the stress in this chapter is on observable similarities and differences between Hindus and Christians and this means we are not attempting to explore at any great length, changes in perspective or understanding which were not reflected outwardly or visibly in Christian behaviour. It is, however, always possible to do the same thing for different reasons — in this case, for Christians like Hindus to continue *practising* caste, but for different reasons. The Lutheran missionaries had in fact argued along these lines — that 'the holding of Caste in the Native Churches is essentially different from the holding of Caste among the heathen.'[36] These views reflected the arguments of high-caste Christians themselves including the dissidents who seceded from Anglican churches in Tanjore and Trichinopoly. They argued that caste was originally a civil institution but that the brahmans gave it religious sanction and meaning.[37] In becoming Christian, converts like themselves rejected this 'brahmanized' religious interpretation and reverted to caste as a purely civil or secular institution. Though vellalas and other Christians might continue to practise caste (so the argument ran) their understanding of caste had changed and could no longer be described as 'heathenish' or Hindu. 'Those native Christians who have not yet overcome their caste prejudices,' stressed the Lutheran missionaries, '. . . and who are anxious to maintain their original social precedence, do so not from a dread of internal or external defilement, but for reasons of cleanliness or pride.'[38]

Even though many of the missionaries were not prepared to go as far as their Anglican colleagues in opposing caste among Christians, they were hoping at the very least for a decline in caste feeling. They were also critical of the custom of early marriage and were anxious to promote the remarriage of Christian widows. What then were the results of these further attempts to modify Hindu practice?

Table 9. *Percentage of Widows within Different Age Groups in the Hindu and Christian Population*[39]

Age	TANJORE			
	Hindus 1881	Hindus 1901	Christians 1881	Christians 1901
0–9	0.15	0.02	0.03	0.01
10–14	0.43	0.32	0.12	0.15
15–19	2.15	2.63	1.23	1.33
20–39	15.04	15.70	12.52	13.07
40–59	57.07	56.63	53.51	52.90
60+	91.02	90.39	88.14	87.00

Age	TRICHINOPOLY			
	Hindus 1881	Hindus 1901	Christians 1881	Christians 1901
0–9	0.06	0.02	0.03	0.02
10–14	0.48	0.24	0.11	0.12
15–19	2.34	1.83	1.95	1.06
20–39	16.84	14.07	13.24	11.90
40–59	56.69	53.20	53.24	48.62
60+	88.89	87.47	87.62	83.22

Census returns show that the proportion of widows among Christians was slightly lower than among Hindus, as Table 9 indicates. Census returns also suggest that the proportion of males to females (in the 60+ category and sometimes in the 40+ category as well) was slightly higher among Christians than among Hindus. Christian men were living a little longer than Hindu men and it is quite possible that the smaller proportion of widows in the Christian community was at least in part due to the fact that a smaller proportion of women was becoming widows in the first place.

But a second and perhaps equally important explanation may lie in the higher rate of widow remarriage among Christian women.

If this was in fact the case, how far was this due to missionary influence and teaching and how far to other factors in the Christian community? Is there any evidence that high-caste Christian women drawn from castes traditionally opposed to widow remarriage were beginning to defy the system, or were these marriages confined to the lower castes who had always accepted the remarriage of widows?

Certainly a few high-caste Christian widows were bold enough to break with tradition and remarry. One such widow was remarried in Negapatam in 1835 (the first such instance recorded in the Anglican mission in that part of the country)[40] and about ten years later two Catholic vellalas were remarried in Trichinopoly.[41] Inquiries in the Anglican mission in 1867 also elicited the fact that one or two widows in Tanjore and Vediarpuram and a few more in Kumbakonam and Nangur had also remarried in defiance of custom.[42]

Table 10. *Christian Marriages and Widow Remarriages; Tanjore District, 1866 – 1900*

Place		Total No. of all marriages	Widow remarriages	Percentage	Widows married to widowers	Widows married to bachelors
Anglicans						
Tanjore	1866 – 1900	216	3	1.4	1	2
Catholics						
Tanjore	1877 – 1888	1,635	82	5.0	65	17
Tanjore	1889 – 1898	525	55	10.5	44	11
Kumbakonam	1882 – 1900	595	19	3.19	16	3
	Total	2,971	159	5.35	126	33

But these cases were extremely rare — rare enough in the case of Catholics to cause a sensation and fierce and prolonged opposition[43] and rare enough in most other cases to be recorded and remembered long afterwards. Indeed, an analysis of marriage registers in Tanjore district confirms the impression that nearly all the widows who were remarried in the Christian community continued to be drawn from those castes which had always practised the custom. One hundred and fifty nine or 5.35 per cent of the 2,971 marriages noted in three different churches during the period 1866 – 1900 involved the remarriage of widows. (See Table 10).

Information on the caste of these widows was available in 150 cases. In all of them the widows involved were low or (more frequently) outcaste women drawn from groups the majority of which already practised widow remarriage (see Table 11).

Table 11. Number of Christians in Each Caste who Remarried[44]

pariahs*	83	chakkiliyans*	1
valangais*	11	shanans	11
pallans*	39	udaiyans	1
kallans*	1	totties	1
East Indians (Eurasians)*	1	vannas*	1

* = those castes which permitted remarriage

In remarrying, at least 91 per cent of these widows were following traditional caste custom and even in the case of the shanans (8 per cent) it is by no means certain that the Hindu members of the caste always discouraged the practice.[45]

If therefore there was a higher rate of widow remarriage among Christians this would seem to be not so much because widows were breaking with Hindu tradition but more because of the peculiar social composition of the Christian community which, as we have seen, included a very high proportion of low and outcaste people who, unlike high-caste Hindus, tended to accept and practise widow remarriage.

The census returns also show some difference in the age at which Hindu and Christian girls were married. The percentage of Hindu and Christian females married within the age groups 0 – 9 and 10 – 14 were as shown in Table 12.

The first point to note is that infant marriage was more prevalent in both communities in Tanjore where brahmans were more dominant and influential than in Trichinopoly. Secondly, some Christian girls were

Table 12. *Percentage of Married Females*[46]

Year	Age	Tanjore		Trichinopoly	
		Hindus	Christians	Hindus	Christians
1881	0 – 9	1.8	0.6	1.37	0.38
	10 – 14	21.32	11.29	16.45	10.34
1901	0 – 9	0.64	0.16	0.69	0.09
	10 – 14	14.34	6.43	14.13	7.00

married by the age of ten and a very much higher proportion between the ages of 10 – 14. Even so, early marriage was much more common among Hindus. Indeed, the chances of a Hindu girl in either category being married was *at least* one and a half or two times greater than it was among Christians of the same sex.

The reasons for the lower incidence of early marriage among Christian females lay once again partly in the different social structure of their community. A higher proportion of Christians were drawn from those sections of the community (untouchable and lower-caste groups) where early marriage was less commonly practised than among brahmans and higher castes[47].

But growing opposition to the custom was apparently also having an effect. While the practice was declining among Hindus, it was declining at an even faster rate among Christians who were, of course, exposed to missionary teaching and preaching on the 'evil' effects of early marriage.

Furthermore, an analysis of over four thousand entries in marriage registers in five churches over the period 1866 – 1900 suggests differences in practice between Anglicans and Catholics — one per cent of Anglican and 13 per cent of Catholic females marrying below the age of 14 (see Table 13).

The lower incidence of early marriage among Anglicans may also be due to the fact that Anglican missionaries and pastors were able to provide more effective teaching, pastoral care and supervision than Catholic clergy who frequently complained of lack of staff and resources in their attempts to look after a scattered and very much larger Catholic population.[48]

Finally, how far did the Hindu and Christian communities differ in literacy and education?

In spite of the fact that the Christian community included a high proportion of castes traditionally deprived of educational opportunities, literacy and educational levels among Christians in Tanjore and

Table 13. Age of Marriage: Christian Girls

Place	Date	Total number of entries	12	12½	13	13½	14
Anglicans							
Tanjore	1866 – 1900	216	1		2		22
Vediarpuram	1866 – 1900	100					8
Catholics							
Trichinopoly	1874 – 1881	989	30	1	159		186
	1893 – 1900	683	5		73		147
Tanjore	1877 – 1888	1,635	12	12	150		275
Kumbakonam	1882 – 1900	595	8	3	58	1	118
	Totals	4,218	56	4	442	1	756

Table 14. Percentage of 'Educated' in each Community[49]

Year		Tanjore Hindus	Tanjore Christians	Trichinopoly Hindus	Trichinopoly Christians
1871	Those who could 'read and write'	8.8	7.7	5.9	5.5
1881*	'Educated or under Instruction'	11.2	11.2	8.1	10.4
1891*	'Learning and Literate'	11.8	12.8	7.9	12.1
1901	'Literate'	10.0	11.5	6.2	10.1

* Excluding the 'not stated' category

Trichinopoly began to match and finally outstripped literacy and educational levels among Hindus during the period 1871 – 1901, as Table 14 shows.

The census of 1901 also gives the number of literates in English, the percentage among Christians being inflated because of the inclusion of Europeans and Eurasians. If, however, for the sake of analysis, we assume that all Europeans and Eurasians (1.2 per cent of the Christian population in Tanjore and 1.4 per cent in Trichinopoly) could be placed in that category and separate them out, the percentage of literates in English in the remaining Christian population was still higher than among Hindus, as seen in Table 15.

Table 15. *Approximate Percentage of Literates in English 1901*[50]

District	Hindus	Indian Christians
Tanjore	0.70	2.19
Trichinopoly	0.15	1.14

If one takes the region as a whole (the number of literates in Tanjore and Trichinopoly districts being taken together) then the results are as given in Table 16.

Table 16. *Number and Percentage of Literates From Each Community*

Community	Number	Percentage of total population	No. of persons Literate in English	Percentage of Total No. of literates in English
Hindus	3,359,167	91.05	21,024	78.94
Muslims	166,372	4.51	710	2.67
Indian Christians	161,484	4.38	2,744	10.30
Europeans and Eurasians	2,155	0.06	2,155	8.09
Total	3,698,178	100.00	26,633	100.00

Of those literate in English, 10 per cent were Indian Christians even though they were no more than 4.38 per cent of the population. If one was an Indian Christian in this region the chances of being literate in English were four times greater than if one was a Muslim. They were approximately three times greater than if one was a Hindu, even though the Christian community contained a far higher proportion of depressed-class people. Christianity therefore represented the very best route to literacy in English and this was also usually accompanied by a growing familiarity with Western middle-class values. Census returns do not give literacy in English by religion and caste in 1901. However, in view of the fact that, in 1871, 44 per cent of Christians in the region were drawn from the depressed classes, it is not unlikely that some of them were literate in English and that Christianity, by providing a greater opportunity for literacy in English, also provided some sort of social mobility for depressed-class people, not through the caste system, but into the ranks of the modern Western-educated community.

Table 17. Education by Sex and Community Percentages

Year		Sex	Tanjore		Trichinopoly	
			Hindus	Christians	Hindus	Christians
1881*	'Educated or	M	22.50	18.89	16.17	17.37
	under Instruction'	F	0.51	4.02	0.49	3.88
1891*	'Learning	M	23.80	20.61	15.93	19.81
	and Literate'	F	0.57	5.52	0.48	4.87
1901	'Literate'	M	20.16	18.11	12.22	15.71
		F	0.73	5.52	0.51	4.57

*Excluding the 'not stated' category

Table 17 showing education by sex and community reveals other important differences between Hindus and Christians — especially with respect to females.

The proportion of 'literates' or 'educated' Christian males was lower than among Hindu males in Tanjore, though higher in Trichinopoly. The proportion of 'literates' or 'educated' Christian females was, however, very much higher in both districts when compared with the percentage of Hindu females in the same category. In fact, the proportion of girls and women in the Christian community who were literate or sharing in the process of education was *at least* seven times higher than among Hindu females in Tanjore and eight times higher than among Hindu females in Trichinopoly.

During the second half of the nineteenth century Christians in the Kaveri delta were, in some ways, not much different from Hindus —

despite the fact that Christianity had been introduced into the area as early as the sixteenth century. Most Christians continued to practise their caste customs. Furthermore, the differences between the two communities, including the age at which females married and the rate of widow remarriage, can be explained partly on the grounds that the Christian community contained a higher proportion of low and outcaste members.

Nevertheless, as we have attempted to show, differences between Hindus and Christians were becoming increasingly apparent and most dramatically with respect to women. The practice of early marriage was declining at a faster rate among Christian than among Hindu females, some high-caste Christian widows were defying traditional bans on widow remarriage, and educational and literacy levels among Christian women far outstripped levels among Hindu women. Furthermore, the Catholic community as a whole (males as well as females) was beginning to stir after many years of internal dissention and neglect and to attract the attention especially of the more Westernized Hindus. The relocation of St. Joseph's College at Trichinopoly in 1883 was a crucial factor in this development reflecting a determination on the part of the Jesuits (to some extent responding to pressure from below) to catch up with Protestants by providing, for the first time in Southern India, an effective system of education in English at the college level. Writing from Trichinopoly in 1895, Fr. G. I. Sewell, who had been actively involved in these developments, remarked that

Pagan Magistrates and Judges who before despised Catholics as poverty stricken and ignorant know St. Joseph's College Trichinopoly as one of the leading educational establishments of the Presidency and are proud to acknowledge their obligations to it by kindness and civility to our Missionaries. They see too the long list of names of successful candidates who annually pass the public Examinations from our College and far from looking on Catholics with scorn occasionally seek their favour while Catholics are beginning to assert their claim to equal privileges in the social scale with their pagan neighbours.[51]

While it appears that the Christian community was beginning to develop a new image as well as characteristics of its own, one may well ask why changes (or at least outward and visible changes) among Christians, especially those associated with caste and marriage, had not been more apparent.

Part of the answer to this question may lie in circumstances connected especially with the Catholic Church which had the support of the great majority of Christians. Catholic missionaries and priests, including those who were most anxious to bring about these changes, were too few in number to influence greatly or effectively supervise the large number of Catholics scattered throughout the delta. And added to these problems were the effects of the Goanese 'schism' which continued up until the Rome – Lisbon concordat of 1886. Not only were the Jesuits and Goanese priests frequently preoccupied with each other, but because of the rivalry between them, as well as between Catholics and Protestants, discipline among converts was extremely difficult to maintain, missionaries having to act with extreme caution for fear of driving their flocks into the arms of opponents.

But the main reason for the lack of visible change probably lies in the attitude of the committed as well as nominal Indian Christians many of whom could see no good reason why they should change practices such as those connected with the caste system. As we have seen, their views found support and even encouragement among many of the missionaries — not the least of whom were the Jesuit fathers. Among high-caste Christians were many who not only feared ridicule, loss of status, difficulties in marrying their daughters and other problems if they gave up caste, but who could not see any serious religious or theological objections to the custom itself.[52] They argued that caste among Christians was a purely civil distinction comparable to class in Europe. They shared the view of early Christians who declared that they would 'avoid the things alone that Scripture hath forbidden' and they held that, far from being objectionable from a religious point of view, the retention of caste was in fact essential if they were to continue to exercise a Christian influence over their own kith and kin. The maintenance of caste, together with the preservation of *some* of their other social and cultural customs, was seen to be an important factor in the continued respectability and further expansion of Christianity in the delta.

NOTES

1 See Appendix 7.
2 Appendix 14.
3 These calculations are based on the population by religion of the principal towns, *Census of India*, 1881, Madras, Vol. III, pp. 274, 279; 1901, Madras, Part II, Vol. XV – A, p. 21.
4 *A.R.S.I.*, Maduré, 1005 – 111, 46.a. See also L. Besse, *La Mission du Maduré*, Trichinopoly 1914, pp. 79 – 86.
5 *Census of India*, 1871, Madras, Vol. II, pp. 31 – 5.
6 According to Government estimates in 1842, 9,383 Catholics adhered to Goanese priests and 18,943 to French (Jesuits) in Tanjore and between 3 –

THE CHRISTIAN COMMUNITY IN A HINDU SETTING

4,000 to Goanese priests and 19–27,000 to the Jesuits in Trichinopoly. (Onshow to Sec., 28/3/1842, *M.R.P.*, Ra. 303, Vol. 43, 4/4/1842; Bishop to Sec., 16/4/1842, *M.R.P.*, Ra. 303, Vol. 44, 21/4/1842.)
7 *A.R.S.I.*, Maduré, 1001 – VII, 5 (P. Louis Garnier, 1842).
8 See Appendix 9.
9 For Jesuit attitudes towards caste see especially *A.P.F.*, Vol. V, 1844, p. 189; Vol. XXV, 1864, pp. 294, 295; *L.N.*, Vol. XXIII, No, CXX, July 1895, p. 162.
10 *A.P.F.*, Vol. II, pp. 291–2.
11 A. Launay, *Histoire des Missions l'Inde*, Paris, 1898, vol. II, p. 380.
12 *A.P.F.*, Vol. XXXI, 1870, p. 66.
13 Besse, op. cit., *A.P.F.*, Vol. V, 1844, p. 191.
14 Besse, op. cit.
15 Shembaganur archives, *Memoranda Missions Negapatnam* (1839).
16 Hardgrave, op. cit., p. 168.
17 For Lutheran views on caste see especially K. Graul, *Explanations concerning the principles of the Leipzig Missionary Society with regard to the Caste Question*, Madras, 1851 and W. H. G. Herre, 'The Evangelical Lutheran Mission', *HF*, Vol. IX, October 1888, pp. 111–7.
18 For the attitude of British Protestant missionaries see G. A. Oddie 'Protestant Missions, Caste and Social Change', *I.E.S.H.R.*, Vol. VI, No. 3, September 1969, pp. 259–91 and D. B. Forrester, 'Indian Christians' Attitudes to Caste in the Nineteenth Century', *I.C.H.R.*, Vol. VIII, No. 2, December 1974, pp. 133–9.
19 Percival, op. cit., pp. 485–96.
20 Supra, Ch. 1.
21 Percival, op. cit., pp. 496–502.
22 *L.M.S.*, E. Crisp to Sec., 28/7/1834, S. I. Tamil, Box no. 6.
23 *U.S.P.G.*, India C 1835, No. 15000. *Reports of the Missionaries of the Incorporated Society for the Propagation of the Gospel . . . for the years 1836, 1837, 1838, . . .* Madras 1839, pp. 25–6 (Report of the Tanjore Mission for 1835).
24 Ibid., p. 44 (Report of the Tanjore Mission for 1837).
25 *M.Q.M.J.*, Third Quarter of 1852, No. 9, New Series, Vol. II, esp. pp. 424–7, 430–1.
26 *Digest of S.P.G.Records*, London 1893, p. 514.
27 Statistical Tables of Protestant Missions . . . 1881.
28 *Reports of the missionaries . . .*, p. 35. See also Schreyvogel's comments on the secession and return of 60 sudras to the Trichinopoly congregation. *Report of the Missionaries. . .*, pp. 57–9.
29 *Inquiries made by the Bishop of Madras*, 1868.
30 Ibid., pp. 10, 11, 16, 23, 25, 26, 34, 35, 45.
31 Ibid., pp. 10, 19–20, 22, 26, 35.
32 Ibid., p. 36.
33 Ibid., p. 36.
34 Supra, Ch. 7.
35 *U.S.P.G.*, J. L. Wyatt, Paper read at the S.P.G. Meeting, Madras, 29 January 1891.

36 K. Graul, *Explanations* . . ., p. 1.
37 *U.S.P.G.* C/IND/GEN – 6 Copies of Documents concerning an argument between the Tanjore congregation and the Rev. L. P. Haubroe, Feb. to May 1829. Petition to the Ven. Fr. Thomas Robinson Archdeacon of Madras from the undersigned men of Tanjore Congregation, 26 February 1829; D. B. Forrester, 'Indian Christians' Attitudes . . .'
38 *H.F.*, Vol. IX, 1888 – 89 (October 1888), p. 113.
39 *Census of India*, 1881, Madras, Vol. II, pp. 44 – 51, 56 – 9; 1901, Madras, Part II, Vol. XV – A, pp. 55, 56.
40 *Reports of the Missionaries* . . . p. 25 (Report for 1835).
41 P. J. Bertrand (ed.) op. cit., Vol. 2, pp. 146 – 153 [Canoz to Bertrand, Trichinopoly Feb. and 7 Nov. 1844].
42 *Inquiries* . . ., pp. 10, 26, 35, 45, 46, 60.
43 *A.P.F.*, Vol. XXV, p. 310.
44 *Census of India*, 1891, Madras, Vol. XIII, pp. 146 – 52; E. Thurston *Castes and Tribes*, Vol. VII, p. 298.
45 Hardgrave, op. cit., p. 107.
46 *Census of India*, 1881, Madras, Vol. II, pp. 44 – 51, 56 – 9; 1901, Madras, Part II, Vol. XV – A, pp. 55 – 6.
47 On the incidence of early marriage among different Hindu castes in the Kaveri delta see especially T. V. Row, op. cit., pp. 167, 169 and *Census of India*, 1891, Madras, Vol. XIII, pp. 145 – 152.
48 Bertrand (ed.) op. cit., Vol. 2, p. 114; *A.R.S.I.*, Maduré, 1004 – 11, 33; Shembagnaur. Diary of Nanjur, 1896 – 1897 (8 July 1896).
49 *Census of India*, 1871, Madras, Vol. II, pp. 252 – 4; 1881, Madras, Vol. II, pp. 392 – 3; 1891, Vol. XIV (Madras) pp. 109 – 33; 1901, Madras, Part II, Vol. XV – A, pp. 92, 93.
50 *Census of India*, 1901, Madras, Part II, Vol. XV – A, pp. 92, 93.
51 J. Ar., Maduré, 1005 – x, 11. Sewell to Fr. General, Trichinopoly, 19/2/1895.
52 See especially *U.S.P.G.* C/IND/GEN – 6 Copies of Documents . . ., (1829); Forrester, 'Indian Christians' Attitudes . . .', *H.F.*, 1888 – 89, Vol. IX, p. 114.

10

HINDU REVIVALISM AND THEOSOPHY

A DAWNING OF CONSCIOUSNESS

Among the factors contributing to Hindu revivalism in south India in the second half of the nineteenth century was a determination to defend Hinduism against the encroachments of Christian missionaries. Alongside a desire to close ranks and keep the enemy at bay was also an attempt to rediscover the roots, the original teachings of Hinduism, and to 'revive' and strengthen adherence to what were considered to be the fundamentals of the faith. Both these elements, of defence and rediscovery (the latter usually involving some kind of reformation or desire to return to a golden age), were reflected in the developments in the Kaveri delta *prior* to the arrival of Theosophy in the early 1880s.

Symptomatic of a desire for reform was the formation of a branch of the Veda Samaj in Tanjore in 1865. This Society which was founded in Madras and modelled, at least in part, on the Brahmo Samaj,[1] was primarily a theistic organization for the worship of 'the Supreme Being, the Creator, the Preserver, the Destroyer, the Giver of Salvation . . . the one only without a second.' Members were expected to sign a covenant which listed fourteen pledges. Among the more significant of these was the promise to free themselves 'from the superstitions and absurdities which at present characterize Hindu ceremonies' and to discard 'all sectarian views and animosities.' They also promised never to violate 'the duties and virtues of humanity, veracity, temperance and chastity,' gradually to give up all distinctions of caste, and to promote a variety of changes and reforms in Hindu society, including widow remarriage and female education. But also significant as part of an attempt to rediscover the faith in its pristine purity was the pledge to study 'the Sanskrit language and its literature (especially theological).[2]

According to the Rev. A. R. C. Nailer (S.P.G.) the Tanjore branch of the Veda Samaj had between 20 and 30 members at its inception. Most of the members were boys belonging to the highest classes in the S.P.G. high school. Meetings were held on Saturday evenings for prayer when members met 'to offer up petitions to one Lord, whom they recognise as their common Father, their creator, and Preserver.'[3]

While some young men, exposed to Western ideas and missionary teaching, were attempting to grapple with the problems of faith through a greater understanding and readjustment of their own tradition, others directed their efforts towards attacking Christianity. Most of their hostility appears to have been directed against the Protestant system which they correctly perceived as a greater and more immediate threat than the Catholic movement.[4]

As early as 1836 the Rev. Thomas Cryer reported that there was considerable opposition to Methodist missionary activity in Negapatam:

> The tracts I have given have been torn to pieces and thrown in the air before me, — angry disputants have struggled for hours to overthrow my assertions concerning Christianity and idolatry, — the baser sort have hooted me from street to street, — and in some instances I have been compelled to hear blasphemies against our blessed Redeemer.[5]

Opposition was also mobilized from time to time against mission schools, especially Methodist institutions which, up until the 1890s, were probably the most successful in the area in winning high-caste converts.[6] There were several periods of considerable excitement and tension in Mannargudi,[7] but the most dramatic incidents and sustained resistance occurred in Negapatam, which was not only the location of a well-known Methodist high school, but also the chief centre of Methodist operations in the region.

In 1854 the police had to be called in to protect the mission house after the conversion of the head pupil and, because of the extent of hostility, the young man was sent to Madras for baptism.[8] More conversions and rumours of conversion followed[9] until, in 1877, anti-Christian feeling reached a peak of intensity. Early that year Balakrishnan, the fifteen year old son of a brahman pleader, asked his parents' permission to receive baptism. This was refused; he was beaten, confined to his quarters and, finally, sent away from Negapatam.[10] When, shortly afterwards, a second brahman, Venkatraman (who came from the nearby town of Tiruvalur), also asked for baptism and took refuge in the Negapatam school, the brahman community was plunged into uproar.[11] Balakrishnan's father and other brahman lawyers appear to have been especially active in organizing anti-Christian opposition. A complaint was lodged against the missionaries for 'kidnapping' Venkatraman and about two hundred pupils, including nearly all the brahmans, were withdrawn from the school 'in less than a fortnight'.[12] Subscriptions were raised and an opposition 'Native' school was established to provide Hindus with an education free from the influence of Christian teaching.

This incident, apart from leading to the establishment of a rival school, also encouraged the revival of attempts to disrupt street preaching. During the next eleven years, prior to the formation of the Negapatam branch of the Hindu Tract Society in 1888, there were intermittent attempts to disrupt missionary activity. These included the organization of rival 'services' just opposite the Methodist preaching places where victory went to 'the noisiest',[13] and incidents of stone-throwing. Eventually, in about 1882, a local 'Hindu Missionary Society' was established headed by two men, one of them calling himself 'the minister' and the other styled 'the catechist'.[14] According to the Rev. J. M. Thompson, their plan of operation was to establish an anti-Christian preaching hall and to circulate anti-Christian tracts. Whenever possible they also attempted to interrupt missionary meetings by raising objections and producing arguments such as those based on Bradlaugh's writings or drawn from Theosophical publications which were beginning to circulate in the region.

THEOSOPHY IN SOUTH INDIA

The Theosophical Society was founded in New York in 1875. Its founders, H. P. Blavatsky, a Russian woman of noble descent, and Colonel H. S. Olcott, a veteran of the American civil war, journalist and lawyer, were both involved in the new Spiritualist movement which was developing in the United States. The central teachings of the movement, which began to take an organized form in the second half of the nineteenth century, were not only that communication with those who had 'passed into the higher life' was possible, but also that attempts should be made to contact these 'higher' spirits.[15]

Though the Theosophical Society grew out of Spiritualism, including an interest in psychic phenomena and other aspects of the occult, its work gradually came to incorporate a wider range of activities and interests. By 1885 research into the world of spirits was no longer, at least officially, such a dominant concern. At its annual convention held in Madras in 1885 the Society declared that its objects were

To form the nucleus of a Universal Brotherhood of Humanity, without distinction of race, creed or colour.
 To promote the study of Aryan and other Eastern Literatures, religions and sciences.
 A third object pursued by a portion of the members of the Society, is to investigate unexplained laws of nature and the psychical powers of man.[16]

These objects were reiterated, with some minor modifications, during the remaining part of the nineteenth century.

Initially the Society made little headway in the United States and, partly because of difficulties there and the founders' interest in Indian religion, 'the twins', as they liked to be called, set up their headquarters in Bombay in 1879. The Society opened its first branch in South India at Tinnevelly in 1881 and, influenced by the favourable climate of opinion in the South, financial and other considerations, moved its headquarters from Bombay to Adyar, Madras, in 1882.[17]

The appeal of Theosophy in the south, apparent even before Olcott's tour of the Kaveri delta in August 1883, was partly due to the timing of its arrival. Its advent coincided with the growth of political activity and the rising tide of nationalist feeling in many parts of the Presidency. While the hopes and expectations of the Western-educated élites were aroused by Ripon's liberal policies, including plans for local self-government announced in May 1882, other developments were creating considerable unease and dissatisfaction. These included the blunders and apparent insensitivity of Grant Duff's Madras administration and especially, after 2 February 1883, sustained European opposition to the Ilbert Bill which was designed to give Indian magistrates and judges the same rights as their European colleagues to try Europeans in criminal cases.[18]

Of particular importance for the future of Theosophy was growing Indian resentment of European arrogance and claims to racial and cultural superiority. An increasing sensitivity on the part of Indians to adverse comments and criticism was linked with an open-minded if not uncritical enthusiasm for anyone, especially Europeans, who would defend India's religious and cultural heritage.

Furthermore, there was continuing unease at the apparent decline of Hinduism and the progress of Christianity. The gradual withdrawal of the Company's supervisory role over the management of Hindu religious institutions, the cessation or disruption of temple-cart processions, the obviously deteriorating fabric of temples, reports of mismanagement and misappropriation of religious endowments and of corruption and intrigue in *maths*, not to mention the more sensational reports of conversions to Christianity — these and other developments were hardly encouraging signs for anyone concerned with the future of the Hindu religion. In many parts of the country Hindu critics of Christianity were already locked in confrontation with Christian missionaries and, as in Ceylon, the Theosophists were welcomed with open arms as allies in the struggle against the forces of Christianity.[19]

Certainly there could be little doubt about the Theosophists' anti-Christian credentials. While Olcott and Blavatsky insisted that the same underlying truths were to be found embedded somewhere in all religions, even in early Christianity, they were quite uncompromising in their assaults on contemporary Christianity. While in America Blavatsky shocked Christians by her verbal attacks on the Christian Church[20] and included criticism of Christianity in *Isis Unveiled* first published in 1877.[21] In a letter to Dayananda Sarasvati, in the following year, Olcott wrote that the Theosophists had 'openly proclaimed themselves as enemies of the Christian religion'.[22] The *Theophist*, the Society's principal journal which commenced publication in 1879 and reached many subscribers in South India, included numerous articles, not only attacking historical Christianity, but highlighting the dangers of Christian missionary activity.[23]

After their arrival in the South Olcott continued to expand on the evils and dangers inherent in the Christian movement. Speaking at Tuticorin, a centre of Protestant missionary activity in Tinnevelly district in 1882, for example, he declared that

Christendom has as fine a moral code as could be wished for; but she shows her real principles in her Krupp and Armstrong guns and whiskey distilleries, in her opium ships, sophisticated merchandise, prurient amusements, licentiousness and political dishonesty. Christendom, we may almost say, is morally rotten and spiritually paralysed.[24]

In contrast to these assaults on Christianity he continued to reiterate the message that ancient Hindu literature, science and religion was not only worth studying, but superior to anything produced elsewhere.[25]

To Hindus who had for so long been subject to Christian propaganda and who were almost beginning to expect the demise of their own religion this was an exhilarating moment. As one contemporary expressed it, 'India the tutored' was about to become 'India the teacher, no longer sitting at the feet of Europe, but dispensing to the nations from her ancestral store the crumbs of wisdom on which they may nourish their spiritual life.'[26]

But the success of Theosophy was not only due to its message of hope and encouragement at a critical stage in South India's history. Several other factors were probably also important in the spread of the movement. One of these was Olcott's discovery and use of his powers of healing during the early stages of the movement. According to Olcott he discovered these powers (which he linked with mesmerism) while attending a disabled man in Ceylon in July 1882.[27] News of 'healings' in Ceylon and North India soon reached the South where the sick and disabled followed him wherever he went. Writing up notes from his diary some years later Olcott observed that

As the publicity given by the Ceylon Press to my early healings created an importunate demand for repetitions on the Bengal tour, so the exciting narratives of the North Indian papers caused me to be urged with equal pertinacity to exercise the power for the benefit of the sick in South India. They beseiged me at Tinnevelly, as at all the other stations, and some marvellous cures were wrought.[28]

Furthermore, the founders of the movement neither demanded nor expected radical changes in the life-style of their followers. Adherence to Theosophy did not involve a change in religion and, unlike converts to Christianity, those who joined the local branches of the Society were able to continue their ordinary life, living as Hindus.[29] Theosophists were not faced with the prospect of expulsion from caste or loss of status and could, if they wished, continue to follow traditional family and public customs.[30]

Lastly, as was the case with the Arya Samaj in North India, local branches of the organization were allowed a considerable degree of autonomy in drawing up their own rules and in deciding on their own activities, provided these were associated in some way with the aims of the Society and received the Parent Committee's approval.

The effect of Theosophy on the attitude of Western-educated Hindus in many parts of the South is reflected in the words of one correspondent writing in the *Theosophist* who declared that the movement had rekindled in Hindus a love of their own religion, science and literature and had 'unmistakably proved the superiority of Hindu philosophies over all other schools of thought', and that Christian missionaries, who were 'despising Hinduism', had been shown their error.[31] Speaking at Triplicaine, a suburb in Madras, Raganatha Row, the well-known political and social reformer, declared in 1886 that

Six years ago, he, the speaker, could not have ventured to speak publicly, as he was now constantly doing, on our national religions without the certainty of being hissed by his own countrymen, but now, thanks solely to the Theosophical Society and to the Divine agency that was impelling its work — the whole country was aroused to enquire into the Hindu Shastras and religious principles.[32]

THE SPREAD OF THE MOVEMENT IN THE KAVERI DELTA

Ideas of Theosophy and the fame of the founders preceded Olcott's first visit to the Kaveri delta in August 1883. Some of his earlier speeches, his healing 'miracles' and the formation of branches of the Theosophical Society in other parts of the South had already been reported in papers such as the *Madras Mail* and *Madras Times*, while as early as

1880, the *Theosophist* referred to its subscribers in a number of towns in the delta.[33]

Olcott's visit to Negapatam, Trichinopoly, Tanjore, Kumbakonam and Mayavaram respectively from 6 – 15 August 1883 followed much the same pattern as his tours elsewhere. They were more like those of a conqueror returning in triumph than the visit of a campaigner attempting to muster support. The battle, it seemed, was already very nearly won. He travelled by train and, almost everywhere he went, was welcomed by crowds and music on the platform, garlanded and presented with an official address. According to the reports of local correspondents, he was invariably received on these occasions by representatives of the local Western-educated élites. These included notables such as the Munsiff and one of the leading pleaders of Negapatam, the trustee of the Tayuman or Rock-Fort temple, the late Sheristadar of the District Court and a Municipal Commissioner at Trichinopoly and the pensioned Deputy Collector and the Police Inspector at Mayavaram.[34] In Trichinopoly 'almost all the native officials of the district' attended his lecture at the town hall and in Kumbakonam the audience for his first lecture included vakils, professors and schoolmasters, as well as 'a numerous array of schoolboys', *mirasidars*, ryots and merchants.[35]

Nor was initial support for Olcott's movement confined to the Western-educated classes. He appears to have deliberately attempted to enlist the co-operation of the traditional leaders of religion, including temple priests, and attempted to spread his message further among the Tamil-speaking population. He usually convened at least one of his meetings in the towns he visited in the precincts of one of the more important temples. While this must have excluded harijans and many low-caste Hindus from attendance, the crowds (which he claimed varied in number from 2,000 to 7,000 people)[36] could be more easily accommodated than in Western-style halls, while the location itself gave the Colonel an opportunity to associate his movement with traditional Hinduism. At these meetings, where his addresses were more of a popular character than those delivered elsewhere, Olcott spoke through an interpreter. Writing his memoirs some years later he recalled, with particular pleasure, his experience while speaking in the temples at Srirangam and Tanjore. In Srirangam he addressed an audience 'numbering perhaps 5,000 . . . in the inner square in front of the Hall of the Thousand Columns'[37] and at Tanjore he spoke about the truths embodied in ancient Hinduism, from the stone pedestal of the bull-colossus of Nandi in the temple enclosure, 'the multitude sitting on the flagged pavement of the courtyard'.[38]

Olcott's message was what many in his audiences must have come to expect — a panegyric on the truths and superiority of ancient Hindu religion, philosophy and science and, linked with that, a plea to Hindu parents especially to establish Hindu schools and educate their children in the Hindu faith.

The tone and popularity of this approach is clearly reflected in S. A. Saminatha Iyer's account of Olcott's first lecture at Negapatam.

> The first portion of the lecture was highly scientific and was received by the non-educated part of the audience with bewilderment and blind and mute admiration. It was the second part of it that really moved the audience to raptures. As sentence after sentence rolled out, now admining [sic] and holding up to admiration Eastern literature, philosophy and science, again entreating and exhorting young India not to despise the learning and creed of its ancestors, but vigorously to strive for their better appreciation and conservation, and then again deploring and deprecating the work of denationalization which was going on hourly in India under the influence of Western education — the whole assembly was most visibly impressed, and the cheering was prolonged and deafening.[39]

The main variant in the Colonel's lectures apparently lay in what he had to say about the forces which appeared to him to endanger a revival of the fundamental truths of Hinduism. At Kumbakonam, where he discussed religion 'from the point of view of science', his lecture was deliberately slanted to counteract the growth of scepticism and materialism encouraged by the Hindu professors of the local College.[40] While he warned his audience there against overconfidence in the assertions of modern Western science, at Mayavaram which, as we have seen, was an important centre of Lutheran missionary activity, he appears to have been especially concerned with the effects of Christianity. He not only exhorted his listeners to 'know the truth about the Hindu religion, and study the writings of their sages and holy men,' but implored them to 'examine with caution the assertions of those who advocate other faiths than their own, even as any owner of a genuine diamond would do, who is requested by the owner of a counterfeit one to agree to an exchange.[41]

The immediate effect of Olcott's campaign in the Kaveri delta, as elsewhere, was to arouse further interest and renew confidence, especially among the Western-educated classes, in the importance and value of the ancient Hindu scriptures.

A few days after Olcott's visit to Negapatam, S. A. Saminatha Iyer, Secretary of the newly-formed Negapatam branch, remarked that

> The visit of this great philanthropist to our town has already done a deal of visible good to our townsmen. It has already set them thinking about the necessity for getting themselves better acquainted with the philosophy, religion and literature of their country, and has impressed them with a sense of the desirability of social harmony and united action as essential elements in the moral regeneration of the community.[42]

Branches of the Theosophical society were established in Negapatam (5 August 1883), Trichinopoly (6 August), Tanjore (12 August), Kumbakonam (14 August) and Mayavaram (16 August).[43] They were, however, typical Western-style voluntary associations and, as such, had little prospect of attracting the non Western-educated classes including the great majority of people who attended Olcott's more popular lectures. They were, from the very beginning, dominated by an English-speaking élite familiar with the functioning of similar Western-style associations. Furthermore, the level of fees, at least in some cases, excluded the participation of poorer members of the community — the rules of the Trichinopoly branch stating, for example, that 'Every member shall pay a subscription of not less than eight annas a month.'[44]

The great majority of branch members, especially in Tanjore district, appear to have been brahmans. The names of 87 members belonging to different branches of the Theosophical society in the region from 1883 to 1900 are listed in Appendix 10. At least 66, or three-quarters of this number, were brahmans. The small number of non-brahmans becomes even more apparent when one considers key positions on the executive. During the same period (1883 to 1900) at least 45 individuals acted either as President or Secretary in one of the local branches. Forty were brahmans and only five were non-brahmans.

The predominance of brahmans in the local branches, together with their control over most of the key positions in the organization reflects, at least in part, their high degree of involvement in Western learning and education when compared with other castes and classes in the population. For example, in 1888 – 89, over 90 per cent of Hindu students attending colleges in Tanjore district and 89 per cent attending colleges in Trichinopoly were brahmans, while brahmans made up 62 per cent of the Hindu population in secondary schools in Tanjore and 55 per cent in Trichinopoly.[45]

But brahmans as distinct from non-brahmans also had their own special reasons for being interested in Theosophy. The emphasis of the movement was on the exposition and furtherance of brahman culture or what the local branches described as 'the study of Sanskrit literature and Aryan Philosophy'. Had Olcott, Besant and others valued more highly the literature of medieval Hinduism including *bhakti* texts and other works, such as treatises on *Saiva Siddhanta*, then Theosophy may well have proved more attractive to non-brahmans including those with little knowledge of Sanskrit.

Though Olcott and his movement aroused a great deal of initial enthusiasm and interest in the delta, the Society's branches, dominated by brahmans, and composed very largely of lawyers and public servants, were essentially élitist organizations and appear never to have attracted much public support. Some were short lived while others had a fluctuating membership or were largely moribund. Indeed, in 1890, only nine years after Olcott's first visit to South India, the headquarters of the movement in Madras circularized the different branches in an attempt to discover why members thought Theosophy was in decline and deputed C. Kottayya to visit branches throughout the South. Commenting on his visit to the branch at Negapatam in October 1890 Kottayya wrote that

> Like the other Branches I visited, this had its rise and fall. The causes of depression are more or less the same everywhere, — they being (1) death of members, (2) transfer or removal of them to other places, (3) petty jealousies and disputes among the members, caused by the conflict of their worldly transactions, (4) the want of correspondence between the Head-Quarters and the Branches giving instructions to the latter, (5) the tales and rumours circulated against the Society by those ignorant of its real objects, and (6) the non-visitation of the Branches by any officer of the Society after its formation . . . The Branch in question has now only 13 out of 29 members on its roll, — 3 having died, and the rest removed to other places. It has not held meetings for reading, discussion or exposition of Theosophical subjects. . .[46]

Very few, if any, new members appear to have joined any of the branches in the Kaveri delta. Membership of the branch at Mayavaram had declined from twelve to seven 'one having died and the others removed to other stations', while the President himself confessed that he was 'too old' to work for the welfare of the Society.[47] The Tanjore branch was officially described as 'dormant' in 1891, while the situation in Trichinopoly was only slightly more hopeful. Even though Olcott was reported as having 'renewed' the activity of the Trichinopoly section in 1890, in the following year it was included among those branches which consisted of 'a few active workers' but which did not 'make themselves sensibly felt as yet in their locality by any marked activity.'[48] Indeed, the Kumbakonam branch (despite the initial anti-religious bias of the professors and students in the Government College) was the only branch in the delta region which consistently maintained an active programme. It was largely through the enthusiasm of the Secretary, K. Narayanaswami Iyer, that a new branch was formed at Tiruvalur in 1891.[49]

Following reports on the depressed state of the branches in many parts of South India in 1890 the executive of the Society initiated a programme of more regular visitations. K. Narayanaswami Iyer undertook regular tours throughout the delta and, in the 1890s, some of the leading European members of the Theosophical Society spoke at branch meetings in Trichinopoly and Tanjore districts. These included

Bertram Keightley, General Secretary of the Indian Section 1890 – 1897, Sydney V. Edge, the first assistant General Secretary of the same Section, Walter R. Old, General Secretary in England, 1890 – 1891, and Miss Lilian Edger, General Secretary of the New Zealand branch, who toured India with Olcott in 1898.[50] The most notable and important visit was, however, that of Mrs Annie Besant who toured the area in 1893 and who succeeded in arousing some renewed interest in the movement. She addressed meetings in Trichinopoly, Tanjore and Kumbakonam. According to a report of the meeting at Kumbakonam, the town hall was 'full to suffocation' and when Mrs Besant entered the hall 'the whole audience stood up and gave her a cordial welcome'.[51]

If the Theosophical Society never succeeded in recruiting a large official membership, Theosophy, nevertheless, had important effects on the attitudes and intellectual life of many educated Hindus who never became, or perhaps never considered becoming, members of the organization.

As in Ceylon, Theosophy inspired the establishment of many new types of association including, for example, Sanmargha sabhas — some though not all of which were affiliated with the Society. The first of these appears to have been established in Trichinopoly in about 1883 by P. N. Muthuswami Naidu, a non-brahman Theosophist.[52] Its objectives were 'to improve the moral tone of the rising generation by setting to others a good example of morality and diffusing a useful knowledge' and 'to practise universal brotherhood'. Though the sabha in Trichinopoly was open to all persons 'without respect to religion, caste or creed' it appears to have been Hindu in character and ethos. Its activities included the publication of a code of morals for young men and boys under the title of 'The Aryan Virtues', the establishment of an order for meritorious conduct, the running of a Sunday religious school for Hindus and the formation of a library of religious works.

Sanmargha sabhas were subsequently founded in many other parts of India.[53] A sabha was formed in Tanjore and the idea was also taken up by the Methodist missionaries who founded similar associations — one in connection with the Wesleyan college at Negapatam and the other at Mannargudi.[54]

Secondly, Theosophy appears to have had some effect in counteracting the spread of rationalistic or anti-religious ideas — views and attitudes derived very largely from the writings of Bradlaugh, Ingersoll and other Western critics of Christianity. After Olcott's visits, lectures on religious subjects in the main towns in the region became increasingly common. Especially striking was the strength of religious revivalism in Kumbakonam, which partly because of the influence of the professors of the Government College there, had become a well-known centre of rationalist thought and inquiry. Olcott himself was especially pleased with the results of his first visit to Kumbakonam in August 1882 and claimed that, despite the sceptical attitude of the Professors and teachers, his visit there had turned public interest 'into religious channels'.[55] The Kumbakonam branch of the Theosophical Society was maintained as the most viable and active group in the delta, and the high level of religious inquiry and activity in the town was still noticeable some years later. A Kumbakonam correspondent writing in the *Hindu* in August 1888 declared that

We have something like a religious revival among us. In the Porter Town Hall, there is every Friday evening an exposition of passages from some religious book, and the study of the Ramayana and of the other sacred writings of the Hindus is the order of the day.[56]

A third and perhaps more obvious effect of Theosophy was to encourage a much greater and more militant opposition to Christianity. As noted above, Olcott and Blavatsky were welcomed as allies in the struggle against Christianity and the upsurge of violent and widespread anti-Christian activity was one of the most remarkable aspects of religious development in the delta, as well as in South India as a whole, during the period from about 1886 to 1892.

ANTI-CHRISTIAN AGITATION

The new wave of anti-Christian activity which erupted in Tanjore and Trichinopoly districts in 1887 and which was mainly associated with the rise of the Hindu Tract Society in Madras, was different in some respects from the anti-Christian agitation which had occurred before. The movement coincided with similar activity elsewhere in other parts of the Presidency; it was at least to some extent organized and encouraged by leaders who lived outside the locality and, lastly, it was more carefully planned, thoroughgoing, widespread and sustained than any of the earlier outbreaks of opposition.

The Hindu Preaching Society, established in Madras city in 1881, was dominated by high caste non-brahmans.[57] It appears to have remained comparatively inactive until about 1886 when Christian missionaries working in Madras began to report an increase in opposition especially in the streets. The association had some links with the mofussil and its preachers may have been partly responsible for increasing anti-Christian activity which was also reported in some towns in the Kaveri delta, such as Trichinopoly, even before the establishment of local branches of the Hindu Tract Society.

The Hindu Tract Society, whose anti-Christian activities soon came to overshadow those of the Preaching Society, was founded in Madras city in April 1887. It was, in a sense, the brahman equivalent of the earlier association — its leadership being dominated by brahmans many of whom were Western-educated lawyers, teachers and other professionals. Judging from the Society's account of its own origins,[58] the chief causes which contributed to its establishment included the religious revival, Theosophy and a growing awareness of 'the grandeur and perfection of our ancient religion'. But it also owed 'more to the activity of antagonistic foreign influences in our own midst than to any other cause'. It rose into prominence not only at a time when the mainline Protestant missionaries were becoming increasingly active and aggressive, especially in the streets of Madras, but also when the Salvation Army was extending its operations in various centres throughout the South.[59] Its primary objective was therefore to defend Hinduism through the disruption or, if possible, the complete elimination of Christian missionary activity.

Sivasankara Pandiah, a Gujarati brahman, graduate of Madras University, Theosophist and school teacher, was the main force in the movement. He was President of the Society from 1888 to 1891 — and together with Cannapiran Mudaliar, a Hindu preacher connected with both the Tract and Hindu Preaching Societies and Srinivasa Sastrial, Mofussil Vice-President, went on tours of country centres, speaking at public meetings and founding branches of the organization. Twenty-six of these were founded in one year alone (1888 – 1889) — 21 in Tamil and 5 in Telugu districts.[60]

Branches of the Hindu Tract Society were established in Trichinopoly and suburbs and in Kumbakonam in 1888.[61] Srinivasa Sastrial, the Mofussil Vice-President, toured the delta in the following year and, as a result of his visits, other branches were formed at Negapatam, Mayavaram and Tanjore.[62] These local branches were all at places where Theosophical societies had also been established, but, perhaps more importantly, were usually located where Protestant missionaries were especially active.

Membership lists of local branches of the Hindu Tract Society are incomplete, but it is clear, even from limited information, that there was some overlap in the leadership of these organizations with Theosophical societies. In Negapatam, for example, N. P. Subramania Iyer, first grade pleader, was Vice-President of the local Theosophical society in 1884 and Secretary of the Negapatam Hindu Tract Society in 1889.[63] G. Sambasiva Iyer, a schoolmaster, was likewise Secretary of both these local organizations.[64]

Membership of local branches of the Tract Society was drawn from much the same section of the Western-educated Hindu community as the Theosophists. The brahmans were again dominant in key positions — 14 out of 19 of those whose names are known and appear on lists connected with branches throughout the delta were brahmans. According to the Rev. J. L. Wyatt, Principal of the S.P.G. College, Trichinopoly, the movement everywhere appeared to be most noticeable amongst 'the middle classes'.[65] In Trichinopoly many lawyers, schoolmasters, merchants and students joined the society.[66] It was 'teachers and vakils' who invited Sivasankara Pandiah to address a meeting at St Peter's College,[67] Tanjore in 1889. Merchants were the dominant group on the committee at Negapatam (as they were on the temple committee) while in Kumbakonam, Pandiah's lectures in the Government College were attended by students, lecturers of the College, revenue officials and others.[68] Like Theosophy, the movement had some support from the more traditional sections of the population. Meetings were occasionally held in temples[69] and, while on his visit to Trichinopoly in October 1889, Pandiah was received by the temple authorities and *tambiran* of the Rock Fort temple who expressed to him their 'heartfelt gratitude' for his 'indefatigable labours in the revival of Hinduism'.[70]

In one sense, however, the social character of the movement was rather different from that of Theosophy. Although Olcott began his tours by emphasizing his links with the common people, Theosophical societies very quickly became small élite groups largely devoted to the study of Sanskrit literature. By way of contrast, the tract societies in the delta, as well as in other parts of the Presidency, tended to develop a more popularist image. They were primarily activist rather than learned or reflective organizations and encouraged a type of activity which was bound to attract schoolboys, the unemployed and anyone interested in poking fun, especially at Europeans.

While it is true that some of the leaders of the Hindu Tract Society attempted to promote reforms within Hinduism their efforts in this direction appear almost half-hearted when compared with the enthusiasm with which local members, students and others took up the more negative aspect of the Society's programme — the crippling of Christian missionary activity.

One of their first targets was missionary street preaching. Missionaries soon began to report a series of attempts throughout the delta to make their open-air preaching an impossibility.

Reporting from Trichinopoly in 1887, the Rev. V. Gnanamuttu (S.P.G.) noted that opponents of Christianity had begun to conduct rival meetings at the same time and in close proximity to missionary gatherings in an attempt to disrupt them, and that

To keep up attention and to make up for the shallowness of their preaching at the interval of every three or four minutes they yell and shout hideously for a few seconds . . . Their audience is mostly the students of the R.C. and S.P.G. colleges, and the Hindu National School . . . These boys often enjoying themselves with our preachers rush up to our meeting, and yell and shout and so interrupt us. They sometimes go even beyond this, mock us by imitating what we say, personally abuse us to our face, call us bad names, tell us that we bark for being paid, pelt sand, rubbish and stones at us and amuse themselves.[71]

Nor were missionaries of other societies immune from harassment when attempting to conduct public preaching. Officers of the Salvation Army, who commenced preaching in the streets of several towns in the region at about the same time as the upsurge in anti-Christian activity, were also affected by the new aggressive tactics of the Hindu opposition. Writing from Trichinopoly in 1890 one officer declared that

Our open air stand on Friday was surrounded by a yelling crowd who pushed and hustled our small band. When we marched away it was under the fire of a perfect shower of stones, sticks, mud, cow-dung and other refuse, and we arrived at the barracks in a pretty pickle.[72]

In 1887 there were reports of attempts to disrupt missionary preaching in the town of Tanjore as well as in Trichinopoly.[73] In 1892 the Methodist missionaries at Mannargudi stated that the Hindu Tract Society had offered 'repeated and prolonged opposition' to their efforts and that 'a serious assault upon a catechist, frequent abuse, occasional stone-throwing, and religious excitement roused again and again' belonged to the year's experience.[74] In Negapatam the establishment of a branch of the Hindu Tract Society, and Hindu preaching against Christianity there, led to further incidents involving the Salvation Army. Two Salvation Army women who were passing a meeting on the opposite side of the street which was being addressed by a Hindu preacher, were suddenly set upon by 40 to 50 Hindus, pelted with stones and dust and pursued to the gates of the railway station where they were rescued by a Salvation Army Captain.[75]

Alongside the revival of rival Hindu preaching and attempts to disrupt missionary street preaching was the circulation of anti-Christian literature. Tracts and handbills printed in Madras in Tamil and/or English were distributed in the region[76] while, in Trichinopoly, Hindu opponents of Christianity also drew up and circulated Tamil material which dealt in specific terms with the local situation. One such pamphlet included attacks on female mission schools and on the S.P.G. programme of *zenana* visiting.[77] According to the author of this tract

Christianity, 'the meanest of all religions', encouraged almost every conceivable vice and wickedness ranging from the refusal of women to obey their husbands, to sexual promiscuity. Parents were warned against sending their girls to mission schools; and families against being swept away by any feelings of flattery they might experience as a result of the visits of 'white Padre women' who used such occasions to convert Hindu children 'deceitfully, secretly and quickly.' The remedy, suggested the pamphlet, was for Hindus to unite and for Hindu leaders, including the heads of *maths*, to establish girls' schools and thereby prevent conversions.

Last, but not least, there was an all-out attempt to weaken the edifice of missionary higher school and collegiate education — a system which, as we have seen, was very much in the ascendency in Tanjore and Trichinopoly districts.

While some Hindu parents supported the idea of setting up their own schools in competition with missionary institutions, college students themselves were becoming increasingly involved in anti-Christian agitation. A decision by students in the Christian College in Madras to take matters into their own hands resulted in what became known as the Madras Christian College 'commotion' of April 1888.[78] The incident, sparked off by rumours that one of the brahman students was about to embrace Christianity, led to student protest meetings, uproar in some of the classes, several student expulsions and a temporary boycott of the College.

During these upheavals, which were reported at length in the *Hindu*,[79] a meeting of students in Kumbakonam passed resolutions expressing sympathy with fellow-students in the Madras College.[80] In March 1889, just eleven months after the Madras 'commotion', a similar series of disturbances occurred in St. Joseph's College, Trichinopoly. There had been some dissatisfaction among students at St. Joseph's over inadequate facilities and restricted visiting hours in the College hostel, as well as some misunderstanding over the level of fees,[81] but, as in Madras, the main cause of discontent appears to have been an increasing fear of conversion — possibly heightened by the activity of the local branch of the Hindu Tract Society. As in Madras, the students complained that some of their teachers were deriding Hinduism.[82] Linked with this complaint was the charge that the College authorities 'interfered' with students' right to practise their own religion and had, amongst other things, deliberately tried to prevent the students from witnessing a Hindu procession as it passed the College hostel gates on the evening of 14 March 1889.[83]

It is unlikely that the College staff were any more outspoken in attacks on Hinduism in 1889 than they had been in previous years. But they may have been more persistent or even aggressive in attempts to win high-caste converts than was usually the case. On New Year's Day 1889, for example, the Rector of the College, Fr. Faseuille, emphasized the need for the Fathers to make a more determined effort to convert high-caste Hindus[84] and, quite possibly, some students (even if they were not aware that two of their number were already serious inquirers) sensed a greater resolve on the part of the College Fathers to press the claims of Christianity.[85]

Rumours that the students' 'sacred religion' was in danger,[86] and the possibility that the Fathers were out to exert more pressure on students to convert, appeared all the more disquieting in view of the fact that senior students in particular had little option but to remain in the mission-school system. If they withdrew from St. Joseph's they had nowhere else to go except to the S.P.G. College which was also a missionary institution — unless they were prepared to travel or live outside the district.

Protest meetings were organized outside St. Joseph's and, in April, after a series of incidents, the students finally decided to press for the establishment of an alternative Hindu college where Hindu students would receive 'a sound instruction in their religion'.[87] A public meeting was convened on the 20th and a subcommittee, including some of the leading 'gentry' of Trichinopoly, was formed in order to concert measures for the establishing of a national college through the upgrading of the National High School.[88]

In the meantime, tension in St. Joseph's was running high and a determination by some of the more senior pupils to assert their rights through active participation in Hindu rituals and ceremony culminated in a serious breach of discipline.[89] Several young men, including Mahadeva Iyer (who was subsequently converted to Christianity), performed 'against all the rules of the College', Hindu ceremonies within the College precincts. Although Mahadeva Iyer, who was one of the leaders of the student agitation, managed to conceal his involvement in the affair, two other students were caught and expelled.

This latter incident sparked off another protest meeting attended by about 600 Hindu inhabitants. They appointed a sub-committee to draw up a statement to be presented to the College Syndicate deploring the action of the College authorities and expressing sympathy with the expelled students.[90] The College authorities refused to budge and, after the summer recess, classes were resumed as normal.

While it appears from this episode that the students had grievances and their own special reasons for becoming involved in an agitation they were certainly encouraged by the climate of Hindu revivalism and by the presence and activities of the Hindu Tract Society. During the initial stages of the unrest they cabled Sivasankara Pandiah, the Madras president of the Society, for his 'presence and advice'[91] and, in subsequent weeks, several members of the local branch of the Hindu Tract Society, including the local president, L. S. Ramachandra Iyer, B.A., B.L., were involved in activities on behalf of the students who were pressing for an alternative college, or who had been expelled.[92]

But another perhaps even more important factor in the college 'commotion' was the part played especially by the staff of the Hindu National High School who had everything to gain and nothing to lose from the attempt to weaken and discredit a rival institution. Students from St. Joseph's used the grounds of the National High School as a haven for private meetings[93] and, according to the rector of St. Joseph's, in a report to his superior in Rome, the opposition movement was conducted throughout by the teachers of the National High School.[94] They had every reason to expect that, if the movement against St. Joseph's gained sufficient momentum, their school would be raised and improved through the addition of a college department — a proposal which, as we have seen, was endorsed at a public meeting in April 1889.

The wave of opposition and violence directed against Christian missionaries, Christian institutions and converts gradually subsided in the early 1890s. In some places, such as Trichinopoly in 1891, missionaries could report that the situation was almost back to normal, while in a few other towns, such as Mannargudi, persistent attempts were still being made to undermine and counteract the effects of Christianity. The ebb tide of opposition in the delta coincided with the decline of the Hindu Tract Society's activities in Madras itself and with the collapse of the movement in other parts of the South.

One of the more immediate effects of the movement in Tanjore and Trichinopoly districts had been to force some of the missionaries to change their tactics. Commenting on Hindu attempts to disrupt street preaching in Negapatam the Rev. T. E. Darvell (S.P.G.) remarked, for example, that 'in the town itself house to house visitation seems more successful, as a quiet hearing is then obtained.'[95] Furthermore, it was opposition from higher-caste Hindus in towns such as Trichinopoly, Tanjore, Kumbakonam and Negapatam during this period that finally convinced the Salvation Army that they had a greater chance of success among the depressed classes.[96] While the effect of the agitation on mission schools for girls is difficult to access,[97] protests against Jesuit policy in St. Joseph's College in 1889 appear to have had a temporary effect on enrolments.[98] According to the Rector, the attempt to prevent parents from sending their children to the College was a failure.[99] He claimed that, during the crisis, the College had not lost a single pupil but that, on the contrary, the number had grown. However, while it may have been true that no students left the College *during the crisis* which ended in about July 1889, Education Department figures show a clear drop in enrolments by March 1890 (see Table 18).

Table 18. Missionary College and Secondary School Enrolments, Trichinopoly, March 1887 – March 1892[100]

As at March	St Joseph's College				S.P.G. College			
	College	Upper Secondary	Lower Secondary	Total	College	Upper Secondary	Lower Secondary	Total
1887	318	291	303	912	149	179	299	627
1888	348	271	317	936	109	78	219	406
1889	325	324	373	1,022	143	175	–	
1890	270	258	353	881	161	170	168	499
1891	307	283	371	961	193	181	93	469
1892	389	282	389	1,060	212	203	206	621

Enrolments were down 14 per cent in March 1890 on the previous year — a decline *at all levels* including a drop of 17 per cent in the College department. During the same period, enrolments in the rival S.P.G. institution were comparatively stable — the college departments there experiencing a slight growth over the previous year.

As we have argued, the aim of many of those involved in anti-Christian agitation was not merely the disruption of missionary preaching and weakening of missionary institutions but, ultimately, the prevention of conversion to Christianity. An examination of baptismal registers (which was by no means comprehensive) did in fact reveal a drop in the number of converts baptized in five out of six churches during the period 1888 to 1891 compared with the number of converts baptized during the previous four years (see Table 19).

It is quite possible that this decline in numbers in some centres was at least partially due to the growth in anti-Christian agitation.

Census reports, which give a more complete picture, indicate a slowing down in the rate of conversions compared with the rate of increase in the population during the critical period from 1881 to 1891 (see Table 20).

However, census figures also indicate a recovery during the period from 1891 to 1901 when the differential between the rate of increase in the number of Christians and in the population becomes slightly more marked than in the previous decade. Thus, even if the anti-Christian crusade had some effect on rates of conversion (as well as on

Table 19. Converts from Hinduism, 1884 – 1899

	Catholics - Tanjore Congregation under Goa (Adults)	Catholics - Tanjore Congregation under Rome (Adults)	Anglicans - Tanjore, St Peters (Adults)
1884 – 1887	22	36	3
1888 – 1891	17	22	5

	Anglicans - Trichinopoly Christ Church Fort (Adults)	Lutherans - Mayavaram (Adults and children)	Lutherans - Tranquebar (Adults and children)
1884 – 1887	20	756	37
1888 – 1891	6	67	10

Table 20. Percentage Rates of Increase, 1871 – 1901[101]

	Tanjore District		Trichinopoly District	
	Population	Christians	Population	Christians
1871 – 1881	7.93	17.84	1.22	17.65
1881 – 1891	4.59	9.09	12.98	14.58
1891 – 1901	0.76	1.88	5.25	8.89

enrolments in St. Joseph's College) these effects appear to have been fairly short lived.

Even in its initial stages, some aspects of the movement were counter productive — stimulating a renewed interest in Christian teaching. Describing the situation in Trichinopoly in June 1889, for example, the Rev. J. N. Thompson (W.M.M.S.) remarked that, in their evangelistic work, the Methodists had their share of opposition from the agents of the Hindu Tract Society, but he continued

On the whole I am inclined to think they have done us vastly more good than harm. Their opposition proved a capital advertisement for our services, and the tracts etc., they distributed, while supplying their own antidote by their violence & gross misrepresentation also served to attract attention & awaken enquiry.[102]

Furthermore, despite the fact that the number of conversions probably declined during the height of opposition, there were some notable cases of individual conversion. These included at least two young men who had played a prominent part in anti-Christian agitation, but who then changed sides, joining the ranks of the Christian movement. In 1890 the Rev. J. L. Wyatt (S.P.G.) commented dryly on the fact that one of the most active stone throwers in Trichinopoly had joined the Salvation Army 'and is now preaching, imperfectly, the faith he once opposed.'[103] But perhaps even more ironic was the eventual conversion of Mahadeva Iyer one of the ringleaders in the student agitation in St. Joseph's College. As we have seen, his baptism in 1894 (together with that of several other brahmans) was the beginning of a remarkable conversion movement among brahmans.

The failure of the anti-Christian movement seriously to undermine missionary activity or check the spread of Christianity was partially due to the fact that some of the stimulus and support had come from outside the region and that when the movement subsided in Madras this made it more difficult for local leaders to maintain their enthusiasm, find resources and carry on. More importantly, however, the movement never had extensive local support and increasingly lost favour with the educated classes as time progressed. When Pandiah, President of the Hindu Tract Society, visited the region most of his audiences were much smaller than those of Olcott. While, for example, the Colonel lectured to a crowd of 'more than 3,000 persons' in Trichinopoly town hall in 1883, Pandiah was able to attract an audience of only about one-third the size six years later.[104] Both leaders were given an enthusiastic welcome at Kumbakonam.[105] However, in Negapatam, in spite of traditions of anti-Christian activity, the movement associated with the Hindu Tract Society there received much less support than Theosophy and two attempts had to be made to establish some kind of viable local organization.[106]

As in other parts of the South, the movement was largely negative and had little to offer Hindus looking for something with a more positive content. The same scurrilous attacks on missionaries and Christianity, the same trend towards hooliganism in the streets and acts of violence which tended to alienate Hindu élites from the movement in Madras were also apparent in the delta. Moreover, the missionaries had vastly greater resources including full-time professional workers, a highly organized press and reliable financial backing from overseas. They had also developed an educational establishment which, despite being Christian, continued to enjoy enormous prestige among Hindus. Indeed, the great majority of Hindu parents continued to send their children to mission schools even at the height of the anti-Christian agitation and were patently unprepared to fund an alternative educational system. Even in Trichinopoly, where feelings had been running high, the proposal for using the National High School as a basis for the creation of a new and independent college had still not been implemented more than a decade later.[107]

THE CALL TO UNITY AND THE GROWTH OF DIVERSITY

One characteristic feature of the Hindu revival movement in Tanjore and Trichinopoly districts, as well as in other parts of India, was the attention given to the need for unity among all Hindus. Members of the Veda Samaj were pledged to discard all their sectarian views and feelings.[108] Olcott impressed upon his audience in Negapatam 'a sense of the desirability of social harmony and united action as essential elements in the moral regeneration of the community'[109] while Sivasankara Pandiah, speaking in Kumbakonam, condemned what he described as 'blind sectarianism and bigotry leading to caste disputes'.[110]

The emphasis in some of these calls for unity was on the need to eliminate sectarian views as well as on the need for greater harmony and co-operation. There was more than a hint that too many different views and too many different 'sects' within Hinduism were dangerous and that it would be better if Hindus could find some kind of theological common denominator. This idea is clearly reflected in the philosophy of Pandiah's Hindu Theological High School founded in Madras city in 1888. One of the aims of the school was to teach the principles of Hinduism on a 'non-sectarian' basis.[111] Side by side with this stress on the need to identify basic 'Aryan virtues' and teach common fundamentals was the constant reference in meetings and in the press to 'Hinduism' as if it was a distinct entity and something which had to be saved from all its enemies.[112]

The irony of the revivalist movement, at least in Tanjore and Trichinopoly districts, is that while initially it stimulated a greater sense of unity among Hindus, it eventually deepened sectarian and other divisions among them. These divisions became much more apparent in the 1890s after the collapse of the anti-Christian crusade. The collapse of the agitation was itself a clear indication that higher-caste Hindus were united neither in their attitude towards Christianity nor in their understanding of the tactics which should be adopted in attempts to undermine missionary activity. Furthermore, once attention shifted away from a focus on Christianity and more towards the positive teachings within Hinduism some of the more traditional differences began to surface. In harking back to fundamentals, Hindus belonging to different traditions realized increasingly that their roots were different and that what was fundamental and needed to be 'revived' in one tradition was not necessarily basic or fundamental to another. The search of the past could and sometimes did end with an emphasis on different texts in different languages and with the rediscovery, not of a common golden age, but of different origins and ideals.

As already discussed, local branches of the Theosophical Society attracted a very high proportion of brahmans, focused mainly on Sanskrit studies and tended to reflect ideas and traditions familiar in brahman circles. This tendency for brahmans to gravitate towards particular types of religious study was also reflected in the formation of the Advaita Sabha which was established in Kumbakonam in the 1890s.[113] One of the particular functions of this body, which was under the management of a committee of four brahmans, was to examine pundits annually in the Vedanta of Shankara.

But not all Hindus affected by the spirit of Hindu revivalism were interested in these aspects of Hinduism. While, for example, some educated townsmen in Tanjore and Trichinopoly districts attended lectures on 'Aryan Virtues' and on *Advaita* Hinduism, others expressed a greater interest in the teachings of Ramanuja or in *Saiva Siddhanta*.[114] The revival of interest in Sanskrit and Vedic Hinduism in particular could not fail to highlight the special and exalted position of brahmans in Hindu society and prompted further interest among non-brahmans in what they felt were their own distinctive traditions — most notably *Saiva Siddhanta*. In fact, *Saiva Siddhanta* was espoused increasingly as the religion of the ancient Dravidian peoples which flourished independently and prior to the brahman incursion into the Tamil country.[115] Saiva Siddhanta sabhas were founded in various parts of Tamilnadu in the 1880s. In 1883 a Saiva Siddhanta sabha was founded in Tuticorin in Tinnevelly district and a similar association was established in Trichinopoly two years later. In 1898 the latter was still conducting public lectures and also maintained a Free Hindu Religious School.[116] One of the effects of the revival movement, apparent by the end of the nineteenth century, was, therefore, to heighten differences among the Western-educated élites — especially the gap between brahmans and non-brahmans in the region.

Whether the movement widened or bridged the gap between these élites and the rest of the Hindu population is, however, more difficult to assess. As we have seen, Olcott made some attempt to involve a large cross-section of people in his initial meetings. He made a point of associating his movement with temple priests and appears to have avoided the mistake of alienating his audience by criticizing some of the more widespread and popular customs. The Hindu Tract Society also attempted to reach a wider group of potential followers, publishing many of its tracts and pamphlets in Tamil and, in some of these, conducting a vigorous defence of popular practices including the reasonableness of idol worship and a wide range of popular rituals.[117]

The effect of these measures was, however, probably offset by other developments which reinforced the sense of separateness between the Western-educated classes and other sections of the population. The general organizational structure of the movement was quite unsuited for popular participation. Tamils, unfamiliar with English and the niceties of Western-style organization or with academic discussion procedures, were hardly likely to feel an attraction for the various associations and sabhas which sprang up in the 1880s and 1890s — even if they could have paid the fees which were sometimes imposed. The renewed emphasis on Sanskrit studies also served to highlight the gap between the élites (especially brahmans) and lesser mortals. Furthermore, not all leaders of the movement refrained from attacking customs which were especially popular with the lower classes. Speaking in Kumbakonam in October 1889, for example, Sivasankara Pandiah proceeded to enumerate a whole series of 'impurities and encrustations' which he believed tarnished the image of contemporary Hinduism. These included the multiplication of minor deities, 'outward and costly' formalities and festivals in temples, the institution of dancing girls, the 'inhuman' sacrifices of fowls and blind faith in *mantras* and in the efficacy of baths in sacred rivers.[118]

While there was a possibility that the attack on popular practices would lead to a purer and more defensible form of Hinduism and help arrest the drift into irreligion or Christianity, there was also a risk that criticisms such as these would only widen the gap between the leaders of the revival movement and ordinary Hindus.

NOTES

1 The Secretary was expected to place himself in communication with members of the Brahmo Samaj at Calcutta 'whenever it may be necessary'. See covenants and rules of the Society in *The Calcutta Christian Observer*, May 1865, pp. 238 – 40.
2 For an account of the establishment of the Veda Samaj in Madras see Suntharalingam, op. cit., pp. 294 – 6.
3 *S.P.G. Annual Report*, 1866, p. 138.
4 Supra, Ch. 1.
5 W.M.M.S., Cryer to Secs., 15/9/1836, Madras, Box 435.
6 For the proportion of students in missionary as distinct from Government colleges in the area see Appendix 13.
7 *H.F.*, Vol. 1, May 1862, pp. 163 – 6; June 1862, pp. 188 – 92, Vol. 2, April 1863, pp. 133 – 9.
8 *W.M.N.*, 1854, pp. 133 – 6.

NOTES TO CHAPTER 10

9 Ibid., 1856, pp. 194 – 5.
10 Ibid., 1877, pp. 206 – 7.
11 Ibid., 1877, p. 280; *L.N.*, 1878, pp. 54 – 5.
12 Ibid., 1882, p. 223.
13 Ibid., 1880, p. 54.
14 Ibid., 1882, pp. 224 – 5. See also *H.F.*, Vol. V, August 1884, pp. 60 – 1.
15 For the origins of Theosophy see especially B. F. Campbell, *Ancient Wisdom Revived: A History of the Theosophical Movement*, Berkeley 1980, Ch. 1.
16 For a discussion of the changing objects of the Society see C. Jinarajadasa (ed.) *The Golden Book of the Theosophical Society*, Madras 1925, pp. 243 – 50 and H. Murphet, *The Hammer on the Mountain. Life of Henry Steel Olcott (1832 – 1907)*, Illinois etc., 1972, pp. 96 – 7.
17 Olcott, *Old Diary Leaves* (henceforth *O.D.L.*), second series, 1878 – 1883, Madras 1974, pp. 360 – 2.
18 Suntharalingam, op. cit., Chs. 4 – 5. See also the Rev. A. Alexander's address to delegates of the second decennial conference held in Calcutta at the end of 1882 *Report of the Second Decennial Missionary Conference*, Calcutta, 1883, esp. pp. 160 – 2.
19 On the movement in Ceylon see especially L. A. Wickremeratne, 'Religion, Nationalism and Social Change in Ceylon, 1865 – 1885', in *J.R.A.S*, 1969, pp. 123 – 50.
20 Murphet, op. cit., p. 92.
21 *Isis Unveiled*, New ed., California, 1972, Vol. II.
22 S. Ghosh, *The Renaissance to Militant Nationalism in India*, Bombay etc., 1969, p. 40.
23 *Th.* Vol. 1, January 1880, pp. 100 – 1; February 1880, pp. 112 – 3, April 1880, p. 181; Vol. II, April 1881, pp. 160 – 3, May 1881, pp. 174 – 6. Articles included 'The State of Christianity', Vol. 1, April 1880, pp. 181 – 2, 'The Christian Art of War', Vol. 1, June 1880, p. 230 and 'The Decadence of Protestant Christianity', Vol. 1, September 1880, p. 309.
24 Quoted in Suntharalingum, op. cit., 296.
25 Editorial in *Madras Mail* quoted in Suntharalingam, op. cit., pp. 300 – 1.
26 *Report of the Second Decennial Missionary Conference*, p. 161.
27 *O.D.L.*, III, pp. 373 – 5.
28 Ibid., pp. 443 – 4.
29 A. H. Nethercot, *The Last Four Lives of Annie Besant*, London, 1963, p. 17.
30 *O.D.L.*, III, pp. 73 – 4; *Th.*, Vol. II, Sup. May 1881, p. 3.
31 *Th.*, Vol. III, June 1882, p. 235.
32 *Th.* Vol. VIII, Sup., Nov. 1886, pp. V.
33 Copies were being sent to Trichinopoly, Srirangam, Negapatam and Kumbakonam as early as 1880. *Th.*, Vol. 2, Sup., March 1881, p. 140.
34 *Th.*, Vol. IV, Sup., September 1883, pp. 3 – 5.
35 Ibid., p. 4.
36 *O.D.L.*, II, pp. 452, 456, 460 – 1.
37 Ibid., p. 456.

38 Ibid., pp. 458-9.
39 *Th.*, Vol IV., Sup., September 1883, p. 4.
40 Ibid., *O.D.L.*, II, pp. 459-60.
41 *Th.*, Vol. IV., Sup., September 1883, p. 5.
42 Ibid., p. 4.
43 Ibid., pp. 4-8.
44 Ibid., p. 8.
45 See Appendix 11.
46 *Th.*, Vol. XII., January 1891, pp. 247-8.
47 Ibid., p. 249.
48 *Theosophical Society Convention and Anniversary*, Annual Reports, 1890-1891.
49 *Th.*, Vol. XIII, Sup., March 1891, p. XXI.
50 See *Convention and Anniversary*, Annual Reports, 1891-1900.
51 *Th.*, Vol. XV, January 1894, p. 260. For Olcott's account of Mrs. Besant's first Indian tour see *Th.*, Vol. XV, April 1894, pp. 442-9.
52 *Hindu*, 5/11/1885.
53 *Th.*, Vol. VII, Sup., July 1886, CXLI.
54 *Hindu*, 13,27/7, 8/8/1888.
55 *O.D.L.*, II, p. 460.
56 *Hindu*, 15/8/1888.
57 G. A. Oddie, 'Anti-Missionary Feeling . . .'.
58 *H.F.*, Vol. IX, July 1888-June 1889, pp. 304-6.
59 The importance of the Salvation Army in stimulating Hindu fears and opposition is reflected in the fact that the Hindu Tract Society specifically devoted one of its tracts to an attack on the Army. The first Salvation Army group to arrive in India reached Bombay in September 1882 a few years after the Theosophists. The Army was in Madras in 1885 and established centres for work in the Kaveri delta in Trichinopoly, Tanjore and Negapatam in about 1887 (*All the World*, June 1887 p. 188, July 1887, p. 214, October 1887, p. 333). In 1890 the Army claimed that its staff of 131 European missionaries working in India was the largest staff employed by an Indian mission even though the Army was the last to enter the field. According to the same source there were 217 'native missionaries' and, during a four month period in about 1890, 2,169 new converts. 'Of these 74 per cent were heathen, 16 per cent native Roman Catholics and Protestant Christians, 7 per cent Indian-born Eurasians, and only 3 per cent Europeans!' (*All the World*, August 1890, p. 349).
60 Oddie, 'Anti-Missionary Feeling. . .'
61 *Hindu*, 12/3, 10/8, 31/10/1888, 4/2/1889.
62 Ibid., 15/2, 6/3, 21/12/1889.
63 Appendix 12.
64 Appendix 12.
65 S.P.G., J. L. Wyatt, Report for year ending 30 June 1889.
66 *Hindu*, 12/3/1888.
67 Ibid., 17/10/1889.
68 Ibid., 25/10/1889.
69 Ibid., 15/2/1889.

NOTES TO CHAPTER 10   215

70 Ibid., 17/10/1889.
71 *U.S.P.G.*, Series B., Annual Report for 1887.
72 *Indian War Cry*, 5 May 1890. See also 8 September 1890.
73 *U.S.P.G.*, Series B, Nagalinka Gnanapprakasam, Annual Report for 1887.
74 *W.M.M.S.*, Annual Report, 1893, p. 58.
75 *Hindu*, 12/10/1889.
76 Ibid., 14/3/1890.
77 See J. L. Wyatt's translation of the second edition of a Hindu tract entitled 'May our girls read in Mission Schools?' (*U.S.P.G.*, Series B, J. L. Wyatt, Annual Report for 1888). See also *U.S.P.G.*, Series B., Nagalinka Gnanapprakasam, Annual Report for 1887 and Report of the Madras Diocesan Committee of the S.P.G. for 1889, p. 51.
78 Suntharalingam, op. cit., pp. 306 – 7; Oddie, 'Anti-Missionary Feeling . . .' pp. 231 – 2.
79 *Hindu*, 7/5/1887.
80 Ibid., 11/5/1888, 3/8/1888.
81 Ibid., 2/5/1889.
82 Ibid., 20/3/1889, 4/5/1889, 29/7/1889.
83 Ibid., 20, 22/3/1889.
84 L. Lacombe, *L'Oeuvre de la Conversion*, p. 28.
85 *Hindu*, 20/3/1889.
86 Ibid., 20/3/4,7/5/1889.
87 Ibid., 4/5/1889.
88 Ibid., 11/5/1889.
89 Ibid., 4/5/1889; L. Lacombe, *A Great Indian Convert*, p. 7.
90 *Hindu*, 24,29/7/1889.
91 Ibid., 11/5/1889.
92 Ibid., 11/5/24,29/7/17/10/1889.
93 Ibid., 11/5/1889.
94 *A.R.S.I.*, 3 February 1890 Maduré, 1005 – VII, 3. Appaswami Anjar, the school's Tamil Pundit, who addressed the meeting in April and two of the five leading members of the Hindu community noted by a local reporter as being present on the same occasion were also staff of the National High School (*Hindu*, 11/5/1889).
95 *S.P.G.Q.R.*, April – June 1890, No. XXIV.
96 F. Booth Tucker, *Muktifauj or Forty Years with the Salvation Army in India and Ceylon*, London, N.D., pp. 100 – 101.
97 Although the Methodists in Warriore, a suburb of Trichinopoly, were able to report early in 1880 that they had had 'the privilege of receiving over a large Brahmin Girls School of 60 to 80 on the rolls from a heathen man', other reports indicate that S.P.G. missionaries had to close several of their schools. They argued, however, that this was necessary, not because of the opposition of Hindu parents, but simply because of 'want of funds'. (*W.M.M.S.* Blackburn to Jenkins, 16/1/1888, *Hindu*, 12/3/1888, *Report of the Madras Diocesan Committee of the S.P.G.*, 1889, p. 63; *U.S.P.G.* Wyatt's Annual Report, 30/6/1889 (71), *The Net*, 1 June 1889.
98 *A.R.S.I.*, Faseuille to P. 3 Feb. 1890, Maduré 1005 – VII, 3.

99 *Reports of Public Instruction in the Madras Presidency*, 1887 – 1892.
100 Ibid.
101 For the actual census figures see Appendix 7.
102 *W.M.M.S.*, Thompson to Walton, 22/6/1889, Negapatam and Trichinopoly, Box 426.
103 *Report of the Madras Diocesan Committee of the S.P.G. for 1889*, pp. 50 – 1. See also *Indian War Cry*, 24 February 1890 and 6 April 1891.
104 *Th.* Vol. IV Sup., September 1883, p. 4; *Hindu*, 17/10/1889.
105 *Th.* Vol. IV, Sup., September 1883, pp. 4 – 5; *O.D.L.*, II, p. 460; *Hindu*, 25/10/1889.
106 *Th.* Vol IV, Sup., September 1883 p. 4; *Hindu*, 15/2/1889. It appears that more than one attempt had also to be made to establish a branch of the Hindu Tract Society at Warriore, (*Hindu*, 12/3/1888, 4/2/1889.)
107 *Hindu*, 1/11/1900.
108 *Calcutta Christian Observer*, May 1865, p. 239.
109 *Th*, Vol. IV, Sup, September 1883, p. 4.
110 *Hindu*, 25/10/1889. The same theme was reiterated in the literature circulated by the Hindu Tract Society. For example, Tract no. 2, 'What Hindus Should Carefully Consider', July 1887, declared that 'Hereafter Hindus should not fight among themselves calling themselves thenkalais, vadakalais, saivites, vaishnavites, advaitins, visihtaadvaitins and dvaitins; they should act as one man and oppose the Christian religion'.
111 *The Duties of the Natives of India to their rulers and their country*, Madras 1888, Appendix, pp. 15 – 16; *Hindu Excelsior Series*, No. XII.
112 See for example, a reference to Srinivasa Sastrial's lectures at Madurai, (*Hindu*, 30/11/1888).
113 *Hindu*, 1/11/1892.
114 Ibid., 14/4/1898; 15, 28/6/1898, 26/7/1898, 12/6/1899; 11/9/1900.
115 K. Nambi Arooran, *Tamil Renaissance and Dravidian Nationalism 1905 – 1944*, Madurai 1980, p. 24.
116 *Hindu*, 15/6/1898.
117 See especially Tamil tracts no. 4 'on the reasonableness of image worship', July 1887 and no. 5 'Why do missionaries condemn other scriptures when they do not examine their own scripture?', August 1887.
118 *Hindu*, 25/10/1889.

CONCLUSION

The purpose of this concluding section is to re-examine, in the light of previous discussion, relationships between religion and society. What were the more constant or enduring aspects of the relationship between religion and society in the Kaveri Delta in the nineteenth century? What was the relationship between religious and social change? How far did social factors and developments stimulate or even inhibit religious change, and in what ways did religious developments affect or impinge upon society in the region?

A fundamental and enduring feature of social life in Tanjore and Trichinopoly districts was hierarchy. As in other parts of India, caste hierarchy in particular had long been affirmed and justified in Hindu texts as a divinely ordained or God-given pattern of social ordering and precedence.

The lines in the *Rig Veda* describing the great sacrifice of primeval man have often been referred to as justifying the particular position of each of the four *varnas* in Hindu society:

> 'The brahman was his mouth
> of his arms was made the warrior,
> his thighs became the vaisya
> of his feet the sudra was born'[1]

The lower classes in the population were again reminded of the exalted position especially of brahmans in the social scale in the *Manava Dharmasastra* or *Laws of Manu*.

> As the Brahmana sprang from (Brahman's) mouth, as he was the first-born, and as he possesses the Veda, he is by right the lord of this whole creation.[2]

In the *Bhagavadgita* Krishna not only affirms his position as 'Lord of the Universe' but also as creator of the Hindu social order,[3] while in the *Dharmasastras* the doctrines of reincarnation and karma are also used to legitimate and justify the caste hierarchy. According to these works, if a man does good deeds he will be born into a high caste while, if he does sinful acts, he will be born into a low caste or even as an animal — a pig or a donkey. Furthermore, not unrelated to this doctrine, which implies that birth in a particular caste is an index of the soul's progress towards God, were notions of pollution and purity — the lower castes, in consequence of their having greater pollution being more distant from the presence of God.[4]

In South India and the Kaveri Delta the notion of an ideal *varna* or class system was, however, considerably modified in practice. Not only were the two middle classes (the kshatriyas and vaisyas) largely absent from the social order, but the position of brahmans as the all powerful and undisputed leaders of religion was more ambiguous than classical literature and some European writers seemed to imply.[5]

As we have seen, brahmans were not the only religious specialists. While they continued to conduct important rituals in the larger temples, non-brahman or 'sudra' specialists, dancing girls and many others also performed tasks important for the well-being, pleasure and contentment of the deity. In some cases, brahmans, together with other high-caste Hindus, were also dependent on inferior non-brahman or outcaste functionaries. The untouchable who beheaded the buffalo in front of Mariamma's shrine and low-caste Hindus who swung on behalf of the village community were all performing rituals which some brahmans clearly felt were necessary, but which they themselves were unwilling to perform.[6]

Secondly, there is a difference between one's position as a priest or religious specialist on the one hand and power to control religious institutions on the other. Those who conducted rituals within the temple did not necessarily belong to the same caste or class of people as those who controlled its management. Even if, for example, brahmans played a key role as servants of the god, one cannot assume that they were the ones who had ultimate control of the institution. Once again, in the case of ultimate control and management (to an even greater extent than in the case of those who conducted rituals), the power and influence of the non-brahman classes was very much in evidence. Indeed, power to control the major religious institutions appears to have depended less on caste or ritual status than on 'secular' factors including wealth and land ownership in local society. It was primarily the landed and commercial classes who were in a position to endow and support religious institutions and it was these wealthier classes, including *mirasidars*, who continued to take an interest in temple management. In Tanjore where a higher proportion of non-brahmans appear to have been *mirasidars* than was the case in Trichinopoly and where non-brahmans had acquired considerable wealth in trade and commerce, especially in Negapatam, they naturally tended to dominate boards and committees. On the other hand, in Trichinopoly, where the brahmans were in a better economic position *vis à vis* non-brahmans, they were correspondingly more conspicuous in the control and management of religious institutions.[7]

But, while in actual practice, brahmans were less dominant in religious affairs than one might have been led to expect, they were naturally conscious of their theoretical position at the top of the caste hierarchy. This is probably one of the main reasons why they, to a greater extent than any other group, were attracted by Theosophy, the leaders of which all preached a revival of Sanskrit studies and a brahmanical form of Hinduism which, if anything, was likely to strengthen the culture and position of brahmans throughout the south — a point which was not lost on non-brahman critics.

It was not only those at the top of the social hierarchy such as brahmans however who attempted to utilize religion — in this case for the purpose of social control. Other groups in the community, even untouchables, were also perfectly capable of making use of the same phenomenon (including religious ideas, institutions and rituals) as a resource and as a method of gaining greater power and recognition in local society.

If some religious ideas could be used to justify and bolster the *status quo* there were other concepts in Hinduism and especially in Christianity, which could be used to challenge the idea of a spiritual hierarchy or attack various forms of injustice or discrimination.[8] It is very difficult to know what impact the preaching of Christian ideas of equality had on low and outcaste Hindus; but it is quite likely that these ideas, together with a knowledge of the care and attention being given to individuals and families, was one of the reasons for the attractiveness of the Christian movement. Moreover, the example of the missionary-pastor who believed he had an obligation to defend and protect his converts especially from the depredations of landlords, and who established schools and took the cases involving persecution or injustice to court — these and other activities, quite apart from preaching, were bound to encourage a greater awareness of individual rights and an increasing resentment of injustice. Indeed, as already mentioned, one of the fears among landlords was that the spread of Christianity and literacy would spoil their workers, encouraging a rebellious spirit and making them difficult to control.

Religion, however, was not only something which could be used for purposes of social control or increased power over others. It was also utilized by individuals, families and caste communities as one among a number of methods of maintaining or improving social status.

Among middle or higher-caste Hindus, office holding, including a position as trustee or member of the temple committee, could greatly enhance the incumbent's status in the local community. The receipt of honours which symbolized one's special relationship with the deity and also the recipient's standing within the worshipping community, was a privilege highly sought-after and one of the major causes of dispute between, for example, tengalai and vadagalai factions in Srirangam temple throughout the nineteenth century. A position either as trustee or as a member of a temple committee also brought with it the possibility of patronage. Furthermore, association with the major temple, especially as a member of a temple committee, was not only useful as a leg up for politicians hoping to consolidate local support, but also on some occasions, a means of amassing a personal fortune and, with that, increased power and influence in the community.[9]

Lower-caste Hindus were also able to maintain or enhance individual or family status through participation in religious festivals. Hook-swinging, for example, was often regarded as a privilege — so much so that the right to swing was in some cases restricted to certain pariah or other families, the young men involved having to await their turn.[10] The adoption of new types of ritual was also seen as a method enhancing or consolidating social status, lower-caste Hindus not infrequently imitating high-caste religious customs (such as the practice of fire-walking) at least partly as a method of achieving upward social mobility.

Religion was not always used, however, in situations of competition and conflict, as a method of asserting individual or corporate rights, of achieving or maintaining social position, or of exercising greater power or control over others. As well as being utilized for these purposes, some of which were divisive, it was also a force for unity — creating a greater degree of social cohesion. Family, caste and village deities were, for example, powerful instruments providing people with a point of focus and strengthening the bonds of family, caste and village. Furthermore, village and temple festivals and other events, such as the Mahamagum festival in Kumbakonam, which attracted pilgrims from more distant places, also acted as a further force of contact and cultural integration. It is this integrating role of religion, especially the part it played in building up and consolidating new identities, which will receive further attention in the concluding section of this chapter.

If then these were some of the more enduring features of the relationship between religion and society, in what way did social factors and considerations (such as those mentioned above) stimulate or even inhibit religious change in the region in the nineteenth century?

Before we address this question we might perhaps say something more about the character and different types of religious change which have been noted and discussed in earlier chapters. Some of these changes, such as the conversion of Mahadeva Iyer, were profound alterations in the inner life and orientation of the individual. For example, notwithstanding the continuities one may be able to detect between Mahadeva's pre and post-conversion religious life and experience, there can be no doubt that, for Mahadeva himself, what was significant about his new-found faith was not its similarity with his previous faith and life in Hinduism, but the fact that it was something entirely new. Describing his intellectual and spiritual struggles which terminated in his acceptance of Catholicism he declared that one of the most significant stages in his journey was reading the *Imitation* and the *Confessions* of St. Augustine which surrounded him with 'a wholly new' moral atmosphere and impelled him to further inquiry.[11]

Traces of this type of inward and revolutionary change, including a wholly new vision of the world, of God and morality (a change which may also have taken place in the lives of some of those who at least outwardly remained 'Hindu') are not necessarily reflected in historical material. There is a great deal therefore which we cannot know. It is difficult to tell, for example, how many other Christian converts experienced with Mahadeva Iyer the same sense of radical transformation. Nor do we know to any great extent what was happening in the hearts and minds of the young men, such as those who joined the Veda Samaj in Tanjore in 1865, or precisely what changes were involved in the life and thought of the students in Kumbakonam who, moved by the oratory and persuasive power of Olcott, gave up rationalism for a renewed belief in the things of the spirit.

Fortunately, however, some of the more general outward and visible signs of religious change are not difficult to document. As we have seen, these included the rise and growth of religious conversion movements involving changes in communal affiliation and religious identity; the emergence of new forms of religious organization, such as Western-type associations for the reform and renewal of Hinduism; changes in the scale and forms of religious defence and organization, such as those apparent in the rise of the Hindu preaching and tract societies, and other changes which took place at the institutional level such as those introduced in the management of Hindu temples which were in turn the result of changes in official religious policy.

Many of these somewhat formal and collective changes were, however, a reflection of other movements and changes at a deeper and more personal level. For example, the growth of the Christian community was itself a reflection of changes taking place in the personal devotional life of at least some individuals whose worship and ritual practice was changing from a focus on Hindu deities to an emphasis on the worship of Jesus, the Virgin or on Catholic saints. Furthermore, changes of this nature which occurred among converts of Christianity were paralleled by similar developments (involving a change in the object or focus of worship) which continued to take place among Hindus. We noted, for example, the rise and growth of cults associated with women who were burnt as satis, the growing popularity of Madurai Viran and revivals in the worship of local and long-forgotten Hindu deities.

Associated with these changes in perception and in the rise to prominence of different deities were changes in methods of worship and in rituals. Some changes in ritual were introduced as a result of sectarian struggle, such as those which resulted from the successful vadagalai infiltration of Srirangam temple, while other changes and rituals were also introduced, at least in part, because of lower-caste imitation of the rituals and customs of brahmans and other dominant groups in the region.

If then these were some of the religious changes taking place in the region in the nineteenth century, what was the relationship between these developments and social factors and change?

One of the most fundamental social developments affecting Hinduism and acting as a stimulus for religious change was the rise of the Western-educated élites — a new generation composed almost entirely of high-caste young men who were exposed increasingly to a whole range of western ideas, literature and learning. Being a product of change, they were, not surprisingly, well aware of the tensions it could bring and of the need to make some kind of adjustment in their thinking and way of life. These were the young men who (while divided among themselves) were conspicuous in pressing for religious and social change. A few of them, like the students in the Government College, Kumbakonam, renounced religion altogether; a few of them, mostly students in missionary institutions were, not only attracted to Christianity, but took the ultimate step of requesting baptism; many of them adopted a more moderate mildly reformist position, or became involved as leaders in movements such as Hindu revivalism or Theosophy. These movements, which were essentially high-caste, élitist and urban, mirrored similar movements in many other urban centres in India.

While the religious changes particularly conspicuous in towns and cities were largely the product of the newly-created Western-educated élites, what of religious changes in the countryside? How important were social factors in the rise of rural movements including, for example, Christian movements in Tanjore district?

Unlike many other parts of South India, Tanjore district appears to have been a peculiarly stable society — most of the dominant families in control in the early nineteenth century retaining their fundamental hegemony throughout the period under investigation. Unlike districts such as Tinnevelly or Nellore (where there were large-scale conversion movements) there were no *great* famines disrupting the social system.

CONCLUSION

Nor do there appear to have been any other new and sudden crises which may have created a widely-felt need for new cosmologies or systems of explanation. On the contrary, the changes which were taking place appear to have been fairly gradual and the explanation for the more obvious signs of religious change such as the growth of conversion movements can hardly be rooted in any theory of a sudden or especially dramatic social breakdown or crisis.

But while dismissing the notion of a new and sudden widespread crisis in Tanjore district it is important to recognize that the depressed classes had long been in a state of almost perpetual minor crisis — socially and religiously oppressed, living from hand to mouth and often on the edge of starvation. What was significant in their case was not a sudden change in their economic and social situation in the nineteenth century but, more simply, the arrival of Christian missionaries who opened new doors of hope and expectation. The potential for a change of religion was there even before the Protestants became active in country areas. Missionary preaching and especially the establishment of permanent mission stations in country areas created an entirely new situation. This included the possibility of an alliance with the mission in ways which would not only modify the effects of an oppressive economic and social system, but which also encouraged the growth of new religious ideas and self-respect.

Religious changes were not only stimulated by social developments (such as the rise of new élites and the establishment of a permanent missionary presence in the countryside) but were also affected by structures within the social system. A desire for religious change was not enough as this could often be undermined by what appeared to be almost insuperable obstacles and opposition. In some cases change was facilitated by the social system while in others it created an almost impossible impediment to any form of protest or deviation.

Family and caste attitudes and pressures were often crucial — the higher one's standing in the social scale the more difficult it was, for example, for Hindus to win family support or approval for any move into Christianity — a phenomenon which was usually associated in the mind of brahmans and others with untouchability. Indeed, one of the reasons for the popularity of Theosophy among the Western-educated élites was precisely that, unlike the act of joining the Christian Church, its acceptance was not perceived as involving a loss of status. Brahmans and other high castes attracted by its teachings were not asked to renounce caste or to make any other concessions which would compromise their status and position as Hindus.

Specific obstacles to conversion at the lower end of the social scale were somewhat different. As the loss of status and ritual purity involved in becoming a Christian was either non-existent or less than it was in the case of high-caste converts there was correspondingly less family opposition. More often than not Christian families in low-caste or untouchable communities continued to interact and intermarry with Hindu members of their own caste in much the same way they had before baptism. The most serious deterrent to conversion usually arose from the attitude of outsiders, village officials, landlords and other representatives of the dominant classes who feared that low or outcaste acceptance of Christianity would undermine their power and control over labourers and other 'servants'.

Not all landlords (the most important dominant group in the countryside) were however opposed to Christianity. Some were neutral or indifferent, while an exceptional few, by taking the initiative in joining the Christian movement, encouraged tenants and landless labourers to follow suit. In these few instances the rural hierarchy (including elements of both caste and class) was operating in favour of religious change.

Some of the factors which determined whether individuals and groups who wished to do so could actually afford to change their religious identity, affiliation or life style are therefore clearly apparent, especially in cases involving possible conversion to Christianity. While some of the pressures at work in brahman households are clear enough and usually operated against conversion, social structures and pressures affecting the life of low-caste Hindus in rural areas operated in a less predictable fashion. When, for example, there was a widespread disposition in favour of Christianity, a great deal depended on the attitude of individual landlords and on whether individual families had sufficient courage, independence or means to survive persecution.

So far we have been considering ways in which social developments, aspirations and needs affected religion — how, for example, religious ideas and institutions were used for social ends. None of this discussion is, however, meant to imply that religion was seen merely or even principally as an effective tool which could be utilized for non-religious purposes, or that the Hindus' or Christians' understanding of the world, including their religious views and sentiments, were unimportant or of little or no consequence to themselves. As we have already implied in previous chapters, religious symbols, ideas and feelings were a powerful force in the life of large numbers of the population. While social factors affected religion, religious belief and feeling affected the social system and it now remains for us to explore and identify more clearly the role of religion in the social process.

In the first place, the East India Company's religious policy of theoretical 'neutrality' (involving, in effect, considerable interference) stimulated further changes in the relationship of various groups and individuals in society to religious institutions — especially their relationship with Hindu temples.

While the management and control of temples remained very largely in the hands of the dominant high-caste groups, British policy had the effect of providing more opportunities for those groups and castes not normally associated with management, to have a greater say in the conduct and control of temple affairs. The new recruits appointed by the district collectors as trustees and managers of the smaller temples in 1842 included merchants, village headmen and temple servants — individuals whose families had never had any connection with temple management. The setting up of the supervisory temple committees further enlarged the arena of public participation and also enabled representatives of some of the lower-caste communities (such as nadars and kallars) to play a part in temple management. Among these men were wealthy landowners such as Doorasamy Moopanar, T. S. Sivasamy Odiyar and T. Punnusami Nadar[12] — the latter also having substantial interests in the salt and liquor trades. The appearance of these men on temple committees was a further sign that wealth rather than caste or ritual status was important if one wanted a say in the management of even the most sacred and prestigious religious institutions. A position on the temple committee, gained largely through wealth and influence, confirmed the incumbent's standing in the locality and, if anything, further enhanced the prospects of already powerful and upwardly mobile families.

A second effect of changes in the religious system, including arrangements for the upkeep and management of Hindu temples, was to intensify and widen the arena of 'sectarian' conflict. One particularly inept decision in relation to vadagalai claims to perform their own rituals in Srirangam, the opening up of the board of trustees to outsiders and the setting up of the Trichinopoly Temple Committee, which came to include vadagalai members, intensified feeling and heightened apprehension among tengalais that one of their most important centres was about to be taken over by their traditional rivals. The struggle between the two groups, which was also occurring in other parts of the south, not only became more intense and violent, but was fought out in a larger theatre — on the new temple committees and through the new legal system, sometimes in ways which further inflamed communal tension.

Another of the more obvious effects of religious and other changes was the continued growth of the Christian community which in 1871 comprised 3.7 per cent and in 1901 4.4 per cent of the total population of the region. Notwithstanding the fact that this community was being constantly enlarged through the recruitment of Hindu converts it was beginning to develop social characteristics of its own. This was partly because the mixture and proportion of castes in the Christian community was different from that in the Hindu community and also because of Christian social teaching and other factors.

It is certainly true that the great majority of Christians continued to operate within the caste system and to marry into their own caste communities, but there were some changes taking place. As we noted, some high-caste Christians, most notably those associated with the Anglican and Methodist missions, gave up caste altogether, while in other instances Christian families terminated traditional marriage alliances with Hindu families. Furthermore, it was hardly possible for high-caste Christians to continue to justify their position in the caste hierarchy in quite the same way as Hindus, by reference to Hindu ideas of pollution and purity or of spiritual inequality. The 'Tanjore Christians', for example, dissatisfied with Anglican policy on the caste issue, clearly dissociated themselves from Hindu theory. 'Histories of the Scripture and of the world', they declared in 1829, 'prove that the Distinction of Caste is not originated from Heathenism, but from the people being divided into different classes' — a development which, they argued, was antecedent to the arrival of brahmanism and the spread of brahmanical teaching.[13]

But if, in spite of these signs of change, the effect of Christianity on caste practices must still be described as minimal, the same thing cannot be said when one explores some of the other social repercussions of the Christian movement. One of the more dramatic effects of conversion emerges through an analysis of the position of women. Practices such as early marriage declined at a faster rate among Christians than among Hindus of the same caste community, while literacy and educational levels among Christian women far outstripped those among Hindu women.[14] Furthermore, conversion to Christianity (including the encouragement of education) opened wider the doors of what can only be described as an educated middle-class culture — a higher proportion of Christians when compared with Hindus becoming educated in English, urbanized and probably also professionals or employees in modern Western-type occupations.[15] It was this middle-class aspect of Christianity, including its association with ideas of progress and modernity, that impressed Western-educated Hindu observers such as one of the Hindu Professors of Kumbakonam College who, speaking in 1887, claimed that Christians were showing Hindus how they could modify the 'absurd trammels of caste', study Western civilization 'in its home' and educate and improve the status of women.[16]

A further effect of religion and religious change was an intensification of ferment, social conflict and even violence. Not all Hindus were, for example, complimentary in what they had to say about Christians and Christianity. The growth of Hindu revival movements, encouraged by the arrival of Theosophy, the organization of Hindu tract and preaching societies and the spread among the educated classes of ideas of nonconformity and change all had the effect of provoking opposition and conflict. While, on the one side, this dissention and strife was a sign of fear and of desperate attempts by those people threatened by change to shore up the *status quo*, on the other side, it symbolized social and religious readjustment — the gestation and birth of new alignments, of new ways of seeing oneself and of relating to the social and religious system.

Religion played an important part in this type of process, in the rise or consolidation of new forms of identity — in the growth of new kinds of identity among the Western-educated élites, in the growth and consolidation of the non-brahman movement and in the emergence of a heightened awareness and sense of purpose among depressed class groups.

As we have noted, the new religious movements, such as Theosophy and Hindu reform and revival movements, helped provide many of the Western-educated young men with a new ethos, ideology and image which not only set them apart from their parents and traditional society, but also, at least to some extent, from each other. Some, as we have seen, became Rationalists, or Theosophists, or followers of *Saiva Siddhanta*, or Brahmos, or Christians, or exponents of some other type of religious tradition — young people who were clearly and sometimes passionately divided on religious issues. And yet, for all this, their religious identity was not totaly subsumed by their allegiance to one or other of these groupings. They were all members of the same steadily growing Western-educated élite and, as part of this wider community, shared many things in common. They were the ones who bore the brunt of cultural contact, who faced similar tensions and problems within the family or criticism from conservative Hindus as they attempted, in some way, to cope with the challenge of a new order and new ideas and styles of life. Even if they were not all involved in reform, they often operated through Western-style associations. Not all were activists, but many of them, though belonging to different religious groups, were engaged in an intense and searching reassessment of the Hindu past and in attempts to enhance and revitalize religious life. Their education through English, questioning attitudes, habits and employment (in cases where they were engaged in modern professional occupations) tended to set them apart, not only from older generations and other members of the dominant class, but also from the mass of the population below.

This gulf was further widened by an increasingly critical attitude towards popular religion. Like the upper classes in early modern Europe who were also influenced by a type of cosmopolitan culture and tended to distance themselves from other classes in the population, they withdrew increasingly from participation in some aspects of popular practice. This tendency to withdraw and condemn was reflected in Sivasankara Pandiah's attack on popular practices while on tour in Tanjore district and in editorials in the *Hindu* severely critical of hook-swinging ceremonies in Trichinopoly and elsewhere. In fact as early as 1853 British officials believed that both hook-swinging and fire-walking were already declining precisely because the educated classes were beginning to withdraw their support and encouragement of these activities. After considering the reports of district officers on hook-swinging, for example, the Government of Madras argued that its attempts to discourage the practice would be aided 'by the example and endeavours of the higher and more educated classes of the Native community' who, even then, in 1854, were opposed to the custom.

Religious ideas and developments not only helped reinforce the Western-educated élites' sense of isolation from other sections in the population, but also encouraged the growth of the non-brahman movement.

Certainly there is not much evidence, at least in the Kaveri delta, of religious differences widening the gap between brahmans and non-brahmans throughout much of the nineteenth century. In fact, what is noticeable, at least up until the 1890s, is not so much conflict but co-operation between the two groups in the management of religious affairs. There is, for example, no evidence of what Kennedy claims was a deliberate attempt by brahmans to establish themselves firmer than ever as 'the secular leaders' especially of the wealthier institutions. If there was conflict between individual brahmans and non-brahmans it was more likely to be over matters of honours and status within the temple, control of resources and sectarian issues than over specific questions of caste. Brahmans and high-caste non-brahmans usually sat on the same committees concerned with temple management, performed rituals in the same temples and worked together in many Western-type religious associations without raising questions about a conflict of interest between the two communities. Co-operation and mutual respect rather than a conflict of aims and views was also reflected in the way in which non-brahman *maths* established special facilities, such as *chattrams*, for brahmans and actively patronized the work of brahman scholars.

Nevertheless, some signs of religious divergence and of conflict between the two groups over religious issues do begin to emerge in the 1890s partly as a result of the influence of the Theosophical movement. As we saw, the emphasis of Olcott, Besant and other leaders of Theosophy was on the exposition and furtherance of brahman culture. Brahmans were clearly predominant both as leaders and as rank-and-file members of local branches of the Society where the stress was on the study and discussion of Sanskrit literature and 'Aryan Philosophy'. On the other hand, the non-brahman *maths* had long placed an emphasis on Tamil rather than Sanskrit and on the study and propagation of *Saiva Siddhanta*. Separate *Saiva Siddhanta* associations were established in the 1890s and there was an increasing tendency among non-brahmans (partly in reaction to Theosophy) to stress and expound the view that *Saiva Siddhanta* was the religion of the ancient Dravidian peoples which had developed quite separately and prior to the brahman 'invasion' of South India. It was in the context of this growing ideological and self-conscious divergence between brahmans and non-brahmans that the communal issue began to emerge as a factor in the elections for the Kumbakonam Temple Committee in 1899.

The role of ideology and of some aspects of religion in the rise of the non-brahman political movement in the twentieth century has been noted by Irschick, Arooran and others. However, what they tend to ignore is the power and importance and, in some cases, the dominance of non-brahmans in the control and management of leading religious institutions. If, in the early years of the movement, high-caste non-brahmans discovered that they were, in comparison with brahmans, poorly educated and underrepresented in the public service, they could not complain, at least in the Kaveri delta, that they had little say in the management of the chief temples and *maths*. Indeed, it may well be that these people became involved in political protest not because they felt deprived of power in religion, but because they wanted political rights and positions in the civil administration commensurate with what they already had within the religious system. In other words, their experience of power and sense of importance in religious affairs made them feel, all the more deeply, their comparative lack of power and influence in the administration and gave added impetus to the non-brahman movement.

Apart from acting as a stimulus and encouraging the growth of the non-brahman movement, religion was probably also a factor in the growth of depressed class consciousness, dissatisfaction and protest. In a recent analysis of 'radical' movements in Tanjore district during the post-independence period, Marshall M. Boulton relates various 'ecological, agro-economic and technological factors to the occurrence of agrarian radicalism'.[17] What he fails to mention, however, were developments in the nineteenth century including the depressed class movements into Christianity in the 1880s and 1890s, which also reflected a great deal of unrest and dissatisfaction and which may well have led to an increased willingness on the part of the depressed-class people to join in protest and agitation. The main areas of recent radical protests in Tanjore district have in fact included those taluks where the strongest mass movements into Christianity occurred. As we have noted, Christian missionaries and pastors encouraged their people to stand up for their rights, to use the courts and resist landlords and others acting in an unjust fashion. We do not know how many Christians and others followed the advice or example of Christian leaders. However, we can no longer assume that protest and agitation were something new in the lives of depressed-class people even in the Gandhian era.

NOTES

1. Translated in A.L. Basham, *The Wonder that was India*, p. 241.
2. *The Laws of Manu*, translated with extracts from seven commentaries by George Buhler, New York 1969, Ch. I, Section 93.
3. *The Song of God: Bhagavad-Gita*, translated by Swami Prabharananda and Christopher Isherwood, New York, p. 51.
4. For further commentary on these teachings from the point of view of an anthropologist see especially M. N. Srinivas, *Caste in Modern India and Other Essays*, pp. 148 – 60.
5. See, for example, J. A. Dubois, *Letters on the State of Christianity in India*, edited by Sharda Paul, New Delhi 1977, p. 48.
6. Supra, Ch. 2, Ch. 6.
7. Evidence taken before the Reforms Committee of 1918 shows that in rural areas in Tanjore there were 176 more non-brahmans paying a tax of 250 Rs. than brahmans (915 compared with 739), while in Trichinopoly the number in each community paying at the highest rate was almost equal (118 brahmans compared with 113 non-brahmans). The economically superior position of non-brahmans relative to brahmans in Tanjore district is also reflected in figures on tax-payers in urban areas. In Tanjore 68 per cent of those paying municipal taxes at the highest rate were non-brahmans compared with 58 per cent in Trichinopoly (*Reforms Committee, Franchise*, Vol. II Calcutta 1919). For further information on the caste of wealthier landowners in Trichinopoly, see Braunstein, op. cit., especially p. 12 and appendix, and on the caste of those in Tanjore, C. J. Baker and D. A. Washbrook, op. cit., p. 24.
8. Hindu ideas challenging the dominant notion of a spiritual hierarchy were expressed in Tamil in the *Tirukkural* and also in popular folk-songs. For the latter see especially C. E. Gover, *The Folk-Songs of Southern India*, Madras 1959, pp. 163 – 5.
9. Supra, Ch. 3.
10. Supra, Ch. 6 and W. T. Elmore, *Dravidian Gods in Modern Hinduism*, Madras 1925, p. 33.
11. L. Lacombe, *A Great Indian Convert*, p. 4.
12. See appendix 3 and also C. J. Baker and D. A. Washbrook, *South India*, pp. 24, 37 and D. A. Washbrook, *The Energence of Provincial Politics*, pp. 115, 187 – 8.

13. *S.P.G.* archives C/IND/Gen-G Translation of Tamil petition to the Ven. Fr. Thomas Robinson, Archdeacon of Madras from . . . men of Tanjore congregation, 26/2/1829.
14. Supra, Ch. 9.
15. For a reference to this process as reflected in the family histories of Christians in Madras see Lionel Caplan, 'Social Mobility in Metropolitan Centres, Christians in Madras City', *Contributions to Indian Sociology* (N.S.) Vol. II, No. 1, 1977, p. 208. See also reference to Christians in *Census of India*, Madras 1901, 1911 and 1921.
16. *H.F.*, Vol. VII, No. 8, February 1887, pp. 247 – 8. See also the statement in the *Hindu*, 15/9/1885.
17. *Agrarian Radicalism in South India*, Princeton, 1985, p. 51. For his definition of 'radicalism' see pp. 8 – 10 and for references to the main areas of 'radical' protest see especially pp. 105 – 6, 141.

APPENDIX 1

ADHINAM TEMPLES, TANJORE DISTRICT, c. 1841 – 1900
(Referred to in N.W. Kindersely's lists of 1835 and 1841)

Dharmapuram Math
Kampaharesvaraswami Temple, Tirubuyanam,* Kumbakonam taluk.[1]
Arunajatesvaraswami Temple, Tiruppananadal, Kumbakonam taluk.[2]
Vaithianathaswami Temple, Vaithiswarankoil,* Shiyali taluk.[3]
Cattanathaswami Temple, Shiyali.*
Sivalogathiagarajaswami Temple, Achalpuram,* Shiyali taluk.
Amritakadesvaraswami Temple, Tirukkadayur,* Mayavarum taluk.[4]
Vilinathaswami Temple, Tiruvilimalalai, Nannilam taluk.
Tyagarajaswami Temple, Tiruvalur,* Negapatam taluk.[5]
Tyagarajaswami Temple, Tirukuvalai [Kivalur]*, Negapatam taluk.
Panchanathisvaraswami Temple, Tiruvadi [Tiruvayyaur], Tanjore taluk.

Tirruppagalur Math (Founded in Tinnevelly)
Akinasvaraswami Temple, Tiruppagalur, Nannilam Taluk.[6]

Madavory Math
Satchanandaswami Temple, Tiruppirambiyam, Kumbakonam taluk.
Curchinasvaraswam Temple, Kutchinam.

Suryanarkoil Math
Mahalingaswami Temple, Tiruvidaimarudur,* [Madhyarjunam] Kumbakonam taluk.[7]

Tiruvavaduturai Math
Athmanathaswami Temple, Avadayarkoil,* Pattukkottai.[8]

Vedarany Math (Jaffna, Ceylon)
Vedaranyesvaraswami Temple, Vedaranyam, Tirutturaippundi taluk.[9]

OTHER ADHINAM TEMPLES NOT INCLUDED
IN KINDERSLEY'S LISTS

Dharmapuram Math
Yogisvaraswami Temple, Kurukkai, Mayavaram taluk.[10]
Siva Temple, Parasaur, Mayavaram taluk.[11]

APPENDIX 1

Tirruppagalur Math
Tiruchankattangudi Temple, Nannilam taluk.[12]
Tirumechiyur Temple

Tiruvaduturai Math
Mayuranathaswami Temple, Mayavaram,* Mayavaram taluk.[13]

NOTES

Key* = referred to as one of the 'most celebrated of the principal temples in the district' by T.V. Row, *A Manual of the District of Tanjore*, Madras, 1883, pp. 228-9.
1. *Hindu*, 18/4/1900.
2. Ibid., 18/4/1900.
3. *M.H.C.*, Reg. App. No. 14; *Hindu*, 1/6/1888, 6/10/1889, 18/4/1900.
4. *Hindu*, 18/4/1900, Hemingway, *Tanjore*, p. 232.
5. Subsequently under control of Tiruppagalur *math*. *M.H.C.*, Reg. App. No. 85 of 1868 and App. No. 64 of 1892; Hemingway, op. cit., pp. 248-9.
6. Hemingway, op. cit., pp. 239-40.
7. Subsequently under control of Tiruvavaduturai math. Hemingway, op. cit., p. 223.
8. *I.O.R.*, P/1426, 1868.
9. Hemingway, op. cit., p. 230.
10. Hemingway, op. cit., p. 230.
11. Hemingway, op. cit., p. 232.
12. Hemingway, op. cit., p. 239-40.
13. Hemingway, op. cit., p. 231.

APPENDIX 2

TRUSTEES OF SOME NON-ADHINAM TEMPLES, TANJORE DISTRICT
(Mentioned in sources dating from 1845 to 1900)

Chakarapani Temple, Kumbakonam*
Narrain Pillai 1845   N.b.

Sarangapani Temple, Kumbakonam
Narrain Pillai 1845[1]   N.b.

Vencatachella Chetty		N.b.
Chucrapany Chetty	*c.* 1856	N.b.
Iyara Pillai		N.b.
Poundareekapuram Krishnaswamy Iyengar[2]		B.

Varahakulam Rengasami Iyengar 1898[3]   B.

Ramaswami Temple, Kumbakonam
Krishnaswamy Iyengar 1854[4]   B.

Rajagopalaswami Temple, Mannargudi*

Ivathory Mudaly	1869	N.b.
Pandurrungy Annachariyar[5]		B.

Strinivasperumal Temple, Nachiyarkovil, Kumbakonam taluk

Neikunnam Chinna Rangayangar	1867	B.
Pathinnoruveli Gopala Reddi		N.b.

Subbraya Mudali		N.b.
Madadevayien	Trustees prior to 1864	B.
Narianappayien[6]		B.

Kayarohanaswami Temple, Negapatam
Sabapathy Chettiar *c.* 1879[7]   N.b.
Mayandi Chettiar 1895[8]   N.b.

Sri Kasturirenga Perumal Temple, Negapatam taluk
Chokappa Mudaliar 1897[9]   N.b.

APPENDIX 2

Kamatchiamma Temple Sambasiva Sastri Sinna Annaswamy Sastri Saminadha Sastri[10]	1900	B. B. B.

Sri Thanthonusvaraswami Temple, Marappanallore, Kumbakonam taluk
Gopala Pillai 1900[11] — N.b.

Sri Chella Pillyar Temple, North Tanjore
Ramaswami Pillai 1874[12] — N.b.

Sivalinga Pillayar Temple, South Tanjore
Nanuvayyan[13] 1871 — B.

Anthecasava Perumal Temple, Kuttalam, Mayaveram taluk
Ramapillay[14] 1845 — N.b.

Temple at Shiyali
Valoo Moodeliar[15] 1864 — N.b.

Others
T. A. Alga Pillai, trustee of a number of temples[16] — N.b.

NOTES

Key* = referred to as one of the 'most celebrated of the principal temples in the district' by T.V. Row, *A Manual of the District of Tanjore*, Madras, 1883, pp. 228–9.
B = Braham. N.b. = Non-brahman.
1 *M.P.R.* Ra 306, Vol. 21A 28/7/1845, 2,6/10/1845.
2 *M.P.R.*, Ra 313, Vol. 74A 21/1/1856.
3 *Hindu*, 19/5/1898.
4 Collr. to Sec. 24/10/1854, M.R.P., Ra 311, Vol. 50, 16/11/1854.
5 *M.H.C.*, Ref, Case No. 14 of 1896.
6 *M.H.C.*, Reg. App. No. 6, 1867.
7 *M.J.P.*, 10/1/1879, Vol. 1426, p. 46.
8 *M.H.C.*, 2nd App. No. 639 of 1895.
9 *T.C.O.*, Disposal No. 682, 15/9/1900.
10 *Hindu*, 3/8/1900.
11 *T.C.O.*, Disposal No. 664, 7/9/1900.
12 *I.O.R.* P/1426.
13 *I.O.R.* P/426.
14 *I.O.R.* L/Parl./Coll. No. 418A Petition 15/9/1846.
15 *H.F.*, January 1846 p. 46.
16 *Hindu*, 26 & 27/4/1889.

APPENDIX 3

TEMPLE COMMITTEES

TANJORE DISTRICT, MEMBERSHIP 1864 – 1900

Year	Members	Occupation, etc.	Brahman or Non-brahman
Tanjore Temple Committee (for taluks of Tanjore, Mannargudi and Pattukkottai)			
1864	Annusastry	Judge of the late Rajah's Court	B
	Harichakrapani Pundither	Judge of the late Rajah's Court	B
	Ramaiyer	Officer of the late Rajah's Durbar	B
	T. Viraswamy Pillai	Sarkele, Govt. Agency Office	N.b.
	Kasinatha Appaji	Pensioner of the late Rajah	?
	Gopala Mudali	Mirasidar of Kottur	N.b.
Negapatam Temple Committee (for taluks of Negapatam, Nannilam and Tirutturaippundi)			
1864	Subbarayalu Naik	Merchant and Savukar	N.b.
	Shunmugam Chetti	Merchant and Savukar	N.b.
	Seventhalinga Chetti		N.b.
	Nainappa Mudaliyar		N.b.
	Aghurappaiyar	Merchant	B.
	Tiyagaraja Mudaliyar	Mirasidar	N.b.
	Venkata Balakristna Chetti	Merchant	N.b.[1]
1868	Subberayalu Neidu		N.b.
	Krishna Chettiar		N.b.
	A. Nainappa Mudeliar		N.b.
	T. B. Calliana Sundarom Mudaliar		N.b.
	Andi Pillay Setty		N.b.[2]
1896-Aug. 1898	P. Krishnier (died 1898)		B.
	Balakrishna Naidu		N.b.
	T. S. Sivavadevelu Odayar		N.b.
	R. Regunatha Row		B.
	R. Sreenivasa Iyengar, *B.A.*		B.

APPENDIX 3

Year	Members	Occupation, etc.	Brahman or Non-Brahman
	P. Rathnasabapathy Pillai, B.A.		N.b.
	M. G. Ramasamy Pillai		N.b.
	Venkatasami Rajah (died 1896)		N.b.
	Thiruvambala Chettiar		N.b.
	Chakkappa Mudaliar		N.b.
	Swayambu Iyer		B[3]

Kumbakonam Temple Committee
(for taluks of Kumbakonam, Mayavaram and Shiyali)

Year	Members	Occupation, etc.	
1864	R. Harri Row	Son of R. R. Venkat Row Late Dewan of Travancore	B
	Ramalinga Tambaran	Trustee of Tiruppanandal Math	N.b.
	Gopu Subbaraya Chetti	Merchant	N.b.
	Chackrapani Chetti	Merchant	N.b.
	Sinniya Tevur	Mirasidar	N.b.
	Chakraviruti Strinivas Chariyar	} 'an Aiyangar of the Ecclesiastical	B
	Strinivasa Pattarachariy	} Order, residing at Combaconum'	B[4]
1884– 1900	Kishnaya Chettiar[5]		N.b.
	S. Ragoonatha Chariar[6]		B
	K. Raganatha Row, B.A.[7]		B
	S. A. Saminatha Iyer (1885-1899)[8]		B
	Kasibari Kondasamy	Tambiran of Tiruppanandal[9]	N.b.
	T. S. Sivasamy Odiyar (1888-1899)[10]		N.b.
	Sreenivisa Iyengar[11]		B
	Doorasamy Moopanar (1888-1898)[12]		N.b.
	Punnusami Nadar (1888-1898)[13]		N.b.
	J. A. Alaga Pillai[14]		N.b.
1884– 1900	Sivaguru Chettiar[15]		N.b.
	C. S. Ramasami Aiyar[16]		B
	Sundaralinga	Tambiran of Tiruppanandal[17]	N.b.
	Ramaswami Pillai[18]		N.b.

APPENDIX 3

TRICHINOPOLY DISTRICT, MEMBERSHIP 1864 – 1900

Year Members	Occupation, etc.	Brahman or Non-brahman
Perambular Temple Committee		
1864 Muttuvengattachella Rettiar		N.b.
Kistna Retty		N.b.
Balagooroo Reddi		N.b.
Gooroomoorty Iyen		B
Saravana Pillai		N.b.
Udaiyarpalaiyam Temple Committee		
1864 Naranaswamy Iyen		B
Samy Iyengar		B
Saravana Pillai		N.b.
Kulittulai Temple Committee		
1864 Sahasranama Iyer		B
Ramalinga Pandaram		N.b.
Rengasamy Iyengar		B
Samy Iyen		B
Marundanoyaga Moodely		N.b.
Musiri Temple Committee		
1864 Gopinadien		B
Annasamy Iyen		B
Naranien		B
Shunmugam Pillai		N.b.
Rengien Chetty[19]		N.b.
1894 Thandavaraya Pillay		N.b.
Kannayiram Pillay		N.b.
Kunju Pillay who replaced		N.b.
Muthusamy Pillay		N.b.
Lakshiminarayana Iyer		B
Venkata Subba Iyer[20]		B
Trichinopoly Temple Committee		
1864 Soobramier		B
Streenevasa Tatachariar		B
Samy Chettiar		N.b.
Vambier		B
Durmadass[21]		N.b.

Year	Members	Occupation, etc.	Brahman or Non-brahman
1889- 1900	K. Sangaiengar[22]		B
	K. Vasudeva Aiyengar		B
	S. Nataraja Aiyer		B
	Pattabiram Pillai		N.b.
	Totta Venkatachella Chetti		N.b.
	L. Krishna Aiyangar		B
	T. Ramasami Chettiyar		N.b.
	S. Krishnama Chariar[23]		B
	Head of Thiruvaduturai Math		N.b.
	Mahalingaswami Chettiar[24]		N.b.

NOTES

1 *Fort St. George Gazette*, 5/4/1864.
2 *MHC*, Reg. App. No. 85 of 1868.
3 *Hindu*, 6/8/1898.
4 *Fort St. George Gazette*, 5/4/1864. See also *M.H.C.*, Reg. App. No. 6 of 1867 and Reg. App. No. 12 of 1867.
5 *Hindu*, 17/9/1884.
6 Ibid., 13/10/1885.
7 Ibid., 1/10/1885.
8 Ibid., 29/12/1885, 28/10/1899.
9 Ibid., 12/8/1888.
10 Ibid., 24/8/1888, 11/11/1899.
11 Ibid., 24/8/1888.
12 Ibid., 24/8/1889, 19/5/1898.
13 Ibid., 24/4/1889, 28/10/1899.
14 Ibid., 23/5/1898.
15 Ibid., 28/10/1899.
16 Ibid., 22/11/1900.
17 Ibid., 11/11/1899.
18 Ibid., 28/10/1899.
19 *Fort St. George Gazette*, 23/2/1864.
20 (*M.H.C.*, Second App;. No. 1530 of 1898).
21 *Fort St. George Gazette*, 23/2/1864.
22 Ibid., 23/1/1888.
23 *M.H.C.*, Appeal No. 22 of 1896.
24 Ibid., 1/11/1898.

APPENDIX 4

TEMPLE LANDS AND INCOME — TANJORE DISTRICT

Income Category	No. of Places of Worship	Area of Land Valies, M.G.	Land revenue Rs. A.P.	Money Allowances Rs. A.P.	Total Income Rs. A.P.
Up to 30 Chakrams or Rs. 46.10.6 p.a.	2247	707.19.45	17610.1.10	8342.5.6	25952.7.2
30-200 Chakrams p.a.	434	6703	33175.0.0	14225.0.0.	47400.0.0
200 or more Chakrams p.a.	176		68931.2.3	79002.1.1	147933.3.4
Adhinam Temples	17	6414	88943.3.3	33581.1.10	122524.5.1
TOTALS	2874	13824.19.45 (91404 acres)	208659.6.16	135150.7.17	343809.15.7

ADHINAM TEMPLES: DETAILS

Adhinam	No. of Temples	Area of Land Valies M.G.	Land Revenue Rs. A.P.	Money Allowances Rs. A.P.	Total Income Rs. A.P.
Dharmapuram	10	2847.2.6	40290.0.11	18057.0.11	58347.10.10
Thiruvavaduturai	1	1158.4.83	16400.14.4	–	16400.14.4
Others	6	C 2409	32252.4.0	15524.0.11	47775.11.11
TOTAL	17	6414.0.10	88943.3.3	33581.1.10	122524.5.1

Percentage of Total for all Temples:
| | 0.59 | 46.4 | 42.63 | 24.85 | 35.64 |

Source: *M.R.P.*, Ra. 303, Vol. 32, 16/12/1841.

APPENDIX 5

CASTES DENIED ENTRY INTO PRINCIPAL TEMPLES, TANJORE DISTRICT, c. 1881 – 1901

Caste	Principal Occupation	Nos. in 1901
Valaiyan	Cultivation, coolie work and hunting	137,216
Shanan (Nadar)	Drawing and selling toddy	35,500
Odde	Tank diggers	3,373
Kuravan	Itinerant hawkers, basket makers, fortune tellers, etc.	5,512
Fisher Castes		
Pattanavan	Sea fishermen and boatmen	8,188
Karaiyan	Sea fishermen	8,737
Sembadavan	Fishermen in rivers and tanks	3,170
Outcastes		
Chaklier	Shoe-makers, leather dressers and tanners	3,936
Pallan	Agricultural labourers	159,855
Paraiyan	Agricultural labourers, village watchmen, scavengers etc.	310,391
	TOTAL = 33 per cent of district population	675,518

Sources: *Census of India*, 1901, Madras, Vol. XV-A, Chapter VIII and Table XIII; T. V. Row, op. cit., pp. 201-206; Hemingway, *Tanjore*, pp. 88 – 9.

APPENDIX 6

PEAK ATTENDANCES AT SOME RELIGIOUS FESTIVALS: ESTIMATES

TRICHINOPOLY DISTRICT			TANJORE DISTRICT		
Town Population Temple, Festival	Year	Numbers	Town Population Temple, Festival	Year	Numbers
Srirangam			*Kumbakonam*		
Pop. 1868=8910	1868	50,000	Pop. 1881=46,295	1873	over 200,000
Vaikantha Ekadasi	1870	20,000	Mahamagum	1885	400,000
Festival	1871	70,000	Festival	1897	500,000
(Dec.-Jan.)	1872	40-50,000	(every 12 yrs)		
	1873	80-90,000			
	1874	25-30,000	*Velanganni* (Nega. taluk)		
	1875	small no.			
	1876	3-4,000	Pop. 1868=2,147	1868	20,000
	1877	8,000	Festival of Virgin	1884	15,000
	1878	20,000	Mary	1885	12,000
		90,000*	Our Lady of	1888	35,000
	1879	45,000	Health	1906	30,000
	1880	10,000	(Aug.-Sep.)		
	1881	small no			
	1882	12,000	*Tiruvadi*		
	1883	5,000	(Tiruvaiyaru)		
	1885	20,000	Pop. 1868=5,837	1868	20,000
	1886	15,000	Saptasthalam	1886	20,000
	1887	5,000	Festival	1887	70,000
	1888	30-35,000	(seven places)	1888	35-50,000
			(Apr.)		
Samayapuram					
Pop. 1868=1,016	1868	30,000	*Mannargudi*		
Mariamma Car			Pop. 1882=17,735		
Festival	1907	30-40,000	Sri	1887	15-20,000
(Apr. – May)			Rajagopalaswami Fest. (Mar.-Apr.)		

APPENDIX 6

TRICHINOPOLY DISTRICT			TANJORE DISTRICT		
Town Population Temple, Festival	Year	Numbers	Town Population Temple, Festival	Year	Numbers
			Tiravalur (Nega. taluk) Pop. 1868=6,000 Sri Tyagarajaswamy Festival (Mar.-Apr.)	1868 1884 1888	10.000 10,000 nearly 20,000
			Ettukudi (Nega. taluk) Pop. 1868=535 Chittraparuvam Festival (Apr.-May)	1868 1884 1885 1888	10,000 30,000 15,000 30,000
			Tiruvadamarudur (Madhyarjunam) Pop. 1868=5,288 Pushyam Festival** (Dec.-Jan.)	1868 1884 1885 1886 1888	20,000 30,000 40,000 40,000 about 10,000

* disputed
** Pushya like Chittra is one of the 27 asterisms (constellations)
Sources: *List of Festivals, Fairs etc., occurring within the limits of the Madras Presidency*, Madras 1868; *M.P.P.*, Ra. 439, Vols. 8-9, (1869) Vols. 272 (1871), 273 (1872), 274 (1873), 275 (1874), 276 (1875), 1038 (1876), 1039 (1877), 1221 (1878), 1393 (1879), 1555 (1880), 1746 (1881), 1925-6 (1882), 2118 (1883), 2347-8 (1884), 2594 (1885(, Z/P/2065, Vol. 3511 (1889), Hemingway, *Tanjore*, p. 250, *Trichinopoly*, pp. 311, 318. J. A. Dubois, op. cit., p. 196, *Hindu*, 12/12/1885.

APPENDIX 7

TANJORE & TRICHINOPOLY: RELIGIOUS COMMUNITIES

Tanjore

Year	Total Population	Hindus	%	Muslims	%	Christians	%
a)							
1856-7	1,657,285	1,521,542	91.81	86,417	5.22	49,326	2.98
1861-2	1,652,170	1,518,075	91.88	80,613	4.88	53,482	3.24
1866-7	1,731,619	1,589,274	91.78	85,211	4.92	57,134	3.30
b)							
1871	1,973,817	1,803,789	91.39	10,270	5.20	66,409	3.36
1881	2,130,383	1,939,421	91.01	112,058	5.26	78,258	3.67
1891	2,228,114	2,022,300	90.76	119,864	55.38	85,371	3.83
1901	2,245,029	2,034,399	90.62	123,053	56.48	86,979	3.87

Trichinopoly

Year	Total Population	Hindus	%	Muslims	%	Christians	%
a)							
1856-7	809,580	742,569	91.72	30,756	3.80	36,255	4.48
1861-2	939,400	869,876	92.56	27,619	2.94	43,905	4.67
1866-7	1,006,826	939,339	93.30	24,529	2.44	42,958	4.27
1871	1,200408	1,115,776	92.95	32,024	2.67	52,222	4.35
1881	1,215,033	1,119,434	92.13	34,104	2.81	61,440	5.06
1891	1,372,717	1,264,037	92.08	38,271	2.79	70,401	5.13
1901	1,444,770	1,324,768	91.69	43,319	3.00	76,660	5.31

a) Quinquennial Estimates
b) Census Returns

APPENDIX 8

BRAHMAN CONVERTS TO CHRISTIANITY

A. JESUIT MISSION
Tanjore – Trichinopoly, 1850 – 1900

Name	Caste	Date of birth	Home district	Father's occupation	Position when baptized	Age when & where baptized	Subsequent employment	Relationship with other converts
1 Appuswamy Iyer	Smarta		Trich.	Village Headman	St. Joseph's then normal school	1891	Hdmstr. Catholic School Revert. to Hinduism	Husband No.2
2 Mrs Appuswamy Iyer	Smarta		"	Parents dead	Wife	c. 1891	Reverted to Hinduism	Wife No.1
3 V. Mahadeva Iyer	–	1869	Tanjore	Domestic Priest	Student St. Josephs	25 yrs 3 Sept. 1894	Deputy Collr.	Husband No.4 Father No.5 Br-in-law Nos.6&9
4 Sarathambal Ammal Iyer and 5 baby Cecilia	Smarta		"	Asst. Insp. of Schools	Wife and mother	17 yrs. 3 Sept. 1894		Wife No.3 Mother No.5 Sister Nos.6&9
6 S. Balachandra Iyer	Smarta	1873	"	"	Student St. Josephs	21 yrs 1 Sept. 1894	Writer St. Josephs Clerk Sth Indian Railways	Br. Nos.4&9 Uncle No.5 Br.-in-law No.3
7 P.J. Doraisamy Iyer	Smarta	1874	"	Pensioned sastri of Raja of Cochin	Student St. Josephs	c. 20 yrs 1 Sept 1894	Business and engineering	Br. No.16

APPENDIX 8

Name	Caste	Date of birth	Home district	Father's occupation	Position when baptized	Age when & where baptized	Subsequent employment	Relationship with other converts
8 L. Doreyappan Iyer	Smarta	c.1879	Tanjore		Student	15 ½ St. Josephs 19 May 1895	Died 1899	
9 Rajasakharan Iyer	Smarta	"		Asst. Insp. of Schools		July 1896	Writer St. Josephs	Br. Nos.6&4 Uncle No.5 Br.-in-law No.3
10 Krishna Row	Maratha					c.1896		
11 Agnes Rukmani (Iyengar)	Sri Vaisnavite	1878			Wife	c.18 yrs Aug. 1896	Died c.1899	2nd wife No.7 sister-in-law, No.16 sister No.15(?)
12 G. Vaidyanatha Iyer	Smarta	1879	Pattukkottai	State Vakil to Raja of Pattukkottai	Student St Josephs	19 yrs April 1897	Tutor & teacher St. Josephs	Br. No.14
13 N. Narayanasamy Iyer	Smarta	1881	Tanjore	Chief Priest of Temple		17 yrs 24 Dec. 1898	Business and railways	
14 F.G. Nateson Iyer	Smarta		Pattukkottai	State Vakil to Raja of Pattukkottai		20 Jan. 1898		Br. No.12
15 Louis Krishna	Vaisnavite					Feb. 1899		Br. No.11? Br.-in-law No.7
16 P.J. Ramaswamy Iyer	Smarta		Tanjore	Pensioned Sastri Raja of Cochin	Student St Josephs	Sept. 1899	Barrister & interp. in Malaya	Br.no.7

APPENDIX 8   247

B. METHODIST MISSION
Tanjore, 1850-1900

Name	Caste	Date of Birth	Home Tanjore District	Father's Position etc.	School	Age when & where baptized	Subsequent employment
17 Subramanyan Iyer	Smarta	c.1841	Negapatam		Head Pupil WMS Schl Negapatam	c.16 yrs 31/5/87 Madras	Teacher WMS Schl. Later Administrator General
18 Kalyana Raman	Smarta	c.1845	Mannargudi	From family of Sastris	1st class WMS Schl	17 yrs 9/3/62 Madras	Methodist Minister (Eventually separated from the Mission)
19 Coopooswamy Row	Maratha	c.1847	Mannargudi	Clerk in District Munsiff's Court	WMS Schl	16 yrs	Methodist Minister (Eventually separated from the Mission)
20 M. Paul	Iyengar (Sri Vaisnavite)		Negapatam	Govt. Official & connected with temple	WMS Schl Mannargudi or Negapatam	1873	Catechist Church of Scotland
21 Vencat Iyer	Smarta	1859?	Nr. Tiruvalur	Sastri	Not in any WMS Schl	c. 18 yrs Aug. 1877 Negapatam	
22 John Narainswamy		c.1867	Nagore		WMS Sunday & Day Schls. Nagore	c.18 yrs 1885 Negapatam	
23 Lakshmi Krishna Subramanyam Iyer	Smarta		Nr. Mannargudi	District Munsif (Judge)	WMS Schl Mannargudi Madras Univ.	21 Aug 1892 Madras	Methodist Minister
24 Ragunatha Rao	Maratha				WMS Schl Mannargudi	Before 1892	Head Master American Presbyterian School

APPENDIX 9

RELIGION BY CASTE

CASTE-HINDU AND CHRISTIAN, 1871

	HINDUS		CHRISTIANS	
	Number	Percentage of Total Hindus	Number	Percentage of Total Christians
Tanjore				
Brahmans (Priests)	126,757	7.03	–	–
Kshatriyas (Warriors)	4,667	0.26	7	0.01
Chetties (Traders)	28,941	1.60	863	1.32
Vellalas (Agriculturalists)	341,154	18.91	7,246	11.10
Idaiyars (Shepherds)	65,636	3.64	105	0.16
Kammalan (Artisans)	54,022	3.00	1,372	2.10
Kannakan (Writers)	1,631	0.09	–	–
Kaikalar (Weavers)	55,172	3.06	327	0.50
Vannian (Cultivators & Labourers)	556,909	30.87	17,880	27.40
Kusavan (Potters)	11,094	0.62	464	0.71
Satani (Mixed Castes)	48,503	2.69	1,068	1.63
Sembadavan (Fishermen)	117,681	6.52	210	0.32
Shanan (Toddy-drawers)	37,539	2.08	3,043	4.66
Ambattan (Barbers)	21,454	1.19	213	0.33
Vannan (Washermen)	14,232	0.79	130	0.20
Others	43,838	2.43	323	0.50
Pariahs	274,558	15.22	32,011	49.01
TOTAL	1,803,787		65,262	
Trichinopoly				
Brahmans (Priests)	31,428	2.82	–	–
Kshatriyaas (Warriors)	3,412	0.31	262	0.52
Chetties (Traders)	21,437	1.92	18	0.04
Vellalas (Agriculturalists)	194,972	17.47	5,881	11.57
Idaiyars (Shepherds)	61,125	5.48	106	0.21
Kammalan (Artisans)	26.502	2.38	1,969	3.87
Kannakan (Writers)	290	0.03	4	0.01
Kaikalar (Weavers)	34,318	3.08	17,676	34.78
Kusavan (Potters)	6,307	0.57	125	0.25

APPENDIX 9

	HINDUS		CHRISTIANS	
	Number	Percentage of Total Hindus	Number	Percentage of Total Christians
Satani (Mixed Castes)	117,604	10.54	4,728	9.30
Sembadavan (Fishermen)	24,212	2.17	162	0.32
Shanan (Toddy-drawers)	4,759	0.43	60	0.12
Ambattan (Barbers)	13,073	1.17	13	0.03
Vannan (Washermen)	12,113	1.09	184	0.36
Others	46,027	4.13	72	0.14
Pariahs	137,606	12.33	19,453	38.28
TOTAL	1,115,776		50,822	

Source: Census of India, 1871, Madras, Vol. II, pp. 87–94.

CASTES-CATHOLIC AND PROTESTANT, 1871

	CATHOLICS		PROTESTANTS	
	Number	Percentage of Total Catholics	Number	Percentage of Total Protestants
Tanjore				
Kshatriyas	–	–	3	0.03
Chetties	562	1.02	301	2.90
Vellalas	5,753	10.48	1,493	15.35
Idaiyars	76	0.14	29	0.28
Kammalan	1,287	2.35	85	0.82
Kanakkan	–	–	–	–
Kaikalar	249	0.45	78	0.75
Vannian	15,852	28.88	2,028	19.54
Kusavan	361	0.66	103	0.99
Satani	751	1.37	317	3.06
Sembadavan	149	0.27	61	0.59
Shanan	2,412	4.40	631	6.08
Ambattan	203	0.37	10	0.10
Vannan	114	0.21	16	0.15
Others	266	0.49	57	0.55
Pariahs	26,849	48.92	5,162	49.74
TOTAL	54,884		10,378	

	CATHOLICS		PROTESTANTS	
	Number	Percentage of Total Catholics	Number	Percentage of Total Protestants
Trichinopoly				
Kshatriyas	32	0.65	230	11.90
Chetties	18	0.04	–	–
Vellalas	5,282	10.80	599	30.99
Idaiyars	106	0.22	–	–
Kammalan	1,946	3.98	23	1.19
Kanakkan	–	–	–	–
Kaikalar	109	0.22	–	–
Vannian	17,310	35.41	366	18.93
Kusavan	125	0.26	–	–
Shanan	60	0.12	–	–
Satani	4,411	9.02	317	16.40
Sembavadan	162	0.33	–	–
Ambattan	13	0.03	–	–
Vannan	179	0.37	5	0.26
Others	63	0.13	9	0.47
Pariahs	19,073	39.01	380	19.66
TOTAL	48,889		1,933	

Source: *Census of India*, 1872, Madras Vol. II, pp. 100–3.

APPENDIX 9

CASTE OF CATHOLICS BAPTIZED, TANJORE AND TRICHINOPOLY, 1841–1893

CASTE	Trichinopoly 1841,42,47, 52,58 Total No. of Entries (1957) %	Tanjore: Congregation under Goa 1874-93 Total No. of Entries (6725) %	Tanjore: Congregation under Rome 1850-93 Total No. of Entries (5017) %	Kumbakkonam 1841-64 Total No. of Entries (5296) %
Vellala - agriculturalists	20.00	0.76	16.00	2.40
Mudaliar - title used by Vellasal, Weavers etc.	–	–	–	0.51
Vadugan - Telugu cultivators	0.89	–	1.30	0.26
Agamudaiyan - cultivators	–	–	1.60	–
Kammalan - artisans including carpenters	5.90	6.30	6.74	1.19
Kallan - cultivators	0.67	1.80	5.60	2.53
Udaiyan [Odean] - cultivators	3.95	10.50	1.90	0.96
Muppan [Sudarman] - cultivators	2.23	–	–	–
Ambalakaran - cultivators, watchmen	2.90	–	–	–
Shanan - toddy drawers including Nadar	–	5.50	7.10	0.93
Vanniyan [Pallis]*	–	–	–	2.49
Kavandan*	–	–	–	0.77
Padiatchi*	–	–	0.86	10.82
Ambattan - barbers	–	–	2.20	–
Vannan - washermen	0.80	1.23	1.20	1.70
Pallan+	8.00	20.00	16.20	3.80
Valangai+	14.90	1.30	1.00	20.62
Pariah labourers etc+	31.80	50.00	37.00	49.00
Chakkiliyan [Sakkalier]+	2.94	–	–	–
Pagati - beggars	2.00	–	–	–
Others	2.36	2.61	1.30	1.70
Anglo-Indians or Europeans	1.56	–	–	–

* Agricultural labourers   + Untouchables, including landless labourers etc.

Source: Baptismal Registers located in St Mary's Trichinopoly; Sacred Heart Cathedral Archives, Tanjore and the Catholic Cathedral Archives, Kumbakonam.

APPENDIX 10

THEOSOPHICAL SOCIETY MEMBERS, TRICHINOPOLY AND TANJORE DISTRICT, 1883 – 1900

Name	Position	1st Year
Trichinopoly District		
D. Ratna Mudialiar (Sowcar; Pres. Town Hall Comm., Trustee of Rock Fort Temple, 1889)	Pres.	1883
L. Krishna Iyengar (Late Sheristadar of Dt. Court; V. Pres. Srirangam Municipal Commission; temple committee member)	V. Pres.	1883
S. Subba Ayer, *B.A.*	V. Pres.	1883
S. Kristnamachariar, *B.A.* (Vakil Dt. Court; member of temple committee)	Sec.	1883
	V. Pres.	1885
	Gen. Council	1886
A. C. Chidambaram Mudaliar	Treas.	1885
T. Pattabirama Pillai (Huzur Sheristadar, 1884)	Member	1883
V. Krishna Rao (First Grade Pleader, later member Trichy. Congress)	Member	1883
T. M. Audinarayana Chettiar, *B.A.*	Member	1883
M. Swaminada Aiyer (Dt. Munsiff)	Member	1883
	V. Pres.	1885
A. Srinivasa Aiyengar (Translator, Dt. Court Trichi, Sth. Indian Railways)	Member	1883
	Sec.	1885
T. P. Ramanjulu Naidoo	Member	1883

D. Muniswami Naidoo (Municipal Commissioner)	Member	1883
P. Durisami Aiyer	Pres.	1887
P. Narasimhalu Naidu Garu	V. Pres.	1887
T. N. Muttukrishnaiyar (Pleader, Munsiff's Court)	Ass. Sec.	1887
P. Subbaiyar, *B.A.*	V. Pres.	1887
Narayanaswami Naidu	Councillor	1885
Pagdala N. Muthaswami Naidu (Aryan League of Honour, 1885)	Ass. Sec. & Librarian	1887
T. M. Sundaram Pillay (Congress Sub-committee, 1888)	V. Pres.	1887
T. Samiah	Delegate Madras	1887
N. Somenathia	Delegate Madras	1887
Bhut Guraswami	Delegate Madras	1887
A. Ramachendra Iyer	Pres.	1890
N. Harihara Iyer, *B.A.*, *B.L.*	Sec.	1893
K. Vasudeva Aiyangar Mirasidar Kodyalam, (member of temple committee and on Standing Congress Sub-committee in 1888)	Pres.	1899-1900
Srirangam		
C. Sambasiva Iyer	Pres.	1900
S. M. Raja Ram Rao	Sec.	1900

Tanjore District

Mannargudi		
Krishna Mudaliar	Pres.	1891
S. Venkatarama Iyer (Municipal Councillor, Mannargudi)	Sec.	1891
B. Viraswamaiyah Garu	Pres.	1897

Puttukkottai

A. C. Kannan Nambiar	Pres.	1898
S. Krishnaswami Iyer (Pleader)	Sec.	1898
S. Ramaswami Aiyer	Sec.	1900

Tiruvalur

Rajagopala Iyengar, M.A.	Pres.	1891
Vaikhynadha Iyer (Second grade pleader), Tiruvalur	Sec.	1891
T. K. Swaminathier (Second grade pleader)	Sec.	1893
T. K. Ramaswamier (Second grade pleader)	Sec.	1894
P. Ratnasabhapati Pillay, B.A. (Temple Comm. 1898)	Pres.	1884
N. P. Subramania Iyer (First Grade Pleader; Sec. of Hindu Tract Society, 1889)	V. Pres.	1883
S. A. Saminatha Iyer	Sec.	1884
N. P. Balachandrier (Govt. Accountant)	Ass. Sec. Sec.	1884 1885
R. Bapoo Pillay	Treas. and Librarian	1884
A. G. Balkrishnah Iyer	Rep. Madras	1886
T. K. Annasami Iyer	Treas.	1883
Mahadeva Sastrial	Hon. Pandit	1883

Negapatam

R. Venkata Ram Iyer	Rep. Madras	1887
C. V. Swayambhu Iyer (Temple Committee before 1895)	Pres.	1890
G. Sambasiva Iyer (Pleader, Sec. of Hindu Tract Society, 1889)	Sec.	1890
S. Chakrapani Iyer	Pres.	1894

APPENDIX 10

P. Kanaka Sabhapathy Sastrial (Second grade Pleader)	Sec.	1896
Kumbakonam		
V. Krishna Iyer	Pres.	1883
S. Krishnaswamy Iyer (Pleader)	Sec. and Treas.	1883
Venkatram Shastrial	V. Pres.	1883
Ragava Iyengar	Comm. on Rules	1883
C. Somsundram Pillay	Comm. on Rules	1883
A. Nilankanta Sastriar	Pres.	1891
K. Narainaswami Iyer (Pleader)	Sec.	1885
M. C. Krishnaswamier (Second Grade Pleader)	Sec.	1892
(Dr.) A. Vaideswara Sastri	Pres.	1895
G. Kaliana	Sec.	
T. Krishnamachariar *B.A.*	Pres.	1896
A. G. Balakrishna Iyer	Sec.	
A. Siva Row		
Tanjore		
N. Subramanya Ayyer, *B.A.*	Pres.	1883
V. Rajagopalachariar, *B.A.*, *B.L.* (District Registrar)	Sec. and Treas.	1883
C. R. Pattnabirama Iyer, *B.A.*, *B.L.*	V. Pres.	1883
K. S. Kristnaswami Iyer	Comm. on Rules	1883
S. Rungaswami Iyengar	Rep. Madras	1887
S. A. Swaminatha Iyer (On temple committee 1885, Delegate to Indian National Congress)	Pres.	1892
(Rao Bahadur) K. S. Srinivasa Pillai (Delegate to Indian National Congress; Besant Comm.)	Pres.	1895

A. Krishna Iyer (Pleader)	Sec.	1890
S. Venkatasubbayyar (Pleader, Vennar Bros.)	Sec. T.V.S.*	1893
T. Sadisiva Rao, *B.A.*, *B.L.* (Vakil)	Sec. T.V.S.*	1899
M. Nataraja Aiyer *B.A.* (District Registrar)	Pres. T.V.S. and Besant Comm.	1897
G. Narasimbachari	Member T.V.S.and Besant Comm.	1899
P. V. Naganatha Sastri	Del. Madras	1899
N. Sarvathama Row	T.V.S. and Besant Comm.	1899
V. A. Vandayar	T.V.S. and Besant Comm.	1899
T. Sambamoorthy Row	T.V.S. and Besant Comm.	1899
S. Krishnaswamy Pillai	Del. Madras	1884

Mayavaram

T. Krishna Rao (Late pensioned Deputy Collector)	Pres.	1883
A. G. Hurry Rao (Town Schoolteacher)	Sec. and Treas.	1883
Sreenivasa Rao	V. Pres.	1883
T. Narianaswamy Iyer	V. Pres.	1883
Ramaswamy Naidu (Police Inspector)	Councillor	1883
Alaga Pillai (Municipal Chairman, temple trustee)	Rules Comm.	1883

P. Narainaswamy Iyer   Rules   1883
                                                  Comm.

Principal Sources: *Th.*, Supp., 1883 – 1900; *Hindu*, 18/8/1884, 29/12/1885, 15/8/1888, 23/5/1898, 9/12/1899.

*T.V.S. = Tathva Veenaraine Sabha

APPENDIX 11

EDUCATION BY CASTE: HINDUS, 1888 – 1889

Tanjore

	Colleges	%	Secondary Schools	%	Primary Schools	%
Brahmans	321	92	3,358	62	6,436	20
Non-brahmans	30	8	2,023	37	25,473	78
Others	–		39	1	687	2
TOTAL	351		5,420		32,596	

Trichinopoly

	Colleges	%	Secondary Schools	%	Primary Schools	%
Brahmans	374	89	1,472	55.3	2,179	14
Non-Brahmans	44	11	1,176	44.2	13,504	84
Others	–		13	0.5	352	2
TOTAL	418		2,661		16,035	

Source: Report on Public instruction in the Madras Presidency 1888 – 1889.

APPENDIX 12

HINDU TRACT SOCIETY MEMBERSHIP, 1888 – 1889

Trichinopoly
L. S. Ramachandra Aiyar *B.A.*, *B.L.*   President
S. S. Venkataramana Sarma *B.A.*   Secretary[1]
A. Panchapagasa Sastry[2]

Warriore
Subramania Iyer (Mirasidar)   President
Nuilusawmy Pillay (Merchant)   Secretary[3]

Tanjore
Gopal Row   President
P. R. Natasa Iyer   Secretary[4]

Mayavaram
A. Sami Aiyer   President
Thiravenkatachariar
Raja Sastrial   Vice Presidents
K. Lukshmana Aiyar
S. Narayanaswami Aiyer   Secretary[5]
(Headmaster)

Negapatam
Greenivasa Sastrigal   Chairman
Ganapathi Pillai
(Wealthy merchant and agent
of the Steam Navigation Co.)   Vice Presidents
Ramaswamy Iyer
(Salt contractor)

N. P. Subramania Iyer
(First Grade Pleader)   Secretaries
G. Sambasiva Iyer
(Schoolmaster)

Subramani Pillai
(Salt merchant)   Treasurer[7]

1 *Hindu*, 12/3/1888.
2 Ibid., 10/8, 17/9/1888. Ganapathi Iyer B.A., B.L., former Chiarman of the Arya Tuthuva Vidyasala invited Sivasankara Pandiah to Trichinopoly, *Hindu*, 17/10/1889.
3 *Hindu*, 4/2/1889.
4 Ibid., 21/12/1889.
5 Ibid., 6/3/1889.
6 Ibid., 15/12/1889.

APPENDIX 13

ENROLMENTS IN GOVERNMENT AND MISSIONARY COLLEGES: TANJORE AND TRICHINOPOLY DISTRICTS, 1881 – 1882 to 1893 – 1894

Year	Total	Government Colleges	Missionary Colleges	Missionary Colleges: Percentage of total
1881	500	271	229	46
1882 – 3	578	249	329	57
1883 – 4	643	209	434	68
1884 – 5	681	211	470	69
1885 – 6	741	222	519	70
1886 – 7	874	246	628	72
1887 – 8	856	237	619	72
1888 – 9	848	231	617	73
1889 – 1890	790	220	570	72
1890 – 1	837	211	626	75
1891 – 2	994	249	745	75
1892 – 3	870	227	643	74
1893 – 4	811	197	614	76

Source: *Reports on Public Instruction in the Madras Presidency 1881 – 2 to 1893 – 4.*

SELECT BIBLIOGRAPHY

I MANUSCRIPT SOURCES

India Office Library and Records

Madras Judicial Proceedings
Madras Public Proceedings
Madras Revenue Proceedings
Board's Collections

School of Oriental and African Studies Archives

Methodist Missionary Society: incoming correspondence and reports
London Missionary Society: incoming correspondence and reports

United Society for the Propagation of the Gospel

Incoming correspondence, reports, etc.

Jesuit Archives, Rome

Incoming correspondence and reports connected with the Madura mission

High Court, Madras

Bundles of documents including judgments, evidence and other related material in connection with appeals from lower courts

Tamilnadu Record Office

Tanjore records

Jesuit Archives, Shembaganur

Incoming correspondence and reports connected with the Madura mission

Church Records located at various churches in Tanjore and Trichinopoly Districts

These include baptismal, marriage and other registers in Tamil, German, French and Portuguese, as well as in English

Anglican
Christchurch, Fort, Trichinopoly
Infant baptismal register 1853 – 77
Adult baptisms 1855 – 97

All Saints, Puttur
Infant baptisms 1886 – 1900
Adult baptisms 1889 – 97
Burials at Warriore 1887 – 1900

St. Peter's Church, Tanjore
Adult baptisms 1875 – 98
Marriage register 1866 – 1900
Marriage register, Vediarpuram 1866 – 1900

St. Peter's, Negapatam
Burial register 1854 – 1900

Kartiruppu (includes Nangur)
Adult baptisms 1865 – 1900

Catholic
Congregation Under Rome, Tanjore
Baptismal register 1850 – 93 (Sacred Heart Cathedral Archives)

Congregation Under Goa, Tanjore
Baptismal register 1874 – 93
B.V. de Dores marriage register 1877 – 88 & 1889 – 98 (Sacred Heart Cathedral Archives)

St. Mary's, Trichinopoly
Baptismal register 1841 – 59
Marriage register 1853 – 60, 1874 – 81 & 1882 – 1900

Parish of Kumbakonam
Baptismal register 1841 – 64, 1841 – 3, 1853 – 9, 1859, 1862 – 4
Marriage register 1882 – 1900

Lutheran
Tranquebar
Baptismal register (general) 1878 – 1900
Admissions register 1880 – 1900
Marriage Register 1878 – 1900

Karikal
Baptismal register (mostly adults) 1896 – 1900
Admissions register 1899 – 1900
Burial register 1897 – 1900

Manikramman
Baptismal register (general) 1888 – 1900
Admissions register 1892 – 1900

Zion Church, Trichinopoly
Baptismal register (general) 1892 – 1900
Marriage register 1885 – 1900
Admissions register 1870 – 4, 1887 – 91, 1892 – 1900

Holy Comforter Church, Tanjore
Baptismal register, Budalur 1852 – 82
Baptismal register (general) 1851, 1863 – 8, 1898 – 1900
Admissions register 1895 – 1900
Confirmation register 1898 – 1900
Marriage register 1898 – 1900

Holy Immanuel Church, Mayavaram
Baptismal register (general) 1883 – 1900
Admissions register 1883 – 1900

II PRINTED SOURCES

(A) GOVERNMENT GAZETTEERS

Imperial Gazetteer, 1908

W. Francis	*South Arcot*	1906	Madras
F. R. Hemingway	*Tanjore*	1906	Madras
F. R. Hemingway	*Trichinopoly*	1907	Madras
L. Moore	*A Manual of Trichinopoly District*	1878	Madras
H. R. Pate	*Tinnevelly*	1917	Madras
C. H. Rao	*Mysore Gazetteer*	1930	Madras
F. J. Richards	*Salem*	1918	Madras
T. V. Row	*A Manual of the District of Tanjore*	1883	Madras

(B) REPORTS, PAPERS, ETC.

C. U. Aitchison (ed.) *A Collection of Treaties, Engagements and Sanads Relating to India and Neighbouring Countries*, Calcutta 1930.
An Abstract of the Annual Reports and Correspondence of the S.P.C.K., London 1814.
Census of India, Madras 1871 – 1901.
M. S. Thiruvenkava Chari (ed.) *A Collection of Papers Relating to Sri Runganathasawmi Temple*, Trichinopoly 1887.
Commons, Accounts and Papers. Papers on the connexion of the Government of India with idolatry, or with Mahometanism.
Evangelisch Lutherisches Missionblatt, Leipzig 1865 – 1900.
History of Indian Railways Constructed and in Progress Corrected up to 31 March 1955. Government of India Ministry of Railways.
Indian Law Reports.
Inquiries made by the Bishop of Madras regarding the removal of caste predjudices and practices, in the Native Church of South India, together with the replies of the missionaries and native clergy sent thereto, Madras 1868.
List of Festivals, Fairs etc. occurring within the limits of the Madras Presidency, Madras 1868.
Madras Diocese Report, 1869, 1889.

Madras Diocesan Quarterly Reports, 1883 – 1902.
Madras Epigraphy, Annual Reports.
Report of the Indian National Congress, 1887.
Report on Public Instruction in the Madras Presidency, 1888 – 1899.
Report of the Second Decennial Missionary Conference, Calcutta 1883.
Reports on the Swinging Festivals and the Ceremony of Walking through Fire, Madras 1854.
Society for the Propagation of the Gospel, Quarterly Report.
Society for the Propagation of the Gospel, Annual Reports, 1854 – 1901.
South Indian Epigraphy, Annual Reports.
Statistical Tables of Protestant Missions in India, Burma and Ceylon, prepared on information collected at the close of 1881, at the request of the Calcutta Missionary Conference, Calcutta 1882.

(C) PERIODICALS

Africa
All the World
Annals of the Propagation of the Faith
Calcutta Christian Observer
Contributions to Indian Socioloty
Harvest Field
Indian Antiquary
Indian Church History Review
Indian Economic and Social History Review
Indian War Cry
Journal of Asian Studies
Journal of Ecclesiastical History
Journal of Economic and Social History of the Orient
Journal of the Royal Asiatic society of Great Britain and Ireland
Madras Quarterly Mission Journal
Mission Field, 1882 – 1900
The Net
South Asia
Theosophist
Wesleyan Missionary Notices

(D) NEWSPAPERS

Atheneum, Madras
Fort St George Gazette, Madras
The Hindu, Madras
Madras Times, Madras

The Times, London

(E) OTHER WORKS

R. S. Aiyar, *History of the Nayakes of Madura*, Madras 1924.
Anon, *A Short History of the Thiruvavaduthurai Adheenam of Thirukkailaya Parambarai*, Adheenam publication No. 163, Thiruvavaduthurai N.D.
A. Appadurai, 'Kings, Sects and Temples in South India 1350 – 1700 AD' in B. Stein (ed) *South Indian Temples, An Analytical Reconsideration*, New Delhi, 1978.
———, *Worship and Conflict under Colonial Rule: A South Indian Case*, Cambridge 1982.
K. Nambi Arooran, *Tamil Renaissance and Dravidian Nationalism 1905 – 1944*, Madurai 1980.
M. Arunachalam, *Guru Jnana Sambandha of Dharmapuram*, Dharmapuram 1972.
P. V. Jagadisa Ayyar, *South Indian Festivities*, New Delhi 1982.
———, *South Indian Shrines*. Revised and enlarged edition, New Delhi 1982.
L. A. Babb, *The Divine Hierarchy: Popular Hinduism in Central India*, New York 1975.
E. R. Baierlein, *The Land of the Tamulians and its Missions*. Translated from the German by J. B. Gribble, Madras 1875.
C. J. Baker, 'Temples and Political Development' in C. J. Baker and D. A. Washbrook *South India: Political Institutions and Political Change 1800 – 1940*, Delhi 1975.
C. J. Baker and D. A. Washbrook, *South India: Political Institutions and Political Change 1800 – 1940*, Delhi 1975.
P. J. Bertrand (ed.), *Lettres Edifiantes et Curieuses de la Nouvelle Mission du Maduré*.
L. Besse, *La Mission du Maduré*, Trichinopoly 1914.
J. N. Bhattacharya, *Hindu Castes and Sects*, Calcutta 1896.
H. T. Blavatsky, *Isis Unveiled*. New ed., California 1972.
F. Booth Tucker, *Mukti Fauj or Forty Years with the Salvation Army in India and Ceylon*, London (N.D.).
C. Breckenridge, 'From Protector to Litigant — Changing relations between Hindu Temples and the Raja of Ramnad' in B. Stein (ed.), *South Indian Temples: An Analytical Reconsideration*, New Delhi 1978.
G. Bühler (trans.), *The Laws of Manu*, New York 1969.
Peter Burke, *Popular Culture in early Modern Europe*, London 1979.
J. Bush (ed.), *W. O. Simpson Methodist Minister and Missionary*, London 1886.
B. F. Campbell, *Ancient Wisdom Revived: A History of the Theosophical Movement*, Berkeley 1980.
J. B. Carman, *The Theology of Ramanuja*, New Haven & London 1974.
Corrie, *Memoirs of the Right Rev. Daniel Corrie LLD, First Bishop of Madras*, Compiled by his brothers, London 1847.
A. J. Cronin, *A Pearl to India: The Life of Roberto de Nobili*, London 1959.
N. Desikacharya, *The Origin and Growth of Sri Brahmatantra Prakala Mutt*, Bangalore 1949.
V. A. Devasenapathi, *Saiva Siddhanta as expounded in the S'ivajnana-Siddhiyar and its six commentaries*, University of Madras 1974.

BIBLIOGRAPHY

J. A. Dubois, *Hindu Manners, Customs and Ceremonies* (Translated from the author's later French MS and edited with notes, corrections and biography by H. K. Beauchamp). Third edition, Oxford 1905.

Anncharlot Eschmann, 'Religion, Reaction and Change: the Role of Sects in Hinduism' in *Religion and Development in Asian Societies, Proceedings of the International Workshop*, Colombo 1975.

J. N. Farquhar, *Modern Religious Movements in India*, Delhi 1967.

G. G. Findlay and W. W. Holdsworth, *The History of the Wesleyan Methodist Missionary Society*, London 1925.

D. B. Forrester, *Caste and Christianity: Attitudes and Policies on Caste of Anglo-Saxon Protestant Missions in India*, London 1980.

R. E. Frykenberg, 'The Impact of Conversion and Social Reform upon Society in South India during the late Company Period: Questions concerning Hindu-Christian Encounters with Special reference to Tinnevelly' in C. H. Philips (ed.), *Indian Society and the Beginnings of Modernisation c. 1830 – 1850*, London 1975.

S. Ghosh, *The Renaissance to Militant Nationalism in India*, Bombay 1969.

G. S. Ghurye, *Indian Sadhus*, Second edition, Bombay 1964.

J. Gonda, *Visnuism and Sivaism: a Comparison*, London 1970.

K. Gough, *Rural Society in Southeast India*, Cambridge 1981.

C. E. Gover, *The Folk-Songs of Southern India*, 2nd ed., Madras 1959.

K. Graul, *Explanations concerning the principles of the Leipzig Missionary Society with regard to the Caste Question*, Madras 1851.

R. L. Hardgrave, *The Nadars of Tamilnad: The Political Culture of a Community in Change*, Berkeley & Los Angeles 1969.

W. Hickey, *The Tanjore Mahratta Principality in Southern India: the land of the Chola; the Eden of the South*, second edition, Madras 1874.

Alf Hiltebeitel, 'Sexuality and Sacrifice: Convergent Subcurrents in the Firewalking Cult of Draupadi' in F. W. Clothey (ed.), *Images of Man: Religion and Historical Process in South Asia*, Madras 1892.

M. Hollis, *Paternalism and the Church: The Study of South Indian Church History*, London 1962.

E. F. Irschick, *Politics and Social Conflict in South India: The Non-Brahman Movement and Tamil Separatism, 1916 – 1929*, California 1969.

P. R. Ganapathi Iyer, *The Law Relating to Hindu and Mohamedan Religious Endowments*, Madras 1905.

P. J. Ramaswamy Iyer, 'Brahmin Conversion' in N. Money and G. V. I. Sama (eds.), *The Story of St Mary's Tope*, Tiruchirapalli 1977.

R. Ramanatha Iyer, *The Madras Hindu Religious Endowments Act (Act 11 of 1927)*, Madras 1931.

N. Jagadeesan, *History of Sri Vaishnavism in the Tamil country (Post-Ramanuja)*, Madurai 1977.

R. P. Auguste Jean, *Le Maduré: L'ancienne et la Nouvelle Mission*, Tome II [N.P.] 1894.

C. Jinarajadasa (ed.), *The Golden Book of the Theosophical Society*, Madras 1925.

J. W. Kaye, *Christianity in India: An Historical Narrative*, London 1859.

A. F. Kindersley, *A History of the Kindersley Family* (printed for private circulation), October 1938.
N. E. Kindersley, *A Letter to the Earl of Buckinghamshire on the Propagation of Christianity in India*, London 1813.
Father Louis Lacombe, S.J. (The Catholic Truth Society of India), Trichinopoly 1930.
L. Lacombe, *L'Oeuvre De La Conversion des hautes Castes au College St Joseph, Trichinopoly*, Rome N.D.
———, *A Great Indian Convert: Rao Sahib V Mahadeva Aiyer*, Trichinopoly 1923.
M. A. Laird, *Missionaries and Education in Bengal 1793 – 1837*, Oxford 1972.
A. Launay, *Histoire des Missions L'Inde*, Paris 1898.
A. Lehmann, *It Began at Tranquebor: the Story of the Tranquebor mission and the beginnings of Protestant Christianity in India*, Madras 1956.
T. V. Mahalingam, *Administration and Social Life Under Vijayanagar*, Madras 1975.
S. Manickham, *The Social Setting of Christian Conversion in South India*, Weisbaden 1977.
A. Mayhew, *Christianity and the Government of India*, London 1929.
A. Meersman, *The Ancient Franciscan Provinces in India 1500 – 1835*, Bangalore 1971.
D. M. Miller and D. C. Wertz, *Hindu Monastic Life and the Monks and Monasteries of Bhubaneswar*, Montreal & London 1976.
M. Moffat, *The Untouchable Community in South India: Structure and Consensus*, New Jersey 1979.
N. Money and G. V. L. Sama (eds.), *The History of St. Mary's Tope: The Origin, Development and Spread of St. Mary's Tope, the Catholic Brahmin Colony, Tiruchi*, N.P. 1977.
C. H. Monohan, *Theophilus Subrahmanyam: The Story of a Pilgrimage*, London 1922.
Chandra Mudaliar, *State and Religious Endowments in Madras*, Madras 1976.
H. Murphet, *The Hammer on the Mountain: Life of Henry Steel Olcott (1832 – 1907)*, Wheaton Illinois, 1972.
H. V. Nanjundayya and L. K. Ananthakrishnam Iyer, *The Mysore Tribes and Castes*, Mysore 1928.
A. H. Nethercot, *The First Five Lives of Annie Besant*, London 1961.
———, *The Last Four Lives of Annie Besant*, London 1963.
G. A. Oddie (ed.) *Religion in South Asia: Religious Conversion and Revival Movements in South Asia in Medieval and Modern Times*, Delhi 1977.
G. A. Oddie, 'Christians in the Census: Tanjore and Trichinopoly Districts 1871 – 1901' in N. G. Barrier (ed.), *The Census in British India New Perspectives*, Delhi 1981.
———, *Social Protest in India: British Protestant Missionaries and Social Reforms 1850 – 1900*, Delhi 1979.
———, 'Anti-missionary feeling and Hindu resistance in Madras: the Hindu Preaching and Tract Societies: c. 1886 – 1891' in F. Clothey (ed),

Images of Man: Religion and Historical Process in South Asia. Madras 1982.
H. S. Olcott, *Old Diary Leaves: The History of the Theosophical Society*, Second Series 1878 – 83, Adyar 1974; Third Series 1883 – 87, Adyar 1972; Fourth Series 1887 – 92, Adyar 1975.
J. C. Oman, *The Mystics, Ascetics and Saints of India*, London 1905.
G. Oppert, *The Original Inhabitants of Bharatavarsa or India*, Westminster & Leipzig 1893.
S. Pandiah, *The Duties of the Natives of India to their Rulers and their Country*, Madras 1888 (Hindu Excelsior Series).
C. F. Pascoe, *Classified Digest of the S.P.G. in Foreign Parts 1701 – 1892*, London 1893.
P. Percival, *The Land of the Veda: India briefly described in some of its aspects, physical, social, intellectual and moral*, London 1854.
H. Pearson, *Memoirs of the Life and Correspondence of the Reverend Christian Frederick Swartz*, 2 vols., London 1834.
K. K. Pillay, *The Caste System in Tamil Nadu*, Madras 1977.
C. C. Prinsep, *Record of Services of the Honourable East India Company's Civil Servants in the Madras Presidency from 1741 to 1858*, London 1865.
S. Srinivasa Raghavaiyangar, *Memorandum on the Progress of the Madras Presidency during the last forty years of British Administration*, Madras 1893.
S. Rajamanickam, *The First Oriental Scholar*, Tirunelveli 1972.
M. Rajamanikkam, 'The Tamil Saiva Mathas Under the Cholas (AD 900 – 1300)' in C. T. K Chari (ed.), *Essays in Philosophy presented to Dr T. M. P. Mahadevan on his Fiftieth Birthday*, Madras 1962.
M. S. A. Rao, *Social Movements and Social Transformation*, Madras 1979.
Robert Redfield, *The Little Community and Peasant Society and Culture*, Chicago & London 1960.
L. Renou (ed.), *Hinduism*, New York 1962.
R. Sathianathaier, *Tamilaham in the 17th Century*, Madras 1956.
B. Stein, 'Social Mobility and Medieval South Indian Sects' in J. Silverberg (ed.), *Social Mobility in the Caste System of India: An Interdisciplinary symposium*, The Hague & Paris 1968.
———, *Peasant State and Society in Medieval South India*, Delhi 1980.
———, *South Indian Temples: An Analytical Reconsideration*, New Delhi 1978.
P. Suau, *L'Inde Tamoule*, Paris 1901.
K. R. Subramanian, *The Maratha Rajas of Tanjore*, Madras 1928.
R. Suntharalingam, *Politics and Nationalist Awakening in South India, 1852 – 1891*, Arizona 1974.
E. Thurston, *Ethnographic Notes in Southern India*, Madras 1906.
———, *Castes and Tribes of Southern India*, Madras 1909.
E. Visswanathan, 'The Emergence of Brahmins in South India with Special Reference to Tamil Nadu' in S. N. Mukerjee (ed.), *Indian History and Thought Essays in Honour of A. L. Basham*, Calcutta 1982.

D. A. Washbrook, *The Emergence of Provincial Politics: The Madras Presidency 1870–1920*, Cambridge 1976.
H. Whitehead, *India: A Sketch of the Madura Mission*, London 1897.
———, *The Village Gods of South India*, London 1921.
B. Wilson, *Religious Sects: A Sociological Study*, London 1970.
H. Yule & A. C. Burnell, *Hobson Jobson*, 2nd ed., Delhi 1968.
B. Ziegenbalg, *Genealogy of the South Indian Gods*, translated into English by Rev. G. J. Metzger, Madras 1869.
K. V. Zvelebil, *Tamil Literature*, Weisbaden 1974.

III THESES

Sara Braunstein, 'British Land Revenue Policy and Social Continuity in a South Indian District: A study of Trichinopoly District, 1801 – 1924'. M.A. Thesis, University of Western Australia, 1976.
V. N. Hari Rao, 'A History of Trichinopoly and Srirangam', PhD Thesis, University of Madras, 1948.

GLOSSARY

Abishekam	a holy bath given to the deity
Acharya	religious teacher
Adhinam	central *math* or monastery exercising control or supervision over subordinate *maths* or other institutions such as temples
Advaita Vedanta	non-dualism or absolute monism; Upanishadic thought systematized by Shankara in the ninth century
Alankaram	decorations such as robes, garlands etc.
Alvars	poet-saint of Medieval Vaishnavism
Amma	goddess; divine lady
Annathan	institution for the distribution of boiled rice
Arccanai	private worship according to the wishes of the individual
Archikar	brahman priest of a saivite temple
Ashrama	one of the four stages of a Hindu's life; a hermitage or retreat
Bhakta	devotee
Bhakti	devotion; doctrinal principle of salvation through devotion
Carnum	accountant
Cawney	a measure of land equivalent to 1.322 acres
Chakram	a South Indian coin equal to 1/16 of a pagoda, the latter being equivalent to 3½ rupees
Chattram	superior rest house for high-caste pilgrims
Choultry	simple building used for travellers as a temporary resting place
Dandi	staff-holding sub-sect of ascetics created by Shankara
Darga	a shrine or tomb of a Muslim saint
Dasanamis	one of ten sub-orders of ascetics created by Shankara
Datum	gift
Devadasis	dancing girls
Devastanam	temple; revenue applied to the support of a temple
Dharmakarta	trustee of a temple
Grama Devata	village deity
Guru	a religious teacher and mentor

GLOSSARY

Homa	a sacrificial ceremony in which burnt offerings were made
Hundi	bill of exchange, draft, cheque; a sealed pot in which were placed offerings for the deity
Inam	present, gift, favour, gratuity — especially a grant of land held rent-free and in hereditary and perpetual occupation
Jeer	spiritual leader of the vadagalai sect
Katlai	a special endowment for a special purpose
Lingam	phallic symbol representing Shiva, normally carved from stone
Mandapam	ceremonial hall
Mandapapati	feeding and entertainment of the deity during halts in his or her procession within the precincts of the mandapam
Mantra	a sacred utterance (syllable, word or verse) considered to possess mystical or spiritual efficacy
Math	residence of an ascetic, or community of ascetics; monastery
Mathapadi	head of a *math*
Mirasi	inheritance
Mirasidar	an hereditary proprietor
Moksha	liberation
Mutt	see *Math*
Nasur	fixed rent
Nattuvan	an occupational term, meaning a dancing master, which was applied to the males of the dancing girl castes who taught dancing
Pagoda	a coin current in South India until replaced by the rupee in 1818 — equivalent to 3½ rupees
Panchayat	a committee of villagers to which a cause was referred for investigation and decision
Pandara Sannadhi	head monk of an adhinam or non-brahman monastic order
Pandaram	a vellala priest or monk
Poonul	sacred thread
Prabandam	hymns of the Alvars or poet-saints
Prakaram	the verandah or passage around the sanctum sanctorum of a temple
Prapatti	resignation or self-surrender
Prasadam	food blessed by having been offered before a deity, which is distributed after worship among those present
Puja	public worship
Pujaris	non-brahman temple priests

GLOSSARY

Puranas	popular Hindu literature including collections of myth, legend and genealogy, varying greatly as to date and origin
Saiva Siddhanta	name commonly used for the South Indian religious system of saivism
Saivites	followers of Shiva
Sampradaya	teaching tradition
Sannyasi	one who has renounced worldly ties, an ascetic; in South India normally a brahman ascetic
Sastri	man of learning, one who teaches any branch of Hindu learning, such as law
Satakopan	honours
Shakti	the wife of Shiva; the goddess who personifies divine power, energy
Smarthas	Tamil saivite brahmans who also acknowledge Vishnu
Srivaishnavites	Tamil followers of the Vaishnava school, especially of Ramanuja
Stullatar	official of a temple, manager
Tahsildar	Indian collector of a subdivision under the European Collector
Tambiran	a non-brahman monk of a saiva *math*
Tengalais	the 'southern' school of followers of Ramanuja
Tirttam	sacred water left over from the deity's meals or bath
Vadagalais	the 'northern' school of followers of Ramanuja
Vaishnavite	follower of Vishnu
Valie	a measure of land containing five cawneys or 6.6 of an acre
Varnas	the four classes of Hindu society, viz. brahmans, kshatriyas, vaisyas, and sudras
Zamindar	landholder, landlord
Zenana	the apartments of a house in which the women of the family are secluded

INDEX

Abishekatlai, 108
Acarya, 86, 98
Adhinam, 70, 99, 101-4, 106-7
adi-dravidas, see depressed classes
Advaita, 13, 211
Advaita Sabha, 211
Advaita Vedanta, 99, 100, 102
Agni Purana, 123
Ahobilam *math*, 27, 100
Aiyanar, 12, 29, 30, 38 n81, 122
Aiyengar, K. S., 91
alankaram, 26
Alexander, Rev. A., 213 n18
Alvars, 83, 84, 86
Amar Singh, 43
ambalagars, 128
Amma, 29
Anglicans, 16
  and caste practices, 174, 175-6, 177, 178, 226
  child marriage, 181
  widow remarriage, 178-9
  and depressed classes, 160
  lapsed converts, 162
anthropology, 4
Apoo, Pillay, 22
apostates, 162, 164-5, 175
Appadurai, A., 7, 26, 85
Appusamy Iyer, 143, 146
Arccanai, 22, 108
Archikar, 88, 89
Arooran, Nambi K., 229
Arya Samaj, 194
Ashramas, 98
Astaksari-mantra, 84

Babb, Lawrence, 8
Badri *math*, 99
Balakrishnan, 190
baptismal registers, 155
Barbier, Fr., 169 n56
bathing, 124
Benares, 43, 109, 113
Besant, Annie, 197, 199, 228
Bhagavad gita, 217
bhakta, 83, 197

Bhattacharya, 84
Bhattas, 68
Bheemanaikenpoliem, 128, 134
Bhuttar, V. A., 90
Billard, Fr., 143, 147, 149
Blackburne, William, 43
Blavatsky, H. P., 78, 191, 192, 193, 200
blood sacrifice, 31, 38 n95
Board of Revenue, 44, 51-2, 53, 88, 106, 107, 110
Bommakka, 30
Boulton, Marshall, M., 229
Bourne, Rev. A., 47
Bradey, Brother, 120
Bradlaugh, 191, 199
brahmans
  brahman/non-brahman gulf, 211, 228-9
Christians, 171-2
converts, 140-50, 190, details, 141
dissatisfaction with Hinduism, 143-4
and the Hindu Tract Society, 201-2
and *maths*, 99-100, 101
obstacles to conversion of, 144-6
effects of conversion on family, 147
and ritual dominance, 8-9
social and ritual position of, 218-9
and temple attendance, 21-2, 31
and temple control, 67-72
tengalai and vadagalai, 84-5
and popular religion, 120
and Theosophy, 197, 219
Brahmos, 226
Breckenridge, Carol, 7
Brihadesvara temple, 41, 43, 70
Burnell, A. C., 75

Caine, W. S., 134
Cameron, N. S., 24, 25, 87
Cannapiran Mudaliar, 201
Carnatic, 16
carnums, 21, 23
Catholic missions
  understaffed, 165, 169, n56
Catholics, 5, 15-17

attitude to caste practices, 172, 174, 175, 185-6
attitude to child marriage, 181, 182
and brahmin converts, 140, 146-50
depressed class converts, 155, 160, 162
factions, 171, 186
lapsed converts, 162
numbers, 144, 171, 221, 225
chakliers, 154
chakrams, 64
Chakrapani temple, 70
chattrams, 41, 43, 109, 114, 228
Chetti, T. V., 91
Chitambaram, 109
Chola, 2
choultries, 25, 109
Christians,
  age at marriage 180
  community, 158, 166, 170
    and caste, 144-5, 171, 173, 174-5, 184-6, 219, 226
    and depressed classes, 155
  education, 181-4, 219, 226
  female education, 184-5, 226
  intercaste marriage, 173-4, 185
  numbers, 144, 171, 221, 225
  population, 136, 153-4, 170
  widow remarriage, 178-80, 185
Chronicle of Srirangam, see Koil Olugu
Chundrashaikarum Pillay, 89
Church Missionary Society (CMS), 16
Coleroon, 1
collectors, 6, 18
Conjamala, Moothey, 89
Conjeeveram, 53, 54, 55, 93, 100
Conversion, 141
  conversion of brahmans, 140
    age, 142,
    and caste practices, 144
    background, 141-2
    Catholic colony, 147-9
    influences on, 142
    obstacles to conversion, 144-6, 147-9, 150
    salvation, 144
    social consequences, 145
  conversion of depressed classes, 154
    change of denomination, 162-3
    change in pattern of, 155-6
    economic factors, 156, 160, 161, 219
    individual rights, 159, 160, 219

landlords, 161, 224
education, 159, 168 n28
group, 156
lapsed 162, 164-5
social factors, 156, 157-8, 159, 219
individual, 155, 209
reactions against, 207, 208
Coorg Mountains, 1
Coromandel, 16
Corrie, Daniel, Bishop of Madras, 53
Cotton, John, 50-1, 60 n49
Court of Directors, 13
Crisp, Rev. Edmund, 54-5, 175
Cryer, Rev. Thomas, 190
Custoory, Rungumpillay, 22

dancing girls, 25, 26, 45
dandi, 99
darga, 33, 125
Darvell, Rev. T. E., 206
dasanamis, 99
Dasara festival, 43, 56 n17
datum, 102
de Nobili, Robert, 15, 154, 172
depressed classes, 154 sq.
devadasis, 25, 36, n45, see also dancing girls
devastanam, 71
dharmakarta, 100
Dharmapuram *math*, 69, 101, 101-15, 115, 116 n41
Dharmasastras, 217
Dickinson, Henry, 18, 35 n32, 87
Doorasamy, Moopanar, 225
Doraisamy Iyer, 143
Draupadi, 128-9
Dravidians, 211, 229
Dubois, Abbé, J. A., 25, 47, 125
Dwarka *math*, 99

East India Company, 13, 15, 18, 33, 40, 224
  and temples, 43-6
  and temple carts, 47-56
Ekadashi, see Vaikunth-Ekadashi
Elanthurai, 127
Esanai, 30
Evangelicals, 5, 46, 54, 56, 57
Evangelical Lutheran Mission (ELM), 16

famines, 157, 222
Faseuille, Fr., 146, 205

festivals, 2, 120, 122-5, numbers attending, 130-4
    and disease, 133
    and railways, 130-1
firewalking, 120, 128-30, 134-5, 228
Forbes, Henry, 128, 133, 134
Forrester, D., 157
Free Hindu Religious School, 211

Ganesh, 28
Ganga, 123
Garrow, George, 87-8
Gnanamuttu, Rev. V., 202
Goa, Archbishop of, 171
gods, 29, 30, 221-2
    village, 29
    vows to, 32
Govindacarya, A., 85
grama devata, 29
Grant, Duff, 192
Guest, Rev. J., 176
Guha, Ranajit, 6
Guru, 98, 100, 103, 104, 110
Guru Jnana Sambandha, 103
Gury, Fr., 173

harijans, see depressed classes
Heber, Bishop, 174, 175
Hindu Missionary Society, 191
Hindu Preaching Society, 200, 221, 227
Hemmingway, F. R., 30, 31, 32, 33, 103, 107, 122, 125
Hepburn, James, 44
Hindu, the, 72, 76, 93, 100, 105, 112, 114, 149, 159, 200, 204
Hindu gods, see gods
Hindu National High School, 205, 206, 210
Hindu revivalism, 189, 227
Hindu schools, 204-5
Hindu Theological High School, 210
Hindu Tract society, 7, 191, 200
    branches, 201
    attitude to Hinduism 211-2, 221
    leaders, 201, 207
    social composition, 202
    reaction to Christianity, 202-6, 208, 227
    decline, 206, 209
Hinduism, 8-9
    and brahman converts 149-50
    and caste, 217, 219, 220
    changes in, 221
    and child marriage, 181
    and Christians, 158
    precolonial, 12
    decline of, 72, 77-8, 192
    East India Company's support for, 54, 55
    East India Company's withdrawal of support from, 58, 64
    and sectarianism, 93, 97 n72, 210-1, 212
    popular, 29-33, 119-20, 212
    and social mobility, 135-6, 136 n5
    and temple cart controversy, 56
    and Theosophy, 195-6
    and widow remarriage, 178-9
Hjejle, Benedicte, 6
Hobday, Rev. James, 26, 56
Hobhouse, Sir John, 57
Holy Comforter Church, 155
Holy Emmanuel Church, 164
homa, 84
hook-swinging, 120, 125-8, 126 (fig), 133, 134-5, 137 n36, 218, 220, 228
Horton, R., 157
Humanitarianism, 55
hundi, 23, 24, 109-10

Ignatius, Rev. I., 157, 176
Ilbert Bill, 192
Indian National Congress, 114
Ingersoll, 199
Irschick, E. F., 229
Iyalore temple, 75-6

Jaganath, 43, 47
Jambukeswaram temple, 18, 20, 65, 68-9, 77
jeer, 88, 89, 100
Jesuit missionaries, 13, 15, 17, 151 n10
    attacks on, 202, 223
    attitudes to Hindus, 35 n28, 143
    and brahman conversion, 140-1, 146-9
    and caste, 172
    and education, 185
    relationship with other Catholics, 171, 186

Kabis, Rev. J., 158, 159
kaikolan, 127
Kalyana Raman, 145
kammala, 172
Kanchipuram, see Conjeeveram
kaniyalar brahmans, 31

Karaikkal, 15, 137, 163
Karnvandaraya Boomadeva, 30
katlais, 105, 107, 108
Kaveri, 1-2, 3 (fig), 7, 86
Kayarohanaswami temple, 70
Kenedy, Richard, 66, 67, 70, 71, 228
Kindersley, N. W., 18, 35 n32, 50-1, 61 n58, n59, 68, 106
Koil Olugu, 27, 95 n28
Konkani-speaking brahmans, 140, 150 n3
Kottayya, C., 198
Krishna, V. Iyer, 72, 114
Krishna Rao, 89
Kumarasami (*tambiran*), 111-2, 113
Kumbaknonam, 2, 16
  festivals, 49, 123, 131
  temple controversy, 71-2, 73, 92, 114, 229
Kumbakonam College, 226
Kumbakonam *math*, 100-13, 114
kurava, 127

Lacombe, Fr. L., 7, 146
Latham, R. M., 87
Laws of Manu, see Manu laws of
Lazarus, Rev. George, 160
Leipzig Mission, see Evangelical Lutheran Mission
lingam, 104
Little, Rev. J., 77
Lushington, Charles, M., 6, 20, 87
Lutheran Churches, 155, 162
Lutheran Mission, 160
  and caste 172, 174, 177, 196
Lutherans, 171, 175-6

Maclean, A., 53
Madras Christian College, 204
Madras Government, 57
Madras High Court, 25, 102, 105, 112
Madras Legislative Council, 72
Madras Mail, 194
Madras memorial, 55
Madras mission, 172
Madras Missionary Conference, 158
Madras Times, 124, 194
adurai Viran, 29, 33, 222
Madyarjunam, see Tiruvadaimarudur
Magali, 122
Magum, 123
Maha Vaidyanatha Iyer, 114
Mahabarata, 128, 129
Madadeva Iyer, 7, 147-8, 149, 205, 209, 220

Mahadevan, Meenakshi Sundaram Pillay, 109
Mahamagum, 43, 47, 123-4, 131, 220
Maitland, Sir Peregrine, 57
Mallamma, 30
mandapam, 108
mandapappatis, 108
Manikaramman mission, 16
Mannargudi, 13
  festival, 49
  mission, 16
mantra kashayam, 104
Manu, Laws of, 98, 217
Maratha brahmans, 141
Maratha rajas, 13, 58-9 n17
Mariamma, 29,
  festival, 30, 122, 125, 127, 128, 130
  temples, 31
mathapadi, 100
maths, 2, 6, 12-13, 17, 65, 98, 99-100
  brahman (*maths*), 204, 228, 229
  control of adhinams, 105-9
  mismanagement of, 112-4
  non-brahman, 101-5
  and non-brahman movement, 114-5
  and pilgrims, 109
  and Tamil studies, 109
  and temple property, 109
Mayavaram, 2
  festival, 123
  Lutheran mission, 196
  mission, 16, 69
Mayuranathaswami temple, 69
Methodist mission, 17
Methodist missionaries, 16-17, 171
  attacks on, 190, 203, 208
  and brahman converts, 140, 144-5, 150, 151 n10
  and criticism of Hinduism, 143
  and lapsed converts, 162
  opposition to caste practices, 174, 226
  and sabhas, 199
Meykandar, 102, 103
Miran Sahib, 33, 124
mirasi, 23, 27
mirasidars, 49, 50, 51, 52, 71, 76, 103, 161, 195, 218
Mission school enrolments, 207, 215 n97
Missionaries, 6
  early influence of, 15
moksha, 98, 122, 123, 124
Monier Williams M., 25, 77, 83, 86, 122
Monism, 143

INDEX

Morangi, 109
Morris, G. L., 68
mudaliar, 68, 77
Mudaliar, T. R., 90
Muktambapuram temple, 50
mula mantra, 104
Musiri, 71
Muslims, 12, 136
Muthuswami, Naidu P. N., 199

Nachiyarkovil temple, 28, 70, 92, 93
Nagore, 13, 33
Nailer, Rev. A. R. C., 189
Narainswami, John, 145
Narayanaswami K. Iyer, 198
National High School see Hindu National High School
Nattuvan, 21, 25, 103
Nawabs of Arcot, 12
Nayakkan Tirumala, 33
Nayaks of Madura, 12-13
Negapatam, 33
  temple committee, 71
  tahsildars, 74, 77
Nelson, Robert, 49, 50, 52, 55, 57, 60-1 n54, 63 n78
Nimmo, Rev. J. E., 30, 47, 123
non-adhinam, 69
non-brahmans, 11 n18
  in temples, 22-3
  maths, 99, 101
  maths and the non-brahman movement, 114-5
  and religious power, 8-9, 11, 22
  temple control, 67-72
  Theosophy, 197
nuzur, 23

O'Malley, L. S. S., 119
Olcott, Colonel H. S., 78, 191
  healing powers, 192-3
  reactions to him, 199-200, 221
  support for him, 195-7
  teachings, 192-3, 202, 210, 211, 228
  tours, 194, 195, 209
Onslow, A. P., 27, 65, 68, 88
Oppert, Gustav, 7, 29
Our Lady of Health chapel, 33

pallars, 154, 155, 173
pallis, 129
Palyaputty, 127
panchayat, 65, 67
pariahs, 154, 167 n16

behaviour as Christians, 173, 176-7
and conversion to Christianity, 155-8
position after conversion, 159, 166, 172, 173
Pandam Sannadhi, 102-3, 104, 105, 107, 110
pandaram, 31, 103, 104, 173
Panguini, 125
paravas, 34 n18, 154
Paumony temple, 44
Percival, Rev. P., 125
Peria Vaidyanatha Iyer, 114
Pidari, 29
pilgrimage, 120-4, 130
Plutschau, Henry, 15
Pongal, 30, 43, 122, 131
poonul, 144
Poreiar, 16
prabandam, 21, 83
prakarams, 25, 41
prapanna, 85
prapatti, 83-4
prasadam, 22, 25, 26, 27
Protestants
  missions, 15-17, 27, 193, 201, 223
  and brahman converts, 140
  and depressed class converts, 155, 159, 165
  numbers, 171
  rivalry with Catholics, 186
Public Works Department, 24
puja, 21, 100, 109
pujaris, 31, 88
Punnusami, Nalar T., 71, 225
puranas, 86
Puri *math*, 99
Puttukkottai, 171

Raganatha Row, R, 194
railways, 130, 132 (fig)
Raja of Puttukkottai, 113
Raja of Tanjore, 16, 40, 49, 50, 123
Raja of Travancore, 113
Raja Gopalaswami, 125
Raja Sarabhoji, 13
Raja Serfoji, 42 (fig)
  attitude to Christianity, 41
  religious activities, 41-3, 46, 59 n19
Raja Shahji, 13
Raja Shivaji, 43, 59 n22
Raja Tuljaji, 13, 41
Rajagopalaswami temple, 70, 93
Rajarajesvara temple, see Brihadesvara

rajas, 13
Ramachandra Iyer, L. S., 206
Ramalingam, 111-2
Ramanuja, 83, 86, 99, 211
Ramaswami temple, 70
Ramaswamy Iyer, P. J., 143, 144, 148
Ramayana, 13
Rameswaram, 41, 43, 100, 109, 113
Ramienger, V, 72
Rangaswami Aiyengar, 67
Rationalism, 78
records, 4-7
Redfield, Robert, 8, 119
Regunatha Row, K, 73, 75
religious centres, 212 (fig), see also festivals
Religious Endowment Act XX, 65-6, 72
Rig Veda, 217
Ripon's policies, 192
Rock Fort temple, 18, 21, 65, 69, 106, 107, 111
Row, T. V., 77

Sabapathi, Navalar, 109
St Augustine, 221
St Joseph's College, Trichinopoly, 17, 141, 143, 146, 185, 204-5, 206, 209
St Mary's Tope, 141, 148, 149
St Peter's Anglican church, 156
St Peter's College, 202
Saiva Siddhanta, 101, 102, 197, 211, 226, 228
Saiva Siddhanta Sabha, 211
saivites, 82, 141
Salvation Army, 17, 201, 203, 206, 209, 214 n59
Samayapuram, 30, 122, 125
Sambasiva Iyer, G., 201
sampradaya, 98
Sanmargha sabhas, 199
sannyasi, 88, 98, 100, 108
Sanskrit, 101, 115, 115 n21, 211, 219
literature, 202, 229
sanscritization, 8, 10 n16, 130
Saptasthalani, 124
Sarangapani temple, 49, 70
Sastri, K. A. N., 8
satakopan, 27
satanis, 68, 95 n17
Saunders, G. W., 87
Schultze, Rev., 16
sectarian conflict, 82-93, 94 n2
Sethu Row, 75

Sewell, Fr. G. I., 185
Sewell, R. B., 53
Shankara, 99, 102, 142, 143, 211
shakti, 29
Shivaratri, 122
Simpson, Rev. W. O., 56, 125
Singer, M., 130
Siva, 47, 102
Siva Jananabodam, 102
Sivasami, Odiyar, 225
Sivasankara Pandiah, 201, 202, 206, 209, 210, 212, 228
smarthas, 99, 141, 143
Society for the Promotion of Christian Knowledge (SPCK), 16
Society for the Propagation of the Gospel (SPG), 16, 77, 171
college, 202
high school, 189
sources, see records
Spiritualism, 191
Sri Amritakadesvaraswami temple, 107
Sri Partasarati swami temple, 93
Sri Tyagarajaswami temple, 25, 108
Srinivas, M. N., 10 n 16, 130
Sringeri *math*, 99
Srinivasa Sastrial, 201
Srirangam temple, 6, 13
employees' positions, 20-1, 23-4, 26
factions, 67, 85-6, 222
festival, 122
management, 65, 67, 68, 70
sectarian conflict, 28, 85-6, 86-91, 92, 95 n28, 96 n49
wealth, 18-20
Sriranganatha temple, see Srirangam temple
srivaishnavites, 82, 94 n6, 99, 141
Srivilliputtur temple, 93
Stokes, H. J., 6, 74, 76, 128, 135
Strinivasa Rau A, 74
stullatars, 21, 23, 68, 88
Subramania Iyer, N. P., 201
Subramanyam Iyer, 145
Suntharalingam, R., 9
Swamy Iyer, 128
Swartz, Rev. C. F., 41, 58 n6

tahsildar, 50, 111
tambiran, 21, 69, 101, 103, 104, 105, 107, 110-1
Tamil
texts, 101

INDEX

studies, 109, 115
Tamilnadu, 4
Tanjore Christians, 226
Tanjore missions, 16, 77
Tanjore temple, 20 (see also Brihadesvara temple)
Tanjore Widows Pension Fund, 160, 163
Tayuman temple, see Rock Fort temple
Temples
  access to, 28
  administration, 20-31
  carts, 43
  committees, 20, 28
    establishment of, 64-6, 90
    factions, 88-90, 90-3, 225
    membership, 66
    responsibilities, 66, 72-3
    social positions of appointees, 67-9, 70-1, 225
  controversy, 46-56
  honours, 26-8
  internal problems, 45
  labour for, 49-51
  land alienation, 44
  mismanagement, 72-4, 80 n47, 81 n59
  offices and servants, 20-3, 46
  pre-British rule, 12-16
  purchase of office, 26
  relations between temples and *maths*, 108
  revenue, 18-20
  servants income, 23-8
  state of repair, 45
  trustees, 20, 28, 64
    mismanagement, 65-9, 80 n37, 225
    personnel, 67, 68-70
  wealthiest, 20, 36 n37
tengalai, 27, 67, 83-93, 94 n7, 99, 220
Theosophical Society, 191-2
  branches, 197
  decline, 198-9
  members, 194-5, 197
  spread of, 194-5
Theosophist (journal), 78, 193, 194, 195
Theosophists, 5, 194
Theosophy, 189
  and attacks on Christianity, 193
  and brahmans, 197, 219, 223
  effects of, 199-200
  ideas of, 194-5
  and social class, 197, 219, 223, 227, 228-9

Therunarayanapuram temple, 75
Thompson, Rev. J. M., 191, 208
Thurston, E., 7, 104
Tirruppagalur, 101, 108
tirttam, 26, 27
Tirupathi, 43, 100
tiruppaniseivar, 25
Tiruppanandal *math*, 72, 101, 108, 109, 111-2, 114
Tirutturaippundi, 32
Tiruvadaimaudur festival, 49, 124
Tiruvadi, 124
Tiruvanaikkaval *math*, 102
Tiruvavaduturai *math*, 69, 101-2, 103, 109
Tiruvalur, 25, 45, 47, 49, 52, 54, 56, 108, 112
  temple, 76
Tiruvayaru, 2
Tranquebar, 15, 16
Trichinopoly missions, 16, 17, 71, 79
Tula festival, 123
Turaiyur, 129

Uttamanabis, 68, 79 n21

vadagalai, 27, 67, 83-93, 94 n7, 95 n19, 99, 220, 222
Vaikunth Ekadashi, 122, 131
vaishnavites, 82, 141
Valambagudi, 127, 128, 134
Vallum, 171
Vanamalai *math*, 100
vanniyar, 129-30
varna, 99, 154, 217, 218
Veda samaj, 189, 210, 221
Vedanta, see *Advaita Vedanta*
Vedantacarya shrine, 86
Vedaranniyam, 124
Vedas, 87, 89, 100
Vedic Hinduism, 211
Vedic sacrifice, 41
Veerasawmien, 89
Veerayyah, Vandayar, 71
Velanganni, 33, 124
vellala, 68, 103, 171-2, 173, 175
Venkatraman, 190
Vigneswara, see Ganesh
Viraraghava temple, 100
Vishnu, 32
Visswanathan, E., 9
Vydeeswaram temple, 112

wages
  agricultural, 24, 37 n57
  temple, 23-8
Wallace, John, 44, 50, 54, 86-7
Wallhouse, M. J., 90
Washbrook, D. A., 157
Wesleyan College, 199
Wesleyan Methodist Missionary Society (WMMS), 16
Whitehead, Bishop, 7, 31
Wilson, Bishop, 175
Winkel, Rev., 160
Wyatt, Rev., J. L., 177, 202, 209

Yellama, 30

zamindars, 113, 123
Zehme, Rev., 161
zenana, 203
Ziegenbalg, Bartholomew, 15, 34 n23
Zion Church, 155

For Product Safety Concerns and Information please contact our EU representative GPSR@taylorandfrancis.com
Taylor & Francis Verlag GmbH, Kaufingerstraße 24, 80331 München, Germany